Sledgehammer Beck

One honest cop vs Sydney's crime bosses

Fia Cumming

Copyright © 2023 (Fia Cumming)
All rights reserved worldwide.

No part of the book may be copied or changed in any format, sold, or used in a way other than what is outlined in this book, under any circumstances, without the prior written permission of the publisher.

Publisher: Inspiring Publishers,
P.O. Box 159, Calwell, ACT Australia 2905
Email: publishaspg@gmail.com
http://www.inspiringpublishers.com

 A catalogue record for this book is available from the National Library of Australia

National Library of Australia The Prepublication Data Service

Author: Fia Cumming
Title: Sledgehammer Beck
Genre: Non-fiction

Paperback ISBN: 978-1-922920-44-7
eBook ISBN: 978-1-922920-45-4

"Corruption in law enforcement has been apparent in Australia virtually since first settlement"—Justice Donald Stewart, Report of the Joint Commonwealth-NSW Royal Commission into Drug Trafficking 1981-1983. Justice Stewart himself served a total of 7.6 years in the NSW Police Force.

PREFACE

This story has been assembled using former Detective Superintendent Merv Beck's day-to-day diaries, newspaper articles and other written materials from the time, filled out by lengthy audio tapes which he made in the late 1990s and 2000s. Information revealed by inquiries and investigations after Beck's retirement has also been included.

Merv Beck's records provide detailed and dramatic evidence in support of his allegations that other police attempted to prevent him doing his duty and to persuade him to deliberately fail.

Beck told part of his story shortly after his retirement. Many years later, as the Wood Royal Commission began to expose the continuing flaws in the NSW Police Force, he decided that the full story should be told.

His story from those times is disturbing, but also inspiring. In the 1960s and 1970s in New South Wales, and especially Sydney, prostitution, casinos and off-course 'starting price' or SP betting on horse racing were popular but illegal vices. As organised criminals took over more and more of these illegal operations in the late 1970s, corrupt police and politicians became involved in ensuring the law was not enforced.

There was big money to be made in all areas, with estimates that up to one third of Sydney's populace indulged in SP gambling at its peak[1].

Against this backdrop, Merv Beck was appointed in 1979 to close the casinos and SP operations. Few believed it could be done: previously police had declared that the casinos were impregnable.

But Beck was an extraordinary policeman who was as daring and cunning as the criminals he was pitted against. Led by him, his squad assailed the gambling outlets with not just the famous sledgehammer but with a suite of tricks and tools that left the criminals flummoxed.

The crime bosses wielded enormous power not only on the streets of Sydney, but in the 'corridors of power' in Parliament and in the Police Force, in the law courts and the boardrooms. But despite threats to eliminate Beck, he survived. Quite possibly this was due to his huge public profile. If Beck had disappeared (like Donald Mackay and Juanita Nielsen), all hell would have broken loose.

---

[1] https://www.afr.com/lifestyle/arts-and-entertainment/sydney-1960s-corruption-theproblem-lay-with-everyone-20170430-gvvk3p

The events chronicled in this book are historic. But like much of history, they can provide insights into what is happening today. Corruption, abuse of power, and failure to impose the law in relation to gambling have remained real threats to legitimate society and democracy over the intervening years and into the 21st century.

In relation to corruption, the depth of decay in the NSW Police Force came into the spotlight after the establishment of the Royal Commission into the New South Wales Police Service, headed by Justice James Wood. The Royal Commission ran for two years from 1995 and uncovered hundreds of instances of corruption including: bribery, money laundering, drug trafficking, and falsifying of evidence by police.

The commission's revelations about the level of corruption resulted in the resignation of then-Police Commissioner, Tony Lauer. After an international search, UK Policeman Peter Ryan—the National Director of Police Training for England and Wales—was appointed to the job to ensure a fresh, clean approach. Ryan's primary job was to implement the wide-ranging reforms recommended by the Royal Commission, including the establishment of a permanent Police Integrity Commission.

Concerns about links between casino gambling and organised crime have also become a matter of great public concern. Since Beck's time, gambling in Australia has expanded massively. A smorgasbord of legal gambling options, including at least one major casino in every state and territory, provide a guaranteed and massive revenue stream to governments and private business alike.

While the casinos are big business and popular attractions, their links with organised crime have come under the spotlight more than 40 years after Beck voiced similar concerns. In the 2020s, a string of damning inquiries in NSW, Victoria, Western Australia and Queensland found Star Entertainment and Crown Resorts unfit or unsuitable to hold casino licences.

In September 2022, the NSW Independent Casino Commission, after a four month inquiry, suspended Star Casino's licence and imposed the maximum $100 million fine. The regulator found the company was "rotten to the core" and had not only allowed infiltration by money launderers and organised crime, but had deliberately covered their tracks. Like the other casinos, however, Star was allowed to remain in operation.

Mervyn Beck died in March 2018 at the age of 96. He was a rare individual, who proved that one man can make a difference.

CHAPTER ONE

"I became who I was meant to be."

Saturday February 13 1982 was the last day on the job for Detective Superintendent Mervyn Lindsay Beck.

The following day would be St Valentine's Day, but Beck's mind was not on romance. It was also his 60th birthday, and under the rules of the NSW Police Force at the time, Beck had no choice but to retire.

At that time he was the Superintendent in charge of the Special Gaming Squad. With the possible exception of the Police Commissioner, he was the most high profile police officer in NSW, both controversial and popular.

His squad was commonly known as "Beck's Raiders", while he was dubbed 'Sledgehammer Beck', because he literally bashed down the doors of a number of illegal casinos and other gambling venues.

In two separate periods leading policing of gaming and betting, the second of which was now ending, he had mounted a tenacious and successful attack on illegal gambling—closing down the casinos, gaming clubs and SP bookmakers which had become a well-known but previously unassailable part of Sydney's underworld.

The most ruthless of the emerging organised crime figures— among them Lennie McPherson and George Freeman—were furious that Beck had been let loose on them. But they did not dare to 'knock him off' because of the inevitable public and political backlash that would ensue.

Many gambling operators also had begrudging respect for the small but incredibly tough and resourceful copper who had beaten them.

They knew Beck was motivated by nothing more than a genuine belief that the system of law, applied equally to all, was fundamental to civil society and democracy.

"I don't drink and I don't gamble myself," Beck said many times, "but I have no moral objection to other people doing those things.

"I am not a wowser. Some of the press called me a wowser but it's not true, and I am not a religious zealot.

"I just believe that if a law exists, it's the duty of the police, as law enforcement officers, to uphold it.

"If the law is wrong, it's the duty of the politicians to change or remove it.

"When I was asked to close the illegal casinos and SP bookmakers, I did my best to close them because they were against the law.

"The politicians in Macquarie Street knew full well what the law was and what my job was. The law was there to be changed at their discretion."

Beck's main concern about illegal gambling in Sydney was its role in the organised crime empires, and his view was shared by many investigators at the time. In his highly respected expose *Drug Traffic: Narcotics and Organized Crime in Australia*[2], Dr Alfred McCoy referred to gaming and betting as the strong arms which directed a flow of money to the illicit drug trade.

Beck recalled, "Many people said to me, why did you come on so strong?

"Well, I only came on as strong as the law demanded.

"I do believe, though, that illegal gambling was not the innocent pastime many people would have us think. Organisers of crime were involved in it. The gambling provided money for investment in other illegal activities, like narcotics. Illegal gambling also robbed the public purse. Large sums of black money were not declared for tax purposes.

"The SP man was no longer your local friendly barber."

The crime bosses, and their cronies, knew that Beck's middle-of-the-night onslaughts would come to an abrupt end with his retirement. They had counted down the days, and now the time had come.

Beck had also counted down the days, but not with any great joy. Unlike most people retiring after careers spanning 36 years, Beck's last day was not spent tidying up his office and farewelling friends over a long lunch before an early departure.

Nor did he take the day off, although that would have been reasonable given what he did the night before.

---

[2] Alfred W. McCoy. Harper & Row, 1980

He worked the late shift on Friday night, and it was a successful night. He used the 10 pound (4.5 kg) sledgehammer to gain entry to illegal gambling premises in the City of Sydney, and several arrests were made. His men jokingly referred to the hammer as 'the key', because it opened so many doors.

Then Beck joined a late night police raid on a city hotel, which was open after licensing hours.

Among the 40 people arrested, several recognised Superintendent Beck and shook his hand.

"You're retiring tomorrow aren't you? I read it in the paper," a welldressed middle-aged man said to Beck. "Just my luck to get busted on your last shift! Good luck with life outside the force— time to go fishing!"

But it was not quite time to contemplate fishing, golf and more time with his wife, Elsie. Despite the late finish, Beck snatched only an hour of sleep that night. He arrived home at 4 am on Saturday morning and changed into his pyjamas. When he lay down, Elsie stirred enough to acknowledge his presence. He gave her an affectionate pat, but before he let his eyes close he set the radio alarm clock for 5.30.

It was a typical Beck move. He drove himself hard and the fact that his career was ending was a reason to work harder to get the job done, not to back off. He believed in his work, and he did not want to leave his position with any stone unturned.

Although it was Saturday, there was much to do before his final exit. He was back on his feet and out the door again at 6 am. After a brief stop at his office in the NSW Police Headquarters, then at the corner of Phillip and Hunter Streets, Sydney, he was out in the squad car in the eastern suburbs with some of his team, planning raids on SP betting operations to take place later in the day.

Saturday passed quickly, and by mid evening all the plans had been enacted and each of the SP bookies had had their weekend spoiled. While squad members attended to the charges, around 10 pm Beck told them he was going out for a last patrol. He went alone, driving from one known location to another.

Each of them had been illegal casinos. But this night, they were dark and unoccupied. They had all been closed as a result of his team's efforts over the previous days and weeks, but Beck wanted to make sure none of them had been cheeky enough to chance their luck by re-opening.

As he left the last on his check list, Beck allowed himself a tired smile. Then he returned to his office and completed the last of his paperwork.

He waited until the stroke of midnight, then the remaining squad members came and shook his hand. There was a hint of tears from some.

Beck himself was not unaffected.

"Good night," he said in a raspy voice as he left the overnight shift and softly closed the door behind himself.

It was officially his birthday, 14 February, as he drove home with a sigh that mingled melancholy with relief, knowing that he was now retired and no longer a serving policeman.

The Sydney newspapers loved to report the daring and colourful exploits of the gaming and betting squad, and in the late 1970s and early 1980s, Superintendent Merv Beck was a household name, one of the most high profile members of the NSW Police Force.

Only hours after Beck had left his office for the last time, Sydney's biggest selling newspaper of the time, *The Sun-Herald,* began circulating with a full page article on Beck's retirement. There was a photograph of him holding the famous sledgehammer and a headline – "Merv Beck Hands over the Key". Journalist Graham Gambie asked the question that many were asking: what would happen when Beck was gone?

"The tireless Mervyn Beck turned 60 at midnight, saying goodbye to the NSW Police Force and to the state's illegal gamblers, whom he had kept in check right through his last 18 hour day," Gambie wrote.

"During these final hours, Supt Beck— leader of Beck's Raiders— added further arrests to the anti-gaming squad's lists, taking the tally since he took over in October to more than 1000.

"The big question, what happens now? Will Beck's successor be as successful? Or will the SP and casino operators come out of hiding like some of them predict and like they did last time Beck left the jo?

"Supt Beck, the man who proved illegal gambling could be checked, said yesterday, 'Sydney's casinos still have their lights out'.

"But he said gambling bosses were rubbing their hands together and boasting 'things are going to be alright after that Beck goes'.

"Supt Beck said, 'They have been a bit desperate over the past few months and think the drought has broken, but I am sure the fellows in this squad will be equal to the task.'

The following day, *The Sydney Morning Herald* also noted Beck's retirement. In an editorial, it referred to him as Australia's Elliot Ness. This was a huge compliment, as Ness was the American FBI agent who pursued Al Capone's illegal brewery operations during the prohibition period. Ness's core team was known as the 'Untouchables' because they resisted attempts to corrupt them, as well as surviving assassination attempts. The parallel to Beck and his squad was clear to those who knew the obstacles they had to overcome to do their job.

Even decades after his retirement, the name Beck's Raiders would ring a bell with many Sydney residents.

When he was asked by journalists or acquaintances to nominate his greatest achievement from his periods on gaming and betting, Beck would quote Winston Churchill's response to a similar question about his life.

"I survived."

* * * *

Merv Beck was not a physically imposing person, but what he lacked in stature he more than made up in determination and strength of character. He was both passionate about enforcing the law, and philosophically committed to it.

His steadfast belief in the importance of the law went back to his childhood, and possibly even before that, as policing was in his genes.

Since the official formation of the NSW Police in 1862, it has been common for sons of policemen to follow in their footsteps. So it was with Apsley Beck, his son Launcelot and his grandson Mervyn.

Beck's father and grandfather were both proud, disciplined, immensely brave and fiercely honest. They instilled in him a high sense of honour and duty as well as the need for physical toughness to get the job done.

Beck was inspired by their history and traditions when his personal values and emotional stamina were under attack. He was also influenced by the knowledge that his father Launcelot Charles had been a small and unimposing man to look at, yet was able to arrest much larger men even when they resisted vigorously— because he was fit, experienced and highly motivated.

Merv's grandfather. Apsley Mills Beck, died 11 years before Beck was born, so they never met. But as a child he often heard stories of Apsley's dangerous and daring exploits, which made a great impression on him.

Apsley was born in November 1864 in Pambula in the Bega Valley. For most of his career, he was a mounted trooper of the NSW Police

Force who worked in country areas. He joined the Force in the early 1880s and in 1888 he was posted to Broken Hill, where he met his future wife and Beck's grandmother, Lucy Howe.

Lucy had run away from her Adelaide home to escape her ruffian stepfather. She took the train to Broken Hill where Apsley was working as a constable and literally fell in love at first sight. Apsley saw her get off the train, looking lost and uncertain, and offered to help. He found her a boarding house and a job. In 1891, they married and their first child, Launcelot Charles, was born the following year.

In that era, the police—like the clergy—were the frontline in maintaining social order. Whether it was industrial trouble or racial tensions, the local policemen had to deal with it. They had to be largely self-sufficient and make decisions for themselves. They were also tough, because the times and their jobs demanded it.

In his later years, Apsley moved to Petersham in Sydney and he died there in 1911. Although he was a protestant, prayers were also said for him in the Roman Catholic Church in Condobolin. In those days of a deep divide between branches of the church, this was a rare tribute.

Two years after Apsley's death, in 1913, Merv's father Launcelot Charles Beck followed him into the Police Force. Like Apsley, Launcelot was a superb horseman. He had worked as a horse-breaker, but at the age of 21 he joined the police to get a steady job and a steady income to support his mother, sister and two brothers.

When he finished his brief training at the police depot in Redfern, Launcelot was told that he was to be stationed at Goulburn. He was also told that there was a troop horse to be taken there. His instructions were to ride the horse down and send his gear on the train.

When Launcelot asked why he could not take the horse on the train, he was told this was not possible as it would cost the Police Department 23 shillings.

Launcelot was given two-and-a-half days to make the journey. It is now about 191 km but in those days was considerably longer, as the bridges and massive earthworks undertaken in the late 20th century have smoothed out mountains and ravines. Launcelot planned his trip well, arriving at a town with a police station not long before night fall on both the first and second day. The local police provided food for both himself and the horse, and somewhere to sleep. He was up again early the next day to continue. He and the horse, who must have been a good one, made it to Goulburn on time to report to the officer in charge, who had been told by telegraph to expect him. Today, only trained endurance horses with support crews would be asked to undertake such a journey.

At Goulburn, Launcelot's main duty was to conduct mounted patrols. The NSW Police Force had only obtained its first vehicles, two motorcycles, in 1914 and horses remained the dominant form of transport[3]. Each morning at 6 am he and half a dozen other mounted troopers would head out to ride around the district and see that all was well.

One morning in 1915 he was returning from this early patrol when he saw two men in Goulburn's main street walking towards him from Baxter's Shoe Factory. He recognised them as wanted for assault and robbery. Beck rode towards the men and told them they were under arrest. He dismounted and stopped the suspects and moved to handcuff them. As he did so, they both attacked him. He struggled with them and as they fought, other people in the town saw what was happening and a crowd gathered across the street.

While they were brawling, Launcelot's police horse wandered across the street towards the crowd of people. A young woman came out of the shoe factory office and saw what was happening. She took hold of the horse's reins and led him across the street towards the constable, who was still grappling with the suspects. Launcelot had one of the men on the ground and was trying to get the handcuffs on him, but his prisoner raised his feet and kicked Beck in the head.

When the woman saw this, she let go of the horse and ran to the side of the street. She picked up a paling which had fallen from a fence and ran back with it to the struggling men. Lifting it as high as she could, she swung the paling at the man who had kicked Beck and struck him on the head and shoulder. The man was knocked off balance, giving Launcelot enough time to get the cuffs on the man he had pinned down. Launcelot then turned to the other man, who seemed intimidated by the crowd and by the woman with the paling. He drew his hand back, preparing to throw a punch but Launcelot was quicker and stronger. He landed a punch on the man's jaw and knocked him down, then took a strap out of his uniform and tried the man's hands together.

Launcelot turned to the lady with his horse.

"I'll look after him," she said with a smile as she gave the horse a pat. "I'll follow you to the station."

Beck dragged the first man to his feet and walked both of the culprits down the street to the police station, with the young woman and his horse following behind.

That young woman was 19 year old Kathleen Ivy Whipp. She had been going home for lunch from her job at the shoe factory. She was just 150 cms (4 foot 11 inches) tall and slightly built.

Launcelot reported her brave actions to his station head, who passed the account on to the Sydney headquarters. Not long after, Kathleen received a letter of thanks from the NSW Commissioner of Police.

She also received the admiring attention of Launcelot Beck. It was a suitable introduction for the pair who would become Mr and Mrs Launcelot Beck and parents to Mervyn.

Decades later, Merv Beck liked to relate this story when asked why he had chosen to become a policeman.

"I think it was bred in me," he said. "I had a courageous father and a courageous mother, I think I became who I was meant to be."

Another story which Merv Beck loved to tell related to his father's posting in Delegate, a small town in the Snowy Mountains near the Victorian border. Launcelot was sent there not long after marrying Kathleen. Financial restrictions during and following World War prevented rapid growth of the Police Department's transport fleet and, even by the mid 1920's, only 13 four wheeled vehicles in total were held by police across the state. Police stations and officers were still classified as 'mounted' or 'foot'.[3]

Part of the job for the mounted police was to escort Chinese goldminers who had come from the Kiandra goldfields on the other side of the mountains and were taking their gold south to sell it. Even in the high country there were occasional bushrangers who were keen to take their own share of the wealth being generated from gold.

There were other occasions when special bravery was required and one of them occurred not long after Launcelot arrived. It became legend in the Delegate area and the following account fills out the story to fit the known facts.

The Delegate River, which runs off the Snowy River high up in the mountains, was in flood due to heavy rain and melting snow. A property owner in the region was very ill. His doctor had been contacted and had provided medicine, which was sent by coach to Delegate, the nearest town. A member of the man's family was in Delegate and had collected the medicine as scheduled but the river had risen so fast overnight that

---

[3] See Police Stations in NSW Cornelius Breen O'Donnell, 1993 UNSW http://unsworks.unsw.edu.au/fapi/datastream/unsworks:35537/SOURCE01?view=true

there was no way for him to get across and deliver the package to the patient.

The relative went to the police station and asked if anything could be done. The station head called Launcelot over and young Beck was keen to assist.

After considering the problem, his first plan was to float the medical supplies across the river on a makeshift raft. When the relative had not arrived back at the station, a worker had been sent to find out what had happened and was waiting on the other side of the river. With a party of supporters and onlookers, Launcelot took the precious package to the river bank with a wooden raft. But the river was flowing so fast that all agreed the plan would not work, the medicine would be swept away and never found.

The situation was becoming desperate. Launcelot decided to take matters into his own hands. He strapped the medicines to his body and led his police horse, unsaddled, down to the river's edge. Then he jumped on bareback and rode his horse to a point on the shore where, he calculated, they would be able to use the current to reach the other side at a place where it was easy to get out. He waved to the man on the other side, gesturing that he should go downstream. The man waved back affirmation and headed off away from the impassable ford and through the scrub downstream towards a small bare area which would serve as a beach.

Barely hesitating, Launcelot then urged his horse into the torrent. Amazingly, the horse did as he was asked and soon they were swimming in the treacherous brown water. They were being swept downstream but also making progress across the river.

They were half way across when disaster struck. A log came surging on the water and collided with both horse and rider.

Launcelot was knocked off, but managed to grab his horse's tail before he was swept away. The horse struggled on, eventually dragging Launcelot out the other side some distance down the river. As onlookers from the town side cheered, Launcelot unbound the package of medicine, which was intact. The station worker raced to meet him, shook his hand and, after a wave to the crowd, ran to his own horse, mounted and took off towards the station. After taking a moment to recover, Beck vaulted onto his horse and followed the worker slowly. There was no way to get back to Delegate for several days until the flood had receded, and he could expect a warm welcome at the station.

Several days later, when the river had subsided, Launcelot and his horse were able to cross at the ford. They rode up to the police station, receiving applause from the people they met on the street and hearty congratulations from the station sergeant.

It was a few years after this, on 14 February 1922, that Kathleen gave birth to a baby boy, who was named Mervyn.

During Beck's childhood he heard the Delegate story many times. It must have seemed like destiny when he heard it again on the day he arrived to start his own career in the NSW Police Force many years later. He was assigned to Philip St Police Station in the heart of Sydney where the station sergeant was Jack Agnew. Agnew had served at Bombala when Launcelot Beck was at Delegate. As soon as he heard he name "Beck" he asked Merv about his father and when the link was confirmed, recalled Launcelot's heroic act in crossing the swollen river.

There were many other true tales about the exploits of his father and grandfather, which made the hardships of Mervyn's life as the young son of a policeman in country NSW more tolerable. From early days, his childhood was a mix of discipline and adventure—a fitting start for someone who would become a soldier and policeman himself. His father and mother were kind and did their best for their children, through some hard times, while imposing firm rules.

Every three years Launcelot would be transferred to a new country town. This meant Beck and his sisters had to leave their friends and start again.

Merv's first school was in Queanbeyan, across the NSW border from Canberra, which he joined aged 5 in 1927. Queanbeyan at the time was the industrial base for Canberra, which was developing fast after being declared as the national capital in 1913. It was in May of 1927 that the Parliament House was officially opened by the Duke and Duchess of York (later King George VI and Queen Elizabeth the Queen Mother). As a senior policeman in Queanbeyan, Launcelot was honoured to become the driver and commander of the first police car issued to the district and one of the first Launcelot had ever seen. It was a Morris Cowley with running boards, one of 143 in the fleet of NSW police motor vehicles at the time. As well as Morris Cowley tourers, the fleet comprised Armstrong Siddleys and Austins[4].

---

[4] https://www.australianpolice.com.au/nsw-police-history-index/motor-vehiclesbranch-1912-1962/

There were many fights among the building workers housed in Queanbeyan. Launcelot would stand on the running boards as the Morris sped to the scene. Some of Launcelot's team had to take the motorcycle or even a bicycle, as the Morris could barely move with five men in it.

Soon after Mervyn started school, however, the family was moved to Nimmitabel in the Monaro high country plains for 10 months to relieve the local constable, who was sick. Nimmitabel is south of Cooma and only about 85 km from Delegate. Despite his youth, Merv retained vivid memories of living there.

"I remember walking to school in the snow with no shoes and socks. I didn't have a coat either so my father gave me a police cape, which dragged on the ground behind me. I can still feel the bite of the cold."

It was not just on the way to school that Merv felt the winter's cold. The Nimmitabel house provided for the family was small. Even though the temperatures were well below zero, Mervyn had to sleep outside on the verandah, with the police cape over his blankets. They were tough times but they ensured that Merv had the physical and mental fortitude expected by his father.

Launcelot himself had not lost his enthusiasm for a challenge. By the time Merv was at secondary school, his father had earned a reputation within the NSW Police as a 'town breaker', and this started when Beck was still a young boy. It meant he was often sent to locations where locals had demonstrated a pattern of violence and resistance to the law which had intimidated their local police. Launcelot seemed to have a particular knack at restoring peace and the rule of law through a mix of physical bravado and strength of will.

This occurred at Launcelot's first posting after Nimmitabel. Merv Beck particularly remembered this place. Weethalle (pronounced WEE-thal-ee) is 526 km west of Sydney in the Riverina. When the Becks arrived it was still a very new town and new community, as it was created after land was set aside there in 1921 for homestead farms for soldiers who had returned from World War 1.[5]

It was still only a skeleton town in 1926, when a temporary school building was provided. The Becks arrived just three years later and had an immediate introduction to the town's rough side.

---

[5] See Wikipedia https://en.wikipedia.org/wiki/Weethalle#History

Merv, then about to turn eight, was playing on the train line (as children did then) with some other kids, when one of them pointed and called out.

"What's going on over there?" They all looked and saw that a fight had started. Then Merv saw that one of the fighters was his father, Launcelot, and his opponent was a much larger man.

Merv set off at a run to find out what was happening, with the other kids in tow. That night his father explained to Kathleen and the family what had transpired.

When Launcelot had walked up to the hotel in his uniform to introduce himself, he immediately found out why the town had a bad reputation.

The drinkers in the public bar had seen him coming through the half glass door. Before he was on the step, the door was pushed open and a huge man came out. He was a wheat 'lumper'—men who would carry and stack bags of wheat weighing up to 90kg. He stood at more than 190 cms (6 foot 3 inches) and was very solid. His name was Dummy Fee.

"If you want to run this place you will have to get over me first," he declared in unfriendly tones.

Launcelot was only just over 70 kgs (11 stone) in his police uniform and leggings. But he did not hesitate.

"Well you are under arrest now!" he replied. Without delay, Dummy leapt forward and swung a punch, which Launcelot ducked and then hit back. The fight was on.

Dummy was no doubt expecting a knockout but he could not get it. They kept swinging and ducking. It had been going on for a full minute and Launcelot was holding his own when one of the drinkers in the pub said to the group, "Let's go out and help Dummy!"

A mob of half a dozen burst out of the hotel. A few people who had been in the street had gathered to watch, as well as the group of children including Merv. Things were looking grim for Launcelot.

Suddenly a small man ran out from a shopfront, yelling wildly. He got between the mob from the hotel and the two fighters.

If his yell didn't get their attention, the square bladed meat cleaver in his hand did. It was Mick Cassam, a Greek immigrant who owned the town's only café.

"If any of youse make a move I'll let you have this!" he shouted. The men took him at his word and halted as one. Beck saw his chance and took a swing which knocked Fee down, then before he could recover whipped a handcuff on his right hand. Fee was so surprised he did not resist as the other wrist was cuffed, then Beck hauled him to his feet.

"NOW you are under arrest!" he declared, to delighted gasps from the kids, a satisfied grunt from Cassam and stunned silence from Fee's supporters.

There was a single lock up room or cell for prisoners at the back of the police house which also served as the police station. Fee had to stay in this cell for about a week, until the out-of-town magistrate arrived to hear the charges.

Each day, Launcelot Beck let him out of the cell and into the yard for exercise, which took a particular form. Merv Beck remembered well how his father instructed Fee to use his free time to dig a massive hole in the ground, which he did. By the time the magistrate arrived the hole was well over two metres long and almost a metre wide, and so deep that Dummy could barely be seen when he was standing in it. The local children who had become Beck's friends were extremely impressed and a bit frightened by this hole, but in time they discovered that Launcelot intended it as a rubbish pit for the family, not a grave for Dummy Fee after all.

Dummy gave Launcelot no trouble during his stay in the cell, and Launcelot ensured that he was let off lightly by the magistrate. The fight and his subsequent civil but firm treatment had given Fee a large respect for the policeman, and a friendship of sorts was forged. From that time, if there was trouble in Weethalle, Fee always provided backup to his 'small' police friend.

While Launcelot was a disciplinarian at home, expecting his wife and children to do as he told them, Merv found him to be fair. He respected his father and some of his deepest beliefs stemmed from the way his father pursued his police work.

Firstly, as Mark Twain stated, "It's not the size of the dog in the fight, it's the size of the fight in the dog".

Secondly, being a good winner and demonstrating fairness and where possible, kindness, was a better way to change people's mind and behaviour than kicking those who were down.

Thirdly, that policing was a hands on business, "and it's better for you to have your hands on them".

Despite the constant moves to a new posting, and despite the drawbacks that sometimes arose from being the policeman's son, Merv knew that he wanted to follow his father into the police. But his sense of duty and lack of fear also made him an obvious recruit to the war effort after Australia entered World War 2 in 1939.

Merv was only 17, so he needed his parents' permission to sign up. Both Launcelot and Kathleen had lost brothers in World War 1 and did not want their son to share the same fate. When Merv turned 18 in 1940, they could no longer hold him back but persuaded him to join the Royal Australian Air Force rather than the Army.

At the age of 19, Merv found himself in the Middle East as an armourer in the famous No 3 Squadron. Their first battle was near Tobruk. They then retreated to El Alamein where another famous battle took place, and from there to Libya, Tunisia and then to Sicily for the invasion of Italy (which was held by the Germans). Beck was one of a select group of airmen flown into Italy to establish the base behind enemy lines from which the squadron supported Allied landings at Anzio and Nettuno.

In North Africa, Beck's squadron came across a camp area on an airstrip which had been occupied by the Germans. In a small dugout, Beck found some papers and photographs that had been left behind. For reasons he could not explain, he kept one of the papers and later had it translated by a British soldier who could read German.

"In the battle of life, one cannot hire a substitute. Whatever work you volunteer to make your own, you must look on as your care for the (human) race."

The words struck a chord with Beck. They showed him that German soldiers were men like him, trying hard to do the right thing. As young as he was, they also gave a focus to his inherent sense of responsibility and purpose, which remained with him throughout his life.

In May 1945 the Germans surrendered unconditionally and the Allied forces declared victory in Europe. Beck went with the squadron to England where he was told he would be an air-gunner for the British RAF, which was forming an air armada to fly to the Pacific and fight the Japanese. While this was still being formed, the United States dropped the atomic bombs on Hiroshima and Nagasaki. World War 2 was finally over and nothing now stood in the way of Beck and his police career.

Beck aged 10 riding "the famous outlaw" Foley, in Nundle.

Mervyn Beck aged 20, in Egypt with the Desert Air Force, 1942.

Beck's grandfather Apsley (mounted, right) with police colleagues.

CHAPTER TWO

Can you fight, son?

Mervyn Beck arrived in Sydney after his war service on 28 November 1945. Within a few days he took himself to the NSW Police Force headquarters and made an application to join, Six weeks later, on 7 January 1946, he was called up to enter training at the Police Depot, as it was then called, in Redfern. He was not yet 24.

Beck's war experiences, his upbringing and the genes he inherited, made him a highly individual policeman from the outset. He was bold, innovative, and a touch rebellious; he was also totally dedicated to his job, and unswerving in his belief in its importance. For Beck, throughout his long and varied career, 'the job' was much more than a way to make money. It was a calling.

Like his father before him, Merv was not a tall man but he made up for that with his stamina, strength and courage. Taking physical risks and defying danger to get the job done was one of the hallmarks throughout his long and distinguished police career. He brought the same approach to a very wide range of crime, from backyard abortion rackets to murder and theft and illegal gambling.

His upbringing and his war experience both helped him to cope with the emotional and physical demands placed on him as a policeman, from the early days. The training consisted of a few weeks of theory lessons, after which the new recruits were assigned as probationary constables at various stations throughout Sydney. Beck was sent to Phillip St station at Circular Quay, also known as Division 4.

The senior officers at Phillip St were hard taskmasters who gave their probationers no leeway on theory or practice. Beck was used to this toughness and respected it, but others found it difficult. "At 2 o'clock in the morning, the senior sergeant would quiz you on the powers of arrest and obstruction and if he asked you a question you had never even heard of, he'd say, alright I will ask you the same question tomorrow night and I want the answer in full. It was a pretty solid way of learning."

The young police were also lined up and inspected for their uniform and 'appointments'—the handcuffs, gun and baton—and knowledge of their duties, their reporting times and to whom they should report. Reporting was done in person at the station at regular times, unless they were fortunate enough to be near Wynyard which had a police call box with a free phone that connected straight to the station. Although Beck and others had been fighting a war overseas, they were referred to as 'son' and told to respect their elders.

They worked a 48 hour week, with only one day off. As well as long hours, they were given poor pay, no overtime payments and little consideration for their lives outside work. Beck was asked to be the best man at a friend's wedding and twice asked for the Saturday off, only to be refused. "Just appreciate your job, son, and take it on the chin. You can't do anything about it," the senior sergeant told him. Many recruits dropped out, but Beck and other ex-servicemen found it easier than military life.

From the start there were exciting, eye-opening and sometimes grim incidents. In his first month as a probationary constable, Beck was on duty at Wynyard Station when a railway officer came running to find him

"Come quick constable, there's been a dreadful accident! There's been a person killed on the tracks!"

The man turned and Beck walked and ran behind him down to one of the underground train platforms. Railway officials were down on the track, behind a stationary and empty train. They waved to Beck when they saw the police uniform. Beck jumped down onto the lines and followed the silent group into the railway tunnel.

About 90 metres from the end of the platform were the remains of a person who had jumped, fallen or been pushed off the train. It was a gory and horrible sight. There were only bits and pieces of what had been a man. It was enough to turn the stomach, even for an experienced person.

Beck had barely had time to take in the gruesome sight when the ambulance officer arrived in a rush. He had a stretcher to collect what was left of the body. But he was on his own. He turned to Beck.

"Give me a hand, we will have to collect the remains and take them back to my ambulance and then to the morgue," he said. He gestured, "You start there constable and pick up what you can, and I'll start over here."

There were no gloves or other protective equipment, just bare hands. Beck took a breath and did what he had to do, grimacing but without comment. When all the retrievable pieces were on the stretcher, the ambulance officer covered them with a tarpaulin.

"I'll take the back and you hop on the front," he instructed Beck, who obliged.

Beck did not realise that the rear position allowed the ambo to raise his end of the stretcher to avoid the remains coming towards him as they walked on the uneven tracks, steps and them up the ramp to the street. In contrast, by the time they arrived at the ambulance, Beck's boots and the backs of his trousers were saturated with the victim's blood. To make it worse, he was only halfway through his shift, with no prospect of a change of clothing.

At the morgue, Beck performed the necessary official duties, booking in the body, and calling the police station to report the incident. He also had to look for any identification on the body parts, which was very unpleasant. Then he returned to Phillip St where he was able to have a shower. By good luck, there was a spare pair of overalls there, which his superintendent allowed him to wear, while he finished his shift at the station. Despite what Beck had been through, there was no suggestion that he be allowed to finish early.

Beck was convinced he had been tricked into taking the front of the stretcher, as the ambo had no blood on him afterwards. He applied this knowledge at a number of incidents which occurred later in his policing career.

A few weeks after this, when Beck had about two months' experience as a constable, there was another notable incident. Beck was at the police call box at Wynyard preparing his report when two naval police came running up, and opened the door, breathing hard.

"Constable, I'm from the navy police. There's been a shooting down at Johnny's!" said one of them.

Johnny's was a night club and bar on the Phillip Street police beat, which was very popular with sailors. When Beck asked for more information, the caller explained: "There's a sailor down there with a revolver, he's fired a shot and another sailor's been hit in the leg. He's down there, and he's still got the gun."

"Well, what are you people doing about it?" Beck responded, knowing that military law could conflict with his police jurisdiction.

"Nothing, we just came to get you."

Not sure what to do, Beck sent the naval police back to Johnny's. He quickly called the station and let the supervisor know what had happened, then headed to the club himself. When he arrived, he found dozens of sailors in the first room, hiding behind pillars and furniture. In one corner, protected by a wall, was a man with blood on his pants, who was clearly the shooting victim.

When they saw Beck, several sailors pointed to the door leading to the bar. Beck moved closer and could see a sailor with his back to bar and a silver revolver in his hand. The two naval police were well clear of the doorway.

"There he is, he's all yours," said the talkative one.

Beck was unimpressed, but said nothing. After a second he walked through the doorway and straight towards the shooter, watching him closely for any sign that he might shoot. If that happened Beck decided he would throw himself on the floor, draw his own revolver and do whatever he had to.

But as he got close, the man stayed still. Beck stopped.

"Give me the revolver," he said firmly.

The sailor looked at Beck, but said nothing. Fifteen seconds went by. Beck leaned forward and quietly took the gun out of the man's hand. He did not resist. A moment later, as Beck placed handcuffs on the man, two detectives from Division 4 burst through the doorway. One of them was senior detective, Sergeant Jack Mervyn Davis. "What's the position here?" Davis demanded.

"I've just arrested this man for firing his revolver." Beck saw two ambulance officers had also arrived and reached the bleeding sailor. "He hit that sailor over there, he was shot in the leg."

Davis told Beck to give him the gun. He and the other detective then took charge of the offender and started to lead him out.

"Leave it to us, we'll fix this," Davis told Beck.

The detectives left. Beck took details of the wounded man, who was then taken to hospital, There was no more to be done. Beck returned to Wynyard and at 1 am, walked back to the Phillip St police station for his dinner.

The station sergeant, Jack Agnew, called Beck over and asked him what had happened at Johnny's. Beck told him the full story.

Agnew then said, "Come and look at this, you don't even get a mention." There in the charge book, where all arrests were recorded, it stated that the armed sailor had been arrested by Davis and the other detective.

Beck was first surprised and shocked, and then rather angry. Agnew told him not to let it happen again.

"Learn something from this," the sergeant advised him. "If you don't watch yourself in this job, people will steal your thunder at every opportunity."

Agnew decided to fix the problem. He wrote Beck's name underneath the other two, with a red line. "Now that will mean you have to go to court and tell your story, which will be good experience for you."

Then Agnew went into the detectives' room. Beck could hear him dressing down Davis and his partner for stealing credit from a probationary constable. Beck could not help but remember this incident over subsequent years, as Jack M Davis worked his way up through the ranks, He became Chief Commissioner of the Commonwealth Police, a post he held from 1969 until the creation of the new Australian Federal Police in 1979.

Perhaps this incident and subsequent advice made a mark on Beck's attitude. While he was courageous and diligent, and believed in discipline as a key to getting the job done well, he had little respect for hierarchy. He had a habit of talking back, and standing up for himself when he believed he was right, which sometimes grated on his superior officers.

This defiant streak showed up during his first year in the force, when he was sent to Penrith— at that stage a town some way from Sydney— on assignment. The Police Department had acquired a former Air Force property at Penrith to become a new residential police college. Beck, still in uniform and based at Phillip St, was one of four young constables from the city selected to live at the site and guard it while it was being refurbished.

They were under control of Sergeant Chisholm, the highest ranking officer at the Penrith station, who would come and see them occasionally.

One of the group, Fred Niemar, had been a shearer's cook and offered to cook for the group. The two others were first grade footballers (in those days amateurs) and they were allowed to take several days off to return to their home towns, Newcastle and Taree, to play matches. When they came back, they announced they had been invited to play for the local team at Penrith, the following day. As Beck had a rest day, Niemar volunteered to stay on duty and to cook dinner.

Beck knew a young lady in Penrith and took her to the football to see his colleagues play. At the end of the match the three young men were leaving when a Penrith constable who knew them, Ian Leading, rode up on a motorbike looking anxious.

Leading told them that Inspector Colin John Delaney from Police Headquarters had stopped by Penrith station and asked for a constable to take him to the new property so he could have a look at the facilities. Leading had done the job. He told Beck's group that Delaney had his wife in the car with him. They had arrived at the camp just as dark was falling, and found the camp deserted and the premises unprotected.

"I can tell you, he was not happy about it!" Leading said. "You guys need to get back there now and watch your backs."

When they heard this, Beck's group wondered why Niemar was not at the property as he had promised. They later discovered that he had gone to the corner shop to buy some tomatoes, right at the time the inspector arrived.

The other two constables turned to hurry back to the camp, but Beck said he would follow later.

"I'm rostered off duty. I'll walk my lady friend home first and then I head straight back." he told Leading.

By the time Beck arrived at the camp after a three kilometre walk it was completely dark. As he approached he could see a car taillight, then a voice called out to him from about 40 metres away. "Who goes there?" As Beck walked closer the voice called out again, "I already asked you, who are you?"

Now Beck replied, "I don't know whom I'm talking to, sir". He was careful to add the "sir" as he knew full well who it was.

When Beck was near to the car he could see the other three constables standing close by. Delaney demanded to know why he was so late back.

Beck told him that he had the day rostered off, and that he had a responsibility to escort the young lady safely home.

Delaney was not impressed.

"Why isn't your bed made?" he demanded.

"Sir, when I left here I had washed my sheets in the morning and left them on the line, and I asked Constable Niemar to bring them in for me, and that's why it's not made." Then he turned to Niemar accusingly. "Didn't you bring them in for me?" he asked.

"No, I did not. I was going to get them after I got back from the shop, but then the Inspector was here and…" Niemar left the sentence Add paragraph break before. "Enough of that!" said Delaney, keeping his stony gaze on Beck. "Why did I find a cigarette stub on the floor of your room?"

Beck knew this was untrue. "I don't know anything about that, I don't smoke," he replied calmly.

Delaney tried again. "I found a beer bottle top in your room!"

"I don't know about that, I don't drink," Beck responded.

Although his trap had failed, the inspector was still irate. He directed Beck to go to the police station, about one kilometre away. The other constables were told to get in his car and they drove, while Beck had to walk again.

Beck did not hurry, hoping that the inspector might have left by the time he got there. When he arrived he was met by Sergeant Chisholm, who was more or less wringing his hands.

"For goodness' sake, just say 'yes sir no sir', don't say anything to upset him," begged Chisholm. "He's not happy, you've all done the wrong thing!"

But Beck was not about to back down to anyone, even an inspector. "Well he was making things up. If I'm spoken to properly, I'll respond the same way!" he insisted, implying the opposite also applied.

Chisholm was beside himself, "Oh don't say that son!" he begged.

Beck joined his three colleagues, who had already been given a severe dressing down by Delaney (who was appointed Commissioner of Police in October 1952) for failing in their duty. Delaney turned to Beck with a face like thunder.

"I don't like your attitude," he began.

"Well I'm sorry about that, sir," replied Beck, "but I fail to see where I have done anything wrong.

"I was rostered off duty, I've told you where I've been. I've given you the explanation for my bed not being made.

"I don't smoke and I don't drink and I can't explain how those things would get there. I can assure you that they weren't there this morning," he could not resist adding.

After a few portentous seconds of silence, Delaney spat out, "Right, the next time Inspector Pine comes up from Parramatta, you will be severely reprimanded by him!"

With that he left. As it turned out, their period on guard duty at the college ended soon after, and they never received a reprimand. Beck and the others returned to their city police stations, thankful to hear no more about it.

The Penrith incident got back to Beck's father Launcelot, as he knew Delaney well. He told Beck he should never talk back to a superior officer. Beck decided his father was right, but he also resolved that when he was in authority he would always speak to his men courteously, and this would get a better result.

Beck did see Delaney again. When Queen Elizabeth visited Australia in 1954, Beck—then on the consorting squad—was part of a contingent of police sent to Wagga to control the crowds. The visiting police were assembled in a large room to be told their specific duties. As each name was called out, the officer would step forward. Police Commissioner Delaney, as he was then, would nod his head as each name was called out, without looking at the person.

When the inspector started to read the names of the Sydney police, the first two got the usual nod. Then he called out, "Detective Beck, Consorting Squad". Delaney's head shot up for the first and only time and he looked around the room. "Where?" he asked, then he saw Beck. He did not say anything, but Beck did not get the nod. Then the next name was called and Delaney looked away again.

Afterwards, a dozen other police asked Beck, "What have you done to Delaney?"

"Nothing, we're mates!" he grinned.

* * * *

After his stint at Penrith Beck returned to Phillip St. Around this time in late 1946, policing of various duties was being shaken up and a new squad, 21 Division was formed to deal with street violence.

As a probationary constable, Beck did not have a right to join the division, but put in an application anyway. In due course he was asked to report to the Division head, Inspector Harry Boswell.

"Well son," Boswell greeted him, "I've got your application to join 21 Division." He then looked Beck up and down. "By gee son, you're not very big, son!"

"Well I suppose not, Mr Boswell," replied Beck, before he then noticed that the Inspector was shorter than himself.

Boswell saw the look and knew what it meant.

"Don't get any smart things in your mind about me!" he demanded. "Well—you're not very big, but can you fight son?"

"I think I can, when I have to. I've done some boxing, in the Air Force," responded Beck.

After more questions like this, Beck made a suggestion. "Look Mr Boswell, have you got someone you'd like me to fight, to see if I can?"

"I'll ask the questions, you just give the answers," retorted the inspector. But Boswell liked his pluck.

"Look, I'll give you a go son and if you can take it, this is going to be rough and tough and you've got to expect the worst. Our job on the 21 Division is to clean up the crime wave that exists in NSW following the war, there's decent people out there being knocked about and the streets are full of hoodlums."

This sounded good to Beck. While he had no intention of picking fights, he had never run away from one either. One of his favourite sayings, which he had picked up from an old 'copper', summed up his view that getting physical was an important part of policing. "Every person who joins the police, what he needs to bring him down to reality is a belt across the mouth from a hoodlum," the older man had told him, and Beck kept it in mind.

Before joining 21 Division, Beck first had to learn how to drive a motorbike and side car, which was the vehicle used by the new squad. As soon as he could do this, Boswell kept his promise and he was transferred. Beck was one of several young officers to join the division, each paired off with a senior officer.

When a call came in to 21 Division for assistance with some trouble on the streets, anywhere in Sydney's growing suburbs, a team would be sent. They would report to the local police station in the area and consult them on what needed to be done.

For these young police, 21 Division was a test of their suitability for criminal work. Each member of the division submitted a weekly return, detailing their arrests for criminal offences (as opposed to misdemeanours), and at the end of their stint, the best of them would be allowed to sit an examination and become detectives.

The patrols went all over the city, and inevitably carried out a high number of arrests, although they were under orders only to arrest if necessary.

Beck started with Allen Fitzgerald, who was renowned as an outstanding swimmer and member of the North Steyne surf club. Beck was also an excellent swimmer and got on well with Fitzgerald. They arrested numerous louts and hoodlums, drunks and other troublemakers.

Often there were fights involved. On one occasion Beck and Fitzgerald arrested two people at Manly wharf who were attempting to break into a car. The first prisoner was placed on the seat of the sidecar and the other was ordered to sit on his legs for the short journey to the local police station. This was the customary way of dealing with two prisoners and one bike with sidecar. One policeman, in this case Fitzgerald, would ride the bike while the second, who was Beck this time, would sit on the mudguard and hold onto the sidecar.

The offenders were taken to the police station and put in the dock for charging. When the uniformed constable was searching them, he found that the man who was sitting in the seat of the sidecar had two wallets—the second one belonging to his partner in crime who had been on his lap. When the constable showed both wallets to the pair in the dock, the man who had been robbed was furious. He launched at his companion and a fight ensured right there in the police station. After Beck and his partner broke it up, the wallet owner demanded that his 'friend' be charged with theft, to the amusement of the police.

Beck later worked with a senior constable named Bruce Jackson, whom he also regarded highly. Together they got into and out of a lot of scraps, including a major ruckus at Luna Park.

Local police had reported large crowds at the amusement park, at Milson's Point on Sydney Harbour, and many of them were American, British and Australian servicemen. When Beck and Jackson arrived they saw a group of about eight unruly British sailors, all of them Liverpool Irishmen (Liverpool had a very large population of people of Irish descent). They were using indecent language towards a group of young women, so Jackson walked over to caution them.

Instantly, the group turned on Jackson and Beck, and the battle was on. Jackson quickly grabbed the ringleader, whacked a handcuff on him and then put the other handcuff on himself. The cry then went up, "Get his keys!"

As quickly as he could, Jackson took his keys from his pocket and threw them over the low wall and into the harbour. The sailors then angrily belted and kicked at Jackson, while Beck was doing his best to restrain them, but the odds were too great. Beck had singled out a Petty Officer and arrested him, but as soon as he grabbed and held the man, the rest of the mob attacked him and snatched their mate away. Beck then ran after him and tackled him, and was attacked again. This happened a number of times. At one time, Beck was picked up bodily and thrown against a playground merry-go-round and held by several sailors while the Petty Officer punched him.

The American and Australian servicemen had seen what was happening and joined the fray. There were now more than 500 people involved in the brawl. Police cars and motorbikes appeared from all directions, but as soon as the police left their vehicles they were attacked by a mass of people.

Meanwhile at the core of it, Beck was determined to get the Petty Officer. Despite his many bruises, he kept following him and at every opportunity, would grab hold of him, only to be pulled off again.

Eventually the fight became so big that the Petty Officer was separated from his mates, and suddenly he realised he was vulnerable. He ran up under the Harbour Bridge, with Beck in pursuit, threw himself to the ground and wriggled under a big car (in those days cars were higher off the ground). Undeterred, Beck crawled in after him. The sailor had taken a rock in with him and kept hitting Beck in the face with it, but Beck refused to back off. He swung his hand with the handcuffs in it and gave the Petty Oficer 'a stroke'. Finally Beck got the better of his opponent and was able to drag him out into the open and put the handcuffs on him. The sailor kept up the struggle but Beck pushed and dragged him back to where his police cycle and sidecar was parked, and put him in the sidecar. As was customary when prisoners struggled, Beck shoved the man into the sidecar head first.

As Beck took off he saw police caps being pelted into the harbour in the ultimate mark of disrespect. He also saw several motorbikes roaring off with prisoners in the sidecars. One motorbike ridden by a sergeant had two Australian soldiers in the sidecar, but while Beck watched, a third soldier ran out and stood in front of the bike, trying to force it to stop. The bike did not stop and the soldier was hit by the sidecar and sent flying into the crowd like a catherine wheel.

Meanwhile, Jackson had been belted and kicked by the angry crowd, until he was rescued by other police and taken to North Sydney Police Station.

A large number of people were arrested as a result of the brawl, and the incident was written up in *The Bulletin* magazine under the heading "Mug Coppers". The Petty Officer arrested by Beck was sentenced to four months' jail, and Beck was given compensation for his torn coat, but not for the physical beating he suffered.

Despite their many aches and pains, the next day Beck and Jackson turned up for work as usual. They were riding around on the motorcycle when a police car pulled up next to them. "Are you Beck?" asked an officer and Beck replied in the affirmative.

"You've got to get off the bike," the officer told him.

"It's believed you've got a fractured skull. They've just had a look at the X-rays after this blow-up last night. So hop in the car and we'll take you down to the station."

As it turned out Beck's skull was not fractured, although he did have severe bruising, and so he did not even have a day off work.

It was far from unusual for Beck to be hurt in the course of his duties, and rarely did he get any sympathy.

Around this time Beck had another encounter with a superior officer, thanks to his stubborn streak.

He and Jackson were out on the police motorbike one evening at North Sydney. Beck parked the motorcycle opposite a hotel that they were going to check for illegal gambling. The parking space was just in front of a car in which the driver was sitting at the wheel. As the two policemen walked away, the driver called out to them.

"Hey, you, fellow—get back here!"

Beck replied, "Are you talking to me sir?"

"Yes I am," said the driver angrily. "How do you expect me to get out of here if you've parked in front?"

Beck looked at the space and there was plenty of room. He told the driver so, adding that the cycle was parked in accordance with the law.

The driver was not happy. "You would say that, wouldn't you? It's rubbish. I'm telling you, move that motorcycle so I can get out!" Beck looked at the cycle again.

"Sir if you can't get your vehicle out of there, the question may arise as to whether you should have a licence!" Then he signalled to his partner and they walked away.

The next morning Beck and Jackson were called in before Inspector Harry Boswell, who had taken a formal complaint from the man in the car. "I've received a complaint from a thorough gentleman, a friend of mine, a solicitor," he began, and Beck and Jackson's hearts sank as the Inspector launched into the other motorist's version of the incident.

This version was most unflattering of Beck, and he did not think it was at all fair. Brashly, he spoke up: "With all due respect sir, I don't think that fellow was a gentleman by the way he spoke to me."

Boswell's hackles rose. "If I say a person is a gentleman, that's it as far as you are concerned," he riposted. "Do you get what I'm saying?" Beck did not get it.

"I can understand what you're saying from what you have been told," he said cautiously.

"But sir, our explanation is not at fault. And I must repeat, this man was not behaving like a gentleman, he was angry and unreasonable."

Boswell was not impressed and told Beck so, at some length, then eventually ordered him and Jackson to get out. Beck was nearly to the doorway when he looked back and Boswell caught his eye. "Have you got something else to say Beck?" he growled.

Beck did not take the cue to keep his mouth shut. "Only that that fellow was not a gentleman!" he insisted.

At that, Boswell picked up the nearest object, which was a copy of the thick, heavy Police Rules and Instruction Book, and threw it violently at Beck. Beck dodged and the book hit the side of the doorway and burst into a myriad of sections which splattered on the floor. Boswell glared at Beck. "Now you two can get busy and put that back together!" he ordered.

It was a very thick and complicated book, full of amendments and it took fully three hours to put it back together, during which Jackson made it very clear to Beck that he did not appreciate his bravery. The experience made Beck, always confident of his righteousness, think twice but did not shake his faith in his judgement. He insisted that, while he had been outspoken, he had also spoken the truth and had the right to defend himself.

The fact that a senior officer had thrown a heavy object at two younger police drew no comment at all.

As well as crowd control duties, 21 Division when it was established was made responsible for policing illegal gambling. On weekends the younger constables were sent out to find illegal SP (Starting Price) betting shops and sometimes they would be taken to Chinatown for raids on Chinese gaming houses. This was Beck's first experience of policing illegal gambling.

Illegal SP bookmaking was a contentious area of the law. Betting on horse races and everything else had been a feature of colonial life since the First Fleet. When the Great Depression hit in the early 1930s, a day at the races became a luxury that few ordinary Sydney workers could afford. Instead the punters turned to the neighbourhood SP, leading to a boom in off course betting. The result was a dramatic downturn in the tax revenues from the legal totalisators, and for this reason the NSW Government ordered the police to crush the SP bookmakers.

Between 1930 and 1936, 20,000 arrests for betting offences were made in Sydney, mainly in the inner city working class slums. But the public did not support the crackdown. SP bookmaking (a generic term for all illegal off-course betting) was a major issue in NSW politics during the 1930s, with no less than three Royal Commissions but still no political resolution.

While the conservatives insisted that SP was a social evil, the Labor Party made political capital by defending the illegal operators in Parliament, arguing that it was nothing short of hypocrisy to allow the wealthy to have their bets at the racetrack while the poor were treated as criminals for doing the same thing. SP betting survived, and the postWorld War 2 boom in telecommunications made SP betting easier and more available then ever via the growing telephone network rolled out by the federal Postmaster General's Department.

In the late 1940s, numerous small illegal bookmakers operated from hotels and houses in many suburbs of Sydney. These were local operators who knew their clientele personally—a far cry from the massive operations set up by organised criminals decades later.

When Beck and other members of 21 Division were assigned to gaming and betting duties, they were allowed to take the police car instead of the cycle and sidecar. There would typically be four of the younger constables and a sergeant to supervise. Dressed in casual civilian clothes, their job was to blend in with the crowd at suspected venues to catch the SPs in operation. Knowing that they were being targeted, the SPs had become cunning and all had lookouts watching for police. Some operated in well-known premises, but others had found locations which were hard to approach and easy to escape from, which made it difficult for the police to make arrests.

One such place was in Redfern. It was like a shopfront with a front window and a solid iron and wood door. Bettors would have to go to the window, which was lifted up, the money was offered and taken and a card given in return, then the window would come down. A lookout would stand outside the window scrutinising each person as they arrived and while they were lining up to place their bets, to make sure they were bona fide gamblers and not undercover police.

The team in which Beck was working had driven to Redfern, but the sergeant in charge of them was pessimistic about their chances. "If you can get into this place you'll be the only one that can do it, but I doubt it," he said to Beck, and he explained the set up. "You can't penetrate through the doors because by the time you got in there you wouldn't find anything, so you've just got to get in there the best way you can."

This was a challenge which Beck found irresistible. He strolled down towards the betting shop and there was a queue of a dozen or so people waiting to get a bet on. One of them was a woman, carrying a shopping bag. Beck placed himself next to her and started to make small talk in a friendly way, as though he was with the woman. He kept his back to the betting window and the lookout so he could not be identified as a stranger, and gradually moved down towards the door as the queue moved.

When he got within a few people of the window, he assessed the defences and decided that the only way to get in was to wait until the window went up and take them by surprise, by running forward and throwing himself inside. He was preparing himself for the right moment when he saw the lookout staring at him with a suspicious look on his face, no doubt thinking that he had not seen Beck before. The lookout was standing in front of the window. But just then the window went up and Beck decided to take a gamble. He ran and dived straight for the window; but as he did, the lookout saw him coming and quickly grabbed the window and slammed it down.

It was too late to stop Beck though. He crashed through the glass, cutting his ear, but he was on the inside. In fact he landed on top of two of the clerks, who had not had time to move away, and before they could do anything Beck declared loudly, "I am a police officer and you are under arrest!"

As soon as they heard that, the startled clerks submitted. Then the rest of the 21 Division team came running up and all the people involved in the operation were arrested.

It was a coup for Beck and a pointer to his future. The sergeant who had given him the challenge could not believe it, and every time he saw Beck from that time on he would talk about 'the window'.

On another occasion when Beck went out with that sergeant, however, the sergeant had been drinking quite heavily. The team was on its way to Mascot late one afternoon with the sergeant in the passenger seat. He turned around to look at the three young constables in the back seat, including Beck, as the car stopped outside a house. "You!" he ordered Beck in his drunken voice, "Go in there and bring out the woman that's betting in there."

Beck got out of the car and walked inside the gate. The front door of the house was open and a radio was on, playing music not racing or even another sport. Beck walked inside and found a woman ironing.

"What can I do for you?" she asked him, calmly.

Beck replied, "I'm from the police, I understand you are carrying out illegal betting here."

The woman shook her head. "No love, you've come to the wrong place, in the wrong street - the place you're looking for is in the next street, about the same place, opposite."

There was no indication of SP betting. Beck thought she was telling the truth. He excused himself and went back to the car where he told the sergeant what had happened.

"There's no activity there at all," Beck said. "And the woman tells me we're in the wrong street, and the house we're looking for is in the next street opposite this one."

But the sergeant was angry. "When I tell you to bring someone out, you bring someone out," he ordered.

"I can't do that if it's not the right thing," countered Beck. The sergeant said, "You get in the car, don't talk to me!" They drove off, but the sergeant refused to check out the other house suggested by the woman. They went back to the 21 Division headquarters at Redfern, where Beck later found out the sergeant had reported him to Inspector Harry Boswell.

Boswell called Beck in, but he knew him well enough by now to listen to what he had to say. "I understand, son, that you went into the house and you said there was nothing doing there after being sent in and told there was," he said.

"Yes that's right, sir and I don't think you would want me to bring somebody out that wasn't committing any offence as I saw it," replied Beck.

Boswell then asked if Beck knew the address of the house they had gone to, and he did. Boswell looked up his records, then he called the sergeant in. The woman was right, and the sergeant had sent them to the wrong address. When the sergeant had gone, Boswell turned to Beck.

"You're not real keen on this SP work, are you son?"

"Not greatly," replied Beck. "I don't particularly like it and if it's going to be like today." He left it to Boswell to guess the rest.

"Look," said Boswell, "I'll tell you what I'm going to do. I'm going to send you away, up to the mountains, and I'll give you some money." He pulled some notes out of his pocket and proceeded to give Beck detailed directions. He was to go to Katoomba and meet an informant, to whom he should give X amount of the money. The informant, said Boswell, worked for him spotting gambling operations.

"When you go up there, you join him, you book yourself into one of the tourist places, you'll be up there for several days, and you look after him and give him expenses money, for drinking and so on."

He gave Beck more than 40 pounds (which in those days was worth about the same as $1000 today). Beck did as ordered and went up to Katoomba and met the informant, and spent some time with him. The informant had been told that Beck would look after him and indicated that he liked to drink, so Beck took him into a hotel.

The informant ordered a schooner of beer, then Beck asked for a lemonade. The informant was shocked. "Nah!" he cried, "You can't come in here and drink with me and have a lemonade!"

Beck said he would drink what he liked. The informant was puzzled. "Why don't you have a beer?"

"I don't drink," replied Beck.

"God, fancy sending a bloke here that doesn't drink," said the other. "For God's sake, at least have something with a bit of colour in it that might look like beer!" suggested the informant. So Beck ended up drinking litres of ginger ale, in an effort to keep up with his companion.

Despite his habits, he was a good informant and turned up eight different illegal operations in Katoomba. Beck took note of their locations and the security they had. Boswell had instructed him to leave town on the Saturday morning, which was race day, and start walking down the road towards Sydney, where he would be met by a Sergeant Fred Hanson.

Inspector Boswell had told him to start walking at 9am and said Hanson would meet him within about one kilometre.

Beck had walked seven kilometres and still there was no sign of Hanson, so he sat on the side of the road and waited. Finally, after another hour Hanson (who later became Commissioner of Police) and his team arrived with the police car. Beck got in, then made it clear what he thought of their poor timing.

They went to each of the places nominated by the informant, and made a total of eight arrests.

One of these places was a factory, the boundary of which was blockaded with barbed wire and other fortifications so the only entry was through the driveway of the fire station next door. Beck pointed this out to Hanson who said it was no problem. But when the police went to go through, the firemen came out and stopped them. "We're police," said Hanson, "on police business and we need access through here to get to where we're going".

But the firemen were resolute. "Well you're not coming through here!" they insisted.

Then there was an argument, and at one point Hanson threatened, "Look if you blokes don't get out of the way we'll move you!", which only caused more tempers to flare. At last common sense prevailed and the firemen backed down, allowing the police team through to the factory where they were found the SP betting under way and made a number of arrests.

On his return to Sydney, Beck reported to Inspector Boswell. Boswell was pleased with his work and asked if Beck had looked after the informant, which Beck said he had. "Alright then," said Boswell, "I'll send you away again."

"Oh by the way, Mr Boswell, I've got some of that money you gave me, left over," said Beck.

To Boswell's surprise, Beck took about 11 pounds, or more than a quarter of the original expenses, out of his pocket. Boswell looked at Beck and then at the money, then snatched it out of Beck's hand.

"Next time, don't be so bloody silly!" he said, from which Beck understood that if there was any left over, he was supposed to keep it for himself.

Illegal betting was even popular on the yacht races in Sydney Harbour. As part of their duties at 21 Division, several of the young constables would be taken down to assist the water police patrolling Sydney Harbour and its foreshores. The raids on 'floating bookies' were always fruitful and arrests were made both on the harbour and on land, although the penalties dealt out by the magistrates, especially in nearby Waverley Court, were sometimes paltry.

On one occasion they were directed to board a passenger ferry which was steaming across the harbour, following the regular boat races. There was a merry crowd on the ferry, including SP bookmakers who were doing a good trade.

Beck was just crossing from the police boat to the ferry when a surge of water swept the two boats together. Beck's leg was over the side and the surge swept the smaller boat up and against the ferry his leg was caught between the two vessels. Beck cried out, partly from pain and partly from fear. To his own amazement, when the force of the wave passed he was able to clamber onto the ferry. His leg was only bruised. Beck has always regarded it as a miracle that his leg was not crushed irreparably at that time.

Beck was working with uniformed police who had not been trained in criminal work, but with each partner they would pick it up as they went. It was a school of hard knocks, not only because of the blows they took in making arrests, but because of the way the way their charges were often treated in the courts.

Beck and his young colleagues, however, regarded each court case as a learning experience, especially the way the barristers would conduct their cross examinations. It was better in their view for a suspect to plead not guilty, and go through the trial, as a test of their skills. If the trial lawyers could not make the police stumble in their evidence, they were well pleased.

After Beck had served the required 12 months at 21 Division, Inspector Boswell personally congratulated him.

"Son, when you started off I didn't think you could make it, you were too inexperienced, you were a probationary constable," he said. "However, I've been going through the record of arrests and they are second to none." Then the normally grumpy old Boswell shook Beck's hand and gave him a wink and a bit of a grin, and Beck's probationary period was over.

* * * *

To move up the ranks to Constable First Class, after two and a half years of service, young police could sit a written examination. Similar written exams were also required to attain higher ranks.

But during Beck's time there was one way to get the promotion early. This was to do exceptionally well at the course run by the recently opened Penrith Police College. It was a six-week, intensive residential course, from which the constables returned home on the weekends. A mark of 90 per cent or more gave the constable the right to move up a rank without waiting the full two and a half years. Beck was keen to move up, so enrolled in the college course and studied hard.

While he was attending the residential course, Beck wanted to take part in a regular weekend shooting competition with his friend Bruce Jackson. They were both members of the police rifle club and were part of the official Police team. On most Saturday afternoons, when they could be spared from other duties, they would compete against other clubs and against the Army team at the rifle range at Long Bay.

Normally, the shooting competitions were regarded as part of official duties, and Beck and Jackson were allowed to use the police motorcycle to travel to the contest.

Because he was off normal duties and at the college, Beck checked with Inspector Boswell about using the motorcycle. Boswell said as Beck was prepared to give up his free time to represent the force, he was fine to use the bike.

Beck was driving the bike with Jackson in the sidecar as they rode through Enfield enroute to Long Bay, with the two 303 rifles across Jackson's knees. Suddenly a car travelling in front of them to the left cut across from close to the footpath to make a right hand turn, cutting off the motor cycle. The driver made no signal. Beck saw something coming out of the corner of his eye and swung the bike as best he could, but the violent swerve tipped the sidecar, which lost balance and took the cycle with it.

The bike and sidecar crashed on their sides through a fence and down a small bank on the other side, coming to rest next to a train line.

Beck and Jackson were dazed and cut, and the bike and sidecar were upside with unknown damage. As the pair sat up and assessed the situation, the motorist who had caused the crash came through the fence towards them. To their amazement, he was not apologetic.

"You'll be in trouble, I'm from the police!" he claimed. Shaken as he was, Beck was not so easily confused. "Don't be silly, we're police!" he fired back.

The motorist scoffed at this and repeated his claim. Just then another constable, Ralph Masters came along on a Safety Bureau motorcycle and took charge of the accident scene. Beck told him what the car driver had said, and Masters promptly arrested and charged him with assuming the designation of a police officer.

Beck and Jackson ended up in Blacktown Hospital for the weekend. But despite their injuries, the young constables were required to be back at the police college in time for the parade at 8.30 on the Monday morning. It was the examination period, they had done some of their tests the previous Friday and there were more on the Monday and Tuesday, which they could not miss.

Beck's ankle was cut and swollen after the accident, so that he could not even get a shoe on it. He had black and blue bruises all over his body and one side of his face was scraped and bleeding. Getting to the college on time was a challenge at the best of times, as Beck lived at Harbord on the northern beaches. He had to get a bus to Central Station, then a train to Penrith. By running like hell, he could just make it to the parade ground in time.

Running like hell was not an option on that day, however, so Beck left home a lot earlier than usual. He could just drag his foot along to make slow progress to the bus stop, and then to the train platform. Finally he arrived at Penrith and started the slow arduous trek to the parade ground, while the other trainees ran ahead.

As he approached down the street and through the entrance to the ground, he could see the trainees lined up. In front of them, with his back to Beck, was the Inspector, Paddy Cashan. Coming closer, Beck could hear him delivering a lecture about how not to behave.

"Now when you people go home at weekends you must realise that you are not on duty, you can't drive departmental motor vehicles, and one of your colleagues, I understand he's in hospital, he's ridden this police bike and turned it over and he'll be in all sorts of trouble," the Inspector said. "He's in the middle of his exams and he's done this."

As the assembly saw Beck approaching a murmur started up and Cashan turned to see what was up. On cue, he declared, "And here he is!" Cashan took Beck into his office and scrutinised him. Had the Government medical officer cleared Beck for duty? Beck conceded that he had not.

"No sir, it happened on Saturday afternoon and I've been to the hospital and they just told me, it'll get better," he said.

Cashan, who still thought Beck was in the wrong, organised for him to be taken to the government medical officer in Penrith. When Beck explained to the medical officer that he was not on general duties and was only hoping to sit his exams, he was able to return and complete his course.

Beck was also able to see Inspector Cashan and set the record straight about his use of the police motorcycle. When Cashan learned that the other motorist had been charged with traffic offences and impersonating a police officer, he was very relieved and changed his opinion, to Beck's relief.

Jackson had also been injured but not too badly and he also was able to return to duty. The two constables were able to claim damages, but only for their clothing. Beck got 20 pounds to compensate him for his sports coat, but nothing for his twisted ankle and bruises.

As a plain clothes trainee detective constable, Beck's first posting in 1947 was at Manly, a seaside resort in Sydney's north very close to the house Beck had bought with a war veterans' loan, in Harbord.

At Manly, through a mutual friend, he met a girl called Elsie Mitchell and fell in love. They married on April Fools' Day, 1949 – delaying the nuptials until after midday to avoid bad luck. The Becks went on to have three girls, Elizabeth, Pauline and Charlene, and one son, Mitchell— the same configuration as Launcelot Beck's family. Elsie, then a typing teacher knew that Merv was dedicated to his career. She supported him in everything, believing "whatever makes him happy, makes us happy".

Detectives worked in pairs, and Beck's first senior partner was a much older man, Mike Connors. Each pair of detectives had to keep a record of their criminal arrests, setting out the different types of incident—break and enter, armed robbery, and so on—and the details. This record was given every six months to the detective sergeant, who would check it and pass it on to the CIB.

When Beck and Connors handed in one such report listing 70 or 80 serious offences, Beck was approached by another detective who was not pleased. He told Beck that he and Connors should "break it down a bit" and stop making so many arrests. Beck refused to take the hint.

Inevitably, as his experience grew so did the realisation that not all of his police colleagues shared his defined sense of right and wrong, or his determination to enforce the law.

This did not worry Beck unduly. He remembered the advice he had received from his father: "Always be your own man, even if it makes you unpopular with your fellows. Do your duty at all times and you'll win."

It was no surprise to anyone who knew him when Beck passed the various tests to become a plain clothes detective. In 1953 he was assigned to another specialist area, the consorting squad based at the Criminal Investigation Branch (CIB). The CIB was then located at the rear of the Central Court of Petty Sessions, which had its front entrance on Liverpool St in the heart of Sydney's Central Business District.

Consorting legislation had been brought in during the time of the razor gangs in 1927. The law made it an offence to consort or associate with a reputed criminal, known prostitutes and people having "insufficient lawful means of support". If police knew (or claimed) that someone had a reputation as a criminal, they could book and fine any person seen with them on any occasion, without providing evidence of criminal activity. People who had been booked seven times under this law, including homeless people, could be arrested and were liable for up to six months jail.

It was a harsh law, but Beck regarded it as a way of controlling 'the criminal element', although he was also well aware that the big money and the big criminals were elsewhere. The consorting squad's main targets were prostitutes, pickpockets and organised criminals.

Many of his arrests during that period were of pickpockets at various race meets, including horse races at Randwick, Clarendon near Richmond, and in country towns, and the greyhound races at Harold Park. But he and the rest of the squad were under instruction to ignore any illegal gambling they encountered, as this was a job for 21 Division and to some extent, the Vice Squad.

A memorable incident, and one of the first of Beck's exploits to be reported by the Sydney newspapers, occurred in early September 1953, Beck was the most junior officer in his patrol when they were called to a suspected robbery at La Perouse about 3 am one night. Beck was told to wait in the car, and was typing up a message from the wireless, when he saw a man run down the street, collide with the police driver and push him over, then run off. Beck jumped out and went in pursuit.

The man ran down onto the dark beach at La Perouse and into the water, up to his shoulders. Beck ran to the edge and shone his waterproof torch on the man. "Come on out, you can't get away!" Beck called. The man said nothing. He started to walk through the water, laboriously, parallel to the beach and away from Beck. Beck decided there was nothing for it, he would have to go in after him. He started to take off his suit while walking and talking to the man. When down to his underwear, he dug a hole in the sand and buried his police revolver so that the offender could not get it if it came to a struggle.

Gritting his teeth Beck then walked part way into the cold winter water, but the suspect kept moving away. After a minute of this Beck decided he had no option, and started walking further out into the water after the man.

Realising that his game was over, the burglar turned and started to swim out into Botany Bay. Two hundred and fifty metres out was a large round mooring buoy, and moored to it was a punter, a large vessel. The man swam towards it, with Beck following him.

After 80 metres they came to a lot of cork floats and ropes on top of the water, covering an area about half the size of a tennis court. The offender kept swimming through the floats and Beck followed.

Beck still had the torch, tucked into the back of his underpants so he could swim. The burglar reached the buoy and retreated to the back of it, with Beck on the other side. Beck reached back for the torch and shone it on the man, calling out to him not to be silly and to give up. By that time, Beck could see the car lights coming down the beach towards their location and was confident that back-up was near.

Each time he tried to approach, the burglar would swing around to the opposite side of the buoy. Beck quickly got tired of the game and devised a new approach. Turning the torch off, he stuck it back into his underpants, took a deep breath and dived under water. There was just enough light for him to see the surface. He swam about 6 metres around the buoy and came up next to the man, to his surprise. As Beck surfaced he grabbed the man around the neck.

As they struggled, Beck managed to retrieve the torch. He shone it in the man's face and then grabbed him by the hair on the back of his head. As the man kicked and splashed, unable to strike him, Beck declared, "You're under arrest and I'm taking you in!"

There was still the technical issue of how to get the man back to the shore. Beck swam sidestroke, pulling the man along by his hair. He struggled for a while and then stopped, allowing Beck to make a few metres progress, then struggled again, on and off.

It was hard going for Beck. After 25 minutes he was within 40 metres of the beach, where a police truck and his Car One were waiting for them with the headlights shining on the water to guide Beck. Then another swimmer appeared, a uniformed constable who had fortunately been wearing a football jersey underneath his uniform. Together, Beck and the constable then pulled the man onto the beach where he was quite grateful to be arrested and shoved into a police car as he was exhausted and on the verge of hypothermia. It was discovered that he was a wellknown criminal with 28 convictions for breaking, entering and stealing and wanted for a number of offences.

Beck meanwhile was still dripping wet and increasingly cold. He hurried down the beach to collect his clothes and retrieve the revolver from where he had buried it. But as soon as he put his clothes on, they became wet too. He was shivering. He hurried off the beach to Car One, which was a bit warmer.

The team leader directed the car to La Perouse Police Station so that Beck could change, but when they arrived they found there were no spare clothes. There was no suggestion that Beck knock off early, and he was not going to ask. Bedraggled and cold he finished his shift with a blanket around him. He was still wet when he caught the early morning bus to Circular Quay and then the ferry home to Manly.

Only a few hours later, the Sydney afternoon tabloid newspapers, *the Daily Mirror* and *the Sun,* both carried large stories about Beck's dramatic swim to make the arrest.

Beck then discovered that the floats he had swum through were attached to shark bait hanging low down in the water, to attract the many sharks which frequented the bay.

The detective sergeant leading Car One team was very impressed with Beck's efforts.

"What you did out there, not many would do that," he said. "I am going to put a report in about you, I think it was an outstanding effort and I think you should be commended."

The sergeant's report went up through the system but for unknown reasons, went to a traffic superintendent for assessment. This superintendent recommended only that Beck "note the comments of his senior officers that they were pleased with his efforts".

The Car One sergeant was furious with this brush-off. He went in person to confront the superintendent. "Would you swim out into Botany Bay through shark infested waters in the middle of winter? I wouldn't!" he exclaimed angrily.

"Don't you come into my office and tell me how to do my job!" the superintendent barked. He ordered the sergeant out and threatened to take action if he pursued the matter. Beck was disappointed but also happy that his sergeant had made the effort for him.

Beck remained on consorting for three years. He enjoyed the work because he had a natural interest in criminal psychology and behaviour.

It also gave him some interesting insights into a darker side of policing, as he had his first experience of a politician attempting to influence the outcome of a criminal charge.

At this time, Beck's partner on the Consorting Squad was Detective Clive Wells, who was held in high regard by Beck and others.

One of their arrests was a man who had tried to pick pockets in the old Lottery Office in Barrack St Sydney, a small office which was always full of people and was a favourite haunt for pickpockets. Beck was sent down there to observe. He saw a man acting suspiciously in the crowd and recognised him as a suspect. Beck followed the man as he left the Lottery Office and went up King St, where he got on a tram. Beck got on the tram too. As they travelled further up King St, Beck saw Wells standing on the corner of Castlereagh St. Beck waved to him, Wells saw him and he got on at the next stop. Together they followed the suspect to his house in Waverley, and then they arrested him.

After the pickpocket was released on remand, Wells was contacted by the Labor Member for Bathurst and NSW Chief Secretary (a ministerial position), Gus Kelly. Kelly's portfolio was responsible for vice, gaming, racing and licensing, all areas of great interest to Sydney's major criminals. It was a matter of frequent comment on the Consorting Squad at the time, in the early 1950s, that Minister Kelly was friendly with various criminals.

Wells was told Kelly wanted to meet him to discuss the case. Wells was nervous, suspicious that Kelly wanted him to drop the charges. He asked Beck to go with him.

When the time came, Wells and Beck met Gus Kelly in the grounds of Sydney Hospital, next to the State Parliament. Kelly had been contacted by the pickpocket, and now he asked Wells what could be done for the man. Wells and Beck said they could not help, as the matter would have to go to trial. Kelly did not look pleased, but did not press the point and the two young police left without further ado.

As it transpired, however, the case was adjourned indefinitely, and the charge never went to court. Wells and Beck had no doubt that Gus Kelly had used his considerable clout to get the man, a common thief, off the hook.

There was a story, well known on the consorting squad, that Kelly had a map in his ministerial office showing the location of illegal SP operators. In 1997 the story was told to the Royal Commission into NSW police corruption by former Commissioner, Tony Lauer.

Lauer said SP operators would meet Kelly in his office. Kelly would pull down the map, which was folded up, and say, "You can have the areas not shaded". Lauer said Kelly had been making the offer in exchange for large bribes "pretty well from the time I joined the service" in April 1955. Kelly was Chief Secretary for a record 13 years from 1952[7] and died at his Mosman home in 1967.

Like Lauer, Beck and his colleagues on the Consorting Squad, believed every word of this story.

In 1953 Beck also went on a three month interchange duty to the Victorian CIB. While there he had his first success in a murder investigation. He and a Queensland Detective Sergeant, Mervyn Chalmers also on secondment, arrested a criminal named Leonard

William Elliott, for the murder of an elderly man near Bathurst in NSW. The victim died from choking after Elliott stuffed his socks down his throat. Elliott then ran off with the victim's valuable coin collection.

Beck and Chalmers tracked down Elliott in Victoria, and found the leather bag with the coins hidden outside his lodging house.

Elliott was 28 years old at the time and with no fixed address. He was tried at Bathurst Court in October 1954. He was found not guilty of murder but guilty of manslaughter and sentenced to 15 years imprisonment. When released, he made the news again in a strange way. On the day of his release, he left the jail at 11am and at 2pm he was caught clumsily trying to break into a house. Elliott told police he could not cope with the outside world and wanted to be locked up again. He was back in time for the prisoners' evening meal, and later died in jail. This was not an uncommon experience for long term prisoners, as portrayed in the 1994 American drama film, *The Shawshank Redemption*.

Through the late 1950s and 1960s, Merv Beck worked enthusiastically at his detective duties, maintaining his high personal standards for determination and dedication to the job. He undertook varied duties, including several homicide inquiries.

He got on well with most of the police with whom he worked directly, but the same was not always true of the senior officers who in many ways determined their fate.

Like most detectives, Beck was particularly disappointed by the calibre of the police appointed to run the Criminal Investigation Branch, the division which in theory was reserved for the most talented and skilled detectives. It was common knowledge among the detectives. that some of the CIB chiefs over the years were 'running with' the criminals. Even those who were not considered 'crooked' were unimpressive and seemed to do little to stand up against corrupt influences.

In Beck's view, these officers were letting down the force which meant so much to him.

One of the few CIB chiefs who stood out above others was Detective Superintendent Jack Flint, whom Beck and his fellow detectives found to be straight down the line and a good judge of the merits of his detectives. Flint was also a hard man and an old-fashioned disciplinarian.

In 1956, the Police Department decided to handpick a group of detectives to be placed in the Vice Squad to boost its investigation strength. The Vice Squad had small groups of police at the various city police stations. Beck and another detective were sent to Regent St police station, which had a three-man Vice Squad led by a sergeant.

Their arrival was resented by the existing Vice Squad members, who did not feel the need for any detectives in their midst. Beck found that the senior officers were constantly sniping at him and his colleague Lance Gardner, nit-picking or as they would say, pinpricking, over petty issues.

Gardner had come to the Vice Squad from uniformed duties and became one of Beck's close friends. He later became a police lecturer until his sad and sudden death in 1975. By coincidence they both lived near Manly, Gardner at Dee Why and Beck at Collaroy. They would both rush to catch the last bus home after finishing the late shift.

Beck and Gardner were both committed to investigate whatever crimes they could, which did not always win favours with their colleagues. One such incident occurred when the young constables decided to investigate the theft of a valuable Persian carpet.

Beck and Gardner had arrived at work two hours early, at 4pm instead of 6pm, to follow up a lead on the theft. When they arrived at the office, a sergeant saw them and asked why they were there early. They explained that they were going out to Vaucluse to talk to the woman about the stolen carpet. The sergeant told them sourly it was not a Vice Squad matter. Beck ignored this.

"We're detectives and it's a criminal matter and we're going to do what we can to solve the crime!" he said firmly.

The lead they had received was a good one. They located the stolen carpet and made arrests. But rather than praise, the next day when they came onto duty, there was a memo from their Inspector, Ron Waldron. He demanded to know why they had come on duty when they were not rostered on, whether they had sought permission, who gave it, and finally, why they had not signed off their duty pad at 2am—when they had left to catch the last bus to Manly. No mention was made of the fact that they had solved a crime.

Beck and Gardner wrote an official report in response to the memo, detailing their reasons, and the results. It was an explanation, not an apology, finishing with the offer to donate the extra two hours pay they were due, to a charity of the Inspector's choice. They presented the report in person and waited while the Inspector read it.

Waldron was not impressed. He tore up the report in front of the young police and angrily threw the scraps in the bin.

But Gardner was not intimidated. "That is an official report and cannot be thrown away like that Inspector," Gardner said. "You should send it to the Commissioner and if you don't, I will."

Waldron looked keenly at Gardner, but said nothing. Then he turned to Beck who—for once—seemed the less belligerent option.

"You take your young mate outside and try and talk some sense into him," he directed.

Beck did so, and after a long talk, Gardner agreed to drop the matter. For a while after that, the sergeants at the Vice Squad left them alone, but the young detectives knew that their presence on the Vice Squad was resented.

Often, the Vice Squad work was morally challenging. The squad would carry out dawn patrols, as they were known, on low grade lodging or rooming houses, which they referred to as 'bug houses'. The police would knock on the door, waking up the manager and announce themselves, then go to each room and open the door. Inside they would often find a couple in bed, and often enough the woman would be a prostitute and/or the man was a missing person, a criminal or wanted for criminal offences. Stolen property was often found in the rooms as well.

Beck considered many of the prostitutes whom they arrested to be victims of their violent pimps. In the days before drug addiction became the routine way to keep 'working women' under control, the pimps would often assault them and even kick them in their genitals if they stepped out of line. The pimps' behaviour was in Beck's view a good enough reason to eliminate prostitution.

Not all of the women, however, were victims. One night, the consorting squad received information from the Victorian Police that two criminals were hiding in Surrey Hills premises occupied by a prostitute. Beck and three others were instructed to go and check out the property. After surrounding the place as best they could, they knocked on the door and demanded entry.

The prostitute appeared at a window above the front door and looked down at them. She was known as 'the Horse' because she had a big mane of hair and a rather a large head. She was a volatile type at the best of times, and she refused to open the door to the police.

While they were arguing with her, one of the police could not resist making a joke. "Bring up a bale of hay for the Horse," he called out, followed by laughter from below and a stream of abuse from the woman above. The Horse then punctuated her response by picking up a chair and throwing it out the open window towards the assembled police, followed by an assortment of other items. One of them was a chamber pot (toilet) which landed on the bonnet of the police car and bounced into and through the windscreen, tossing out its offensive contents.

Before she could do any more damage, a sergeant forced open the door and the police ran into the house. They quickly found the two suspects and arrested them and the Horse, who remained defiant and unrepentant despite the wind blowing on her in the police car through the hole in the windscreen.

The energy and enthusiasm which Beck and Garland brought to their work soon got them into trouble again.

A sergeant in the vice squad was responsible for the squad's gaming and betting duties. Gaming and betting was outside Beck's normal duties, but when the sergeant went on leave, he gave Beck and Gardner an assignment. He left them a list of four names, each of them an SP bookmaker, and instructed Beck and Gardner to attempt to arrest them while he was away for three weeks.

They set about their task with gusto. During the first weekend of the sergeant's absence, Beck and Gardner took the initiative and arrested not three but eight SP operators.

Once again, instead of praise Beck received a remonstration. The sergeant was informed and immediately came back to duty, telling the two young detectives in no uncertain terms that they had exceeded their authority.

Although he was remonstrated, the arrests must have won Beck praise in some quarter. Soon afterwards he was transferred to North Sydney as the officer in charge of both vice and gaming matters in the district, ranging from indecent exposures in public toilets, to SP bookmaking. Beck was the only officer at North Sydney working in these areas, so it was a chance to learn much about both aspects of the law.

Race days were busy. On these days, Beck was assigned a working companion from the Vice Squad. Together they were responsible for finding SP bookmakers in the North Sydney district, and making arrests. The companions he would be given were always young constables who were learning on the job, known in the force as 'peanutters'.

"Why am I getting all these young peanutters to help and not someone who knows the game," Beck asked his senior sergeant after a few months. The response surprised him.

"The young fellows are fine. We don't want to give the bookies too much trouble," the sergeant said. Looking Beck in the eye, he continued, "And don't you get carried away either. Just do what you can, we don't expect any upsets."

At this time, during the late 1950s, although 21 Division's Gaming Squad and other police were supposed to keep watch on them, SP bookies were not an issue of major concern for the law enforcement authorities, and in general SPs were viewed as a source of harmless fun. One SP who came before the courts was given a character reference by a police officer, who said he was a decent citizen "and by no means a welcher", meaning he did not break his word. The magistrate hearing the case declared his sympathy for the SP before giving him a 25 pound fine instead of the maximum six months sentence.

Beck, however, found it impossible to do this or any other job half-heartedly, and so he took full advantage when, by chance, one of peanutters who was regularly sent to help him on Saturday race days turned out to have especially useful talents.

The young constable was Ken Rimmer, a tall, thin fellow who got on very well with Beck. He also had a very good memory for numbers. When Beck realised this, he devised a strategy that proved very effective against SP bookies.

Beck and Rimmer would go down to the public phones at North Sydney or Crow's Nest in the late morning or early afternoon. Many homes were still without telephones and mobile phones had not been invented. The public phones usually had lines of people waiting to make a call and place their bets. Rimmer would get in the queue, pretending to have some bets to lay and chatting to the other callers. Once he was next in line he could see through the glass of the booth as the numbers were dialled—on the round number selector with the finger hole for dialling—and also hear snatches of brief speech as bets were laid.

Writing down the numbers was out of the question, as his cover would have been blown. But Rimmer was able to remember the six digits used by the previous caller while he made his own dummy call, then hung up and left the area to find Beck. Beck would write down the number and they would head to another public phone to test it.

"Hello, is Tom there?" Beck would ask, pretending to have a wrong number.

"No mate, no Tom here," said a voice at the other end.

"Oh, sorry I was given this number. Are you sure Tom's not there?"

"Mate, either place a bet or get lost, you're wasting my time!" would come the reply, and Beck would hang up with a grin to his partner.

Over the course of a few hours every Saturday Beck and Rimmer would identify a number of SP numbers. On the following Monday Beck would go in person to the Postmaster General's Department, widely known as the PMG, which operated the telegraph and then telephone network before Telecom and then Telstra.

The PMG's investigation branch would check the numbers against their records and supply the address at which the phones were connected. On the following race day, Beck would obtain a warrant for searching those addresses. Often when he was on the premises he would take a phone call and confirm that the caller wanted to place a bet, before making his arrests.

This technique worked very well, and several SP operators were brought before the courts in the course of a few weeks. The penalties handed out to them were mixed, as were the reactions from Beck's police colleagues and from the PMG department.

After the initial flurry, Beck and Rimmer found that the PMG was becoming less helpful, and even obstructive. The official in charge of the investigations branch started to argue that he did not have time to check out the numbers the young policemen supplied, and made up other excuses for not helping. Beck began to suspect that there was a link between the official's behaviour and the attitude he was getting from the Vice Squad at Police Headquarters. It was made clear to Beck by his senior officers at North Sydney that the Vice Squad was not thrilled with his success. He was told that he was "going overboard" and making too many arrests, and that he should just "go steady".

To get around the blockage, Beck approached another section of the Police Department (the administrative and policy arm of the Police, which was merged with the Force in 1987) which also had access to the PMG to obtain contact details on the holders of telephone numbers. This section had no problem getting the names and addresses out of the PMG and were happy to hand them straight over to Beck.

After he had been in the North Sydney position less than four months, Beck had arrested 35 SP bookmakers. Instead of receiving praise for this success, he found himself transferred back to criminal work. His replacement in gaming and vice within the North Sydney branch was a senior sergeant, four ranks above Beck.

Beck did not mind returning to criminal work, which was his first love, but his stint in gaming and vice had been interesting. When he was called to head 21 Division many years later he drew on his experience at North Sydney.

In 1960, when he was 38 years old, Beck was promoted again. He was now a detective sergeant, and was transferred to Regent St station where he served until 1967.

The work was varied and included several homicides. One of these, in February 1961, involved a 21 year old woman from Waverley who was charged with murdering her husband by stabbing him as he lay naked in bed. Beck gave evidence that the woman, Norma Roberts, had told him that she had argued with her husband after they came home from a nightclub where they had been drinking.

The husband repeatedly struck her, even after she tried to end it by going to bed. She got up, went to the kitchen and got a carving knife, then stabbed him in the stomach.

But Mrs Roberts told the jury her husband had got in to "a terrible rage" after she spoke to a friend at the nightclub. She claimed she did not remember getting home or anything else, except waking up with the husband leaning over her and hitting her.

"I don't know where I got the knife and I don't remember getting the knife," she said.

The jury found her not guilty.

Another murder case in 1964 involved the death of a blind baby, Suzanne Maree Marshall, found dead in her crib at the Royal Alexandra Hospital for Children in Camperdown. The murder was only discovered after her body was exhumed, a month after burial, and found to contain a high dose of cyanide.

Beck led the team of police who interviewed hundreds of people, including doctors and nurses and parents of other children in the ward at the time. The case received extensive publicity, but despite several theories, there was no resolution. In January 1967, a man in Gunnedah in northern NSW claimed to have information and Beck re-opened the case. Despite his best efforts, and his own suspicions, Beck was unable to solve the case. Many decades later, he remained sad for the baby and her parents,

Dealing with emotion was important to his work. Beck and his police colleagues found themselves constantly challenged by drama, pathos, and anguish. Occasionally, this was balanced with a dash of humour.

The latter came to fore on one occasion in 1965. Beck and his partner at Regent St were called over to Glebe Station to help in the investigation of a spate of shop robberies, believed to be the work of two men known to the police.

They went to the home of one of the suspects in Chippendale, where he lived with his mother. The man was not home so they questioned his mother about his movements and an associate with whom he had previously been involved in several robberies. The mother strongly denied any knowledge of her son's whereabouts and became quite abusive. She claimed, as most mothers in the circumstance did, that the police were picking on her innocent son and his young friend.

Beck and his partner did not accept that and warned her to behave herself and just answer the questions as they were just doing their job, provoking another outburst.

Unfortunately for the mother, during the heat of the argument the ceiling of the room in which they were standing gave way, and down tumbled the son and his criminal mate, falling right at the feet of the startled police officers.

They had been hiding up there while the mother was denying everything, but when they fell a large quantity of stolen goods came down with them. Beck and his partner quickly recovered from their surprise and slapped the handcuffs on the suspects, who were later charged and convicted, along with the mother who was charged with hiding them.

In 1967 Beck and three other police were stationed at Camperdown, a sub-station of Regent St. There was a high crime rate in the area, but Beck knew that serious criminals never undertook crimes near their homes because this would attract police attention. So he and his team chose not to limit themselves to the immediate area, instead following their inquiries wherever they led, throughout the city.

Working in pairs, they were making a large number of arrests, including 86 criminals arrested for receiving stolen goods within a three month period. Normally it was very difficult to nab receivers, and putting them out of business was very satisfying for the police because it made life more difficult for the remaining thieves.

As well as making many arrests, Beck and his team were also getting a lot of information from the receivers about armed hold-ups, frauds and other crimes, which they were obliged to pass on to the armed holdup squad and fraud squad.

Many more arrests were made on the basis of that information. But Beck's team was never given credit in the charge records for supplying the tip-offs, although this was the rule, and after a while this became a major source of irritation to them. They began to wonder if it would be better to keep the information to themselves so they could also make the arrests.

Beck would call the Regent St police station each morning and call through their crime reports. The detective sergeant in charge of Regent Street, or his deputy, would relay this information to the CIB along with the combined divisional crime reports.

The Camperdown team's record was so impressive that Ray Blissett, the CIB chief at the time, rang Beck one day to compliment him.

"I always thought that was an area where there's a lot of criminals," commented Blissett, not realising that very few of the arrests by Beck's team had been made in the local area.

The second in charge of the station, Ray Goldsworthy, was always astonished when Beck rang him and reported on the previous day's activities.

"God strike me pink," he said more than once. "What are you getting all these charges for, what are you getting so many for? Don't you realise you are making it difficult for these other guys who are not able to get onto these things?"

Beck would reply, "Well, the crimes are there, and that's what we get paid to do." Goldsworthy was never happy with Beck's response and Beck was never happy with his comments, but they had to tolerate each other.

The three detectives working under Beck were as keen as he was. Beck could hardly believe that they were told to slow down to make life easier for others. A high arrest rate became a hallmark of Beck's career, whatever his position.

"That was just the way I worked," recalled Beck. "I just took it that if I was to be a policeman and hopefully a good one, which I tried to be, that the more offenders I removed from society the better.

"I just followed any leads that we got and I was persistent. As a result, over the years I have dealt with a huge number and variety of crimes—from 17 murders to rapes to pickpockets, consorting offences such as scandalous conduct, burglary, break enter and steal, and conspiracies.

"I have arrested criminals who were so entrenched I was able to charge them with 150 offences of break enter and steal.

"Added to that there were stabbings, gun offences, car thefts, attempted murders, false pretences, and all kinds of assaults of a criminal nature, arson, building site thefts, fatal accident investigations, and illegal abortions."

As Beck's career progressed, his hard work, high success and insistence on doing the best job possible were often a source of annoyance to other police, including superior officers. One reason was the existence of a conspiracy to disguise the true extent of crime in Sydney and NSW.

The phrase 'by the book' had its own meaning in the NSW Police at that time. It was a reference to 'Paddy's Book', the ledger of crimes and arrests kept by every police station. Every incident such a break and enter, hold-ups and burglaries were recorded in the book, along with the outcome.

The book was the station's official working record, but many (and sometimes most) of the incidents recorded in it were not copied in to the official police reports which were forwarded to police headquarters and eventually, made public.

From the early 1960s, Beck knew that crime statistics were being falsified every day. The number of crimes reported to police was being systematically understated to make the rates of arrest look much better than they really were.

The discrepancies made Beck and a lot of other decent police very uneasy. They would talk about it and threaten to circulate the real figures, which they knew would be of great interest to the insurance industry as well as the general public.

But when these rebellious conversations were heard by more senior police, they were quickly quashed. Any detective who talked about problems with the official reports was threatened with a return to uniformed duties. Beck and his friends concluded that the cover up was sanctioned, if not mandated, by the most senior levels of police to impress either their political masters, the public, or both.

The insignia for the NSW Police Force was changed in 1959. It remains the same today. Its Latin motto 'culpam poena premit comes' translates as 'punishment swiftly follows crime'. Beck and his colleagues wished that the motto was closer to the truth.

Beck himself did his best to make it so. From Regent St he was transferred to Manly in 1968, very close to home for him. The same year there was an armed holdup in a furniture shop. Beck was the only detective at the station when the call came through as the others were all out on jobs. He drove to the furniture shop and spoke to owner, who was able to give a good description of the offender. Any armed hold-up was a serious crime so, to alert other police, Beck circulated the description over the police radio and also sent the report through official channels.

This was normal procedure, but when the division's detective sergeant returned to the station and learned what Beck had done, he was furious. He abused Beck in loud terms for not recording the crime in Paddy's Book, claiming that Beck had now saddled him with a crime that he had little chance of clearing up. His tirade of abuse ended with a stern warning that Beck was not to circulate news of any crime in future, without conferring with him first.

On another occasion Beck had arrested an offender in his district. Under questioning, the man admitted he had been involved in a number of previous robberies in other parts of Sydney. Beck drove the man out to the western suburbs, where he pointed out a number of premises that he said he had robbed. Beck wanted to add these burglaries to the charges, but when he followed up he found that none of the robberies were on the records at police headquarters or the Criminal Investigation Branch.

Annoyed, but also determined, Beck drove to the police station closest to several of the robberies and asked to see the station's detective sergeant, who would know about the robberies. He was out on a job, but undeterred, Beck sat down and waited for him. He wanted to see Paddy's Book. The sergeant when he returned retrieved the book from a hiding place. Sure enough, the robberies were recorded in it.

"Don't you think this is a ridiculous situation where we don't report the crimes that are actually happening?" Beck asked the sergeant.

"I have been through a needless run around this afternoon trying to get a fair result for people who have been robbed, which is our job.

"And if we don't let people know about crimes then we will never get public support to increase the force to what we need!" The sergeant did not agree.

"No, I don't think it's ridiculous," he replied tersely. "This is what we have to do, and I'm not changing anything. It's reported in this book and that's what the way I am going to do it."

Paddy's Book had been instituted by the police Criminal Investigation Branch to make the performance of the police look better than it was. But over the medium to long term it became a hindrance to good policing. As the crime rates were officially very low, there was no political rationale to increase police resources. Hence Paddy's Book directly undermined the efforts of uniformed police as well as detectives.

Beck and some of his colleagues continued to push back against Paddy's Book, with no success. But a few years later, the secrets and lies were revealed.

The person most responsible for the revelations about Paddy's Book was a policeman who had much in common with Merv Beck—Detective Sergeant Philip Arantz was courageous, honest and honourable, and was dismayed when he realised that there was widespread corruption in the NSW Police Force. In the early 1970s, Arantz was in charge a project to computerise police records which, predictably, ran into a major issue with the gap between the Paddy's Book records and the official reports.

In 1971 he decided to break the code of silence which had allowed the deceit to go on for many years. He leaked official figures to the *Sydney Morning Herald* showing that reported crime in 1971 was 75 per cent higher than the official 1970 figures, a discrepancy too large to be explained away as a 'crime wave'.

Both the Premier, Sir Robert Askin, and Police Commissioner Norman Allan refused to admit the truth, instead attacking Arantz and attempting to discredit him. In an appalling breach of civil rights, not to mention justice, Arantz was immediately certified mentally ill by the Police Medical Officer, Dr Morrie Vane, and forcibly admitted to a psychiatric hospital where he was kept for three days.

After being released. he was charged with misconduct, and in due course was dismissed from the Police Force in January 1972. Dismissal meant he was not eligible for the police pension which all serving officers could expect.

Although it was well known within the Police Force that Arantz was being punished for exposing an official cover up, no one dared to take up his cause. It was not until a decade later, in 1982, that Arantz was finally vindicated and set on the path to restitution.

At the time, in the early 1970s, the persecution of Arantz by his police superiors and by the Government acted as a further warning to other police to keep quiet about any rorts or irregularities in the force.

Many police also believed their Commissioner, Norman Allan was corrupt, and bending the crime statistics was probably the least of the crooked happenings under his command. But as is often the case, smaller more mundane crimes can be easier to prove, and so it was with Paddy's Book.

This was the environment in which Merv Beck pursued his career, and as the years went on, little changed. Unlike many, Beck was not disillusioned by the dishonesty he saw in others, but nor was he oblivious to it. He became wary and made his own judgements on whom he could trust in the force. He had little direct contact with the highest echelons, this included the various commissioners and their powerful deputies.

At Manly, Beck continued to prove himself a tough and thorough investigator. In July 1970 he was in charge of another homicide case: Peter Kiel, described as a wealthy Sydney farrier (Horse hoof trimmer and shoer) was found dead in a burning cottage at Ingleside.

On another occasion, he saw through a window a crazed man throttling a woman. Without hesitating, Beck punched through the glass, startling the man who let go of the woman's throat, saving her life, while Beck clambered through the window. His hand was cut badly enough to leave a permanent scar, which he considered a very small price.

In 1972 Beck was appointed to head criminal investigations at North Sydney police district, leading a team of 20 detectives working in North Sydney and Mosman and surrounding areas. The appointment was written up in the local newspaper, with the heading "Crack Detective heads crime team".

"Det Sgt Beck has wide experience in criminal investigation, and has led many major crime inquiries," the paper said. "He was previously stationed at the C.I.B, Manly, Darlinghurst, Regent St and Eastwood.

"Det Sgt Beck said this week he hoped to step up crime fighting efforts in the area.

"'To do this, we will need to seek the co-operation of residents and business,' he said. "With this co-operation we can keep this area what we all want it to be. The Detective office is open 24 hours a day for anyone seeking advice on security and crime prevention.'"

At the start of April 1973, Beck was again in the local newspaper—leading the hunt for a bomb hoaxer. In the previous weeks, local police had been called out to 70 bomb scares in the Spit Junction area, including five in one morning, mostly targeted at the Classic Theatre and local banks

True to his word about involving the community, Beck issued an appeal to the public to come forward with any information that might put an end to the hoaxer's fun. The hoaxer had wasted thousands of police man-hours and excessively annoyed local business, he said. It was just another example of the variety of work that Beck encountered.

Shortly after the Arantz affair, Norman Allan retired after 10 years as Police Commissioner. Allan nominated Frederick Hanson as the man to succeed him, and in mid-November 1972 Hanson took the top police job. There was no Police Minister at the time, and it was widely accepted that Premier Robert Askin had given the job to Hanson.

Hanson was known as 'Slippery' after he was promoted ahead of more than 1000 more senior police. He was a scoundrel with a reputation among police for being open to bribery.

Rumours and allegations of corruption against police began to multiply, both within the force and in the public, as soon as Hanson took charge. Like his predecessor, Hanson was extremely close to Premier Askin and they worked to advance their mutual interests.

Merv Beck was one of the police who was impacted by the deepening mirk in the force, not long after Hanson's appointment. In November 1973, Beck was waiting for his promotion to the rank of inspector, which was due the following year, when he received word that it might not go ahead as smoothly as he expected.

The bad news came from Detective Superintendent Victor Moore from the Criminal Investigations Branch, who called Beck at North Sydney police station.

Moore said two other police were also due for promotion to inspector, whom he named, but there was only one vacancy at the CIB, where a new inspector would normally expect to be posted. Beck wanted the position and knew that he was more senior than the other two, so was not prepared to give it up easily.

"I am senior to those two you mentioned and I will back my record against theirs," he said. Moore said there would be a meeting of senior officers shortly and the position would be discussed.

A few days later another Superintendent, Jack Christy rang Beck. Christy had known Beck since he was a probationary constable and Christy was a sergeant in the police armoury. Beck had been an armourer in the air force, and over the years they had become good friends.

"I have been reliably informed, Merv, that they don't want you at the CIB when you are promoted to an inspector."

Beck was taken aback. "Can you tell me why not?" he asked.

"They are frightened what you will see if you go there and what's more, what you would do about it when you did!"

The message was echoed by two senior CIB police known and trusted by Beck, Superintendents Fred Bradstreet and E.E. (Ted) Cannacott.

Cannacott was appointed head of the CIB just two months later, in January 1974, and remained there for two years. Beck had worked with Bradstreet on the abortion task force.

Cannacott and Bradstreet now told Beck that, although they personally wanted him, they did not have the power to ensure his appointment. Others with influence were determined not to have an officer with Beck's reputation, at the CIB. Beck was not trusted to turn a blind eye to what he might see there, and doubtless their fears were well placed.

Cannacott conceded that any decision he made would be overruled by the Police Commissioner Fred Hanson, who was himself strongly opposed to Beck's appointment to the CIB..

Beck was not entirely surprised. Cannacott had previously confided that he was having difficulties, and these continued after his promotion. His authority was constantly being undermined by senior CIB officers who reported his decisions to Fred Hanson, who promptly overturned them. As a result, the CIB squads had virtual carte blanche to choose their own men—allowing them to choose only those who would not rock the boat. All detectives aspired to be a detective inspector in the CIB, the pinnacle of crime solving. But Beck and the detectives he trusted also had reservations about becoming part of a closed shop which, according to common knowledge, was rotten and needed a thorough clean out.

Disappointed with his superiors, Beck wrote around this time: "It seemed a definite policy was followed to pass over any officer who did not comply or conform and take part in the organisation that existed within the police service to control those avenues from where financial rewards could be gained."

It was a hard thing for an ambitious police officer to accuse his superiors and colleagues of being corrupt and 'on the take' from criminals, and even harder to contemplate that his own career was being jeopardised because he was too honest to accept corrupt practices. Although he said it in a roundabout way, that was precisely what Beck now believed.

He knew of many cases where the CIB had failed to solve crimes and punish offenders when the evidence was there. Good detectives who tried to work within the CIB had told him they found it hard going, or worse. If they tried to resist the force of the group which was close to Commissioner Hanson (known as Hansonites), they were persecuted.

Some had been reverted to uniform as a punishment, others quit the force altogether in their frustration.

But Beck also knew that there were some police who were willingly drawn into the CIB culture. Many of the senior detectives at the CIB were known to Beck. Some were good at their work, but their corrupt activities threw a dark shadow over their achievements as far as Beck and other police colleagues were concerned.

They were often active, intelligent police but they changed in the CIB. In police circles, to say someone was 'fed corn' meant that he had been given a small bribe and had developed a taste for more, in exchange for unquestioning loyalty. As the corn eater progressed he was able to demand and receive payments directly from the criminals, and so the system was entrenched.

(Years later, the disorder within the CIB had become so obvious that the whole Branch was closed down by Commissioner John Avery. Beck and many other police believed this was 'throwing the baby out with the bathwater', as it left NSW as the only Australian police force without a CIB. But it may have been inevitable given the notorious history of the branch.)

Just as disturbing to Beck and Cannacott was the knowledge that the decent detectives at the CIB could be relied on by the Commissioner and the Hansonites not to make rouble for them. Beck also knew detectives in this situation, who had joined the police force with him and worked with him over the years.

Beck could not condone their participation in the 'code of silence' about corruption. But with widespread suspicion about the Commissioner himself, and a history of persecution of those who spoke out, it appeared pointless to fight, even for someone as forthright as Beck.

Among the many rumours that circulated through the force was a story told to Beck at this time by a police sergeant he believed to be reliable.

At Police Headquarters, there was a self-contained flat for personal use by the Commissioner of Police during long days and nights of work. The sergeant told Beck that a Newcastle hotel owner, who was also an SP operator, was on very good terms with Commissioner Hanson, as well as with other police including the sergeant himself.

The SP operator had confided that Hanson often allowed him to spend the night in his police unit. The same SP operator also had in his possession the police seniority list, an official document showing each police officer, by name, date of birth and rank. Using the list, the SP operator and his colleagues could learn when certain police were due to retire, and others due to be promoted. It was very useful information for anyone who wanted to ensure that police they counted as "friendly" were put into positions with influence over policing related to that person's business interests.

* * * *

A few months after his rejection by the CIB, Beck demonstrated his skill and bravery in a dramatic and courageous arrest.

Detective Sergeant Bruce Trees (who was to work with Beck on gaming and betting in the future) made a formal report on the incident which set out the course of events in detail.

Trees was working at Mosman Police Station (part of the North Sydney Division) and under command of Beck who was then a Detective Sergeant First Class.

On 12 February 1974, Trees recounted, he was in Beck's office about 11.30 am when a message came over the police radio network that two offenders had been disturbed breaking into a block of home units in Kirribilli. A short time later he heard a call from car 6/3: "6/3, urgent, urgent. We are being fired upon. Could you send further assistance!"

Trees and two other police, Detective Symonds and Sergeant Third Class Slade immediately jumped into their police car and drove to the units in McBurney Lane, Kirribilli. A number of police were present and said the two burglars were close by, and on foot. Trees and his companions made a quick patrol of the areas but found nothing. They met another officer, Constable Barrett, outside a block of units in Peel St. Barnett told them he had handcuffed one of the offenders and was holding him when the other, Anthony Lachman alias Jan Prcak, suddenly appeared from a doorway and held a revolver at his head.

"Let my mate go or I'll blow your head off!" he demanded. He was holding a long barrelled revolver and Barrett complied. The men then ran off, with the first man still handcuffed. Barrett then discovered that another police officer, Constable Murray, had not been so lucky. He had also had a revolver put to his head by Lachman, but had decided to fight and in wrestling to get the gun out of the burglar's grasp, had been shot in the hand. Other police including a Detective Sergeant Riley then pursued Lachman and exchanged gunfire as they tried to stop him.

After hearing this account, Trees told Symonds to go with him and they set off on foot. At the front of the Peel St units they found a trail of blood, which led to a laundry block at the back of the units. It appeared that one or both of the offenders was in there, and the man with the gun had probably been wounded by police fire.

At the rear of the units Trees and Symonds were joined by Beck, who had climbed over a fence from Peel St, and another senior officer, Superintendent Bill Purcell. Trees, Beck and Purcell cautiously approached the laundry block and could see more blood on the bottom of the laundry door and the paving.

Purcell called out to whoever was in the laundry block.

"Police here! We have you surrounded. Come out now with your hands up and leave any weapons behind!"

There was no reply. Purcell repeated his demand, with the same response.

Purcell gestured to Trees to move to the rear of the laundry. When he got there, Trees saw a louvre window at the top of the wall, with several garbage cans resting against the wall.

Trees moved across beneath the window and picked up a long handled shovel. He smashed the louvers and yelled out.

"Police here, lay down your arms! You are surrounded by police and if you don't come out, serious injury may follow."

Again, there was no reply. As it was too dangerous to try to approach the window, Trees moved back to the front of the laundry.

Beck then took up a position immediately to the left of the laundry door, with another man, Senior Constable Hartnett slightly to his left. Purcell was behind Trees and to Tree's left.

At Purcell's direction, Trees then tried to force the laundry door open using the shovel, but without success. Beck kicked the door, but still it did not open. Then they tried together, with Trees using the shovel and Beck kicking, and the door swung open.

Inside were the two burglars. Lachman/Prcak had his left knee on the toilet to steady himself, and the revolver in his left hand. It was pointed at Beck and Trees, while they had their revolvers pointed at him. The police could see that the gun was loaded as the bullets were visible in the chamber.

"Drop it, drop it!" demanded Beck. Lachman said nothing and kept the revolver aimed at them. Beck repeated the demand and he and Trees started to move closer to the men.

"Back, back or I shoot!" Lachman screamed at them.

Beck again told him to drop the gun and he and Trees continued to inch closer. Lachman turned the gun slightly in Trees' direction. Beck seized the moment, instantly striking out with his gun and hitting Lachman's weapon, which fell to the floor.

Trees and Beck then struggled to overpower Lachman. They pushed him to the door where he was seized by Purcell and Hartnett. The second offender, who was still handcuffed, kept saying, "Don't shoot, don't shoot!". Beck then picked up the revolver which lay on the toilet floor. It was a .45 Webley six chamber revolver, fully loaded.

Once the men were disarmed, Beck and Trees handcuffed them and led them from the toilet block to await the police van. Superintendent Purcell stepped forward and told them they were under arrest. before turning to several journalists who had heard the calls on the police radio and arrived at the dramatic scene.

Trees reported: "I firmly believe that, but for the actions of the members of the service mentioned above, this offender may well have made further efforts to discharge his firearm. Fortunately, when he was momentarily distracted, Detective Sergeant Beck was able to strike the weapon and knock it from his grasp, avoiding what may well have been a fatal shooting of either one of us."

Lachman/Prcak and his accomplice were charged with assaulting police while armed, and break enter and steal. It later emerged that Lachman had previously shot at a homeowner when he was caught in a unit in Kirribilli in 1971, and that he was wanted in Victoria for shooting and wounding a person in similar circumstances. He was a very dangerous man.

Two weeks after the incident, the head of Number 6 Division recommended consideration of official recognition for "bravery, coolness and devotion to duty" to Purcell and Beck as well as Detective Sergeant Riley, and Constable Murray.

After further reviewing the events, on 23 May 1974, Deputy Chief Superintendent Jack Christy of the Metropolitan Area Office wrote to the Commissioner about the Kirribilli incident and subsequent favourable newspaper coverage. Christy recommended that Beck, Trees, Riley, Murray and another constable be granted Queens Bravery Awards for conspicuous bravery, and that Purcell be given a favourable mention in his service register.

Although there was no question about the events of the day and the bravery that Trees and Beck had shown, the recommendation was shelved. Purcell received a favourable mention but Beck, Trees and the other three received nothing, Beck was especially disappointed for Trees. He suspected Commissioner Hanson had rejected the recommendation as soon as he saw the name "Beck", and the other police were collateral damage.

Shortly after this Beck applied for a tour of duty with the Australian contingent of the international police peacekeeping force in Cyprus. He lodged the application although he knew he was not strictly speaking eligible. Beck was pleased and not entirely surprised when Commissioner Hanson himself gave approval for the overseas services. It gave Beck a chuckle, as he was sure he was allowed to go just to get him out of New South Wales where he was regarded as a nuisance by the Commissioner and his Hansonites.

The move was a very positive one for Beck. The United Nations Peacekeeping Force in Cyprus (UNFICYP) had been established in 1964 to prevent further fighting between the country's Greek and Turkish Cypriot communities. It was one of the world's longest-running peacekeeping missions, with Australians serving in military, civilian and policing roles from its inception until 2021.

For Beck, Cyprus was like a breath of fresh air because he was able to do the job the way he saw fit, to the best of his ability. He quickly distinguished himself and in May 1975 became the Commander of the 11th Australian contingent, a position he retained until his tour of duty ended, working closely with the British contingent. The appointment also meant he was appointed as a special Commonwealth Police officer by the then-Australia Police (the name which replaced Commonwealth Police in March 1975) for the duration of his secondment.

While it was a peacekeeping force, without combat duties, it was not without risks. Only five days after Bec arrived, a NSW police constable who had flown over with him to join the Australian contingent was killed. Constable First Class Ian Ward and a Turkish Cypriot civilian died when the Landrover they were in hit a landmine on 12 November 1974. Another NSW constable and four young Turkish Cypriots, including three girls, were injured by the blast.

There were also occasional confrontations. In one incident, a Turkish soldier was aggressively blocking the road that Beck was travelling. The Turk had a pistol; Beck had none. Each told the other to "step aside". In the end, the Turk backed down. Beck said later, "I knew I just couldn't give in to this officer, although he was armed and I was not."

The Commander of UN Forces in Cyprus at the time, General Prem Chand, was impressed by Beck and grateful for his skilled interventions.

"Peace-keeping is particularly difficult for the civilian police, as they have nether power of arrest nor statutory authority in Cyprus to carry out recognised police functions," the General wrote in his formal assessment of Beck. "Problems can develop if the mission of the United Nations is not fully appreciated and accepted. Chief Superintendent Beck was singularly successful in having contingent members adjust to requirements and in ensuring that they produced their best efforts at all times. I regard Chief Superintendent Beck as a very effective Commander who carried out his duties in a most competent and satisfactory manner."

General Chand awarded Beck the United Nations Medal[6]. It was an honour Beck of which was particularly proud.

After 12 months, however, Beck's tour of duty was over and he was flown back to Sydney. Almost immediately, he was reminded of why he had been so pleased to have a break from the NSW Police Force.

As a matter of courtesy, Beck was advised to report to the Commissioner and pay his respects. Beck arranged an appointment to see Hanson in his office at 10am the following Tuesday.

He arrived at the appointed time and was advised by the senior public servant managing the office to wait. After 45 minutes, the official came back and told Beck that the Commissioner of Police was "indisposed" and would not be able to see him.

"Is he sick? Beck asked.

"No, he's pissed. He's too drunk to see you," the official said with an apologetic smile.

Beck did not see Hanson on that or any other occasion about his return to state duties, but given his behaviour, he did not think he missed anything.

Around this time, reports of Hanson's appalling behaviour began to become public.

In the 1974 New Year's Queen's Honours list, Hanson had been awarded a Commander in the Order of the British Empire (CBE). Those who worked with him, like Beck, knew he deserved nothing

---

[6] *Sun-Herald* 17 February 1982

of the kind, but it was many years before the truth leaked out into the public domain.

In 1985 a Royal Commission was established jointly by the Federal, Victorian and NSW Governments in to illegal phone interceptions (tapping) by the NSW Police. Retired Superintendent E.E. (Ted) Cannacott gave evidence to the Royal Commission that when he was head of CIB between 1974 and 1976, he gave a daily briefing on telephone taps to Assistant Commissioner (Crime) R.T. Stackpool, who then briefed Hanson. But that only occurred when Hanson was there on duty, and in the first eight months of 1974, Hanson had turned up for work in the office on average just two days out of five working days each week. In *Can of Worms*[7] in 1986, journalist and author Evan Whitton said Hanson was described during his time as Commissioner as "a 'playboy,' who liked a drink and a good time".

In mid-1975 some of the gossip came to light. An illegal casino at West Gosford was raided by police on 4 July. Freelance commentator Tony Reeves, in an interview on Triple J, implied that Hanson had a financial interest in the casino. Hanson sued the ABC and won. The ABC apologised and settled on undisclosed terms of 9 February 1976.

Hanson said: "I'm so bloody happy it doesn't matter[8]."

When Beck returned, Sydney's inner city community was still in shock over the disappearance on 4 July 1975 of Juanita Nielsen, a member of the family who owned the Mark Foy's retail chain. Nielsen and the independent community paper she published, *NOW*, had become the leading voice of opposition to high rise development in Victoria St in King's Cross and other areas of the inner city. The protest movement and 'green bans' were costing the developer millions of dollars a year. Nielsen was last seen at the Carousel Cabaret on Roslyn Street in Kings Cross, owned by the increasingly powerful crime boss, Abe Saffron.

Beck knew about the Nielsen case only from what he read in the newspapers. He was not involved in the investigation, or perhaps it would have had a different outcome. He was assigned back to Manly, Number 14 Division, as an assistant commander to Senior Inspector Keith Paull, with whom Beck had worked over many years on various

---

[7] Can of Worms: A Citizen's Reference Book to Crime and the Administration of Justice (1986) I

[8] Ibidem

criminal matters. It suited Beck well. He was able to spend more time with his wife, Elsie, and their children while he applied himself to solving crime and arresting suspect with typical enthusiasm.

The mystery surrounding Juanita Nielsen continued for many years. Her body was never found and no one was ever charged with her murder, although three men were charged with conspiring to abduct her a week or so earlier. One of those, Eddie Trigg, pleaded guilty in 1983. He was the last person seen with her. Both Saffron and his club manager, Jim Anderson had connections with the frustrated Victoria St developer, Frank Theeman,

Eight years after she vanished, in November 1983, a coroner and jury found that Nielsen had died "on or shortly after" the day she was last seen. They also found "evidence to show that the police inquiries were inhibited by an atmosphere of corruption, real or imagined, that existed at the time". In 1994 the Commonwealth Parliamentary Joint Committee on the National Crime Authority also criticised the NSW Police investigation, and emphasised links between Nielsen's presumed murder, property developers and the criminal milieu at Kings Cross[9].

---

[9] http://adb.anu.edu.au/biography/nielsen-juanita-joan-11241

Beck being presented with the UN Medal in 1975
by General Prem Chand, UN Commander, Cyprus Peacekeeping Force.

CHAPTER THREE

"Frankly, there's no one else we think could do it."

Despite the attitude of some of his superiors, Merv Beck's reputation as a policeman of fearless integrity continued to grow. Most of those who worked with him recognised his combination of personal courage and leadership ability, in rare quantities.

Politics in NSW changed dramatically in May 1976. It was six months since the Whitlam Labor Federal Government led by Gough Whitlam had been dismissed, and replaced in the subsequent election by a new conservative government. But voters were prepared to give the new-look leader of the state Labor Party, the slick, witty Queen's Counsel barrister Neville Wran, a chance. Wran had scraped into the ALP leadership in 1974 and his lucky streak was repeated at the election, where Labor won by the narrowest of margins—one seat, in turn won by a mere 74 votes. The conservatives' 11 years in power, 10 of them under Robert Askin, were over.

Policy on gambling emerged as a serious political issue after the election of the Labor Government. A month after the election, Premier Wran announced that casinos would be legalised in NSW. Wran also made it clear he had no moral objections to SP bookmaking, revealing to the media that as a boy he had worked as a 'penciller' for an illegal SP bookmaker.

In the face of the ensuing controversy, however, Wran backed down on the casino legislation and promised concerned church leaders that he would hold an inquiry before making such a move.

Illegal gambling was possibly the most visible aspect of the developing organised crime underworld in Sydney, Australia's largest city.

Drugs and gambling had gone hand in hand since the 1920s, when legal restrictions and bans created attractive opportunities for blackmail and corruption. As international syndicates took over in the 1970s, trafficking in illicit drugs exploded. Illegally earned money needed to be disguised and exchanged. Sydney's illegal casinos and SP bookmakers provide a perfect way to 'launder' these ill-gotten gains.

Australia's first legal casino had opened at Wrest Point in Tasmania in 1973. Its success prompted energetic lobbying by its operator, Federal Hotels, to convince other state governments to allow casinos to attract tourism. The Northern Territory Government announced its plans for a Darwin casino (which opened at the Don Hotel in 1979).

The potential revenue to be raised by expanding gambling turnover was very tempting for many governments. The NSW Government had been making money from gambling in some form since World War 1. By the 1970s, NSW was well established as the 'gambling state', with more forms of legalised gambling than any other Australian jurisdiction and double the level of discretionary spending on gambling[10].

But the line was still drawn on casino style gambling, illegal or SP bookmaking and games of chance in clubs.

Even with the restrictions imposed by defamation laws, the national and Sydney media were able to reveal enough about Sydney's illegal casinos, and the links between overseas casinos and organised crime including the mafia, to ring loud warning bells.

Another major problem for the new NSW Premier was his Commissioner of Police. Fred Hanson.

Despite his victory against the ABC, Hanson was damaged by the case. After the Liberal-Country Party was swept out of office in May 1976, the allegations of corruption in the NSW Police Force and mishandled murder investigations increased.

On 17 September 1976, an influential federal political insiders' newsletter, *Canberra Survey*, published an article headlined: "NSW Police, politicians are Corrupt". Although no names were named because of defamation laws, it was a bold piece of journalism. While nothing of the magnitude of the association in the US between presidential candidates and the mafia had occurred in Australia, it said, "the story

---

[10] Jan McMillen, *Risky Business: The Political Economy of Australian Casino Development* (PhD Thesis, University of Queensland, 1993), p.255. quoted in NSW Parliamentary Library Research Service, "NSW and Gambling Revenue" by John Wilkinson 1996

of corruption and criminal associations in the police force of NSW, and among some senior politicians, is sordid and alarming…"

As well as smaller suburban casinos, it said, Sydney City had half a dozen major casinos which operated openly. "Plushly decorated, they attracted to their various gaming tables prominent politicians, lawyers, senior media executives, and the ever-present criminals, standing over the entire operations, providing 'protection' against assaults by the other criminal elements and against raids by the police…

"Surveillance of the Goulburn Club shows that it continues to be a central point for criminals, police and some politicians to get together. Lennie McPherson has been there, at the same time as an Inspector of Police. Two different plainclothesmen visit regularly each week. In the carpark opposite anonymous packages are changed from the boots of criminals' cars to the boots of other cars. This corruption continues.

"One most senior police officer is known to have 'farmed out' the operations of a major casino in industrial Wollongong, while he is also part-owner of a casino in a northern coastal resort. The same officer attended the opening of the plush 22 Club or the Palace at 22 Rockwell Crescent, Pott's Point, a couple of years ago. He also recently attended the funeral of a prominent gambling club operator who had a share in the 22 Club.

"With such widespread corruption, reaching as it appears to into very high levels of the force, it is not surprising to find criminals exerting undue influence on the activities of large sections of the force and frequently on the course of justice."

In September 1976, Premier Wran had made good his promise of an inquiry into casinos in NSW. Edwin Lusher—like Wran, a member of the exclusive group of senior barristers designated as Queen's Counsels or QCs— was asked to make recommendations to the government on their legalisation and introduction. Wran made it clear that in his view the inquiry was concerned with how casinos should be legalised, rather than if they should be. It was the first public inquiry to systematically consider the relative merits of public or private casino ownership and management for Australia.

Commissioner Hanson had made it clear he did not much like the new Labor Government, nor its intention to legalise the casinos. He retired prematurely on 31 December 1976. Hanson said he had stayed on only long enough to ensure that the man he wanted to succeed him was chosen.

That person was former rowing champion and multi-Olympian Mervyn Wood, confirmed as the next Commissioner of Police on 1 January 1977.

* * * *

Beck had been assigned to the Mona Vale station as Inspector Third Class, his first command position. It was in Beck's words "a pleasant little station" and Beck was happy in his work throughout 1976, despite occasional frustrations.

But one day in mid-May 1977, Beck received a phone call from Police Headquarters in the city.

He was told to attend a meeting at 9 o'clock the next morning. Beck wondered why he was being summonsed, and was more surprised when he was met by the then-Deputy Commissioner Jim Lees, who introduced him to three senior officers—Deputy Chief Superintendent, Frank Ferris, and Superintendents Eric Power and Reg Douglas.

The three superintendents told Beck they had a job for him, a disciplinary job. Darlinghurst police station, which included Kings Cross, had fallen into a state of poor discipline and poor policing.

Although others had been sent to head the division, they had failed. Beck, they said, was known for his belief in discipline.

"We've selected you because we think you are the man most likely to succeed in cleaning up the mess at Darlinghurst," Ferris told Beck.

"Frankly, there's no one else we think could do it.

"We trust you, and we know you're tough. But we're not going to pretend it's going to be easy.

"In straight language Inspector, you are requested to go there and make a bastard of yourself."

Beck did not embrace his superior's suggestion on how he should do the job.

"I am prepared to accept the appointment. However, I am not prepared to make a bastard of myself in doing so," he replied.

"But that's what it needs," Ferris insisted. "We need someone who is strong and can tighten discipline in the place. It needs to be corrected."

Beck was not moved by flattery. He knew that Darlinghurst was regarded as a punishment posting. But Lees and Ferris were right that he liked a challenge, and he really had no choice anyway.

"Alright. I'll take on the job and I won't disappoint you. But I'll do it my way," he responded.

Darlinghurst was run down in morale, staff and resources, and a blight on the NSW Police Force. It covered only a small area, including College St, Woolloomooloo, the Sydney Cricket Ground, the Sydney Showground and part of Moore Park, Oxford St as far as Paddington Town Hall, King's Cross, Rushcutters Bay and up to Edgecliff. But this was the heart of Sydney's night life, a hot bed of bars and clubs as well as illicit activities. There was so much 'action' in this small area that Darlinghurst, with 200 police, had the largest staff of any station in NSW.

Beck's assignment was to restore discipline, improve operational results and correct the division's overall performance. But enforcing the law in 'Darlo' would not be an easy job, even for disciplined police. It was a rough area that tested police physically, mentally, and morally.

It was flattering but also disturbing for Beck to be told by his senior officers that he was the only one that they trusted to do such a 'clean up' job. It reminded him of his father Launcelot's career as a town breaker, but it also depressed him. The force executive clearly had a low opinion of most police around Beck's rank, and Beck did not disagree with their assessment.

"I always thought that it was pathetic that I was considered unusual, that there wasn't a dozen officers who were held in the same high regard and considered capable of doing a job like Darlinghurst," recalled Beck.

"But from what I've seen of some officers in this job, it is a shame that they held those positions."

At 6.30 am one week later, on May 23 1977, Beck arrived at Darlinghurst station. He had taken special care, with the help of his wife, Elsie, to ensure his clothes were immaculate. He wanted to give the impression from the start that he expected high standards.

He quickly discovered that high standards were not the norm at Darlinghurst. While he had been led to believe the station was not running well, it was far worse than he had imagined.

He was the first permanent officer in charge of the station for some time, as none of those who had been offered the job wanted to keep it. One of the temporary officers in charge was Senior Inspector "Bumper" Farrell, who had recently retired from the position. Beck had been at Darlinghurst 17 years earlier and had worked with Farrell on the Vice Squad and on several murder investigations around the Cross. Bumper had a big reputation and it made an impression on Beck that even a cop as experienced and resilient as Bumper had not been able to pull Darlo into shape.

Violence, drunkenness, and drug taking were a constant problem in the area, with more than 100 drunks arrested every night, mainly for their own safety. Assault and robberies were very common, as were con artists and prostitutes (male and female) working around the strip joints and various odd shows. People constantly went missing, and there were many people in the area who were wanted on warrant.

All of this made for a huge workload for the Darlo police, and when Beck met his new team they seemed overwhelmed. As soon as he walked in he saw that the station was untidy and many of the police on duty at the time were in the same unkempt state. Most were sitting on desks or leaning back in their chairs smoking. Some of them kept talking when the new officer in charge walked in. Beck regarded this as disrespectful, to himself and indirectly, to the public. He did not like it at all.

He had called a meeting for mid-afternoon when most of the staff were on duty. Beck told his new colleagues that the station was under new management. He said discipline would be brought up to an acceptable standard and he expected them all to be neatly uniformed.

To back this up, his first action was to introduce duty parades three times a day. As each new shift arrived, the men were inspected for their appearance. Before Beck's arrival, inspections were very rare and the Darlo police resented Beck's new regime. Even the uniformed officers thought it was old fashioned and unnecessary to dress well. Beck ignored their hostility.

Drinking alcohol at the station had also become a bit of a problem. A drinking group had turned one of the cells into a bar, with a bar fridge stocked with beer. Others were going to the pub during their lunch and dinner breaks and on the way home, wearing only part of their uniforms to make this less noticeable.

Alcohol was not the only temptation. There was a lot of illegal gambling in the station precinct. Ironically, given what lay ahead for Beck, an attempt was made early on to persuade him not to bother about the gambling outlets.

A well-known businessman who had previously met Beck, visited him at the station. In the privacy of Beck's office, he proposed a friendly deal.

"Well inspector, you know that there are certain places in this district where people can go for a bit of fun, a bit of a flutter on the games," he said.

"There's some concern around that you might take a harder line against the gambling and betting operators than your predecessors. "This may just be a rumour," he added with a smile, "but I've been asked by certain parties at the Cross to make a discrete suggestion which I'm sure you will find quite acceptable.

"They are willing to give you $500 a week, in cash, and all they want in return is for you to just not worry so much about that side of things and leave the status quo.

"There's plenty of real crime around so I don't think you will have any trouble keeping busy without troubling my friends."

Beck stared at the man for a few moments, then slowly shook his head.

"I'm sorry, you've got the wrong idea. I am not at all interested in that proposal."

The businessman looked surprised, but Beck's face made it clear there was no room for negotiation. He showed him out.

Beck also discovered that paperwork was often considered an optional extra at Darlinghurst. Police at the station referred to doing things 'the Darlo way', which meant taking short cuts in procedures wherever possible, because of the volume of work and unusual situations. Sometimes it worked well, was efficient, and made common sense. But it had become so entrenched that young police at the station did not even know they were taking short cuts and did not realise the potential hazards of some practices, such as failing to bring some complaints to official notice. Correspondence such as traffic offences and accident reports was invariably late and often lacked important information.

Station record books had to be updated and mistakes corrected. The miscellaneous property and exhibits for evidence were in an appalling mess, with items unlabelled, unprotected and unsupervised. The Darlo way was that the station's police could 'borrow' items from the exhibit room, on an honesty system. Drug exhibits were mingled with the firearms exhibits and could be found scattered throughout the station, often in officer's lockers.

By the end of October 1977, when Beck had been there for five months, the station was still returning property to owners which should have gone back to them as far back as 1975. Even prisoners were complaining that the money in their wallets and pockets had been short-changed. Members of the public interviewed at the station or even by phone frequently complained about the way the police had spoken to them.

Constables would wander in to drop off or pick up property on a trust system which the senior police condoned although they had no control over it. Yet many of the exhibits concerned were drugs or firearms. Property which should have been in one of the exhibit rooms was also found in various places around the police station or in lockers used by individual police.

Sorting out this mess was a tedious and time-consuming job which Beck assigned to several senior police who were sent to Darlinghurst to work with him. One of their first tasks was to install a new system of double locks on the exhibit room, and to ensure drug exhibits were well labelled and secured. General security at the station was tightened too, as members of the public had been allowed to wander in and out freely.

Internal discipline and morale was another entrenched problem. There was tension between the more senior ranks and the constables, who had little respect for their superiors. A number of senior constables and sergeants had been subjected to a departmental inquiry and had been awaiting the outcome for months. Their bitterness and the fact that they were still on staff had a bad effect on the rest of the station.

A few young constables had been at Darlinghurst for three or four years with very little training. Beck did not like their manner, nor their lack of interest in their work. Some of them seemed to look up to the senior constables whose records and behaviour were far below the standard that Beck - and Police Department procedures - expected in terms of grooming and uniforms, following proper procedures, and personal behaviour. The younger police considered these senior constables to be 'hard core' and 'cool'.

Beck tried to be fair. After discussing the position with these young constables he arranged for them to be transferred to other stations, for their mutual benefit. Others he called into his office and told them to toe the line and take his direction, or face disciplinary action.

"I invited everybody to discuss their problems with me. I adopted my usual policy of being fair, firm and friendly and I didn't embarrass anyone in the presence of others," Beck recalled. "If I had anything to say to them about their work, I'd speak to them individually. That was my method of operation, then it remains between the two of you."

Taking people to task was one thing, carrying out disciplinary action was another. The station's sergeants and officers were initially reluctant to assist Beck. Several told him they had refused to take part in any disciplinary action, because the station's previous leaders had not supported them and that had left them isolated.

Beck assured them that this would not happen under him, provided they acted correctly and performed their duties as required. A number of these men including Sergeant Ted Bunt, Sergeant John Harding, and Inspector Coulson made the decision to back Beck, and proved to be keen, trustworthy and willing to work the long hours expected of them by Beck.

Even with the support of these senior members of the station, Beck was determined not to be 'a bastard' as Ferris and Lees had suggested. He stressed to his officers that demands and punishments should be fair and not overly harsh.

He also went to lengths to get to know his most junior staff. He regularly called in the 38 probationary constables at the station to discuss their problems with him privately over a cup of tea. On the first occasion, a number of the constables were so surprised that they almost laughed when offered tea instead of the usual beer or scotch favoured by previous officers in charge. But they quickly found that Beck's approach not only kept them focused but allowed them to raise issues with Beck that were concerning them, and get honest and open responses.

It was Beck's view, which he pressed on these and other junior officers who served with him, that as police they occupied their ranks on loan on behalf of the public, before passing them on to others.

"What you do with those ranks will remain with you for the rest of your lives," he said.

Not all the station police were happy about this new broom. Anonymous notes questioning the sanity of some of Beck's new procedures were sent to non-commissioned officers. Beck also received a number of anonymous phone calls at his home at various times of the night, but considered them a nuisance rather than a threat.

The most disturbing was a mocking call. "It's time you woke up to yourself. The job is a sham!" was all the caller said before hanging up.

When Beck tried to organise a social gathering for the station, the 'hard core' made it clear they were not going to go because it would amount to 'licking the boss's boots'. Some younger police were afraid to go against the wishes of this group.

After about two months, Beck was able to have members of the hard core transferred to other stations. This made his job a lot easier. Beck called another meeting of the division.

"The discipline that I have asked for is not excessive, and its workable even in a very busy district like this.

"You're proving that. It's helping you to do your jobs better.

"I will be staying here and I can tell you now I won't be expecting a higher level of discipline, but I also won't be accepting a lower level. I think we've got it right now and I want to thank you all for your cooperation."

The great majority of the staff accepted that, and Beck felt a lift in the mood and morale at the station. His police began to take a pride in their work. At the inspection parades, there were unofficial competitions to see who had the shiniest boots. A number of young constables working with Beck even complained about the poor appearance and behaviour of police from other Divisions, with whom they had to work at sporting events such as football matches.

Beck worked 10-plus hour days, starting at 6.30 am and ending at 4.30pm, or sometimes 6pm; or for a late shift, starting at 1pm and ending at 11pm or later as required. He consciously chose the long hours.

"The reason being, as senior member of this Division, it enables me to see the men personally on all shifts and affords me an opportunity to correct, advise and encourage where necessary the men under my control, this enabling me to oversight all shifts each day," he explained in a report to Deputy Commissioner Jim Lees.

"Difficulties have been many for all senior men within the Division but have been overcome by patience, understanding and adopting a firm and friendly attitude with the men. Respect is now freely given to Officers and Sergeants alike by the men and women by way of answering to their duties and general behaviour."

Beck's progress reports were read with increasing relief at Police Headquarters. Lees, Ferris and other senior officers were supportive and grateful to Beck for taking on such a huge job, and constantly told him so.

After five months, Beck was delighted with the transformation in the station and its relationship with the surrounding community. He wrote a detailed report on the changes to Deputy Commissioner Lees, and issued a general invitation to senior officers to visit the station at any time and see for themselves. "I am confident that the police at

Darlinghurst are now better disciplined and better turned out that most other divisions," he reported proudly.

The Darlo police were also pleased with their new status. Among the comments Beck received were that he had "made it a pleasure to work at No 3 Division" and that the discipline he imposed was "most essential and is fair" and "long overdue".

Sergeant Second Class Hooper was rotated to work at No 3 Division for two months. He told Beck, "In the past young probationary constables I have spoken to from No 3 Division informed me they once lived in fear when working at Darlinghurst on account of what the more senior police did and they feared they would be sacked if involved in the same behaviour and drinking habits. I am of the opinion (that) the standard of discipline now at Darlinghurst would be of great benefit if conducted throughout the Police Force."

It was a time of social change with more women entering the force and demanding a greater range of duties. Beck's mother had shown him how tough women could be, just as his father had demonstrated that smaller men could be remarkably strong both physically and mentally. Beck warned his men that he wanted the policewomen to be treated with the same respect as they would afford their sisters or their wives. He also spoke to the young women and told them he expected them to behave properly and to come and see him immediately if they had any problems from harassment or discrimination.

One of women working under Beck at Darlinghurst, however, did not think Beck did enough for his female staff. Christine Nixon became an Assistant NSW Police Commissioner under Peter Ryan in 1994 and then Victorian Police Commissioner from April 2001 to February 2009. She was then appointed chair of the Victorian Bushfire Reconstruction and Recovery Authority but stood down in July 2010 after criticism of her response to the Black Saturday bushfires.

In an article in *The Daily Telegraph-Mirror* in April 1994 with the headline, "Top Police Post Goes to Woman", Nixon mentioned her experience when at Darlinghurst in 1977. She claimed that as a woman, she had had to fight to get into positions where she could use her practical police skills, especially at Darlinghurst.

"The senior male officers didn't take kindly to having women around. They put me on the switchboard," she stated in a direct dig at Beck.

It was true that Beck had placed Nixon on the interview counter of the station switchboard although she had regularly presented herself at his office and asked to be sent out on the trucks with the men.

Both at the time and in retrospect, however, Beck denied that he was being sexist. He just did not think that Nixon had the physical presence needed on the night patrol. A truck crew consisted of only two police and neither Beck nor his staff believed that a team would be strong enough for the likely challenges, if one of them was a young policewoman.

Before he took over Darlinghurst, Beck had worked with policewomen for many years. Ironically, one of the places where he had worked most closely with a policewoman was at Darlinghurst, in a previous stint as a detective in 1959. There, he formed a very high opinion of Policewoman Peg Fisher. Later, in gaming and betting, policewomen were also valued members of Beck's squad.

One of them was Lola Scott (then Whalan), who like Nixon had a very successful career. Beck considered her "an excellent and courageous worker as well as a real lady". Like Nixon, Scott was promoted by Peter Ryan in 1994, first to chief superintendent and later, Commander, making her the highest-ranked female police officer in the state. (Scott left the force in December 2002, and subsequently sued broadcaster Alan Jones and radio 2UE in the Supreme Court over two broadcasts in July and August 2001.)

But Beck believed Darlinghurst was a special case because of the frequent violent episodes, and higher importance had to be given to safety than to appearances.

"It would have been folly to place an inexperienced young policewoman in that position where she could be hurt," he said.

"I spoke to the police involved on these trucks regarding the policewomen, and several of them said to me, 'Look sir, every time we go out we become involved with people who resist us and fight us and we are hard pressed to look after ourselves.'"

One constable said, 'We will go through a brick wall for you (Beck), but we couldn't do it if we didn't have the support that's required."

Beck explained this to Constable Nixon, and also that she made an important contribution to the station's new image by dealing with the general public. "All police were delegated to duties according to their ability and in the best interests of the division," he said.

Later, as a retired officer, Beck watched Nixon's progress with interest and some amusement. Beck believed policing had to be learned in the school of hard knocks, and that experience gained in court appearances was invaluable to any police officer, including senior management. All levels needed to know what was achievable and desirable in policing on the street, he believed. Nixon did not have this experience, partly because of her sex. Although he promoted her, Commissioner Peter Ryan realised this and sent Nixon out into the field to get some hands-on experience, learning from people far lower in rank than herself.

While Beck demanded obedience and loyalty from his staff, he also returned it. The late 1970s was a time of great controversy over uranium mining. When the division was assigned to escort a shipment of yellowcake (uranium ore) through the city to the wharves, a superintendent from police headquarters gave Beck instructions that his men were not to engage with demonstrators and not to take action if they were punched, kicked, spat upon, or verbally abused.

Beck replied that he could not agree to allow his staff to be assaulted in any way, and that ordering them to submit to assault went against common sense. After some argument, Beck stubbornly refused to give the instructions to his police, but invited the superintendent to come to the station and tell the men himself. The superintendent declined Beck's offer, and Beck told his men not to accept any abuse from the crowd. As it eventuated the protesters were not violent and the shipment got through without difficulty.

After about five months at Darlinghurst, and having got the station in order, Beck felt it was time to take a more strategic look at the criminal operations in the district by holding an Operation Eagle—the name for a particular type of exercise often used by police in trouble zones. It entailed calling in all available police from the station and outside squads such as the Vice Squad, 21 Division and Highway Patrol to hit the streets for a short, sharp clean up of street offences and other crimes.

The Darlinghurst Operation Eagle was held on Friday and Saturday, 7 and 8 October. Hundreds of people were arrested and charged with a range of offences including traffic offences, while many others were warned for consorting or unruly behaviour. The reaction from local residents and businesses was very positive. An executive at the Chevron Hilton, the upmarket hotel in the Cross, told one sergeant he wished the operation could be held every weekend. He also commented on the 'new look' police at Darlinghurst.

Next Beck decided to take a look at illegal gambling. This was the province of 21 Division, so Beck did not have the authority to conduct raids himself. But he was concerned about the extent of it in his area, and the attempt to bribe him if anything increased his interest.

Beck decided to find out just where the games were being held.

He asked two of his licensing staff to draw up a map and a complete list of gambling locations, which he proposed to compare to the 21 Division records. It did not take them long, and when it was finished Beck made several copies. He submitted the first copy to the office of Commissioner Wood for his attention, and then went to visit Deputy Commissioner Jim Lees, who had become a friend.

When Beck put the map in front of Lees, the senior officer drew breath.

"You had better leave that with me because it's dynamite," Lees said, eyebrows raised.

A few days later, it became clear that word had begun to circulate within the force that Beck intended to launch an assault on illegal gambling, and not all police were happy about it.

Beck was attending an officers' dinner and was talking to other senior officers about his experiences at Darlinghurst when Commissioner Wood came over to the group and asked where the Bradstreet brothers were sitting.

A few minutes later, at the very moment when his fellow officers were congratulating Beck on doing such a good job at Darlinghurst, Senior Inspector Jack Bradstreet (whose brother Fred was also a policeman) came over and interrupted the conversation. He took Beck aside.

"The Commissioner just told me I'm going to be taking your place at Darlinghurst, and you're replacing me at Chatswood," he told Beck.

"What's that all about?" Beck was floored.

"I don't have a clue, this is the first I have heard of it," he said.

Bradstreet did not relish the thought of taking on Darlinghurst, while Beck was dumbfounded that he was being moved—and demoted— when he had just started making a real impact.

The next day, Beck received official word from the same trio who had asked him to take the job— Power, Ferris and Reg Douglas, who was acting Deputy Commissioner while Jim Lees was on holidays.

They told Beck that Commissioner Wood had presented them with the transfer as a fait accompli, and refused to listen to their objections or give any reasons for the transfer.

"Nothing can be done about it. That's all I have to say," Wood said firmly.

The senior officers were apologetic. Beck was dismayed. When he told Elsie and the children, they were angry.

"I couldn't believe it," he recalled later. "It knocked the stuffing right out of me.

"I went home and discussed it with Elsie. She and the girls were up in arms wanting to take it to some higher authority. I just told them a lot of police work was like that, you weren't told a great deal and if the department didn't want to give me a reason there was nothing I could do. They suffered with me."

When Jim Lees returned from holidays, Beck immediately asked him what it was all about. Lees could not offer any sound reason.

"You did everything right, everything we asked you to," Lees said.

But like the other officers, Lees said Commissioner Wood had made the instruction and would not change it; and he was the boss.

Lees did, however, propose a compromise. As moving to Chatswood would have been a step down for Beck, Lees had arranged for him to take over Central Police Station instead—the second largest station after Darlinghurst. Beck asked whether he should do anything differently at Central and Lees said, "No, just do exactly as you've been doing."

On October 31 1977, Beck submitted a lengthy report to Jim Lees, who was then Acting Commissioner, on his five months at Darlinghurst. He made no mention of the sudden end to his appointment, but congratulated every member of the Division for their efforts.

Beck was given just one week to leave Darlinghurst. On the afternoon of his last day he was suddenly called into the muster room. About 60 police were waiting for him. They presented him with a large silver trophy inscribed, "From No 3 Division, in Appreciation". The gesture brought a lump to Beck's throat and a tear to his eyes. He treasured the trophy into his old age.

Two months later, Beck was contacted by Inspector Bradstreet who had taken his place at Darlinghurst. Bradstreet said thousands of dollars worth of drugs which had been seized from suspects, had been stolen from the Kings Cross station. Unfortunately Bradstreet had removed one of the two padlocks on the exhibit room, put there by Beck to ensure only authorised police could enter.

Bradstreet was upset and told Beck he thought Darlinghurst was "too much" for him. This was scant comfort to Beck, and both men hung up feeling depressed.

* * * *

While Beck was cleaning up Darlinghurst, New South Wales was rocked by what many described as Australia's first political assassination.

It was openly stated that Sydney had become the crime capital of Australia, and there was growing evidence that the feared organised crime networks of other countries, including the mafia, had become active in NSW, fuelling the illegal drug market.

Donald Mackay, a resident of Griffith, had been the leading figure lobbying politicians to stop illegal drug deals and marijuana crops in the Riverina. Mackay had also been a Liberal Party candidate for both federal and state parliament. In March 1977 he gave information to NSW Police about a drug crop at Coleambally, resulting in the arrest of four men from Italian families. When Mackay was publicly named in court by a police officer as a source of the tip off (which should not have happened), and discovered the crop was worth more than $25 million, he feared for his life.

On the night of 15 July, Mackay disappeared from a Griffith hotel car park, and was never found. Blood matching his type was found on his van and ground, his car keys were underneath the van and empty bullets were nearby.

Amid intense media and political pressure over Mackay's disappearance, Premier Wran set up a Royal Commission into Drug Trafficking, headed by Justice Phillip Woodward[11]. While this deflected the political and media heat over Mackay's disappearance, the underlying problem remained—a growing, violent underworld linked to the drug trade.

In a case of bad timing, the Lusher report on options for legalising casino gambling was published in August 1977. Although the TAB and state lotteries were being successfully run by government, Lusher recommended that the proposed casinos not be government owned. Instead, he proposed privately owned casinos, controlled by a comprehensive system of government regulation, administered by an 'independent, non-political' control authority.

Lusher also recommended that only small boutique casinos be allowed, like the British club casinos, catering for the top end of the market. He did not approve of the Las Vegas model of large, glitzy venues which attracted people who could not afford their inevitable losses.

---

[11] See http://www.sydneycrimemuseum.com/crime-stories/the-woodward-royal-commission/

Lusher also proposed that casinos be prohibited from advertising, and only a small number of licences be granted. He did not support an ever-growing private casino industry, regardless of the potential for tourism and government revenue.

Ongoing controversy about illegal gambling and growing concerns about organised crime made legalising casinos politically risky. The voters of Sydney were tolerant, but not blind to the scandals. Mackay's murder was still fresh. It was not the time to be seen to be kind to criminals. Premier Wran could sense the mood and sat on the report.

While this was happening, in late 1977, Detective Inspector Merv Beck was getting on with the job of enforcing the law, as best he could, as the officer in charge of the 180 police of Number One Division, known as Central. Its division headquarters were near the Central Court of Petty Sessions.

When Commissioner Wood went on holidays not long after Beck had taken up his new job, Jim Lees became Acting Commissioner. Lees had Beck's confidence and was also at pains to separate himself from Merv Wood.

Lees again asked Beck to do the same good work at Central as he had done at Darlinghurst in cleaning up both crime and his own police.

In response, Beck suggested that as Chinatown was in his new division, he intended to give it a shake-up. Chinatown was a known hive of crime including drugs, gambling and illegal immigrants, and Beck told Lees that he was not prepared to tolerate these criminal activities in his bailiwick.

Beck had noticed some of Abe Saffron's doorkeepers and minders at places in Chinatown. Saffron was part of the new elite of organised criminals in Sydney and a force to be reckoned with. He had been described by the South Australian Attorney-General, in 1976 as "Mr Sin", but was also known as "King of the Cross".

His legitimate businesses, hotels, nightclubs and property development, were founded on prostitution, illegal gambling, protection rackets and almost certainly, illegal drugs (nonetheless, he was never prosecuted until 1987 when the National Crime Authority hit him for tax evasion).

At that point, Beck did not realise that Saffron, like other major criminals, was deeply involved in illegal gambling in Chinatown and elsewhere, but he was sure there was plenty of criminal activity going on.

Over many years, Chinatown had been a favourite after hours venue for Commissioners of Police and CIB chiefs, as well as key members of the Labor Party which had its headquarters in Sussex Street. (The Liberal Party was closer to the Cross, in William Street). The Chinese community was building its financial and political strength, but there were also rumours about activity by the infamous Triads, the Chinese mafia.

The mention of Chinatown changed Lees' attitude. He drew the line firmly.

"I can't approve that," said Lees. "What you're suggesting is that you go outside your area of authority.

"If it's gambling, vice or drugs, it's not your job. You have to leave that to the specialist squads. And that applies to Chinatown and everywhere else."

Beck had no choice but to agree.

Beck had instituted a fortnightly meeting of all the station staff, where he would talk to them and encourage them to raise any issues or ask any questions about their duties and what was required of them.

After one of the meetings broke up, one of the young policewomen was still standing there so Beck approached her. "How are you enjoying your work in the police force?" he asked politely.

"Oh I like it now, but it was difficult when I first started," she replied.

Beck asked what she meant, and the young constable referred to the big charge room in the station. Central was a very large charging station so there was always a crowd in the charging room, with as many as eight police at once plus public servants, offenders and others.

"When I first started working in the charge room, some of the male police would be swearing and using bad language and they would look at me for a reaction and start laughing at me," she said.

"But that doesn't happen now. I fixed that by using the same language myself.

"The same people would then gather around me and say, look, young women should not talk like that, it's not nice!

"So I replied, 'well I am glad you see it that way, remember not to talk that way yourselves!'

"From that time on, I have been enjoying my work as a policewoman, I like being here very much."

For 18 months Beck remained officer in charge of Number One Division, busy with the police duties he had been given.

During this time, public debate and controversy over illegal gambling and connections with organised crime escalated. Beck was not blind to what was going on in Chinatown, including gambling, drug trade, and harbouring of illegal immigrants. But he was still under orders to leave this to others, and reluctantly obeyed.

At one time a photo appeared in a Sydney Sunday newspaper which made Beck both angry and dismayed at the state of the NSW Police. It showed a group of Chinese businessmen and several senior NSW police in a restaurant, where they had clearly had a good time. What made the photograph shocking was that the police had handed their caps and jackets to the Chinese, who had put them on like dress ups.

The photograph suggested that the friendly relations had gone too far. To Beck, with his respect for the uniform, it was a shameful reflection on his superiors. As far as he could see, the photo prompted no reprimands or other repercussions for the police involved.

Beck with the silver trophy given to him by the Darlo Police.

RSL Anzac Day March 1976. Beck second right.
Extreme right is Staveley Frederick Norton ("Dick") Hickson,
father of Jill Hickson who married the NSW Premier, Neville Wran,
later in 1976. Hickson was a squadron leader in 3 Squadron of the
Desert Air Force, in which Beck also served.

At the Police Aero Club at Bankstown Airport,
on the occasion of sponsoring a cadet pilot who later joined
the NSW Police. Beck was a qualified private pilot.

CHAPTER FOUR

Casino Storm Looms

While the allegations circulating in Parliament and elsewhere about illegal gambling and corruption did not seem to harm the Wran Government, the same was not true of the Police Force.

The Nielsen disappearance and other scandals had raised serious doubts about the integrity of the NSW Police. Honest police like Merv Beck were increasingly disappointed by their Commissioner Merv Wood, who had initially seemed promising but now appeared to be little better than his predecessor, 'Slippery' Fred Hanson.

Premier Wran insisted that the police were not being held back from closing the illegal casinos, but whatever the police were doing had little impact. Ignoring the record of the previous conservative government led by Robert Askin, the Liberal-Country Party Opposition found plenty to criticise in Wran's obvious ambivalence to policing the casinos.

A few months after the Lusher inquiry delivered its report, and exactly a month after Beck had been forced out of the Darlinghurst Police Station, *The Daily Telegraph* ran a story on 30 November, 1977.

Under the heading "Casino Storm Looms", state parliamentary correspondent, Harry Potter, claimed the Opposition was going to launch an attack on the Government over illegal casinos using "stunning evidence" from a key official. The article was based on a briefing by Bob Bottom, who was working with Country Party Leader, Leon Punch, on a parliamentary "urgency" motion.

Premier Wran headed off the attack by announcing that he had ordered Police Commissioner Merv Wood to close the casinos.

"I am aware that both in the press and on radio today rumours were disseminated in relation to illegal casinos," Wran said. "This rumourmongering, inspired by members of the Opposition and pursued by them for some weeks, makes it necessary for me to clear the air…"

The "rumours" constituted eyewitness evidence from Leon Punch himself. Punch had seen Commissioner Wood two weeks before, dining at a French restaurant with no less than George Walker, proprietor of the illegal casino, the Goulburn Club. Wood had seen Punch too, and had hurried out of the restaurant.

When the meeting with Walker was revealed, Wood knew there was no point denying it.

"The only way to get information is to talk to people in the game," he claimed brazenly.

It was well-known among police that Wood not only associated with George Walker, but was friends with him. Walker was invited to many official police functions as Wood's guest. According to police present at some of these gatherings, when Wood arrived he would walk straight past his officers to shake hands with Walker.

The official crackdown on the casinos announced by Wran went ahead, but not immediately. With amazing gall, given the media and political interest, Wood announced that he would not start the crackdown until 31 December because he did not want to put 300 employees of the illegal casinos out of work before Christmas.

When the police finally did hit the casinos and clubs in the New Year of 1978 there was a flurry of good publicity for the Government. As soon as the allotted time for the crackdown was over, the casino doors began to open again. Within weeks they had returned to normal.

Soon there were calls for another crackdown—on the illegal SP bookmaking trade. The government-owned and run TAB was struggling to compete with the burgeoning SP rackets which operated in direct competition and without fear.

The TAB Agents Association of NSW had laid 68 complaints to police in the previous 14 months about SP operators working openly in hotels in Sydney and other centres. Now the TAB provided the police with the names of 350 hotels next to TAB agencies, where illegal bookmakers were operating. The TAB's profits went to the Government and into programs to help NSW residents, while the SP profits went into grubby hands. Damning as it was, the list provoked little response.

One report 'guesstimated' the total turnover of SP operators in NSW in 1978 at more than a billion dollars a year—around $5.3 billion in 2020 money. To put this in context, the NSW Government's revenue that year was about $3 billion. Little or none of that came from the illegal bookmakers or casinos, who on the whole avoided paying tax altogether.

Agitation by the TAB for action against their illegal competitors was not appreciated. In early 1978 a note was received at TAB headquarters referring to the chairman of the TAB Agents Association, Dan Mongan.

"A warning to Dan Mongan…he has a price of $10,000 on his head to be destroyed as quickly as possible," it said. A radio journalist who had run a special investigation on the SPs also received a death threat. In view of the disappearances of Nielsen and Mackay, the threats were not taken lightly.

When the NSW State Parliament sat in March 1978, the Opposition honed in on the SP betting industry, organised crime and the NSW police response.

Country Party Leader Leon Punch, renowned for his firebrand manner and again armed by Bob Bottom, kicked off the attack on the Government. Punch said he had received allegations of police involvement in illegal SP operations, and that evidence of this had been provided to Premier Wran in a report compiled by the then-head of the Criminal Intelligence Unit (CIU), Sergeant Tony Lauer.

He alleged that corrupt police were also involved in SP betting, and that police had told TAB agents that they would be bombed by the underworld if they did not stop complaining about SP bookies.

"Is it a fact that the police have been prevented for more than a year now from raiding SP operations, on the order from a senior source?

"Has that order had the effect of particularly protecting the extensive SP operations of organised crime figure George David Freeman?" Punch railed.

Wran replied that no member of the government had given such an order.

"As to George David Freeman—that is a name not known to me," he claimed straight-faced, to guffaws of disbelief from the Opposition.

It would have been hard for anyone in Sydney not to know who George Freeman was. He was a high profile public figure, regularly pictured in the tabloid newspapers and described as a "colourful racing identity".

He had built up a respectable image as a major operator in the racing industry to disguise his real business as the boss of one of Sydney's largest SP operations and an associated crime network. Sydney's punters did not realise that major criminals, including Freeman, were doing deals behind the scenes to alter the odds being offered on horses, fix races by paying off jockeys to deliberately lose, and generally ensure that whatever happened, the public did not make money at their expense.

Punch's questions did not seem to rattle Freeman. The following month, in April 1978, Freeman was seen at the Newcastle races in company with 'Aussie Bob' Trimbole, and an ex-policeman. The Newcastle racecourse detective, Frank Lynch (also an ex-policeman), reported the trio in writing to the chairman of the Newcastle Jockey Club, Roy Mahoney. (Trimbole, born in Griffith, was named by the Woodard Royal Commission in its 1979 report as one of the main suspects in the disappearance of Donald Mackay).

Despite denying all knowledge of Freeman in response to Punch's questions, Wran promised to get Police Commissioner Merv Wood, to look into Punch's claims that the gaming police were leaving Freeman's SP operations alone.

In response, Wood sent Assistant Commissioner Reg Stackpool to 21 Division to investigate. Stackpool uncovered no irregularities and no illegal activities by Freeman.

While no action was taken there, Lauer himself was banished from the CIU to a position at Katoomba where he could not make waves. (Much later, his honesty became a more desirable commodity and he was appointed Police Commissioner in March 1991.)

But the cat was at least part of the way out of the bag. After two years of government denials that organised crime was a problem in Sydney, the Lauer report provided the ammunition the Opposition needed, ably assisted by Independent John Hatton.

At this time, Bob Bottom was briefly employed by the Wran Government. He provided a report, "Report Upon Organised Crime In NSW", which recommended the establishment of Australia's first independent crime commission. The Government shelved the report and Commissioner Merv Wood denied that organised crime existed in NSW, although his Police Minister and Premier, Neville Wran, admitted in Parliament that "organised crime will exist, and to deny its existence would be extremely naïve".

In September 1978, Liberal frontbencher John Dowd revived the comtroversy, this time quoting from the leaked Lauer report. He told Parliament the CIU had completed a report "dealing with the association of one George David Freeman with other persons". Included in the list with whom Freeman associated was the chief stipendiary magistrate of NSW, Mr Murray Farquhar.

Dowd told Justice Minister Ron Mulock that the people of NSW and the Parliament were entitled to know why they had not been told about the CIU report on Freeman, which was by then more than 16 months old.

Mulock's response was that the report was a matter for Neville Wran, who was both Premier and Minister for Police. When further questions were directed to Wran, however, the Premier shut down the debate by denying that he had read the report.

This was unlikely as the report, dated March 1977, made startling claims. It was the result of a covert police operation which involved tapping (listening in on) and taping the phones of a number of suspected organised criminals.

Lauer's report, concentrating on Freeman, concluded that he was operating 20 SP outlets with up to 200 telephone lines, which reported to his office in suburban Rockdale. It said he was also bribing police, and was connected to US organised crime (mafia) figures.

Other tapes captured all sorts of interesting conversations which went far beyond Lauer's report, but very little of their content was revealed until much later.

The continuing allegations made it impossible for Wran to proceed with his stated intention of introducing legal casinos.

Bob Bottom, back in journalism, continued to needle the Government. In January 1979, the influential national current affairs magazine, *The Bulletin,* published an article by Bottom which again raised material from the NSW police tapes.

Under the headline, "Criminals plan to muscle in on Wran's casinos", Bottom noted that Premier Wran argued that legalising casinos would end the long-standing scandal of illegal casinos.

Bottom claimed, however, he had obtained a tape recording which proved that criminals were scheming to take control of the new regulatory regime, so they could own legal casinos, by bribing politicians. Their plot was discussed at a secret meeting of illegal casino owners and crime leaders, including George Freeman, at the Taiping Chinese restaurant in mid-1976, soon after Wran was elected.

Bottom claimed he had obtained a tape made by another big crime player, Stanley John Smith, usually known as Stan the Man, to be played at the meeting, which he labelled the 'Taiping conspiracy'.

Bottom concluded, "Curiously, while talking of bribing and controlling the (casino) Board, Smith insisted that it would remove the stigma of illegality from casinos and remove the criminal element. Yet the tapes confirm the often-suspected link between illegal casinos and organised crime and the dangers inherent in legalisation if not properly and honestly administered."

The Government did its best to stonewall. Police Commissioner Merv Wood dismissed Bob Bottom's claims of a conspiracy as "comic cuts and a laugh".

Further cracks began to appear in the Government's denials. In May 1979, Opposition Leader John Mason revisited the CIU report by Tony Lauer. Mason wanted a proper response from the Premier, so provided him with advance notice of a question he intended to ask that included the addresses of 10 alleged SP operations— in Dulwich Hill, Enmore, Redfern, Marrickville, Rosebery, and Kingsford.

Wran scrambled the police to get a response and Jim Lees, who was again Acting Police Commissioner, provided it. In a minute to the Premier's Department, Lees confirmed that nine of the ten addresses listed were well known to 21 Division, and had been raided many times. Apparently, the raids had little impact.

At the Enmore Rd premises, 21 Division had made arrests on 11 occasions since February 1973. At the last visit during the week ended 31 March 1979, however, "no evidence of illegal betting or unlawful gaming was obtained", Lees said. Likewise, visits to seven of the eight other premises listed between March and May 1979 also found no evidence of illegal activity.

In a bid to change negative public perceptions, the NSW Cabinet quickly approved legislation to amend the Gaming and Betting Act. The new laws were marketed as a move to enhance policing of SP bookmaking, as the maximum fine which could be imposed on SP operators was increased.

But the real import of the changes worked in the opposite direction. The penal clauses were removed, meaning that the courts would no longer have the option of imposing a prison sentence on proprietors of illegal SP operations, which had previously been six months for second and subsequent offences.

This left NSW as the only state where a convicted SP operator could not be sentenced to jail. The government claimed that the new "stiff" fines made up for this, but in practice the usual fine imposed on operators under the new laws was just $50, a pittance compared to the profits being made. Even if the court chose to impose the higher fines, they were regarded by the syndicates as part of their overhead expenses.

To the cynical, the legislation was a sleight of hand, a deception which enabled the Government to announce a stiff crackdown on the illegal betting operations for public relations purposes, without imposing any real damage on them. Even if police succeeded in raising illegal operations and arresting the operators, they were unlikely to be put out of business.

Then, a year after Commissioner Merv Wood scoffed at Bob Bottom's claim that organised crime was operating in Sydney, Bottom got the last laugh.

On 24 May 1979, NSW Chief Magistrate Murray Farquhar had released on bond an American man, Roy Cessna, who had been charged with possession of drugs valued at $1.5 million. Despite the value of the drugs, the matter was listed as a summary matter to be held in the District Court rather than the Supreme Court.

Bob Bottom was investigating the Cessna affair for *the Bulletin*. He heard that Wood had ordered the charges to be downgraded, and rang Wood to ask him. Wood denied it, but did admit he had been contacted by Morgan Ryan, a mutual friend of him and Farquhar, who had questioned the real value of the drugs. (Morgan Ryan was to prove a key player in the later drama over NSW illegal phone tapping because of his friendship with High Court judge Lionel Murphy.)

When the article was ready, Bottom rang Wood's office again, to check the quotes he was attributing to the Commissioner. Bottom read them out to Wood's secretary. When she started to relay the quotes to Wood, the Commissioner grabbed the phone. "Hell," he said to Bottom, clearly agitated. "I didn't think you would quote me!" He then hung up.

Wood was already in deep trouble over the suppression of the CIU report on George Freeman, and emerging revelations about criminal activity by his friend and associate, Murray Stewart Riley. Riley and Wood had been double scull partners at the 1956 Olympics, where they won bronze. They were also both members of the NSW Police Force. After leaving the force, however, Riley became an international drug smuggler with American mafia connections.

Now an unsigned document, allegedly prepared by senior police officers, was distributed to a number of NSW politicians. The document claimed there was widespread corruption in the NSW force and referred to a meeting between Wood and an "illegal casino operator", among other things.

Premier Wran initially tried to brush it off, claiming it would be strange for a police commissioner not to know people in the underworld[12], but quickly changed his mind. On 5 June he announced that Wood had tendered his resignation, effective immediately.

Wran released a portion of Wood's letter of resignation. "I have carefully considered these allegations and others made in recent months and I am most concerned with the effects that such allegations are having on the morale, reputation and standing of the NSW Police Force."

Just a few days later, on 9 June, a fire broke out in the Ghost Train at Luna Park, the fun park situated on prime harbourside land in Milson's Point. Seven people were killed including six children. Almost immediately, the NSW Police investigating the fire claimed it was due to an electrical fault, There was no forensic investigation.

(In 1987, the National Crime Authority reopened the investigation of the fire. Although no new evidence was presented, it was found that the police investigation into the incident had been inadequate, and also criticised the previous coronial inquiry ineffective. In May 2007 a niece of Sydney underworld figure Abe Saffron, Anne Buckingham, provided an interview to *The Sydney Morning Herald* in which she claimed Saffron was responsible for the fire, but subsequently retracted the comments.)

Wood's deputy, Jim Lees, again became Acting Commissioner. The claims against Wood were formally investigated by an assistant commissioner, Jim Black, and Detective Sergeant D. James. The subsequent report was said by the Government to be "inconclusive".

Lees quickly discovered that his power was limited. A few months before Wood's dramatic resignation, in April 1979, Wran had made another important appointment to the senior ranks of the NSW Police. A superintendent from Parramatta, W.A.R. (Bill) Allen, became Chief Superintendent of the metropolitan area, chosen over 16 more seior police. Wran dubbed Allen the police "troubleshooter", although in hindsight, a more appropriate title would simply have been "trouble."

After Wood's departure, Wran put Allen in charge of cleaning up the embarrassing mess over illegal gaming and betting, including casinos. Since its inception in 1946, 21 Division had always come directly under

---

[12] See David Hickie, *the Prince and the Premier*, Angus and Robertson, 1985

the commissioner. While the Gaming and Betting Squad had become its core, the original name stuck and it remained known in the media and in the Police Force itself, as 21 Division.

The special squad was now to be responsible to the man Neville Wran had hand-picked as Chief Superintendent, Bill Allen.

Since 1975, 21 Division had been under the command of Inspector Pat Watson. Watson had now retired and Allen's first job was to find a suitable replacement, knowing that Wran wanted to crackdown on illegal gambling to relieve pressure on his Government over police corruption.

Allen turned to senior officers Keith Paull and Roy Whitelaw for advice. Paull, very experienced and a good thinker, had several suggestions, one of which was Merv Beck with whom he was working at the time. Allen thanked him and said he would get back to him.

Several years later, Beck asked Keith Paull what had happened between himself and Bill Allen at this time. This is Paull's account[13].

"Bill Allen phoned me at 'D' District and asked me to meet him at a suitable place late one afternoon, I suggested Willoughby Legion Club as we met there, where he advised that Neville Wran had appointed him to the position (Chief Superintendent) and made him responsible for suppression of illegal gambling and betting for the State. That he was to report direct to Neville Wran, that he had had a conference with Neville Wran in recent times and that he had almost open access to Neville Wran. That they called each other by Christian names when in private and that Neville Wran had told him to set up a new Gaming and Betting Squad immediately and for Bill Allen to have complete control over its formation."

Allen had asked Paull for a recommendation on who should lead the squad, and Paull had suggested Beck.

Paull added, "Bill Allen told me in strict confidence that he had a very good chance of appointment as commissioner instead of J.T. (Jim) Lees, that he—Bill Allen—would take me up there with him. He asked me to talk to Merv Beck and see if he was agreeable to the appointment."

Paull ran the idea past Beck and Merv's initial response was positive. A day or so later Allen asked Paull and Beck to meet him, again at the Willoughby Legion Club as he wanted the discussion kept confidential. Allen told them that he wanted Merv Beck to take charge of the squad

---

[13] Account recorded in Merv Beck, recorded account provide to Paul Rea 1984

immediately. He said he had run the choice past Premier Wran, and Wran had agreed.

The question remained, was Beck prepared to take on the job? Beck said he would think about it and get back to Allen.

Beck frankly thought it would be a mistake to take on the job. There was too much stacked up against him. Beck was no fool and he knew how bad things were on 21 Division.

After his stint in 21 Division in 1946, Beck had been saddened to see its reputation steadily slip over the following decades, until it was known more for its failures in relation to illegal gambling than anything else.

Being under direct control of the commissioner and being the sole authority responsible for policing illegal gaming and betting gave it great power. In 1954, then Police Commissioner Colin Delaney claimed that Thommo's did not exist—giving Sydney, as one commentator said, "a week of laughter". The lie was repeated in 1969 by Commissioner Norman Allan. In both cases, the commissioner's advice was repeated by the Premier and fed out to the public, which became suitably cynical about the standards of policing in the harbour city.

Beck himself had several times been warned off encroaching on 21 Division's territory. With sole responsibility for policing of gaming and betting, it escaped interference or scrutiny from other police and had become a law unto itself. Many police, including Beck, were suspicious that the opportunities for bribery were too great for the squad to resist and the line between law keepers and law breakers had been eroded.

Beck did not want to be associated with such a mess.

He went home that night and told Elsie, what was proposed, making it clear that he was not very keen. But Elsie was not going to give him a way out. "It's a matter for you yourself," she said.

He still had not made up his mind the next day when he received a phone call at the station asking him to come to police headquarters for a meeting with Acting Commissioner Lees. Beck, like most other police, knew that Lees was not particularly well regarded by the Wran Government, partly (so it was said) because he was a "church man". It was a strange twist that his religious beliefs apparently meant he could not be trusted.

Lees made it clear straight up that he wanted Beck to take the job Allen had offered.

"Could you do me a particular favour, I want you to accept that position on 21 Division," he told Beck. "I do expect to become commissioner and I would want someone in gaming I can trust and rely upon."

Beck respected Lees and wanted to help him. But he had a few conditions.

If he was going to take the job, he was doing it his way. There was no way he was going to allow the job to tarnish his reputation or his record.

He recalled: "My reluctance in taking the position was that those who had been before me did not enjoy a high reputation, nor did the men under them.

"I reluctantly accepted the position, but I also made it known not only to Lees but to Bill Allen that if I took the position I did not want to be told not to go here or there or keep away from these people, or look after those. And I certainly didn't want any political interference.

"I was given the assurance by both that those things wouldn't happen."

In fact Beck was surprised that he was offered the job, given the circumstances of his departure from Darlinghurst. His determination to leave no stone unturned in enforcing the law was well known.

On the other hand, given the magnitude of the problem on Sydney's streets, it was almost certainly true that no other honest policeman would have taken on the job. It remained to be seen whether Beck could actually achieve what he was now asked to do.

* * * *

Once his mind was made up, however, Beck felt positive. There was nothing he liked better than a challenge. An optimist by nature, he decided that the Police Force and the Government were now serious about knocking out illegal gambling, and were relying on him to do this—and in doing so, generate positive publicity. He believed that doing a good job, and being seen to do a good job, would help to restore flagging public confidence in the Police Force as a whole.

He did not expect the obstacle immediately put in his way.

Assistant Commissioner Lees told Beck he would have to form a whole new team in the gaming and betting squad as the Government—ie Police Minister Wran—had decided to remove all of the squad members and "start with a clean slate".

To Beck's surprise, he was not even offered assistance with finding the right people. Keith Paull had given Bill Allen a list of police he believed would work well on the squad, when they discussed Beck; but Allen had done nothing with it.

Now Lees told Beck bluntly, "You'll have to find your own officers. Don't expect me to nominate ones who are going to be reliable, because I can't."

Beck thought Lees' comment was a sad reflection on the force, but probably true.

The decision caused media comment, "Games Squad in New Police Shock", reported *The Sun* newspaper on 9 July 1979. "In another big police shuffle, the 14 man gaming squad has been transferred to other duties," reported Bill Archibald. "This follows the transfer of Insp Reg Edwards, (Acting) chief of 21 Division, and two of his senior officers….

"One man transferred from the squad last week was attached to 21 Division for nearly 15 years."

There were two exceptions. Bill Allen told Beck that two of the squad members, whom he named, would be staying. As Beck was allowed 30 police working under him, this still left him with a big job. Those joining the squad had to be ready, willing and able to immediately leave their current positions and take on a very difficult and possibly dangerous job. Above all, they had to be trustworthy.

Beck turned to his circle of trusted colleagues to provide him with other names, giving precedence to honesty and reliability over experience. Some of those he approached turned down the offer, but most of them accepted the chance to work with an officer as strong and straight as Beck. Beck was also contacted by some officers volunteering to join the squad, usually because they had encountered minor problems in their previous roles. Beck had no issue with this as long as they met his criteria and his judgement proved to be sound as the men flourished under his direction. Initially there were no women on the squad, but when required on raids, police women were called in from other areas.

While the gaming and betting squad was disbanded, 21 Division had various other duties and police in these roles were allowed to remain. One of these other tasks was training young police to be plain clothes detectives, before they were sent out to divisions or squads.

There was a group of six or seven detective instructors, led by Detective Sergeant Grace. They were used on 21 Division in plain clothes, and took the trainees to assist with criminal matters covered by the division including robberies, street offences and brawls.

Beck got on well with this group. Before long he organised to have some of them moved into his gaming and betting team, and in time he arranged for them to gain formal designation as detectives, as Beck believed they were well deserving. Beck also utilized many of the trainee detectives in teams of three led by a senior policeman, on gaming and betting duties.

While he was busy putting his team together, Beck took the time to do some fundamental research on illegal gaming and betting. He found the 1963 Royal Commission report by Justice Kinsella fascinating reading—especially as it was clear that all of its recommendations, except the creation of the TAB, had been ignored by successive NSW Governments.

The establishment of the TAB in 1964 was supposed to be the final death knell for the off-course illegal bookmakers, generically known as SPs although they did not all use a "starting price" system. It was designed to provide betting that was accessible in the suburbs, safe and legal, and also provided revenue to the State Government. This prediction proved to be wrong. The SPs actively fought back against the TAB, even mimicking its marketing ploys such as doubles and trifector betting. They could compete on odds because, unlike the TAB, the SPs pocketed all of their profits.

In contrast to the laughable declaration by NSW Police that SP bookmaking had been stamped out in the late 1960s and early 1970s, it had changed from a cottage industry to a well organised division of organised crime, providing both income and a ready avenue for laundering money from their other activities, including drug dealing, prostitution, car theft, race-fixing, and smuggling guns, wildlife and people.

Almost all of the traditional pub 'pencil men'—characterised by Premier Wran in the NSW Parliament as "Friendly Fred"— had been forced out by operators working for crime bosses. New telecommunications technology had made SP an even more attractive proposition: the introduction of Subscriber Trunk Dialling for interstate calls from Sydney in 1971 allowed the NSW SP syndicates to cover bets laid as far away as Darwin. Large Victorian and South Australian betting networks were operated entirely from phone parlours, containing dozens of phones, based in central Sydney or regional areas.

Beck knew that he could not, and was not expected to, close down the SPs altogether, because the law and the penalties were not strong enough. The jail penalty for SP offences had just been replaced with fines, making it even easier for gambling operators to remain out of the public eye while their minions, often for extra money, would take the charges.

There was also a muddy political situation. In the latter half of 1979, while Beck's crackdown was under way, the NSW State Council of the Australian Labor Party, of which Wran was the NSW Parliamentary Leader, passed a resolution in favour of allowing privately-run casinos, supervised by an independent board.

Despite the Government's hypocrisy, Beck believed very deeply that his job was to enforce the law as it stood. Changing the law was a matter for the Parliament, not police.

Against this background, on 2 July 1979, Merv Beck began his new duties as officer in charge of 21 Division. He was still trying to assemble a team to work with him, but had found seven who joined him in the new offices.

The outgoing gaming and betting staff were clearly not happy about their abrupt dismissal. Almost all of the records on anti-gambling operations throughout NSW had been removed or destroyed.

Beck set about reading what remained, which was mainly letters and newspaper cuttings which the outgoing squad had chosen to leave. There were complaints from members of the public, including City of Sydney councillor Tony Reeves, about various gaming places and lack of police action, and newspaper articles making similar complaints.

Attached to some of the letters were minutes written by 21 Division explaining that these locations had been raided, but the police were unable to get in as tight security made them impregnable. It was clear there would be plenty of challenges ahead for Beck's team.

Already, Beck had been contacted by many people he knew in the media, the Police Force, legal circles, political circles, businessmen and women, and public servants. They offered him support and information, but warned that he was in an area where corruption had become the norm.

As well as disloyalty and treachery from other police, they warned, he could expect firm resistance from some of Sydney's most dangerous criminal empires, run by George Freeman, Lennie McPherson and Neddy Smith among others. These well-meaning contacts also predicted that Beck would run into deep resistance if he tried to police areas like Broken Hill and Newcastle.

Beck took all of this on board. He knew that to succeed, he needed complete loyalty from his squad, and decided from the outset to be open and accessible to his team, including regular meetings and interviews.

To get started, Beck brainstormed with the squad members, and encouraged them to tell him of anything suspicious that they saw or heard. About a dozen of the men who joined him had experience in gaming and betting duties, and on just his third day on the job, a small group of these officers gave him an alarming insight into how the gaming and betting squad had operated in the past.

They had been sent to hotels to look for SP operators, only to be told on arrival that they were expected, as the operator had received a phone call to tip him off. They were convinced that the call had come from the gaming and betting squad office they had just left. What made them most angry was that customers of the hotel, seeing what had happened, believed they were part of this corruption.

Beck reported all of this to Acting Commissioner Lees on 6 July. Bill Allen had instructed Beck to report only to him, and not to Lees, but Beck refused to accept this directive. He told Allen that Lees had also asked him to report to him personally, and he would continue to do so. In fact, Lees encouraged Beck to report to him often, visit him whenever he felt the need and tell him of any interference by anyone, at any time, in Beck's duties.

Even with his background knowledge, as Beck bedded in he was staggered by the extent of illegal gambling and especially the size of the SP bookmaking industry.

SP betting was available at the majority of hotels throughout NSW, either through a bookie on the premises or a visiting one, and there were an increasing number of high volume phone SP betting operations. It came to Beck from a number of sources that buying a hotel or taking over a lease included the requirement to accommodate an SP bookie, and those who rejected the condition were put under such pressure that they buckled in the end.

In comparison, the casinos were relatively small business. At the time of his appointment in mid-1979 there were 24 or 25 large casinos in NSW, 16 of which were in central or suburban Sydney, with others in country areas including Albury, Parkes, Wollongong, Newcastle and the Far North Coast. The inner Sydney casinos were well-appointed and catered for the high end of the market with fine food, fine alcohol and attractive waitresses. Their regular clients included prominent members of society.

Other gambling outlets were more down market. About 400 'ethnic clubs' in fact existed purely for gambling, and various premises offered only two-up, an Australian game in which two coins are placed on a small piece of wood called a kip and tossed into the air. Bets are laid on whether both coins will fall with heads or tails facing up.

While SPs were ubiquitous, the casinos and two-up parlours were the most public face of the gambling. They were sophisticated and confident, assuring clients they were safe from the law. But they had never faced the strategy, determination and physical force which Beck applied to them.

Beck was only a few days into the job when he determined what would be his first target.

It was common knowledge that two-up games that were being conducted around Surrey Hills and Darlinghurst. One of the few records left by the previous 21 Division members showed that they had tried to gain entry to the Darlinghurst premises of the biggest and most famous of these places, Thommo's Two-Up School. But no arrests had been made there for more than eight years.

The challenge for Beck was clear. He was also keen to swoop on the gambling operation as a follow-up to his work at Darlo, which had been cut short after he suggested finding out the players behind the games.

Thommo's had started in 1910 as a mobile operation, and survived and thrived over the decades. Begun by a boxer, it was run by restaurant and casino operator Joe Taylor until his death in 1976. Four or five different groups then ran Thommo's. Some of these may have just borrowed the name to attract clientele, while others were part of a complicated leasing arrangement.

True to its mobile origins, Thommo's moved a number of times, its location always concealed. In the late 1970s its was operated from premises on Commonwealth Street, Wentworth Avenue, at the end of Foster Lane and Reservoir Street near Central Railway. One of the main premises was on Oxford St within 250 metres of Police Headquarters, which was then located on College St (having moved from the corner of Phillip and Hunter Streets in the early 1970s).

Having decided to make it a target, Beck sent three of his team to test the security at Thommo's with a low level raid.

It was well after midnight as the three police, in plain clothes, walked the last 50 metres towards the street level door which they knew led to Thommo's upstairs premises.

As they approached, a security guard dressed in white stepped forward.

"Hey mate, can I help you?" he said with the right mix of courtesy and threat.

The head constable got out his badge "Police, open up!" he demanded.

Before he could do anything else, the police heard an alarm sound upstairs. Then it went quiet.

"Police, open up!" he demanded again.

"Just a moment, mate," the guard said.

Sure enough, after another silent minute the police heard a key turn in the door lock. As the police exchanged glances, not quite believing their luck, the heavy door swung inwards.

Another tall muscly man, this one dressed in black, gestured up the stairs. "This way."

When they reached the first floor they went through another door into a large room. There were a number of tables with chairs scattered around the room. Several dozen men and women were sitting at the tables or standing in artificially relaxed postures.

One man with carefully styled hair and a smart black suit stepped forward with a confident smile. "Good evening officers, what can we do for you?"

The officers looked around and then looked at each other. As the host knew, they could only lay charges under the anti-gambling laws of the day if they could take possession of the hardware used in the gambling games. But there was nothing to be seen.

"We're just having a quiet meeting of our association," the smiling host offered.

"Righto. We'll just have a look around," replied the team leader.

The police scattered around the room, looking under the tables and behind the plush curtains. The host and patrons kept out of their way, remaining silent apart from the odd murmur.

There was nothing to be found. After a few minutes the police regrouped, shaking their heads.

"Will that be all gentlemen?" the host asked with another smug smile.

"Yeah, that's all for now. Thanks," said the leading officer and they walked back down the stairs. The security man let then out and the heavy door shut behind them.

It was clear that when the alarm had sounded, the staff had leaped into action to hide all of the gambling materials in some secret place. It was literally a case of 'no dice' and Thommo's lived another day.

But Beck was not one to be put off so easily. When his men returned empty handed, Beck realised that he was not going to succeed unless he was as cunning as the gambling operator. He immediately began work on alternative strategies.

To Beck, the argument that his predecessors had consistently put forward, that the two-up game was impregnable, was as silly as the suggestion that it did not exist.

A few nights after the failed raid, Beck walked down the darkened street from his office to get a closer look at Thommo's defences for himself.

From 30 metres away he could see the entrance at street level. It was a narrow terrace building on a busy street, where young couples and groups were constantly passing, on their way to nightclubs and restaurants.

Standing on the pavement near the heavy, dark door was the doorman, wearing a white coat like a car valet. While Beck watched, a wealthy looking man and woman walked up to the guard and spoke to him. After a brief exchange he nodded and motioned them to the door. He took a key out of his pocket and unlocked the door to let them in. As they walked through he pressed a buzzer, which Beck realised was to alert another doorman, positioned at the stop of the stairs, that someone was coming up.

The guard was a 'cockatoo'— the term widely used in Australian illicit pursuits for a lookout who could alert the insiders if the police or another threat appeared. In this case he was vetting the arrivals to make sure they were genuine patrons. Apparently most were given the nod, as Beck saw another couple and several single men also let in while he watched.

Beck could see the lights on behind the thick curtains in the upstairs section, but nothing more. He knew it was more than likely a game was under way. He returned to his office, thinking as he walked.

Over the next few days Beck devised a plan and ran it past his men. They were keen, and a few nights later, Beck set it in motion. It was one of Beck's first major raids and he had been on the squad for just 12 days.

About 11.15 pm, Beck and about a dozen men arrived at an arranged meeting place quite close to Thommo's. Two of the men were dressed in jogging gear and shoes which Beck had asked them to bring to work. At Beck's signal they started running down the street, and turned a corner onto Oxford Street. They continued to jog up towards the doorman at Thommo's, a clear target in his white coat.

Instead of passing the doorman, when they drew level with him the police each grabbed one arm and firmly pulled him down the footpath and around the corner.

The doorman was so surprised he did not have time to ring the alarm and although he yelled out, no one inside the Thommo's fortress could hear him. He was struggling and trying to get free, but stopped when his two snatchers identified themselves as police. He scowled and swore when one of the officers took the key to the heavy security door from his pocket.

Beck and half a dozen other men had reached them. Beck took the key and signalled to other members of the squad to join him while the cockatoo remained in firm custody. They walked back to the entrance to Thommo's and Beck put the key in. He looked at his men and nodded as the door opened. Then he pressed the buzzer once, signalling that a customer had arrived. One of the squad members, dressed in jeans and a smart casual jacket, went up the stairs while Beck and the others waited below, listening intently.

There was no resistance from upstairs and the officer, playing his role as a hopeful gambler, passed the second doorman without comment. Inside the large room he found a circle of people several deep, gathered around a clear space where the game of two-up was being played. Instead of standing back to take in the action and see where the game was up to, the police officer shouldered several players aside and walked straight into the middle of the two-up ring.

To the astonishment of the players, he placed his feet on the money they had laid down as bets to stop the game.

One of the players— whose turn it was— shouted out, "Hey, you— get off—this guy is stealing the money!" He lunged forward, his fist drawn back ready to throw a punch, but stopped in shock when the policeman pulled out his badge and loudly declared, "Police!"

When Beck heard this from downstairs, he and the other squad members raced up the stairs, warrant in hand. As their feet pounded on the stairs, not fully muffled by the carpet, the startled gamblers turned to see them enter.

The commotion also startled late-night diners celebrating Bastille Day at a popular French restaurant which occupied the ground floor of the building.

The game was up.

The police quickly moved through the crowd telling each person they were under arrest for illegal gaming and betting. There were 36 gamblers and five staff. The gamblers were a varied lot, including elderly women, some migrants., blue collar workers, well dressed young women, and men in suits.

Some of them yelled at the police, angry and disbelieving.

"How long is this going to keep up?" asked one.

"Will you fellows be back?" demanded another.

"If you persist in gambling then yes, I will be back!" replied Beck calmly.

The players remained unconvinced. "We'll see, we'll see," one retorted, eliciting some laughter.

While this was the first time such comments were made to Beck, it was certainly not the last. Gamblers were as sceptical as the gambling operators that the NSW police would or could keep illegal gambling outlets closed, especially one as well established as Thommo's.

Liquor, cigarettes and food were also being sold on the premises. Two people who were identified as managers were charged with conducting a gaming house and illegal gaming, and also for selling liquor without a licence.

The house was taking 20 cents in the dollar from every bet laid, and bets ranged from $10 to hundreds on each spin, which was a lot of money at the time. While they were talking to the arresting police, some of the patrons complained about the price of a beer, for which Thommo's was charging $1.20.

It was a triumph for Beck's new broom, and a symbolic blow against the gambling fraternity.

Sydney's biggest selling newspaper at the time, *the Sun-Herald*, devoted a full page to the raid with a photo of Merv Beck looking dashing in a Trilby hat. "Glamour gone, it looks like tails now", the headline quipped.[14]

As satisfying as the raid was, Beck knew it was not enough to stop Thommo's reopening on the same or different premises. The penalties that the gambling managers could expect were a trifle compared to the operation's profits, and unlikely to hurt much, thanks to the Wran Government's new legislation removing jail sentences. Whoever was running the Thommo's franchise, moreover, was far from the action. Even a lawyer who had represented the proprietors for more than 30 years, Phil Rooch, claimed not to know who they were.

---

[14] Sun-Herald 22 July 1979

Interior of the Forbes Club where the Raiders made arrests on several occasions, showing the fortified windows.

CHAPTER FIVE

Sledgehammer Beck

Beck believed strongly that senior officers were needed in the field to provide leadership on the spot, where it was most needed. This was especially important while his men were learning on the job, given that they were almost all new to the area of gaming and betting. As a result, he made a point of personally leading the raids on casinos and other gambling establishments which the previous gaming squad had said were unassailable.

His presence was good for morale and discipline. Even in the thrill of the chase, Beck was meticulous about keeping to the rules and was never overly rough with offenders. Many individuals who had been arrested by him at gambling establishments, later said hello to him on the streets or contacted him with relevant information.

The fact that he was there in person also made an impression on the gambling operators. As Beck recognised, these were not stupid people and they knew how to play a game, including making false allegations about police misconduct. When Beck was there to take a complaint on the spot, it was much harder for offenders to invent details after the event.

On the other hand, Beck did not hold back on using physical force on inanimate objects in his way. His attitude to locked doors quickly earned him a nickname— "Sledgehammer Beck".

The sledgehammer had been a traditional tool for police needing to force entry to premises, especially in Europe and the United States. But in Australia, by the late 1970s, they were usually overlooked in favour of more modern powered tools.

Years earlier, Beck had used a sledgehammer when he was a sergeant on criminal investigation duties in Camperdown.

In those days, the heavy hammer, with a head of steel rather than wood, was a practical tool commonly used by determined police.

"I always found when we were raiding places (at Camperdown) that one of the best tactics was to get the criminals when they were asleep in bed, and that's early in the morning," he recalled.

"We would time it, depending on summer or winter, with the predawn hours. We would go to where we knew these people were holed up. Where necessary we obtained warrants and we would have someone knock on the door. But often there would be no answer, so we would burst in the door with the hammer.

"By hitting the lock a good sound blow, it would work wonders.

"I used the hammer myself, in those cases, because I was a sergeant and I led the way with it."

As the head of Gaming and Betting, Beck found a renewed use for 'the key', as he jokingly named the hammer because it opened so many doors. He also renewed his familiarity with late nights and the 'wee small hours'. Between 1 am and 3 am is recognised as the time when the human body clock is at its lowest ebb. Beck chose this time for most of his raids on the illegal casinos and gambling clubs, and he found that the timing was important. Sometimes for various reasons he would deploy even later, in the few hours before dawn, using the cover of darkness for the assault and then taking advantage of the emerging light to assist with the search of the premises.

The first time he used the hammer against an illegal casino was on the last day of August 1979. Beck led his team in a well-planned raid on the Argyle Club in Parramatta.

A complaint had been received from a young couple who had been parked in Argyle St close to the illegal casino. They had been approached by two surly, heavily built men, one on each side of the car, who ordered them to leave the street immediately "or they would regret it". The men were quite abusive and the couple reported this to the local police, who passed it on to 21 Division.

Beck sent two of his men to observe the street and they confirmed that the two men were cockatoos or lookouts for the club, which they quickly determined was located in a building at 99a to 101 Argyle St.

While they watched, a number of men and women went to an upstairs section of the building, where they stayed for most of the night.

Further observations confirmed that it was an illegal casino.

Cockatoos were paid to be very watchful. Beck sent some men to try to get inside the Parramatta casino, but they were challenged and turned away. So Beck carefully drew up an alternative strategy.

Reconnaissance had shown that getting inside the casino would be difficult even if they could evade the cockatoos. It was important for Beck to know the structure of the building, and what he and the men were up against. This included whether the building was brick, timber or a mixture, whether and how the windows were secured, the position of adjoining buildings, and the lighting in the street.

Photographs were made of all entrances, both doors and windows. A rough plan of the building was also prepared, as best as could be done without actually going inside.

Over several nights, members of the inner circle kept watch on the premises, counting the number of cockatoos; the number of people attending, and how many of each sex; and the number of cars parked at the building. The registration numbers of the vehicles and details of the owners were checked on the night of the raid before any action was taken.

Beck also carefully planned the resources he needed to carry out the raid, starting with manpower. On the chosen night, the observation team would go to the area well before the raid was scheduled and report back on what was happening there. The raiding party would follow, preferably around 1.30 am. That was when the premises were most crowded as the illegal games usually did not start until 11pm or midnight.

The raid party itself was divided into teams led by a sergeant. Each team was given a job by Beck and drilled on how they would carry it out, including contingencies. The first team was in charge of arresting the cockatoos, then other teams would be positioned at vital posts around the building. Beck had made it a rule to include some reserve police in his raiding team, who would stay out on the street where they could be quickly called on, or could grab anyone trying to escape.

Vehicles were needed to transport all of these police to the scene. A police truck was needed to carry seized items or exhibits which would later become evidence, and also wagons or trucks to carry people arrested to Parramatta Police Station. Small exhibits would be taken to the squad headquarters in the Criminal Investigations Branch (CIB) building, but larger ones were taken to the police storage facility in the Eastern Suburbs. All had to be entered in the exhibit books and looked away safely.

These police vehicles needed to be guarded during the raid, so that while the raid was on they were not damaged or stolen. After the raid all the equipment had to be returned to its proper storage and accounted for.

A warrant was needed for entry which included entry by force if needed. The warrant could only be granted after the observation team on the night had confirmed that gaming was taking place at the targeted location. Beck or one of the squad needed to obtain a warrant before heading out on the raid.

Special duties were assigned to individual police according to their talents. There were several young policemen who were agile and happy to be sent by Beck climbing on rooves or through windows, if necessary, and assisting wherever they were needed.

Beck also liked to find out in advance, if possible, who was conducting the illegal casino. Doing this often relied on inside information as he could not approach the building owners without the information getting back to the proprietors.

On the night chosen for the Argyle St raid, all members of the gaming and betting squad who were involved had to report to Beck at a given time, before Beck initiated any action. They all knew that a raid was going to happen but had not been told where, or when.

At a certain hour, the observation team phoned in that a crowd of people had gone into the casino, and advised where the cockatoos were too. Beck then made the decision to go ahead and the teams were mobilised.

For this raid, Beck had organised a full range of equipment to assist their entry: hammers, crowbars, an axe, pliers, bolt cutters, ladders and ropes. He had also organised back up to be called on if those instruments failed— police trained in the use of oxy torches and motorised cutting instruments.

Whatever it took, Beck was not going to be turned away.

When the whole party had arrived at the rendezvous point, Beck gave them the instructions to drive to Argyle St— about 15 minutes away. First to go were the team who were going to help the observers to arrest the cockatoos. The others followed, and after leaving their cars took up their appointed positions to the rear and sides of the building.

It was now 2.30 am on 1 September 1979. The club was in the shopping centre, in an older building with high ceilings, at the top of a steep and narrow flight of stairs.

After stationing a few men at the rear, Beck led a small group up the stairs to the first floor. Halfway up was a large steel door, with brickwork surrounding the sides and over the top of it. The door looked to Beck like a police cell door, with an oblong slit in the middle of it at eye level, and a light over the top of the slit aimed to shine on the person standing outside.

Beck knocked on the door. The slit in the door opened and he could see a pair of eyes behind it. Beck's official notes on the raid recorded the following.

A voice said, "What do you want?"

"I am Inspector Beck. Here is my identity, here is a warrant to enter these premises, now open the door," replied Beck.

"I will get the boss," said the voice.

Then the slit was closed.

About a minute later it was reopened and this time there was a pair of glasses with distortedly big eyes looking out.

"What do you want?" asked the man.

"We are police, open the door," said Beck.

"You will have to get in the best way you can, I am not letting you in!" responded the man defiantly, and he slammed the slit shut.

With that, Beck took up the sledgehammer and smashed into the door several times. Then others in his team took it and did the same, but the door was so solid it did not move.

The premises were surrounded, no one could leave. It was simply a matter of getting inside.

Beck looked around and thought of a new angle. He directed his men to use the crowbar to attack the brickwork over the top of the door. This was a lot easier going, and after a short while the bricks had been knocked out and with them, some wires which were sparking dangerously.

Beck pushed the live wires away with the wooden handle of the hammer, and with the help of his police cleared enough room over the top of the door for a person to climb through. Then they lifted a young detective up into the space, with Beck cautioning him to be very careful not to touch any of the wires.

The brave young detective succeeded in getting through and dropped to the floor on the inside of the big door. There was no one there and he removed the bar and opened the door. Beck and his team went through quickly and up a further stairway into a large well lit room. They expected to find the casino there, but all they could see was a small kitchen with some tables and chairs, like a small café, at which sat four elderly Greek people drinking coffee. There was no trace of gaming or any other people.

There had to be a trick. Beck set his team searching the room. On one side was a large curtain, with a stone wall behind it. In the centre of the wall was a solid steel door similar to the one halfway up the stairs. Beck immediately directed several police to stay in the room while he took the others back down the stairs, out onto the street and around to the rear of the building.

The property was protected by a tall galvanised iron fence. There was a gate in it, secured with a padlock. The squad did not even need the sledgehammer to break the lock and get through the fence. On the other side, like some kind of maze, was a small strip of concrete and then another fence, this one made of wooden palings and with a gate to match. The lock on this gate met the same fate and Beck led his men through to the next layer of protection. This was a steel picket fence with a steel shuttered gate similar to the gates used in antiquated lifts. Beck's men broke through this too, and were now looking at a closed door at the rear of the building.

The door was smashed open, revealing a wooden staircase. Beck climbed the stairs to a landing where there was yet another wooden door.

Now Beck took the hammer himself and struck the door near the lock. It sprang open and he stepped through.

Inside was a group of men and women who had obviously been listening to Beck's progress. They were frowning and fearful. In front of them was the frontman who had told Beck to get in the best way he could, and may have been regretting it. His name was Graham "Crocodile" Palmer and he was well-known to Beck.

True to his nickname, Palmer had tears on his cheeks, which were red with anger and anguish as he surveyed the ruined fortifications in which he had placed so much faith.

Palmer began ranting at Beck in a near-hysterical fashion. Then he changed his tone.

"Come on then," he yelled at Beck. "You think you're so tough—come and fight me you bastards. I'll fight you, any one of you—I'll fight two of you at once!"

The gamblers urged Palmer to calm down, frightened he would arouse a furious response from the police, but Beck held up his hand to his men and told them not to react.

He moved closer to Palmer, ignoring his fighting stance, and grabbed him by the arm.

"Keep quiet and come with me," he told Palmer, as he led him into an adjacent room.

After shutting the door, Beck looked at Palmer sternly. Palmer now looked perfectly calm.

"What was the matter with you in there, Palmer?" Beck demanded.

Palmer shrugged. "Look, don't take any notice of me, I'm only putting this on for my people. They expect me to be tough!"

Beck asked Palmer about the casino. It was lavishly decorated and furnished, and Palmer claimed it had cost almost $80,000 to set it up. Beck believed him. There were eight very beautiful, professionally built gaming tables. The gaming room was fully carpeted, then stylish tiles led to the kitchen area where a European style chef was producing fine food. There was also a fully equipped bar. The whole place was air conditioned, which was rare at that time.

When Beck had enough information he led Palmer back to the gaming room. The gamblers were huddled in groups, some appearing defiant and others devastated. The police were firm but respectful and had given the offenders the standard warning that they need not answer any questions unless they wished to do so, as anything they said could be used in evidence against them.

When Beck returned, a very well-dressed mature aged woman came forward and spoke to him in a shaking voice.

"Are you in charge of this lot?" she demanded.

"Yes," replied Beck civilly. "Can I help you?"

The woman shook her finger at him in indignation. "You have got no idea what it's like to be in here, listening to the dreadful banging of those hammers! The building was shaking, my head was swimming!" She hesitated, then cried out, "and look what you're doing to me now!"

Beck followed her gaze to the floor and realised that the poor woman had wet herself in fear, with puddles forming in the floor.

Beck called over one of the team and asked him to soothe the woman and help her fix her clothes as best she could. Then the woman and all of the other clients, 32 in all were taken downstairs and out to the police paddy wagons. They were taken to the Parramatta police station, where they were charged. Beck's team accompanied them and assisted with fingerprinting, taking of personal information, bail inquiries, checking identities and names given, and photographing the offenders.

When they had gone, Beck turned back to Palmer.

"Where are the instruments of gaming that you were using, the cards and dice and other material?" Beck demanded.

Palmer, not learning from his earlier mistake, threw his head back. "You'll have to find them!"

So Beck's team began a thorough search, looking under rugs and throughout the kitchen. They found nothing, until one of them noticed an overhead air conditioning duct and climbed up to look in it. Sure enough, there were all the gaming implements.

Palmer had been watching the search. Realising that the game was up, he admitted that the implements had been hidden there. Then Beck informed him that the eight gaming tables would also be taken away, as evidence.

The tables were very expensive. Small ones were costed at $3000 each in late 1970s money, whereas large ones such as Palmer's could be as much as $12,000. The tables were one of the biggest costs in setting up a gaming place or casino, and Palmer was not keen to lose them.

"Well I've got you there if you want to take the tables," he said with satisfaction, "because they were built in and they can't be taken out." But Beck smiled wryly.

"Remove the tables," he told his team. "Take them apart if you have to!"

Palmer was correct, the tables were too wide to fit out through the doorways. So to his horror, the police used their tools for a new purpose, taking the tables to pieces which were then removed.

By now Palmer was furious, and his anger made him indiscreet.

"I could have got those people out of here while you fellas were banging on the doors, and round the back gate," he boasted.

Beck saw a chance to learn more.

"I doubt that, Palmer. How would you do that?"

Palmer took the bait. "I'll show you."

He led Beck to a concealed doorway which led from the casino into the neighbouring florist within the same building.

"All I had to do was lead the people down here, out this little door and out into the street while you were doing your best to get in." Beck tried to look impressed, but only for a moment.

"I'm sorry to disappoint you," he said then. "But if you look across the street there, see those shadows?"

He beckoned towards them and out came half a dozen of his men, who had been placed there in case they had to catch people trying to leave the premises.

Palmer opened his mouth, but this time, said nothing.

After the people arrested at the Argyle Club had all been charged and the equipment all accounted for, Beck and his team headed back to their quarters to attend to the paperwork. By then it was quite late in the morning, about 4.30 am, as the raid had not begun until 2.30am.

The tip-off from the young couple in their car had been very valuable, as the gaming and betting squad had not known about Palmer's club until then. Whatever records of it had been previously held by 21 Division, had been destroyed before Beck arrived. Beck had no doubt that this had happened, as Palmer was well known for paying for protection. He also boasted about his mates in the police force and was a frequent attendee at gatherings of the so-called 'barbecue set', which soon after this became of great interest to Beck.

For a hardened criminal, Palmer was an interesting character. He had a reputation for acting the tough guy, as he had done during Beck's raid, but it was also well known that this was just an act, and often when he was confronted by police he was very nervous. Business cards were unusual in those days but Palmer carried a mock card, listing his services as various types of nonsensical crime but also including rape.

When Palmer appeared at court over the Argyle Club, he pleaded guilty. The fine he received was just $1000—a far smaller loss to Palmer than his precious, and extremely valuable, gaming tables, the loss of face among the gambling fraternity and of course the huge profits which he had enjoyed. A few years after the casino raid, Palmer was sent to jail for 16 years for drug offences.

After the Argyle St raid, Beck and other members of his team regularly used 'the Key' to get through the defences built around casinos and other gambling venues. To the gamblers inside, hearing the boom and crash as the hammer did its work was an unnerving experience, and the woman at the Argyle Club was not the only one to lose control during a raid. Many of the people who cowered behind the steel doors said each blow had sent involuntary shivers of fear through their bodies and their minds.

But it was not Beck's intention to harm or intimidate anyone except the gambling operators. After listening to a number of these accounts from frightened gambling patrons, Beck— who was kind at heart—

talked with his team about how to achieve their goals without putting the fear of god into their targets.

Beck had taken the view throughout his police service that he should go as hard as it took, and no harder, to make an arrest. If people gave him difficulties, he responded in kind and Beck's determination and toughness was legendary, but he always avoided violence where possible.

Once the arrest was made, he was always polite and friendly to those arrested.

He insisted that the squad do the same. When they gained entry to gambling premises, they reassured people that they would not be harmed. This was very successful and a number of people arrested were friendly to Beck and his men, until they were placed in custody in police cells and charged.

Another time when the squad had arrested a mixed group of gamblers, two women and a man piped up and asked to see the famous sledgehammer which Beck's team had used to get in.

"They were shown it and they looked upon it as though it was some symbol of authority or something amazing, but to us it was just a tool that was used and had to be used," mused Beck.

The sledgehammer did not come into play in every raid. It was only used when it was absolutely necessary to damage the building to gain entry. On a couple of occasions the squad entered the wrong premises, but the hammer was not used and no harm was done. The circumstances were fully explained and compensation was paid.

In general, however, Beck believed that illegal operators knew what the consequences would be, if they made it as hard as possible for police to enter, and refused to let them in. This was certainly the case as the team settled in to their work, attracting constant publicity.

The team's responsibilities followed the natural division between the two aspects of illegal gambling. The casinos operated at night, especially in the very late hours, while the SPs operated during the day, on dates when horse races were being run. On race days, the first shift of the gaming squad would focus on SP bookmakers, while the second shift targeted the casinos and illegal gaming houses at night.

At the end of the racing day, the night shift crews would come in for a briefing by Beck on the night's targets and to be assigned their duties and sorted into teams of two. Each shift had to follow up their field work with paperwork and court appearances.

The workload was huge. Shifts were long and sometimes, extremely long. Beck himself worked virtually around the clock to ensure he was there to supervise and support his squad during both shifts and across all of their work.

During the day he stayed at the squad office, monitoring and directing all operations. His teams would contact him on their car radio or using public phones whenever they made an arrest or if they needed assistance of any kind.

All information gathered by the team went to Beck for assessment, so he knew where the potential targets were, and could redirect police as needed.

Beck personally took part in important raids wherever possible. This often meant accompanying several teams over the course of a night, at midnight and then well after midnight, to see how they worked. He made a point of helping with the arrests and followup paperwork and even testifying in court.

On nights when raids on casinos were planned, Beck's routine for the squad began with a solid meal, early in the evening so that the rest of the night was free for work. The men would all eat together as a mark of solidarity, in a quiet café or restaurant. They rotated between various eating places so that they would not be easily spotted.

The dinners were virtually the only time the squad had to relax together, and Beck enjoyed listening to the fellows, as he called them, talking about any and everything.

"I'd just sit there and listen to their talk," he said. "And I could see they were in good humour, they were in good spirits, they were friendly and stuck together. I was very proud of this team and they should be very proud of themselves to this day."

With the meal under their belts, they quickly went into action. Beck sent the undercover officers out to make observations in areas where they knew or suspected a casino was operating. When they were satisfied that illegal gambling was under way they would report back to Beck, who would organise signing of a warrant. He would then gather the team and conduct the raid.

At the end of the shift, where possible, the squad members would all return to base and sit down for a round table conference on what they had seen and what it meant, and share whatever other intelligence they had gathered. The conference was an important part of Beck's management style, ensuring that his men all felt part of a team that shared their successes— and their limited failures.

In between raids, the squad was also busy. Beck had a list of targets to be visited on the night for observation prior to a raid, and other leads to be followed.

Beck knew well that he had to be scrupulous in adhering to the police regulations at all times, given the intense scrutiny on him and his squad. He had promised to report to Acting Commissioner Lees every day, with the results of the previous 24 hours' duties and details of the raids, including the circumstances of the arrests. Some of this information was also provided to his official supervisor, Bill Allen.

Beck was happy to brief Lees as his feedback was always positive. Lees also asked Beck to pass on his appreciation to the members of the squad, and this was good for their morale. On the other hand, drawing up the report added another component to Beck's workload. Writing a synopsis of the squad's day and night activities, and delivering it in person to Lees at Police Headquarters took time. On nights when raids were carried out, Beck would never get more than three or four hours' sleep.

Following Beck's unstoppable lead, the new gaming and betting squad quickly learned to push the boundaries to get the job done. Sometimes their raids involved physical feats, courage and downright risky behaviour. They also became skilled actors as they audaciously role-played their way through the defences of gambling establishment.

To Beck and his men it was all part of the job and fortunately their risks ended in laughter more often than injury. The gasp of surprise when they made a spectacular entrance was a reward in itself.

Two examples of this dare-devil behaviour were raids on ethnic clubs featuring the young sergeant, Allan Peake.

Very soon after Beck had taken over 21 Division, before word had got around that he was really serious, Beck had led a team to an ethnic club near Bankstown, but had not been able to get inside. They had knocked on the door and rung the bell, with no response, although they could hear voices and knew that games were being played upstairs.

The only entrance was through the very solid front door, and at the top of the stairs was another door. There seemed to be no way of getting in upstairs either, as there was no verandah or awnings, just a sheer brick wall. Even the adjoining buildings were plain and offered no assistance.

Beck obtained a warrant and returned to the club, but he still had no way of getting in. He knocked and called out. The police could clearly hear the gambling taking place inside and the gamblers could see Beck and his team. But their only response was laughter at the discomfort of the police outside.

Sergeant Peake had checked out the back of the building. He came back and told Beck he thought he could make it to the first floor by climbing a drainpipe. Beck was happy to accept his offer so they went round the back to watch his progress.

The drainpipe was very thin and the only window was high, about 10 metres up. Beck and the other police held their breath as Peake gradually climbed up, with the pipe creaking and groaning as though it would break at any moment and send Peake crashing down.

Finally Peake reached the window and to the relief of his watching team members, wriggled his way in and disappeared.

It turned out to be the toilet, but fortunately it was not in use at the time.

Peake picked himself up and gingerly opened the door. He could see the games proceeding, so he walked out into the middle of them and declared himself to be a policeman, showing the warrant and ordering them to open the front door.

Everyone in the club was stunned. They knew the police were outside but having foiled them before, they had felt secure, and now were plainly shocked that one had managed to get inside.

Many of them were so nervous that there was a run on the toilet which Peake had just exited.

Eventually the principal opened the front door to let Beck in, and the players were arrested and gaming equipment was seized. Before they were taken to the police station the principal came up to Beck and, in his thick accent, attempted some sort of deal.

"Pleez, pleez if you come back you wonta finda door locked!" he promised. Clasping his heart, he added, "Promise, pleez, if you coma back, you won't send no one througha shithouse, I have bad heart!"

On another occasion, Sergeant Peake and a partner from the squad were trying to get into a club, where they knew gaming was going on. A number of previous attempts had been made by squad members, without success, as the alarm would go up in the foreign language and the gambling would be disbanded.

Sergeant Peake and his partner were in the lane outside the club, mingling, when a police truck unconnected with 21 Division drove across the mouth of the lane.

Peake, pretending to be a lout for effect, shouted out, "Keep going, you big fat bastards!"

The crowd in the lane liked the comment, but unfortunately for Peake, it was also heard by the police in the truck. The truck turned into the other end of the lane and an enormous sergeant leaped out and grabbed Peake.

"Now what have you got to say about the big fat bastard?" the giant man demanded.

The crowd scattered while Peake squirmed. When there was no one close Peake hurriedly explained to the other sergeant that he was undercover and what he was doing, and asked him to maintain the pretence by putting him into the paddy wagon. The enormous sergeant was more than happy to comply. He unceremoniously picked Peake up and bodily threw him into the van with, in Peake's view, a bit too much realism!

Peake was released a few streets away, sporting a number of new bruises. Meanwhile his partner was also having fun, after scattering with the rest of the crowd. He ran and found himself on the railway tracks where he stopped and looked around,

As none of the other gambling crowd were in sight he was just about to start making his way back to the club when he felt cold steel in his ear. It was a revolver, held by a railway security officer who took his job very seriously.

When the partner had also talked his way out of the situation, he and Peake finally got back to 21 Division where their adventures caused much amusement among their colleagues.

Painful though it was, Peake's acting did pay off, when the pair returned to the ethnic club the following night and were accepted by the in-crowd and allowed entry, leading to a successful raid.

While raiding the casinos required breaking down doors, locating and breaking SP bookmakers was a very different type of operation.

Less than three weeks into the job, on 21 July, the squad raided an SP operation in Tweeds Heads at the Queensland border. The operation was reputed to be one of the biggest in Australia, with a turnover of $100 million a year.

Beck's success was recorded in *the Sunday Telegraph* on 22 July. "In raids on the ring's Tweed Heads headquarters over the last two weekends, five arrests have been made. But police said the SP bosses had escaped the raids and had 'shut up shop'.

"The operation has been working out of a block of Tweed Heads flats for years—right under the noses of local police. ... Some bets recorded in books seized by police were as high as $20,000.

"The raids carried out at three premises are seen as part of the concerted bid by the revamped 21 Division to stamp out SP in NSW. The old Gaming Squad was transferred en masse only days before the raids were carried out."

* * * *

It had been Bill Allen's recommendation that Beck be chosen to lead 21 Division, and Beck had expected vigorous support for his crackdown from Allen and Commissioner Lees. But it did not take long for Beck to become uncomfortable with Allen's supervision of the squad's work, which soon turned to interference.

It was clear that the two men had different expectations about how Beck would carry out the crackdown and how thorough it would be.

From the start, Allen attempted to tell Beck how he should and should not do his job.

One of his first instructions to the new squad was that the Government did not require premises raided by Beck to be declared 'common gaming houses' under the law.

After a place had been found to be used for illegal gambling, supported by convictions, an application could be made to the Government through official police channels, usually the Commissioner, for it to be declared a common gaming house.

Once this occurred, the property was legally off limits. Any person found on the premises at any time was liable to be arrested, without the police having to obtain direct evidence that illegal gambling was taking place.

This was obviously a very powerful tool against the illegal operators, but successive governments were reluctant to use it. Allen made it clear to Beck that if he prepared applications, the Government would not proceed with them.

Other police told Beck of many problems they had experienced in attempting to use the gaming house provision, over many years. One senior detective found that his report on a certain premises kept getting lost. It was only after he had submitted it to the then-Commissioner a third time that he received a satisfactory answer. While this was going on, the place was still being used for illegal gambling. Such delays, according to what Beck heard, were not unusual.

Now the pattern was being repeated. According to Allen, the Government was not interested in putting the casinos out of action in the long term, which meant the squad would have to make repeat visits if they wanted premises to stay closed. Given the low court fines that were being given out, closure was the best punishment available.

Even SP bookmakers and casino operators were getting off with fines that were mere tokens compared to their turnovers, as the Wran Government had changed the Gaming and Betting Act to remove the option of a jail sentence for offenders.

The differences between Allen and Beck became heated over Beck's plan to raid the well-known casino at 680 Darling St, Rozelle (also said to be in Balmain by Beck and many others). The casino was the very first that Beck had in his sights, and the men he had assigned to observe it were satisfied that gambling was being conducted every day and night.

The casino had been operating for some time and was owned and managed by a man named Bruce Hardin. Hardin was an associate of George Freeman, Lennie McPherson and other heavyweight criminals, but also had close associations with many police at both senior and lower levels, including former 21 Division police, and politicians.

Like most of his colleagues, Beck was aware of the connections. He also knew that, before he had taken up the job, many casino operators or SP bookmakers had been tipped off a week or two in advance when it was their turn to be raided by the police. When the 'show' raid did take place, some of the staff would take the rap as fall guys, providing a mutually acceptable outcome for both the police and the principals, the 'big fish', who seldom saw the inside of a police station.

This only confirmed Beck's keenness to raid the casino. But when he told Bill Allen, Allen immediately declared the place was off limits. It had special status, Allen claimed.

"Don't go near that place at Rozelle," Allen told Beck.

Beck asked him why not, explaining that his men had been watching the place and had reported that it was definitely operating as a casino.

"As soon as I get the strength to do it, which is now, we're going to knock it off," he said.

Allen shook his head.

"No, you can't do that," he proclaimed. "That's an order. The Premier doesn't want you to do it!"

Beck thought this was very suspicious, whether or not it was true.

"The Premier? Why would he say that? Why didn't Wran tell me that himself?" he demanded.

Allen was getting angry.

"You just remember who you are! I am your boss and you do as I say!"

But Beck continued to demand a reason why the Rozelle premises could not be raided.

"You told me to take this job. I am doing the job.

"That means closing illegal operations and that means the Rozelle premises!"

Allen knitted his brows.

"The Premier wants to get some people out of there before it is raided," he growled.

"Really. Well you had better give me some names," Beck replied.

It was a bold move, but to his surprise Allen obliged. He named Bruce Hardin, the proprietor, the Labor MLA for Balmain, Roger Deegan, and the Liberal MLA for Parramatta, John Abels.

This was very interesting but also alarming information to Beck. He looked at Allen with even greater indignation.

"If the Premier wants to warn these people, which is curious, all he would have to do is give them a phone call before we raid it," he said.

"This order is no good to me. I told my men in good faith that I was assured by you people there would be no interference, and that we can go anywhere."

Allen was not interested in what Beck thought or what he told his men.

"You wait till you get the green light. You understand? You stay away from Rozelle until you are told it's okay.

"That means the red light is on until I say!"

Beck had no choice but to obey his superior, but he was outraged. He considered the order a licence for the casino to operate with impunity, which he found mortifying given the promises he had made to his men that they would operate without fear or favour.

Beck went back to his squad and told them that they were not going to Rozelle that night. But he instructed them to keep watching the place, and even placed a man in a school ground opposite, from where he could see all the comings and goings.

Beck also made himself a massive nuisance to Allen. Every day he would go to the Chief Superintendent and berate him, saying his men were frustrated and just did not understand why they were being restrained.

Beck suggested that if the order did indeed come from Wran, he wanted to see the Premier so he could tell Beck to his face. Allen did not like this idea one bit.

"You remember your place Beck!" he repeated. "This is the Premier you are talking about.

"You don't tell him what to do, and you do what you are told. He will tell me when you can go there and I will tell you."

But to Beck it was just not right that people who were clearly breaking the law were being allowed to get away with it.

As the days passed and the green light still did not come, Beck's relationship with Allen deteriorated to open hostility. After two weeks of conflict over Rozelle, Beck had had enough.

Beck went to Lees and complained. Lees was sympathetic but, to Beck's great disappointment, said he could do nothing against Allen, even though he was the superior officer.

"What can I do about it, look who put him (Allen) there," Lees protested, referring to Wran.

Beck was despondent. This was not what he had expected from Lees. He could not abide the thought of working with hobbles restricting him.

Beck then told Lees he thought it might be best if he was transferred out of 21 Division, because he could not get on with Bill Allen and did not want to have anything to do with Allen, given his attitude. He had seen enough of the way 21 Division had policed gaming and betting in the past.

Lees would not hear of it.

"I can't move you, if I moved you now there would be a hell of an outburst about it! Politically, we just couldn't do it."

"Unless you do something about it you may have an outburst anyway," Beck replied.

"If Bill Allen continues to talk to me and treat me in the manner he does, I fear I'll do something— by way of giving him a good belt in the mouth!"

Lees laughed.

"Yeah I know you would. But I don't want you to do that, what I want you to do is just bite the bullet and keep doing what you're doing so well."

Despite his disappointment, Beck could understand that Lees was in a tenuous position. He was still Acting Commissioner of Police, not yet confirmed in the position, and there had been strong rumours that Wran did not want him. If Lees was too strident against Allen, it could well cost him the job, which neither he nor Beck wanted to happen.

So Beck went back to Allen and laid it on the line.

"If this is the way you are going to run things, you'd better get yourself another man, because I'm not prepared to accept this," he said baldly.

Allen disliked Beck intensely, but he also knew that getting rid of him so early in his appointment would attract huge public attention which would be bad for Wran and for himself.

"I'll see what I can do," he growled.

He told Beck to go back to his office while he contacted the Premier.

Two hours later he rang Beck.

"You've got the green light for that place, you can go there now," he said.

Beck was sceptical, wondering if the casino would also be given a green light in terms of a warning, but immediately mobilised his men. Under the cloak of darkness, as usual, they swooped on the Rozelle premises. To Beck's disgust, for the first time in weeks the doors were open and the usual bustling premises were empty, apart from two cleaners.

Within days, Beck's men had discovered another premises just down the road from the Darling St casino, and being run by the same people.

He wrote at the time: "A large gambling casino was going day and night near the city, but for two embarrassing weeks 21 Division were told not to take action as the Premier wanted to get his friends out before the police took action. The time lag is not reasonable apart from anything else, that is if in fact the Premier did issue those orders.

"When I accepted my present position to police gaming and betting I did so on the condition that I would have a free rein to take action wherever illegal gaming and betting is found,

"I made this clear to Allen and Lees and they agreed this would be my position, yet it appears Allen is ignoring my views and making it difficult. I complained to Lees on numerous occasions, who appears to have difficulty in the fact that Allen has been chosen to control my actions."

In fact Lees seemed powerless to stand up against Allen, despite his private praise for Beck. Lees also shrugged off Beck's concerns about other serving and retired police scheming to undermine and discredit him and his men.

In contrast, many friends and honest police including Keith Paull and Roy Williams, who was in charge of the police radio section at that time, warned Beck to be careful. They shared Beck's concern that the hostility was adding to the strain and stress on members of 21 Division carrying out their duties, some of whom were already visibly affected.

It was clear to Beck by now that substantial sums of money were being paid to protect illegal gambling. From information told to him by SPs and other gaming operators, Beck deduced that it could total up to $5 million a year ($27 million in 2022 money). Much of this, he was led to believe, was delivered in cash, and the place where most transactions too place was the City Tattersall's Club in Pitt St.

'Tatt's' was a popular venue for many police, as well as bookmakers and others. Soon after he took over the division Beck was told by a senior officer, Cec Abbott, (who later became Police Commissioner[15]) not to take action there.

"I'm telling you this for your own good," Abbott insisted. "The people in Tatt's are a lot more powerful than you.

"Don't take them on, Beck. It's not worth it, you'll be the loser!"

Never one to take a hint, Beck responded, "I can assure you action will be taken if we find any illegal activities!"

"Well, you've been warned what will happen if you do," Abbot told him gravely.

Beck decided to make up his own mind. He asked police who had been in 21 Division before his time about the club. They told him that money was exchanged at Tatt's every Monday, which was 'settling up' day for bets placed and won with legal and illegal bookmakers, and other transactions. The gaming and betting squad itself, they claimed, had a sergeant who would go to City Tatts each Monday. After a long lunch and many drinks, he would appear in the squad's office in the late afternoon with a bag of money.

Beck sent a pair of observers from the squad to the club several times on Mondays to see if there were any people of interest there. The observers recognised a number of SP operators, registered bookmakers

---

[15] Cecil Abbott was Police Commissioner from 31 December 1981 to 7 August 1984.

and also a number of off duty police with an interest in horse racing. They reported back that these police had recognised them within a few minutes of them entering the club. But they saw no illegal activity, and no action was taken.

At the end of July, after three weeks on the job, the squad encountered its first failure which seemed likely to be the result of a tip-off to the gambling operators.

With the Wednesday race meeting at Randwick underway, Beck led his team to a first floor office in Bayswater Road, Rushcutters Bay. Carrying a warrant, but receiving no response to their demands to open, they broke down the door.

There was no one there, but there were 40 phones connected and computer equipment ready to record bets. A journalist was tipped off about the raid and it was reported in *The Daily Mirror* two days later, on 27 July.

"The Gaming Squad has closed down a big Sydney SP business—before it could get started!" reporter Bill Jenkings wrote.

He added, "Even the longest established and wealthiest SP operators in Sydney are worried about Insp Beck's raids. It seems unlikely, according to those in the know, a new big business would come into existence when the heat is on as it is at present…Insp Beck has already made a number of important arrests and has thrown Sydney's big SP business into confusion."

While Jenkings described the raid as a success, Beck was disappointed and concerned. He had no doubt the SP operator had been tipped off in advance about the raid, resulting in the empty office and no arrests. When this happened again soon after on a casino raid, Beck suspected he had a new problem to contend with. Was there a spy in his squad leaking information to the illegal operators?

Despite these setbacks, by early August the squad had arrested hundreds of offenders and sent them before the courts.

The SP bookies were no longer game to trade openly from hotels and public betting shops, but nor were they prepared to give up the game.

Some of them tried new methods such as open line telephones and accepting bets on a verbal agreement rather than writing betting slips. They also became more adept at destroying evidence when the police suddenly appeared.

The casino operators did not have the same agility. One after another, Beck and his men had exposed the illegal casinos and arrested their staff and patrons. But often they did not stay closed. Some were relocated but most reopened on the same premises, relying on more complex security measures. The doorkeepers became much more wary in screening newcomers to try to prevent infiltration by one of Beck's team.

Copying the casinos, big ethnic clubs operating in Sydney installed heavy wooden and steel doors which could be both manually and electrically operated, and also started to employ cockatoos. The hefty investment was justified by the profits they were making from the illegal; games, especially manila, rummy and iftica.

It was clear from the start that the illegal gambling operators did not expect the police blitz to last long.

During the first few weeks, Beck and his team were often met with genuine surprise. The illegal gambling operators knew that a crackdown had been ordered, but had clearly not expected anything as thorough as Beck's attentions. They had not had to deal with determined police action for a long time; Beck and his men found premises that had been in operation for 18 years and had never been visited by police.

Initially, the squad was greeted with scornful comments like "Beck won't last five minutes" and "he'll be gone within a month."

"What's all this business about, we've been told nothing like this will happen," was another common reaction to a raid.

The surprise turned to indignation and anger when it became clear Beck was not letting up.

A number of casino and SP operators told the squad members they were making a mistake.

"You should talk to your higher-ups."

"You'd better cut this out, the pollies won't have a bar of this."

"Mate, my connections are gonna do something about this Beck, this has gone on too long!"

A couple of those arrested named members of the NSW Parliament and said these politicians would talk to Premier Wran and ensure Beck was removed.

Similar comments about pro-gambling MPs were relayed to Beck by journalists. It was said that several Labor MPs had indeed complained to Wran about the crackdown and demanded that the previous easy-going attitude to illegal casinos and SPs, be restored. But the Government was also under pressure from the Opposition and others to be tough on crime, and refused to bow to the demands.

(Some of the MPs named by the irate SPs, who were backbenchers at the time, remained in Parliament for many years and annoyed Beck, in his retirement, with their hypocrisy over policing and in particular, illegal gambling.)

The response from gambling operators was understandable. Until then, they had nothing to fear from 21 Division. Beck and his men were keen to prove the old days and old ways were gone, and the crackdown was genuine and permanent.

The squad members became regular racegoers and developed a detailed knowledge of racing and bookmaking. They kept an eye on race meetings throughout the state as well as the major metropolitan meetings on Wednesdays and weekends.

SP bookmaking was taking place in a variety of locations. As well as hotels and offices they could be located in clubs, shops, derelict buildings, farmhouses, homes, factories and even caravans and sheds—anywhere that telephones could be connected.

Hotels were the logical place for Beck's squad to start their hunt for SPs. They would go to a particular hotel and work through the different bars and lunge areas looking for the SPs while trying not to be conspicuous.

They soon discovered this was not easy and the SPs had some tricks to throw them off the scent.

One of them involved a stranger walking up to a young constable after he had entered a hotel looking for the SP.

"Your mate wants to see you," the stranger mumbled into the policeman's ear, before moving off. The constable took this at face value and went through the hotel until he found his colleague and went to ask him what was up. This was just what the SP wanted, as he now knew the identity of both police on the premises and did not open for business until they had left.

Another constable was caught out when he was observing the hotel in his undercover clothes. He was drinking in the beer garden wearing shorts and sandals. The SP operator noticed his white legs and feet—usually covered by his uniform. "What station you from officer?" he asked. The policeman started to reply before realising his cover was blown.

While the casino raids required a larger number of men, Beck would send teams of two or three police out into the field to follow the leads of SP operators.

The sudden onslaught of police soon after Beck took over Gaming and Betting had an immediate impact on SPs, with many operators and assistants being arrested over a wide area.

There were a very small number of local operators still running their own SP businesses. They included a woman, large in character and in person, operating in Bondi. Beck nicknamed her Big Nellie.

When the Raiders crashed through the door of her premises, the lock flew across the room and landed near the woman. Big Nellie was too shocked to say anything, except "Shit!" The police could not help laughing and Nellie joined in, although the raid was probably the end of her business.

In most cases, the syndicates had made it impossible for sole or small operators like Nellie to stay in business. Sometimes they became 'partners' under duress, still operating their SP business but giving a large percentage to the syndicate. If this was not agreeable, the syndicates used whatever force was needed to put the competition out of business.

Resistance was just not worth it for the small operators. Knowing that they had no law to protect them; acceptance was the easier way out.

One former bookmaker confided in Beck that he had tried to resist an unacceptable proposal from a syndicate and had been threatened. Then a fire broke out at his premises, which put him out of business. This man alleged that there were also police involved. Beck arranged for him to be interviewed by detectives from the Internal Affairs Branch, but he backed out of it, too frightened to reveal who was involved.

Stories like this inspired Beck to be as ruthless on the illegal SP operators as they were to their clients. Within months, he had persuaded thousands of punters to quit their illegal bookmakers and head to the legal TAB instead.

As early as 28 August 1979, the *Daily Telegraph* reported "TAB booms as police crack down on SP men."

"The 21 Squad's blitz on illegal SP betting is pouring hundreds of thousands of dollars weekly into the State Government's coffers," reported Geoff McCamey.

"The three-month crackdown has increased TAB turnover by at least $1 million a week. The Government is believed to be earning more money also from lottery ticket sales, soccer pools and poker machine tax as gamblers look for an alternative to SP betting."

The constant media coverage made Beck's successes even more galling to some and made the squad more vulnerable, if they did slip up. Beck impressed on his team how important it was for them to stay focused and disciplined.

After they had been working together for a month, Beck was satisfied with nearly all of his team. The squad had settled into its demanding routine, working well together, and most raids were successful. The few more senior police Beck had been allowed to include in the squad impressed him with their support and enthusiasm during raids, and greatly helped in the task of moulding a successful team.

The bond they formed was real. Beck had chosen them personally, and he led them in all aspects of their duties. They valued his advice and he valued theirs. The respect was mutual and quickly developed into friendships.

While he was a man of action, not words, Beck's praise for his team was eloquent.

"I am proud of my men, they stand tall and strong," he told Lees.

But there were two notable exceptions, Sergeants Bradbury and Hermes were the only two former members of the anti-gaming squad allowed to stay under Beck. Bill Allen had instructed Beck to keep them.

Beck found the pair to be lazy and unreliable. If the squad had a leak, he was sure they were the source. But he had no proof.

Beck knew that someone within his squad was talking to Allen behind his back, because comments that he had made to the squad about raids were on several occasions repeated back to him by Allen. Allen had also taken skewed information from his spies and used it against Beck without asking for a proper explanation. Beck had every reason to suspect Hermes, who remained in close contact with Bradbury and Allen.

On one occasion Allen asked Beck about SP bookmaking in Wollongong. Beck mentioned some premises and the next thing, heard that Allen had sent Bradbury to that place. Another time, Allen sent Bradbury to a country town on SP duties, knowing that Beck's team was heading for the next town to raid a large SP operation. When the raids were less than successful, Beck was furious.

His distrust came to a head in August when information was called in to the squad about a large SP phone outfit at King's Cross. Bradbury took the call and he and Hermes decided to act on it. Against orders, they did not inform Beck or any other squad members. Instead, they told Bill Allen.

The pair turned up at the SP operation to make arrests and found it in full swing. But there were only two of them and they had no contingency plans. The phone operators and other staff jumped up and ran off before they could be arrested, leaving the equipment behind.

While Bradbury went outside to meet Allen, Hermes remained in the empty office. He was wondering what to do next when a man came through the front door into the SP office. He had a plastic bag and started to pick up pieces of paper and put them in the bag.

"What are you doing here?" Hermes demanded. "Do you work here?"

"Nah, I'm only the cleaner," the man said innocently. "I don't know anything about what they do here."

"Well you'd better leave right now, this is a police raid," Hermes said.

The man did not argue. He took his plastic bag, quickly left the office and disappeared onto the street.

When Bradbury came back soon after with Bill Allen, Allen demanded to know where the SP operators were.

"They've all gone!" Hermes bemoaned. "Even the cleaner."

"Even the cleaner?" asked Allen suspiciously.

As later became apparent, this 'cleaner' was the head of the SP operation. After initially fleeing with his staff, he had boldly come back to see whether the police had gone. Thin as it was, his act was enough to fool Hermes.

Any blunder by the Raiders was potential news. A journalist from the *Sydney Morning Herald* found out about the bungled Kings Cross raid. This journalist, however, knew and respected Beck and strongly supported the crackdown on illegal gambling. He rang Beck about the story and, to Beck's lasting gratitude, agreed not to publish it.

Beck wrote at the time, "Bradbury has blown several jobs and it took me a great deal of effort to convince the newspaper people not to write them up in a Keystone cop manner in order to preserve the good name of the division."

Beck carpeted Bradbury and Hermes and gave them a stern disciplinary talk. Hermes was a huge man, weighing close to 130 kgs (18 stone), but this made no difference to Beck.

After the failed Rushcutters Bay raid on the SP network, and the Kings Cross incident, Beck conferred with his senior men. They agreed that Bradbury and Hermes could not be trusted. As they were still part of the squad, Beck did his best to cut them out of important discussions. He referred to them as "those few treacherous people that we walk around".

For a month there were no suspicious incidents. Then in September, Bradbury crossed a line and the tensions came to a head.

Beck learned that the two-up premises at North Sydney had opened up again, despite being raided twice previously.

Beck sent a team to observe the premises from nearby properties. Two of the police hid in the grounds of a school located opposite the premises. They phoned back to say that the two-up game was in progress. Several of the police also climbed onto a nearby building from where they could see the game through the windows of the gaming premises.

Coupled with the previous raid on the premises, and his knowledge of the legal requirements, Beck was confident he had enough information to get a search warrant to raid the place again.

It was quite late, but there was a Justice of the Peace at the local Ambulance headquarters before whom the police could swear that the information in the warrant was true and correct. This was needed for the warrant to be valid.

Beck called over Bradbury and told him that the information in the unsigned warrant was correct, ie illegal gambling was being conducted at the premises. He directed Bradbury to go to the JP and get the warrant signed.

To Beck's astonishment, Bradbury refused.

"I'm not satisfied there's a game over there and I'm not going to get a warrant," he claimed, implying that his fellow team members were liars.

Beck thought perhaps Bradbury was not familiar with the procedures for getting a warrant at that time of night. Beck assured him that the correct procedure was being followed and explained the situation.

It was established legal practice for police seeking a warrant to act on information provided by other police in the field. They had to swear the information was true, based on reports from their colleagues. The only alternative was to witness the events themselves, which would take extra time and resources. This was not only impractical in many circumstances, but distasteful as it implied that members of the observation team were unreliable.

But Bradbury still refused to do as he was told, in defiance of his superior officer. Beck changed tactics.

"Right," said Beck, "you stay here, you can answer the phone. You're not coming with us!"

Then he turned to another sergeant.

"How long would you take to get this warrant?"

"By the time I get out that door," the sergeant replied, "I'll be back in 10 minutes."

Beck gave him the go ahead and the warrant. The sergeant hurried away and, true to his word, was back within 10 minutes with the signed document. Beck took the warrant and signalled to his team to head to the cars. As pre-arranged, they drove quickly to the two-up school, where they proceeded with the raid and made numerous arrests.

The following day, Beck considered what to do about Bradbury. He could not tolerate such deliberate disobedience and obstruction.

Bill Allen had wanted Bradbury and Hermes on the squad so Beck decided to make them Allen's problem. Still fuming, Beck went to the Chief Superintendent and told him what had happened.

"I'm not prepared to have him on my squad a moment longer," Beck said firmly. "He's your man—he's only on the squad because you insisted.

"Now you make up your mind.

"You can take him or lose me— and I'm not fussy about which it is." It was the second time that Beck had threatened to quit 21 Division. Allen could tell that he was serious. He thought for a moment.

"Look, ring the inspector over at Chatswood and see if he'll take him over there," he suggested.

Bradbury had been at Chatswood before. Beck knew the inspector there, who had worked under Beck. Beck rang him and told him that Allen wanted to send Bradbury back.

The inspector said he already had enough sergeants. Moreover, he did not want Bradbury.

"Sorry Merv, I can't do that," he apologised. "I've had him before, he's a troublemaker and I don't want him at my station!"

Beck went back to Allen and told him that Chatswood was not an option, and repeated that Allen had the choice of either removing Bradbury or removing Beck.

Without any other immediate options, Allen told he would take Bradbury in his office. Bradbury stayed there as Allen's sidekick for about 10 months. During that period, as far as Beck could see, he did virtually no work although he was a second class sergeant. Others said Bradbury's main job was to carry beer for Allen.

(Many years later, when Beck was in retirement in 1997, he recalled this incident in a submission to the Royal Commission into the NSW Police. Beck was subsequently called to give evidence before Justice

Wood on the problems he had experienced, including his clash with Bradbury over getting the warrant.)

While Beck was pleased to have got Bradbury out of the squad, Allen spoiled the victory as much as he could. He ordered Beck to supply Bradbury with one of the division's cars, and to provide one or two men to assist Bradbury when he wanted them. This was doubly irritating as Beck was short of men.

Allen would frequently ask Beck, who had little option but to answer, what was happening in regard to different gaming places. When a place was due to be raided, he would send Bradbury there at the same time, although he was no longer part of the team, which the squad found very disruptive.

Hermes remained a thorn in Beck's side, and despite his complaints to superior officers, he could not get him removed. Instead, Beck ramped up his internal security measures even further to try to prevent breaches.

He became careful about what he said on the telephone or in his office, in case someone was listening, and adopted new procedures to tighten security before raids.

Only a handful of sergeants would be included in the planning for any one raid, while the rest of the raid party would be informed at the last minute.

He also introduced a diversion to make it harder for anyone observing the squad to guess where a raid would be made. The raiding party was split consisted of a number of small teams, each with a car.

Each car would head in a different direction—towards the western suburbs, south, north or east, in case anyone was watching or trying to follow. After driving for a while, the cars would do a loop and retrace their paths, at a leisurely pace, before going to a rendezvous point nominated by Beck where they would meet him.

No stopping was allowed, or leaving the vehicles for any reason, including making a phone call or going to a shop. The rule was the same for all. Beck thought it was the best thing for all of his team: if a casino operator was tipped off, all of them would be under suspicion.

Beck also told Commissioner Lees that he intended to keep details of future raids closely guarded. He would no longer give advance information to Lees or other superior officers—meaning Bill Allen.

Lees had to make a choice between pleasing Allen, an upcoming senior officer, and a man he trusted. He agreed to Beck's request.

* * * *

Thommo's was not the only two-up "school" in Sydney. Others included Melton's Two-Up, at 18 Albert St Strathfield near the railway station, and a Crow's Nest school at 302 Pacific Highway. The Strathfield premises was raided twice by Beck's team and the Crow's Nest premises three times over the course of a few months

Each time, Beck and his men devised a ploy to get past the club security.

Taxi drivers were invaluable unwitting assistants. On one occasion, Beck asked one of the young trainee detectives to act out the part of an interstate tourist looking for some gambling action. They sent him out to Kingsford Smith Airport, where he went inside the terminal, waited for a planeload of passengers to arrive and pick up their luggage, and then walked out of the terminal among them to the taxi rank.

He hailed a cab and pretended to be a bit of loudmouth in search of some nightlife and games, stressing that he was from interstate. The taxi driver took him to the Crow's Nest place. The taxi driver, who knew the place well, introduced Beck's man to the gambling place's lookouts and explained that he was from Melbourne.

It was 3 o'clock in the afternoon and there was no game, but the lookouts were keen to look after him. When he said he had no hotel, they took him inside and rang a nearby hotel to book him a room, and told him to come back later that night.

The ploy had worked, and the undercover cop rang Beck from his hotel room to tell him.

"Hi boss, it worked. I'm in," he said with satisfaction. "I've been accepted as a player and it's all set up, I'm joining a two-up game at 11 o'clock tonight."

Once again, Beck was able to make the raid using the evidence and knowledge of having a player on the inside.

With so many race meetings being held across the state, race days were hectic for the Gaming and Betting squad. Beck's sent teams running from one place to another, making arrests and then heading to another area to catch another SP while bets were being laid. There was no point trying to catch several operators in close proximity as news of a raid spread rapidly and the SPs would go to ground.

Towards the end of the race day, as the last races were on, they would drive back to the place they had first raided. Often, word had gone around that the squad had been and gone, so the bets were on again.

Beck greatly enjoyed using strategy to outwit his SP targets.

"It did cause confusion to them and it upset their nervous systems, many of them told us this," he recalled.

"After years of token policing, most of them had been doing business night and day for years. Then suddenly overnight there is a change, banging on doors and locked windows with iron bars, police coming in through windows and off rooves!

"They said it was enough to give them nerves, see doctors, employ lookouts, plant themselves in new premises to try to dodge arrest. They'd even complain to me, 'many of our clients are too frightened to turn up, what is the place coming to?' It was quite amusing."

Less amusing was the impact of gambling on many people who had lost money. Beck's team learned that it was usual for a betting group to have its own regular clients, men and women, and to provide loans to players who were losing. Gamblers caught by Beck's team revealed that they usually had $800 to $1000 on loan every week, at interest rates which were 25 to 30 per cent—for just three days.

If the money was not repaid at the end of that time, the debt collectors would come around and rough up the defaulters, often using the old-fashioned gangster method of kneecapping, ie a belt across the knees with an iron bar which was extremely painful, and a warning to hurry up or they would get that again, and more.

Beck and his men spotted people they had seen previously in the Surry Hills and Darlinghurst games, limping around on sore legs. Some they even found taking part in other games, trying to win back their losses. They would not explain how they came by their injuries, believing that far worse pain was probable if they became informers.

To Beck, the violence that accompanied the gambling scene was more reminiscent of the United States than Australia.

"Thommo's had a folksy legend but it was no different from most other illegal gambling, including SP," said Beck. "Behind them stood the enforcers, the criminals and thugs ready to carry out whatever brutal work was needed to protect the business.

"This form of protection is really gangsterism or just plain standover tactics at least. The criminals refer to this as selling insurance, to give it a respectable façade."

A takeaway food shop owner from Marrickville who was an inveterate gambler provided Beck with an example of this violence. He had lost $1000 playing the card game manila one night. He wanted to keep playing and try to claw his way back, so the house lent him $500 on provision that it was paid back within three days. He lost that as well.

At the end of the three days he did not have the money and knew he was in big trouble. He was working at his takeaway shop making hamburgers when he got the first warning, a telephone call saying time was up and asking if he had the money. He said no and within minutes a large chunk of concrete came flying through the shop's plate glass window and landed on his stove among the sizzling hamburgers. This was the warning.

In fear for his life, the man managed to scrape together the money, possibly from relatives, to keep the gambling thugs away. When the police, investigating the breakage, found out about the debt he insisted he could not lodge a complaint because it would not be worth his life.

* * * *

Like a good sports coach, Beck knew he could not afford to let his team become tired or jaded so they lost motivation and no longer enjoyed their work. He took the time to look after their wellbeing in terms of resources, physical preparedness, mental attitude and morale.

As hard as the job was physically, the most difficult aspect was morale. In contrast to frequent positive comments from Jim Lees, the media, and from many parts of society, the squad was subjected to hurtful and worrying sniping from some of their own police colleagues. Some nasty comments reached them indirectly, but some were made to their faces. These comments, and other attempts to prevent the squad doing its work, were disappointing but not surprising to Beck.

On several occasions, in the first month of their operations, members of the squad were verbally abused to their faces by former members of 21 Division who claimed the squad would 'crash' very soon as a result of their efforts.

Some rank and file police in various areas were also openly hostile to Beck's team, abusing them with insults, swearing, sarcasm and threats. A sergeant from the gaming and betting squad was at the Cleveland Hotel in Redfern when he was spotted by a couple of off duty police who were having a beer. They called out to him and then started to abuse him over the work of the squad. The sergeant returned the fire with spirit, telling them they should be ashamed of their attitude for failing to support their fellow police.

The same treatment was given to another sergeant at the Graphic Arts Club in Regent St Sydney, which was directly opposite the Regent St police station. A number of senior police there condemned the squad, and Beck in particular, for applying pressure to the gambling operators.

Even the wives of squad members were subjected to abuse. One wife received several indecent phone calls, in which the caller referred to her husband's work on the squad. Another wife happened to be at an event with a man who was related to an SP bettering operator. The relative made it clear he thought Beck and the squad would be short lived. "Your husband's a fool if he sticks with Beck," he told the startled wife. "I can tell you now, within two months your bloke will either see what side his bread is buttered on, and take the money, or he'll be on a hiding to nothing and his life will be a misery."

The policeman involved was furious that his wife had been spoken to in this manner. He told Beck who assured him the squad would stay strong if they remained united.

Beck himself was not immune to the harassment. Some senior police told him to his face that his work was not important and he should back off. Ignoring the blight that gambling could become for many people, and the links with the drugs trade, they claimed SP bookmakers and casino operators were not doing any harm. They also demanded to know how long it would be before the crackdown ended, as they clearly believed it was finite.

When Beck told them that he was acting under orders from Acting Commissioner Lees, who in turn had been directed by the Government, one of these police officers replied, "Well in that case, it certainly would not last long".

One of the most memorable predictions that Beck would fail was delivered by former superintendent of the NSW police force, Allen Clarke, in a conversation that became relayed back to Beck

Clarke was a racing fan with a number of contacts amongst the SP bookies. He asked one of them what effect Beck was having on his operation. The SP said he was giving it up, because it was not worth his while to carry on and get arrested. Clarke's response, relayed to Beck later by the same SP betting operator a few months later, was one which Beck never forgot.

"You should carry on just the same, for Beck will be crushed like a cockroach under your foot in two months' time," Clarke claimed.

Beck was highly amused by the cockroach reference. He had seen the former superintendent on several occasions in the months between him making the remark, and Beck learning about it. But he never said anything to Beck's face.

Another of Beck's contacts relayed the same story to him, and he believed it to be reliable. Beck got the impression that the SP operators thought considerably less of Clarke, and no less of Beck, as a result of Clarke's intemperate comments.

CIB Chief Ray Goldsworthy did not say anything disparaging to Beck's face either, but made it clear what he thought of Beck's work.

For unknown reasons, Lees had directed Beck to supply his daily synopsis of the division's arrests and activities to Goldsworthy. But the first time Beck turned up to provide the details, Goldsworthy told him in person not to bother.

"I'm not that interested in gaming and betting," he drawled arrogantly.

Beck in typical fashion did not take this well.

"Well I'm not that interested in telling you either, but I've been directed to by the Commissioner!" Beck replied.

Under sufferance, Goldsworthy cast an eye over Beck's morning report.

His eyebrows shot up when he saw the numbers.

"God struth, it's just like the old days when you were at Regent St!" Goldsworthy exclaimed.

"You don't know how to go steady, do you Beck?"

Beck tried to draw Goldsworthy on why he thought there were too many arrests and why going easy was a good idea. Neither he nor any other police questioned about this by Beck would provide their reasons.

In fact Beck was more surprised by Lees' instruction to report to Goldsworthy than by Goldsworthy's reaction. It was well-known that Goldsworthy was friendly with illegal gambling operators, including Bruce Hardin, the operator of the Rozelle casino which Beck wanted desperately to close, but had been ordered to leave alone.

Goldsworthy and Hardin had been seen together several times, enjoying dinners on Hardin's yacht in Homebush Bay.

Connections such as these between his superior officers and criminals were depressing.

Beck wondered how extensive the networks were and where they led.

"If each connection was followed it would produce a map like the British Rail grid," he told Elsie one night.

Beck also began to receive anonymous calls on his home phone.

"Often I would just get home and get into bed and the phone would ring and it would be an anonymous call.

"I knew this was just another means of keeping me awake, to wear me down.

"But I couldn't take the phones off the hook because I had men about (on duties).

"In these ungodly hours the enemy would always know that if I wasn't at work I was probably trying to get an hour's sleep, but I insisted that the men could ring me at any time and at all times.

"Actually I would have done better to have a bed in the office but I thought that would look a bit ridiculous and I wanted to drop in at home just to make sure things were alright.

"Then I would work that day and see that the court matters and the exhibits were in order and arrange the duties for the day shift people, and look for targets for the following night. I would do the day's work and then I would go on into the night.

"While ever these (gambling) places were there, I wanted to be there on the raids because that was my leadership style."

It also made good sense. It was less difficult for false allegations to be laid if Beck was there.

The problem was demonstrated after one particular raid, on a new casino at 65 Waratah St Kirrawee in Sutherland Shire. The casino had only been open for a matter of weeks. It was located in what looked from the outside to be a modern factory, and was clearly designed to be police-proof.

Beck's observation team reported that the modern building would not be easy to penetrate. Beck decided to bring in the 'big guns' in the form of several undercover police from the CIB, and the Police Rescue Squad. They were keen to help.

The raid took place about 11.15 pm on Thursday, 26 July. It was written up in *The Sun* newspaper the following day.

The paper reported: "Rescue Squad police began cutting through a (steel) mesh door after detectives called out to be let into the casino. When the steel door was cut away, detectives used sledgehammers to break open locks. While detectives arrested people inside, other police loaded equipment from the casino onto the (police) truck.

"Police used sledgehammers and bolt cutters to open the safe.

"Furniture from the lavishly decorated casino was also taken. The casino has thick pile carpet, wood panelling on the walls and ceiling and a chandelier in the main hall. It has a two-up pit with cushion-covered benches surrounding a green baize floor marked 'odds and evens.'"

Twenty-nine people were arrested in the raid. One man was charged with attempting to organise a common gaming house, and two more with aiding and abetting. The gamblers, including one woman, were all charged with being in premises suspected of being a common gaming house. They were held in cells at Sutherland Police Station until 5 am, when they were bailed out.

After the raid, Beck snatched a few hours' sleep. By 8.30am, he was back on duty to oversee the court appearances and other matters. Twenty-seven of these charged forfeited bail when they failed to appear in Sutherland Court that day, but all were subsequently convicted.

During the raid, as well as gambling equipment, cash and coffee machines, the police had seized boxes of liquor and wine. The court made an order that the alcohol be returned to its owner. Unbeknown to Beck, one of his sergeants, Fred McHardy, took it on himself to follow the court order (so he thought). He went back to the casino premises to drop off the property, instead of keeping it stored for the required time to allow an appeal.

When he got to the casino, the manager was not there to receive it. McHardy, looking for an alternative, went to the business next door, where the man in charge said he knew the casino operator well. When McHardy said he had some things to return, the businessman volunteered to take them and pass them on. McHardy handed over the alcohol and obtained a signature from the businessman to confirm that he had taken charge of the goods.

Some days later, however, the club principal (who died not long afterwards) laid a complaint with the Police Ombudsman against Sergeant McHardy. The complaint alleged that the liquor and wall fittings had been taken by Mahardy and never returned.

Beck asked both Lees and Whitelaw to ensure that the matter was investigated by 'honourable police', as he put it. He suggested that Keith Paull oversee the investigation, as Beck knew Paull would correct any bias against him.

The businessman who had accepted the alcohol was prepared to give evidence. He told the inquiry McHardy had definitely given the boxes of alcohol to him, and he had signed a statement to that effect. This put McHardy in the clear on that score, but there remained the question of the wall fittings. As they were not on the club walls, it looked as though it might be hard to prove McHardy's innocence.

Fortunately, the last of the police to leave the casino on the morning of the raid had been the scientific officer. As he went out, he took a general photograph for context, and then he locked the door behind him and the keys were handed back to the proprietor. That last photo proved very useful, as it showed all the light fittings in place just as they should have been.

The photograph was proof the second allegation against McHardy had no foundation, and was no more than an attempt to disrupt the squad. The scientific officer was also interviewed by senior police from the CIB, who reported their findings to the ombudsman.

Soon after, one of Beck's valued sources advised him that the whole complaint was a set-up instigated by Pat Watson, a former head of 21 Division, to try to blot Beck's copy book. Beck was later told by Bob Bottom that Watson was a close associate of ex-policeman and former State MP Tim Walker, who had been a bagman, ie collector of bribe money, for Robert Askin. Walker had attended the Kirrawee casino opening and so, according to unconfirmed rumour, had former swimming legend and later State MP, Dawn Fraser.

While Walker had avoided Beck's raid, it appeared he had called in a favour from Watson who was more than happy to put a knife into Beck's back.

There was more fallout from the Kirrawee raid.

The undercover men who had assisted with the raid (and found it quite fun) were under command of CIB Superintendent Jack Palmer. Palmer was on leave at the time of the raid, but broke his holiday as soon as he heard that some of his men had been used on gaming and betting.

He called Beck in and told him he was not to use any of the CIB staff without permission in advance from himself or his assistant officer, Reg Stevenson. While Stevenson was well known to Beck and had several times assisted him, Beck rejected the proposition straight out.

"No way will I tell you in advance where and what we're doing, and that is on the instruction of the Commissioner of Police," he replied somewhat hotly.

"I will use the undercover police whenever it suits me. They are a police facility and if I need them, I will use them. If you want to know about it—well you'll be wakened at 3,30 in the morning because that's the most notice I'll be giving if I am forced to tell you!"

Palmer glared at Beck. He was not going to back down.

"They're under my command, inspector, not yours."

Palmer followed up with a form instruction to his detectives not to provide any assistance to Beck, without his permission. Beck complained to Lees, but the Acting Commissioner was not prepared to take sides.

"You'll have to make do with your own squad. You can designate some of them for undercover work," Lees suggested.

"My advice is to keep away from the CIB. Keep it close, use the men you know you can trust."

Beck was disappointed but followed Lees' advice and quickly put together an undercover team which performed to a high standard. It included Geoff Owens, then a junior officer, who went on to become a well-respected superintendent and expert on organised crime.

Beck had also called on members of the Police Rescue Squad to gain entry to the casino and to force the safe. It was the first time he had called for their help with gaming and betting duties. He knew the rescue squad had been used by 21 Division in the past because he found a file—one of the few which had not been destroyed—which included an account of a sergeant from the rescue squad climbing onto the roof of a gaming premises at Rozelle, at the request of gaming police of the day, enabling them to gain entry.

Beck thought it only right and reasonable that he be allowed access to the same resources.

Assistant Commissioner Brian Doyle, who was responsible for the Rescue Squad, was normally a strong supporter of Beck's squad. But the report in *The Sun* had unnerved him. He complained to Lees that the Rescue Squad should not help Beck's team any further, because it might damage their positive public image.

When this got back to Beck, he was very disappointed, It was astonishing to him that helping his squad could be construed as bad for the public image of the police. He also saw no reason why the Rescue Squad should not be available to assist when needed.

In fact, he pointed out to Lees, withholding the rescue team would be contrary to the police rules—on which all detectives were examined in detail during their written examination. The rules stated clearly that Rescue Squad and equipment were police facilities, available to all police. Beck remembered the question in his exam, and the answer.

He was entitled to use the Rescue Squad's officers, trucks, cutting gear, ladders and other items.

Once again, Lees was not prepared to force the issue. He told Beck only to use the rescue equipment "if necessary", and not to use Rescue Squad members. Beck regarded this as unhelpful. He wrote in his personal diary, "These matters are working against my efforts".

While he knew corruption was alive and well in the NSW Police Force, Beck was nonetheless continually disappointed by immoral behaviour of former and serving officers. The Kirrawee allegations were false, but they were damaging.

After just one month in the job, despite having to train an all-new squad, Beck was having a huge impact on illegal gambling. Yet, as he wrote in his report to Lees on 7 August, he had serious concerns about the response of his police colleagues.

"Without exaggeration, a day would not pass at this squad (without) well-meaning police, some members of the public and telephone calls from the press warning of the opposition (within the police) to the work carried out by this squad," he wrote.

"Firstly it should be considered in this day and age police have a far more difficult task in the performance of their duties than in the past, brought about by various attacks on police by the media, civil liberties and other groups. Nevertheless the tasks performed are most necessary and essential irrespective of the difficulties confronting the individual police officer.

"Steps have been taken to instruct all police engaged on the various duties at this squad to perform their duties with as much care as possible and at all times consider the consequences when dealing with members of the public.

"As far as I am concerned the men are responding well to the calls made upon them. Taking into account the great number of people arrested, premises searched and inquiries made, there are few occasions where better duty could have been performed.

"It is most unfortunate that judgments have been made recently of some members' performance of duty without the full facts being known.

"It has been found that normal difficulties that are experienced in the performance of police duties are being bandied about by other police in an endeavour to discredit the present efforts to suppress gaming and betting."

Beck's insistence on following crime wherever it took him also brought criticism in late August. Beck was approached by an informant, a former detective working as a security guard, to investigate a large theft of liquor from the Tooth's Brewery.

There was good reason to believe the theft was an inside job by workers at the brewery, but the management did not trust the local police. The security guard did not know Beck, but knew he would do a good and honest job of the investigation. Beck assigned the job to 21 Division's instructing detectives.

The team of six senior detectives were responsible for training young police to be detectives, through on-the-job criminal work. The leader was Detective Sergeant Bill Grace, who was highly regarded by Beck. Grace's team did an excellent job investigating the brewery theft and several employees were charged. The delighted brewery management came personally to thank Beck.

Some other police did not like Beck stepping outside the immediate boundaries of gaming and betting. A very senior officer at Police Headquarters complained to Assistant Commissioner Brian Doyle about the brewery job, claiming Beck had stolen the job from the local police.

Doyle's attempt to stop Beck using rescue squad resources was still irking Beck. When Doyle called him about the brewery job, Beck was annoyed.

"The brewery manager told me he couldn't trust the local police, because when they were called in over a similar matter previously, nothing happened," Beck said.

"He was considering laying a complaint against those police, but instead 21 Division was approached.

"My detectives got a good result, they solved he crime and saved the force from embarrassment.

"That's a win for everyone, so I see no reason for any police to complain."

Doyle was not won over. He told Beck to stick to his special duties, even though the instructor detectives were never intended to work on gaming and betting.

As tough as he was, Beck felt this was very unfair. He had made the correct inquiries to ensure the brewery job was not being investigated by any other police, before assigning it to his team.

"It is galling, when the team is working well, that we are being sniped at by senior officers," he wrote in his notes at the time. "In my view crime has no barriers providing there's no one else working on it."

It seemed the upper echelons of the NSW Police did not share this view. As had happened may times before in his career, instead of praise for his energy and initiative Beck was criticised for cleaning up the mess left by his police colleagues.

* * * *

It had quickly become clear to Beck and his team that telephones were the lifeblood of the SP betting industry.

Telecom (later Telstra) had been created a few years earlier by the division of the PMG's department into the Australian Postal Commission and Australian Telecommunications Commission. Telecom was at that time 100 per cent owned by the Australian Government and the nation's sole telecommunications carrier.

The SP industry was reliant on phones for two reasons: to get updated information on horses as the basis for its odds, and to give customers access to lay on bets.

The heart of an SP operation is its price service, providing constant updates to the bookmakers on the latest quotes on offer for each horse in a race. With long distance dialling, races in Sydney, Melbourne and the bigger regional centres could all be covered.

In the late 1970s, several major price services existed to provide prices to Sydney SP bookies.

Each service would have agents at the Sydney racetracks, one of whom would be carrying a 'bug' or micro transmitter in his pocket. The agents would ask on course (legal) bookmakers about odds, which would be picked up by the transmitter and relayed to another agent in the carpark.

As Melbourne prices were announced at the Sydney racecourse, the price team could also pass on what was happening at the Melbourne races. Once the prices had been received at the service base, they were sent by teleprinter to Darwin, where SP betting was legal. SP bookmakers in other jurisdictions could get the odds through a simple phone call to Darwin.

The bookmakers would then pass their own odds on to their customers, by phone. Usually three calls were given for each race, reporting the fluctuation in prices. A separate price service was offered for Brisbane races.

But while phone networks had lifted the betting shops to new heights, they also gave them a new vulnerability as their phone numbers could be traced.

Telecom was obliged to assist with police inquiries, and the requests from the gaming and betting squad were routine. But the squad quickly realised they were getting a lot less assistance from Telecom, than they should have been.

Telecom officers in the investigations section increasingly claimed they were unable to discover who owned certain numbers, or where they were physically located—precisely the information Beck needed.

The squad had tested the numbers, pretending to be SP customers, and knew that the bookies were operating.

Yet the message would come back from Telecom that there were no such numbers, the phones were not connected.

In other cases, after the gaming squad had made inquiries, SP operators had apparently been warned about the squad's interest in them and planned raids by the squad came to nothing.

It was no great surprise when Beck's squad received a number of reports that senior Telecom investigations officials had been seen lunching with the former head of the 21 Division, Pat Watson, another former 21 Division member and chief superintendent in charge of country NSW, Ted Quill.

But they were surprised when SP operators spilled the beans on their deal with Telecom officials when they were being arrested.

"Oh I knew you were making a check on my phone number, we had a phone call," one boasted to the arresting police. Another revealed the date and time he was tipped off.

Beck provided information about his problems with Telecom to Bob Bottom, who published an article in *the Bulletin* in September 1979.

Following the article, an official from Telecom investigations phoned Beck and asked him to assure the state manager that relations between Beck's squad and Telecom were good and proper and nothing of the kind described by Bottom was going on.

Beck was not inclined to give any such assurance. He knew what Bottom was saying was true, and had told him so. He also knew that Telecom's investigations section included some ex-police, who in Beck's view were a similar mix to the Police Force—some good, some bad and some in between.

Beck raised the matter with Lees, who agreed that providing the statement that Telecom wanted would be factually wrong (which Beck refused to be), and would also prevent Beck from giving evidence to the contrary at a later date, if an inquiry was launched.

In fact a minor inquiry was held, by a QC named Wilcox who later became a judge, and Beck supplied information. It did not take evidence under oath, and did not result in any meaningful change.

Beck took his own action to get around the problem. Beck and his team soon worked out which officials were honest and gave them correct information. These people even admitted to Beck's team that there was corruption among their colleagues. When these people were on duty, Beck and his men went straight to them to check the SP numbers.

If a reliable person was not on duty, Beck would use a different tactic. He would arrange for members of the Drug Squad, Vice Squad, the Special Branch or other police units to contact Telecom and get the numbers checked for him, without letting on why the addresses were needed. This worked every time.

In these ways, Beck managed to get the information he needed for a while. But when Beck's men stopped calling, the investigations branch became suspicious and rang Beck to find out what was going on. Beck had to devise a new ruse to throw the investigations section off scent.

He got his staff to invent lists of phone numbers to feed to the section, which were routinely submitted, while the numbers they were really interested in were checked elsewhere.

Once, it came back that the phone number given to the investigations unit to check belonged to a branch of the Salvation Army. Beck and his men had to make a quick excuse, and were relieved that the investigations staff had not worked out what was going on.

At the same time, the illegal SP operators had excellent access to phone technicians.

It was not uncommon for Beck's squad to find 30 phones in the big operations that they raided. The highest number was 40, found in the premises in Rushcutters Bay which had been evacuated before Beck's raid.

As fast as the squad knocked them out, they would bounce back up. Usually they would set up in other premises initially, then when the coast seemed clear they would go back to the first location, as they were very keen to restore their lucrative businesses.

In many cases, the phones were operating again within a day or two – whereas at that time, Sydney households were waiting for days or even weeks for new connections or repairs.

It was clear to Beck that none of this could happen without assistance from inside Telecom. This was confirmed by a technician who admitted to a friend—who passed it on to Beck— that he and other technicians 'on the take' would go into the telephone exchanges in very quiet times, usually very early mornings, to fix lines for the SPs.

The informant said they could also provide temporary lines for weekend use only. The technicians would go in on Saturday and divert lines from businesses which closed at midday. Late on Sunday, they would restore the line to the legitimate owners.

According to the technician informant, the pay for a weekend of work like that was $1000 (a fortune in this days). This was also the going rate for installation of two to three safe lines.

The informant said the price had gone up sharply after Beck took over, because of the greater urgency and risks associated with the work. The SPs were prepared to pay top dollar for good service and equipment because the phones were essential to their profits.

A source also told Beck that some of the bigger SP syndicates employed their own phone technicians, who were former Telecom employees. They used call diverters, which were rare and cost $700 each at the time, to switch betting calls from the registered address to a secret location. The device had to be installed at the address where the telephone numbers were officially connected.

Beck's squad found this technology was in very widespread use by bookies in the Newcastle area. On one occasion his squad members rang the number and it was answered. At the time they were looking through the window and could see the phone sitting there unattended, confirming that the call had been diverted.

The hundreds or even thousands of phones in use by the SPs across Sydney and NSW were disguised in many ways. Normally, Telecom records would show only one legitimate phone at a location, but when Beck's men arrived they would find a large number of them, with adapters to plug in even more if they were needed.

After weeks of bruising raids, the SP operators realised they needed to lift their game to get Beck off their back. Moving their operations to new premises was a successful ploy, but only worked for a short while. With vast amounts of money at stake, as well as their professional pride, they adopted a variety of new defensive tactics.

One of these was to set up an office that looked just like an SP hub, but was just a decoy. These decoy premises would be complete with rows of telephones which (unlike the ones in the Rushcutters' Bay premises) were not connected. Snippets of false information would be fed to squad members to cause them to investigate.

While the fake premises were being raided and uncovered as a hoax, the real one gained valuable time to operate.

"We found quite a few premises which were dummies as we called them, equipped with telephones that were a bit older and had probably been used in the past," said Beck.

"We knew it wasn't real but we took away the equipment and telephones anyway. If we didn't, knowing how fast these operators could move, they would probably return there in the belief that we wouldn't be back because we thought it was a dummy.

"We actually did go back to these places and there were several cases where we found fresh telephone systems had been installed.

"It was one of those cat and mouse situations and we had to be vigilant at all times."

Beck realised that the SPs were not the only ones who could use "dummies" to confuse the opposition. There were too many race days and too many SP operations for his small team of men to cover them all. So he would contact hotels in country towns indicating that a team would be staying there after they had conducted a raid on illegal bookmakers.

They had no intention of going to that town, but as Beck hoped, the message about the squad quickly spread. The effect could be seen in a sudden surge in TAB takings in the relevant towns, as punters decided to take a safer route and avoid a potentially embarrassing encounter with the law.

One or two SPs even went out of business in this way, as their takings crashed on the basis not of raids, but rumours spread by Beck.

As their acting skills were paying off in relation to casinos, the squad also applied them to flushing out SP bookmakers working in hotels and other established premises.

Generally three police would work together, a senior man and two constables, one of whom would sometimes be a policewoman.

They introduced signals to communicate with each other across a room, such as holding their hands in a certain way, or touching their face or their ear. They had signals for "keep away from me", "leave the hotel now", "sit and watch", and "have suspect in mind".

One of their ploys involved diversion tactics to break the ice in hotels where SPs and their offsiders were on the alert for police. One was a fruit and vegetables ruse, which, unlikely as it was, proved very successful.

They used it first at a large hotel on the NSW Central Coast. The squad knew the hotel allowed an SP bookmaker there on race days, but clients were closely screened and strangers excluded.

One of the young constables, dressed in casual clothes, bought a plastic bag of oranges and took it to the hotel in question. He entered one of its bars and ordered a drink, placing the oranges on the bar, and was promptly told by the barmaid to remove them.

The constable did so, but then put the oranges back on the bar and received the same rebuke. This went on a number of times until the other customers joined in to support the barmaid.

While this was going on, the SP operator entered the bar and took a good look around the bar. He watched the game being played with the oranges and apparently found nothing suspicious, so started taking bets. Then the cheeky customer with the oranges revealed his real identity, and arrested the disappointed SP.

At another hotel, one of the older squad members dressed in very plain clothes entered the hotel carrying a large pumpkin and after settling down at the busy bar made it known in a loud voice that he had got it for a terrific bargain. When he revealed how much he had paid, the other drinkers laughed at him, at which the pumpkin man argued back in a joking manner. He then produced a cabbage from a bag and told everyone how cheap it was, causing a new round of hilarity.

While this amusement continued, an SP who operated in that bar accepted a number of bets, until the pumpkin Man— mirroring his colleague with the oranges—abandoned his vegetables and arrested him.

On another occasion two young constables, a man and woman, were sent to a hotel where illegal betting was being played and went to the snooker room, where they started to play a game.

The young woman was an excellent player and had soon attracted the attention of a crowd of onlookers. An SP operator who had been busy in another room joined the audience to cheer on the woman, only to be arrested by her and her partner after she had won, as both were police constables and had had a clear view of his activities, in between potting balls.

Beck was full of praise for the police women who helped with the squad's work, especially Lola Scott whom he described as "a very important and most efficient member of the raiding groups with me".

Bruce Hardin's casino in Darling St Rozelle.

CHAPTER SIX

"Why don't you take the money and leave us alone"

Beck had been in the job only a few weeks when his attitude to corruption was tested.

Hints that bribes were there for the taking were made regularly to Beck and his men by people they arrested and others. The big SPs and casino operators were too smart to approach Beck directly but used intermediaries, usually people who had met Beck in passing, to put out feelers.

The intermediaries were also careful to distance themselves from any attempted bribery. Usually they would raise the issue in an oblique, roundabout way, but there were two notable approaches It was probably no surprise to Beck that both related to Chinatown.

Chinatown had long been a feature of Sydney's colourful inner city. In the late 19th century opium dens operated in the same areas where Chinatown persists today.

In the 1970s, Chinese and European illegal gaming houses operated alongside legitimate business houses, restaurants and hotels and frequented by people of all walks of life, including senior police, politicians, business executives and criminals. Drug deals, illegal immigrants and the growing presence of the Chinese triads gangs provided the seamy underside to the area best known for cheap and excellent restaurants offering exotic fare not found in other parts of the city.

The few 21 Division records that remained when Beck arrived, revealed many complaints over a long period of time about gambling in Chinatown and Haymarket. Raids had also been carried out there, but they seemed to have no impact.

Beck was keen to tackle it, especially as he had been prevented from taking on the Chinese underworld in the past. He also knew that some of Sydney's leading criminals were involved in the areas. Surveillance by his squad had found Abe Saffron's henchmen at the Fuk Lee Club in Dixon St. They had also located other gambling premises at numbers 70, 71 and 33 Dixon St.

As Beck had discovered when he was at Darlinghurst, police intervention in Chinatown had for years been strictly controlled. There had been police raids on illegal clubs and casinos over the years, but they appeared to be just for show.

Beck had found a report by a former senior sergeant in 21 Division stating that attempts in August 1968 to gain entry to a gambling premises in Dixon St had failed. The report convinced him, if he needed further convincing, that his predecessors in gaming and betting squad before him had not been trying very hard.

Compared to the casinos and other gambling places, Beck and his team found the Chinese clubs were easy targets. They did not have the same fortified doors and secret entrances as the other casinos, and no cockatoos or hefty security guards. The police officers they met no resistance and simply walked in.

When Beck's squad started to raid them, the Chinese gambling proprietors were as surprised and shocked by Beck's appearance as those in other parts of Sydney and NSW. They made no secret of the fact they had previously been protected because they paid bribes, and seemed to believe this immunity from police interference was a right, not a rort.

"Why don't you take the money and leave us alone, like we've been paying over the years?" one operator said to his face.

While the remark was made in the heat of the moment, it was not long before more considered offers were made to Beck.

The first came via a police superintendent from the city district who came to see Beck at his office in Police Headquarters. The superintendent had brought a friend who was a businessman at the markets, then at Haymarket, who was waiting outside the office.

The superintendent said his friend would like to have a chat with Beck. Beck agreed and the policeman brought him in and introduced him. Then he excused himself, leaving the two men to talk in private.

"It's nothing to do with me and I'm not offering anything," the businessman opened.

"But the people of Chinatown are very nervous or apprehensive about what damage you might do to their businesses.

"There are various people who are interested in doing some business with you.

"Now, you might be approached with various offers of course." He hesitated and leaned forward confidentially.

"They would be prepared to pay you $2000 a week if you don't go there or send anyone else there. It's up to you whether you accept them or not."

Beck frowned.

"You're speaking to the wrong fellow," he replied bluntly.

"Understand—it's not me," the man protested. "I'm not making any offer.

"But I'll do this for you. I can make a phone call for you and you can speak to the person who answers it, and he'll go on with it." Beck was losing patience.

"I've got no intention of speaking to anyone on the phone about this, I don't want to speak to you— and I'm very disappointed that you would even think that I'd be interested in this!"

Beck left the room, asking the man to wait, and hurriedly called Commissioner Lees. Lees asked if he had taped the conversation. Beck did not normally use a recorder, but agreed this was an occasion to do so.

He got one from his secretary and put it in his suit pocket. Armed with the recorder, Beck went back into his office in the hope of trapping the man into repeating his offer. But he found it hard to reopen the conversation and the man was too cunning to say anything incriminating. The meeting ended awkwardly.

Looking back some time later, Beck said: "If I'd stayed there long enough, and it wouldn't have been too long, I could have been a millionaire.

"But then again you've got to have a shave and look yourself in the mirror, and that's not my caper."

Given the amount of money on offer from just one area of Sydney, and given the number of SP bookies, ethnic clubs and casinos which had existed before he took action, $1,000,000 over four or five years could certainly have been achievable.

This would have been a worthwhile investment by the illegal gambling industry if it reversed the big drop in income being suffered at Beck's hands.

Another businessman who approached Beck said some Chinese were using a building that he owned, and they did not want to be disrupted by Beck.

This businessman decided to make a more formal proposition to Beck.

"Look, Detective, I own a premises down there in Chinatown and the Chinese, they rent these premises from me and they're using them for whatever purposes they want. From time to time, they have a lot of people playing cards and I know that you've made arrests there." The businessman paused.

"What is the position if I go down there to examine my premises to see if they're alright, and you come along and you raid the place, and I'm in there—what is my position when illegal gambling is taking place?" Beck was not going to take the hint.

"If you're in there, you would be charged with being found on premises used as a common gaming house. You would be arrested," he said.

"That's no good to me," replied the businessman, hoping for another answer.

"Well if it's no good to you, the best thing for you would be to never be there, because if those premises continue to be used for gambling they will be raided," Beck replied uncompromisingly.

"Can I ask you something?" continued the businessman.

"As long as it's reasonable," said Beck. "What's the problem?"

"Did you know former Commissioner Norman Allan?"

"Yes, I knew Commissioner Allan," said Beck warily.

Allan (Commissioner from 1962 to 1972) at that time had been retired for some time, and in fact he had died a few years before this, in January 1977. Beck knew he had been a friend of the Chinese for many years, and had taken a close personal interest in any police matters in Chinatown. Even as an inspector or a superintendent, Allan would often ring low ranked police conducting routine inquiries in Chinatown to ask whether they were intending to arrest anyone and if so, what were the circumstances.

Years earlier, Beck had himself received one of these calls. Knowing Allan's connection, he had done his best to reveal as little as possible. Many other police told Beck in detail about instances where Allen had interfered with their inquiries in Chinatown, to protect people he knew, and gave the suspects information about the police inquiries and how to stymie them.

The businessman went on. "Well, if you knew Mr Allan you would have known he had very strong friendships with the Chinese people.

"Tell me this, if it was good enough for Mr Allan when he was commissioner to be looked after and to accept things from the Chinese, why is it not good enough for you?"

Beck smiled humourlessly.

"Number one, I don't do business with anybody.

"Number two, I'm telling you now, if ever I find you down there in circumstances where you should be charged, you can certainly expect to be!

"Now I'm asking you to leave my office, and don't come back.

"What's more, there's every likelihood that I will be able to have your premises declared a common gaming house and if that happens, you'll have no income from that premises for quite some time."

Despite Beck's annoyance, the businessman decided to have one last try. Perhaps he knew the Wran Government was unlikely to ever issue a common gaming house declaration.

"I hear you, Detective, of course. But I have to tell you, before I go, there are people down there, they are prepared to pay you any money you like.

"All they want is to get a fair go and be allowed to get on with their business without too much trouble.

"And when I say this to you, I am offering you nothing," he added quickly.

Beck showed him the door.

The encounter left Beck feeling disturbed, angry and wary. It made him shudder to think he could be considered open to bribery. The reference to the former commissioner was particularly galling. It was one thing to hear stories and gossip about corruption and another to have a stranger talk about cash transactions.

At this time there were plenty of stories of corruption circulating in Sydney society and they were getting more specific. Rumours that had been suppressed for years by draconian defamation laws, bubbled closer to the surface.

On 16 August 1979, Independent NSW MLA John Hatton used parliamentary privilege to claim former Premier Askin and former Commissioner Fred Hanson had allowed organised crime to become established in Sydney.

Particularly in the late 1960s, Hatton said, "the real penetration of organised crime by overseas gangsters, mobsters and mafia took place. Shopfront gambling and rackets came of age, large corporate fraud, consumer cheating, securities frauds and prostitution became rife and in some ways have continued.

"I have no doubt that ex-Premier Askin and former Police Commissioner Frederick John Hanson knew and may even have encouraged these activities,."

In retirement, Askin replied that he had never been involved in any criminal activity during his political career. His response was nonetheless damning.

"When I first took office as Premier, Police Commissioner Norman Allan saw me and asked what my policy was about organised crime," Askin protested.

"I asked him what the policy had been under the previous Labor Government. He said, we have no chance of eliminating these illegal activities and we do our best to keep them under control. So I said, that seemed to be the best course to follow."

Another story doing the rounds in Sydney at the time was that Norman Allan and Bob Askin had taken part in the opening celebrations of a new illegal gaming premises in the late 19860s. This gambling palace was also in Chinatown. The Premier and Commissioner of Police had allegedly christened the new casino by tossing two-up pennies. This story was later published in journalist David Hickie's 1985 book *The Prince and the Premier*.

In between his very demanding work schedule, Beck was following the public commentary about police corruption and illegal gambling very closely. He hoped the time was finally coming when the rot would be exposed and cut out, and that he would be a catalyst for change,

But he had known from the start he was blazing a trail in dangerous territory. This became obvious when he and his squad targeted certain gambling hot spots in Chinatown.

But when Beck saw Lees in late August for a routine meeting, the Acting Commissioner had a disturbing message. He advised Beck that it was likely he would be approached by Bill Allen and told not to take action in Dixon St in Chinatown until November.

"How would you feel about complying with such a request," Lees asked carefully.

To Beck, the suggestion was outrageous.

"I can't agree to that at all, and you know it," he said indignantly.

"If I agreed to that restriction, I and the squad would be criticised for being just like our predecessors, and that would be true.

"Why would Allen give such an order?"

Lees replied, dead pan, "Because Premier Wran will be attending a dinner in Chinatown."

Beck could hardly believe this answer. Attending a dinner did not have any relevance to the activities of his squad. Nor did one dinner need to impinge on the squad for weeks. Still, Beck had faith in Lees and could not bring himself to reject the excuse out of hand. He realised that the Commissioner was in a difficult position. But he was not going to comply with an order just on a rumour.

"It seems very odd," he said more circumspectly. "Surely you could contact the Premier yourself and find out whether he agrees with this or whether Allen was making it up?"

Lees was conciliatory. Of course, he said, Beck should continue to take whatever action in Chinatown he felt necessary. But no, he would not ask the Premier about the proposed ban on raids in Chinatown.

Lees' response virtually guaranteed a showdown between Beck and Allen over Chinatown. Beck wrote that night, "My opinion is Allen is making approaches on behalf of the Chinese offenders in Chinatown and due to my objections to keep away has sought Mr Lees' assistance… I really believe and I think it's only common sense that if Mr Lees had gone to the Premier and told him of the difficulties we experienced and that Allen was directing me to do this and that in his name, I thought it might clear the air in some way.

"If the Premier had admitted it to the Commissioner, which I don't think he would, it would show I believe the extent of the protection being given to these people. On the other hand he might have been prepared to sacrifice Allen and say 'no that's not correct and I will have him removed.'"

As it was, Beck could only wonder whether the Premier's name was being taken in vain. But he was not going to comply so readily with what he considered to be an inappropriate directive. He spoke to Deputy Commissioner Roy Whitelaw, who agreed that the squad should do its duty wherever it was needed, including in Chinatown. This gave Beck the imprimatur to stand up to Allen.

As Lees had foreshadowed, on 28 August Allen saw Beck and asked him to keep away from Chinatown. Allen said Premier Neville Wran might be embarrassed if Beck made a raid down there, among the many gambling houses, because Wran liked to go and have dinner there and also because the Chinese had held a dinner for City of Sydney Lord Mayor, Nelson Meers.

Allen claimed that the Premier wanted to be able to visit Chinatown and mix with the local businesspeople, without being "embarrassed" by what the gaming and betting squad had been doing.

Beck had accepted Allen's direction on Rozelle, but he was not going to steer clear of Chinatown without a better reason.

"Look, if Neville Wran wanted a dinner down in Chinatown he would only have to say and the Chinese would run up to Macquarie St and carry him down on their shoulders. And he wouldn't be going into these gambling places if he had a dinner there," he argued.

"So, replied Allen with irritation, "isn't it enough that I tell you not to go there?"

"No, it is not," was Beck's firm reply.

"You just remember who you are!" snapped Allen.

"I have accepted my present position in the belief I would not be prevented from attending any area!" Beck insisted. "Chinatown is a hotbed of illegal gambling and other activities. Allowing illegal gaming to continue there would be a poor reflection on me. And as I have applied myself and the squad to other areas where the same offences are being committed it would be remiss of me to stay away from there."

Allen was seething. "Well, you do what you f….ing well like and see what happens!" he said.

"I will continue to attend to Chinatown on a regular basis, as agreed by Mr Lees and Deputy Commissioner Roy Whitelaw!" Beck insisted.

Allen looked at Beck grimly but did not say any more. Beck left without it being mentioned further.

The conversation signalled the end of Beck's attempt to have normal relations with Allen. From that point on, they mutual dislike was obvious and communication between the two was virtually non-existent.

Without help from Lees, Beck had no way of checking whether Allen said was correct or not. He decided to warn his men about Allen's directive, and not to target the area but not to avoid it either. Allen could, possibly, have had Beck removed for disobeying orders, but given Lees and Whitelaw's support for Beck, any move to remove him would have been extremely messy and caused a political problem for the government.

Beck also told his sergeants about his conversation with Allen, and explained his actions, knowing they would pass it on to the other men.

Openness was crucial to his style of leadership and from the start, when Allen told him to avoid the Rozelle casino, he realised that he would need to be totally honest with his men about the circumstances in which they were working. Given the loyalty he demanded, the men needed to know that it was not their leader who was holding them back, and they were as upset as Beck himself at the limitations.

Despite Allen's order, a number of Chinatown premises were raided. One raid took place at 1.30 am on 30 September, when Beck led his team to 71 Dixon St. They arrested 45 people playing illegal games of Chinese dominoes, mahjong and fan tan. Beck returned to his office at 5am and finished his report at 5.30am.

He was back on duty at midday, organising the squad for assignments in country areas and taking calls from his men in the field.

Allen adopted an unpleasant, uncooperative attitude after Beck told him that he could not comply with his request. But Beck did not care.

He was amused when senior police who had been cadets with Allen told him Allen had been unpopular even in those days and was often nicknamed Piggy because of his manner. Beck agreed with the description as in all his dealings with Allen he had never seen him smile.

* * * *

With the long hours and intense work, Beck's own police were working more than a fair day for their pay, but they were enjoying the work. So many people were arrested the squad and brought into the local police stations for charging, that the local officers on duty could not cope. Beck's men would help with the fingerprinting and the rest of the processing required, as much as possible. In most cases the local police worked well with them.

Attending court with the many offenders picked up in race day raids was, however, not able to be delegated and was very time consuming. The squad always tried to have court matters adjourned to dates when there were no races scheduled, so they were at full strength on race days.

The SPs had their own tactics for making proceedings as long and inconvenient as possible for the squad, even when they had no hope of beating the charges. Chief among these were pleading not guilty, seeking adjournment to race days to ensure some of the squad were not out in the field, and making claims of police brutality, violence or damage to goods. These legal tactics were employed often and had a definite impact on the squad, which was already understaffed for the workload Beck gave it.

It did not take long for Beck to discover that these tactics were being encouraged by treacherous police, serving and retired, who understood how aggravating they would be to the squad.

The police who were advising offenders on how to make life difficult for Beck were, in Beck's view, worse than the offenders themselves.

Wherever possible, while he was on gaming and betting duties, Beck made a point of befriending the people arrested by his squad and many interesting conversations resulted. Often he detected, beneath their resentment at being arrested, a respect for the job that was being done by the squad. Several people told him as much, stating that they knew something had to be done about gaming and betting in NSW as it was out of hand.

A number of SP bookies, after being arrested, even warned Beck that it was the police who had previously been receiving protection money, not the gambling operators, he had to watch out for. These SPs openly admitted that they had paid their way in the past, to police and politicians, for who they had little respect.

A man who admitted he had been in charge of a large SP betting operation with several outlets, told Beck that he should not surprised by anything some police would do to obstruct his squad's crackdown.

When Beck asked this man what he thought about these tactics, he said the police who had been looking after the "betting game" for a long time had become reliant on the extra money to fund a lifestyle well beyond their police paypackets. In return the SPs were assisted in various ways. They would be told in advance when they were to be raided, and if times were hard they would be left alone for longer periods with no action.

Police on the take had bought units or other properties, or expensive boats, and now had loans which they could not repay thanks to Beck. The SPs and casinos were refusing to pay when their contacts could no longer provide protection, so the crooked cops had very personal veste interest in getting rid of Beck.

"They have to do something to stay on the payroll," the SP operator said, "so you can expect a lot of stick from your own mates. The Government has brought you in to clean things up and cool the heat on them, but it is known you will be gone soon."

Several people told Beck that after being arrested, they had been told by other police to plead not guilty, make allegations of mistreatment and seek court adjournments to race days to tie up the squad and keep them from making raids out of the field. This undermining from other police was even reported in the media.

One of these occasions happened after a successful raid on an SP premises at Haberfield. Some SP operations were based in normal suburban houses, and this was one. Beck's squad had checked the phone numbers and knew the premises were being used for SP bookmaking, and had a warrant to enter.

When Beck and two sergeants arrived at the address they could see the suspects, a man and a woman, through the window.

"Police here," Beck called out, and his sergeants held their badges up to the door. The people inside could see and hear them, and reacted quickly. Instead of opening the door as requested they started to grab piles of paper and run into the next room, the kitchen, where they stuffed the incriminating evidence down the garbage disposal unit.

The front door was magnificent with leadlight glass and the rest of the house was equally impressive. It was big and the gardens and appointments reeked of money. Beck and his men were taken aback and were reluctant to take up the hammer and just smash the lovely door to gain entry.

Eventually Beck decided he would have to force the door. He asked one of the sergeants to kick it open, but do as little damage as he could. The sergeant ran towards the door and raised his foot to kick it, but unfortunately for him it had been raining, and the foot on the ground slipped on the concrete and he went over backwards.

As he went down he desperately grabbed at a small palm tree in a large pot which was standing next to the door, but his weight pulled the tree out of the pot and into the air, and as he fell he brought the tree down on his head and the soil fell out all over him.

He was not hurt, just dirty, and after copping a laugh from his colleagues they quickly got on with forcing the door open, and ran inside. The man dropped what he was doing and ran into a bedroom.

He threw himself under a bed, a desperate and futile move. The police knew he was there and despite his struggles, pulled him out by his arms and legs.

The woman, who had more presence of mind, yanked the telephone out of its connection on the wall to stop any calls coming in, before being arrested.

The police gingerly put their hands down into the insinkerator and managed to rescue some of the betting papers, to be used as evidence. They also plugged the phone back in, hoping that it would ring so that they could speak to callers, accept some bets and record that for evidence in their notes.

The man and the woman caught in the raid, who lived in the luxurious house, were agents for a big time bookmaker at Randwick. They sought an adjournment for their court appearance but did not try to have the matter moved to a race day. They turned out to be more honourable than their boss would have liked.

Some days after the arrest, they contacted the squad and revealed they had been approached by other police. These police had asked them to make as much trouble for Beck as possible. But they said they were not going to act on the advice, as they did not think it was right. They had been arrested fairly and were quite happy with their treatment.

Beck asked these people to tell him the names or positions of the police who had advised them to make trouble, as he hoped to take action again them, but they politely refused. They said it would not be worth their lives to expose the crook cops, and they were afraid to go any further than they had.

Beck' kept a copy of the handwritten speaking notes he used in one of his regular briefings to squad members, in September 1979.

"The best answer I consider that can be given to our critics is to keep arresting their friends, the SP operators and gaming fraternity. And it is true, I think you will agree, that nothing generates criticism as much as success.

"(On the other hand) we appear to have some forces working against us and I am sad to say to you some of our fellow police officers in several instances are well to the fore (in this). I want you to maintain your composure at all times and ignore those abuses by disloyal police.

"Now more control will be placed over your whereabouts for at all times there is a need to know where you are. For in this type of work as you will realise, we can be called upon to carry out raids at very short notice. Therefore I will want to know where you are and how many people I have at my disposal. And for that, notice will be taken of where each man is and how long it will take to have him contact me once my direction goes out to him.

"I want you to ensure that you do not give up the TAB employees or any other people who may pass information on to us about illegal operations. It is the duty of the TAB people to report opposition to the TAB, for they work for the government and as we do, we all work for the people of this state.

"I want you to know that as far as I am concerned, your work has been excellent. It has been achieved over these last two months by men of this squad which has astounded the critics, heartened the great majority of good police and brought praise to you from many worthy people.

"Watch your drinking and driving at all times when you are working, for it is realised that there are times when you enter hotels on duty, you are obliged to mingle with the drinkers and partake there, but be very watchful of that, don't be embarrassed or bring discredit on the force as a result.

"As you are aware, each one of you have been and will continue to be spoken to by me at regular intervals regarding your personal matters if you need any assistance, any personal difficulties you have doing your duties here or problems at home, I want you to tell me about these matters and how they affect you and your duties. For the work performance here is heavy, and will remain heavy until we get on top of the situation.

"I want you to foster a good working friendship with business people and I want you to at all times be friendly with people, be a good listener (sic) and accept all information graciously and maintain security of that information at all times.

"If you as individuals receive information, I want you to immediately report it to me, and as far as I am concerned, you and I— unless there is a need for others—will be the only ones that have access to that information. That is important, for we don't want information to leak out of the squad where innocent people may be blamed. And if we restrict it and confine it to limited areas we can maintain far greater security in regard to that matter and we owe that to those people.

"I want each one of you to have your say here today and let's face up to any difficulty we might have as a team. And rather than grumble or be critical about matters that you don't like or think could be done better, my door is always open and I am always prepared to listen to you, and I think you realise that and I am very pleased with your efforts.

"I know that quite a few of you have said to me, and asked me, how did I think you would perform in your duties. That's why I have introduced these little talks that we have together, because I want you to know that if I think well of you I'll certainly pass that on to you, I think all people appreciate kindness and a word of help and advice, we all need that.

"I want everybody to be more careful in what you say to people who are arrested. Treat all briefs that you have as a plea of not guilty until such times as you know otherwise. Don't take risks, don't be slap-happy about things, tighten up your defences at all times. Refrain from any action that reflects adversely upon our squad and indeed yourselves."

On any measure, the squad was performing very strongly. But in contrast, the legal system was very weak. It was a great annoyance to Beck and his men that there were no longer prison terms for gambling offences, and some magistrates routinely let people off with the minimum fine of $50.

While this may have been fitting for ordinary gamblers, especially first time offenders, it as an insult to Beck's squad and to the legislation when applied to operators of major facilities, many of whom had organised crime connections. They were defended by expensive lawyers and Beck had no doubt their employers covered both the legal fees and the fines.

The trivial punishments handed out to gaming offenders were exemplified in September 1979.

In late August, two of the squad members including Detective Sergeant Tomic had done a good job in locating and entering a very large SP operation in a building 217 Thomas St, Ultimo.

There were 12 women and two men with a large switchboard in full operation. It was a well organised operation which had been operating for years with no raids from police, run by the large and powerful Crowley and Buckley (C and B) syndicate. The syndicate was well connected and many State MPs including former Premier Bob Askin reportedly had accounts and regularly bet with them, as well as former senior police.

C and B was a well-run, savvy operation. It was the first SP to use walkie-talkies to lay off money on-course, to reduce the starting price offered by legal bookmakers, and offered this service to other SP operations for a fee.

When Beck raided, the three phone operators who were taken to court were women aged 66, 68 and 74, who sat in court weeping and sobbing. Although it was clear to Beck that their fines would be paid by C and B, Magistrate Flynn took pity on the women and fined them a token of $50 each, despite the size of the operation.

At the end of the court appearances, Beck remembered a phrase which he had read somewhere.

"There are moments of crisis in any man's life when he is overwhelmingly compelled to piss against the wind."

It became somewhat of a personal motto during his period on 21 Division, as he doggedly ignored the difficulties and got on with the job as best he could.

Much later, after he retired. Beck was reminded of the raid on C and B. Beck was a guest speaker at a function at a large Sydney private school, which was attended by about 500 people. After his presentation, almost all of the audience members lined up to have a word to him.

At the very end of the line was a man who introduced himself to Beck as a principal of C and B. This fellow told Beck that he had been informed before the raid by a member of the Gaming and Betting Squad, whom he named, that Beck had a blackboard in his office with C and B written on it. Beck added bits of information about the operation as it came to him.

This was most interesting to Beck as the story was right, and the man before him had not been arrested during the raid. The police officer named had remained in the force until shortly after Beck's retirement.

At the other end of the scale were people who were regular gamblers and regular losers and had no money to spare. When Beck advised one person he had arrested to see a solicitor about the charges, the offender said he was better off without one. He said he had seen a few solicitors in his time, and did not have much time for them. When Beck asked why not, the man said he had yet to find one who was worth the money.

"When you first go and see them, the first thing they do is paint a black picture and how difficult and involved it (the case) would be, and how necessary to go and see them," said the man.

"Once you are on their books, they make you go and find the witnesses and even get statements from them. They're so off-hand… They just look down on me and blame me if they lost the case.

"They're as useless as pockets on a singlet," he concluded.

On the other hand, there was positive feedback from the Government.

When Beck saw Lees on 30 August, the Acting Commissioner told him that the squad's duties were very much appreciated by the Government. The ministers (Wran as Premier and Police Minister, and Minister for Justice and the Attorney-General, Frank Walker) had told Lees they respected Beck's ability and the Government was getting good mileage out of the very strong public reputation which Beck's squad was developing, as their honesty was rubbing off on the Government.

"I am very pleased to hear that," said Beck. "But we could be even more effective

"As the Government wants us to do the best we can, will you issue a directive to all serving police to support the work of the division?"

Lees refused. He told Beck that both he and Premier Wran were aware of the problems the squad was encountering, but offered no assistance.

"I and the premier will keep an open mind and take these things into consideration," Lees offered.

To Beck, this sounded alarmingly like a hedge against the squad's possible failure.

While Beck was well aware of the Premier's ambivalence about gambling, it was a disappointment that Lees failed in many regards to give him the support he had been promised.

"I took the view that the pressure being applied was part of a plan to remove me," said Beck. "However the more pressure and difficulties thrust in my direction, the more I was determined to take the stand I did." Some of the team did not react the same way.

One was a senior sergeant who seemed to buckle as the pressure mounted, although he was not actually one of the field officers. His apparent weakness puzzled Beck, who knew that some of the team were working far harder and under greater duress than this sergeant.

Caring as he did about his men, Beck sought out the senior police medical officer and asked for his opinion. Essentially Beck wanted to know why this one individual was more affected than the others.

The doctor listened to Beck and then leaned back in his chair.

"Men come with various strengths and weaknesses, each with differing capacity for stress and strain," the doctor said.

"To use an analogy, the bravest and toughest might figuratively have four gallons (eight litres) of coping in them, while others have only half a pint (about a litre) or less.

"Even though a man has achieved a senior position, he might actually have a small capacity for stress."

The doctor's insight made an impression on Beck, who always demanded the maximum of himself and those around him.

"So," mused Beck, "often we can be critical of people for their poor efforts and the like, but it could be a matter that they may be working at their full capacity which may be limited?"

"Exactly," the doctor smiled, "it is not really their fault."

As Beck thanked him and stood up to leave, the doctor added: "And I think you're a five gallon".

Goulburn Club fortifications 1979

CHAPTER SEVEN

Untouchable

Within weeks of his appointment to 21 Division, Beck had made an impact not only on illegal gambling, but on public and police sentiment. He had become a household name in Sydney as the media loved to report the squad's activities.

While not everyone approved, cheering him on were politicians, police, media commentators, crime researchers and members of the public who were delighted that the sleaze of illegal gambling was finally being cleaned up. These supporters showered Beck with compliments as the casinos and SP operations closed down, It was quite common for people who did not know Beck to contact him by phone and congratulate him and the squad on the job they were doing.

Some would mention a suburb and ask him to consider going there, to which Beck would always agree and make sure that he did. Another call of appreciation would usually follow the resulting raid.

This sort of exchange with the public was very positive and gratifying. Beck always reported the compliments to his team and they did a great deal to maintain the squad's morale and enthusiasm for their job.

One of these came on August 11 from a Sydney businessman who was not a particular friend to Beck. While this man was known as a bit of a knockabout who included a wide range of people in his circle, he told Beck that people in the community were looking to him to clean Sydney up.

"You and your squad are like Elliot Ness and the Untouchables," he told Beck.

Elliot Ness was the head of the Chicago Police bureau responsible for policing the prohibition on alcohol in the early 1930s. His biggest target was Al Capone, (also known as Scarface) who had built a crime empire based on gambling, prostitution, bootlegging alcohol, bribery, and narcotics trafficking.

The United States' Bureau of Alcohol, Tobacco, Firearms and Explosives says of Ness on its official website[16]: "Special Agent Eliot Ness is one of the most famous federal agents in the history of law enforcement. As a supervisor of an ordinary team of agents, he did the extraordinary. Against all odds, he and his Untouchables broke the back of organized crime in Chicago, a city that was dubbed the "Crime Capital of the World." Ness performed brilliantly as both a crime fighter and a leader in a time of national distress."

The parallel with Merv Beck and his squad was obvious and grew with their achievements, Despite his natural modesty, Beck was very pleased by the comparison, and made a poit of sharing it with his team.

It was noticeable that, after the initial difficulty in securing the right number and calibre of staff to assist him, Beck was now being approached by serving police wanting to join him.

It appeared that hundreds of police of all ranks were loudly applauding the squad's success. To them, Beck was a symbol of the courage to withstand corruption and enforce the law in the best traditions of policing.

In all cases, these were unsolicited requests. Beck detailed a first class sergeant to deal with these requests as a regular part of his duties and to speak to all of the applicants, asking in particular why they wanted to join the hard-working team.

The usual reason was that they wanted to be where they could see a team working together, achieving results and doing their job without fear or favour. A lot of them were young people looking for a challenge, others thought it would be good work experience which could boost their careers.

Some of these applicants were successful, and Beck was pleased to welcome them on board his team, within the constraints of his staff ceiling. Those who were not able to join the team were encouraged to help in other ways and many of them provided information to the squad, in secret.

They were given Beck's direct phone number and were able to ring him direct. Beck would personally take the call and then organise to speak to them on another phone, outside his office.

---

[16] https://www.atf.gov/our-history/eliot-ness

This positive support made it possible for Beck to deal with the hostility and anger that he generated from others, including his official supervisor, Chief Superintendent Bill Allen. Allen had been pleased that Beck was going to take the job, but Beck's fervour, and his success, appeared to be greater than Allen had expected.

Allen had already instructed Beck to stay clear of Chinatown. Now he told Beck that Newcastle was also off limits.

"You aren't needed there Beck," Allen claimed. "The local cops are all over it. Your squad needs to concentrate on places where there aren't police already working o gaming and betting."

Beck knew this was an outlandish claim. He also knew that Newcastle had a history of shady dealings between police and illegal gambling operators. While he was not going to accept the order without a fight, he decided to play a more tactical game.

After discussing the problem with a colleague, he had an idea. Perhaps he could challenge Allen on legal grounds? He contacted the Police Department's legal team and asked them to check whether there were any geographic limits on 21 Division's powers.

To his huge relief, the advice came back that there were no such boundaries. 21 Division was created to police the whole of NSW, so there was no justification for excising any part of it.

Armed with this advice, Beck told both Allen and Lees that the squad would be making raids wherever it felt they were needed, across NSW. Allen had no choice but to grudgingly accept this. Clearly fuming that Beck had outsmarted him, he told Beck he would approve raids in Newcastle on one condition.

"You know as much as I do, Beck, what the lawyers say is one thing," Allen said sullenly.

"They don't tell us how to deploy our police.

"Right now, you're free to go where you want, within reason.

"There's just one condition.

"If you're sending anyone anywhere outside Sydney, you have to tell me in advance.

"I need to know where they're going, what day, and what time.

"And you can also tell me the name of the sergeant leading the raid if you are not there.

"You got that Beck?"

Beck had got it. He did his best not to poke the bear, but he had a question. What did Allen mean by "within reason"? The answer was that Broken Hill was still off limits, just because it was too far away.

It was not what Beck wanted to hear, as he knew Broken Hill was another highly suspect area. But approval for raids in Newcastle and other regional centres was a major victory. He accepted the compromise, and immediately began organising forays across the state, providing as few details as possible, as late as possible, to Allen.

Given the restrictions Allen was putting o his work, Beck again wondered why Allen had sought him out for the job in the first place. It should have been clear to anyone who knew his track record that Mervyn Beck was not one to do any job by halves.

When Beck caught up with his friend Keith Paull, Paull recalled part of his exchange with Allen about Beck which seemed to shed light on the appointment.

"Can he be controlled?" Allen had asked Paull.

"Yes, he can be controlled," Paull replied quickly, not wanting Beck's tendency to talk back to superiors to be held against him. Beck, he knew, was a good police officer who was diligent in carrying out orders and enforcing the law.

When Paull now recollected the exchange, however, he and Beck agreed that Allen was referring to a different sort of control, of the kind that Beck would never accept.

"As far as I am concerned, you do as you are told, which means you can be controlled in the ordinary function of policing," Beck said years later.

"That doesn't include corruption. I was never going to be part of that, and as a consequence I refused to do things that they wanted me to and not to do what they didn't want me to."

Paull also recalled Allen's sly promise to take him "to high places". Clearly, Allen believed he was headed to the top of the NSW Police, and as it turned out, he was almost right.

Another source of tension between Beck and his supervisor was the co-called ethnic clubs. These were clubs frequented by former migrants, mainly Italians, Greeks, Lebanese and Chinese, but their only ethnic connection seemed to be the choice of card games they played. The most popular of these were the banned game manila and blackjack. Chinese clubs offered Chinese dominoes as well as the English games.

There were no social activities and only men were allowed to enter. Food and drink were provided, probably to encourage gamblers to stay longer, and many supplied alcohol although they did not have a liquor licence. It was common practice for the clubs to have their staff take part in games to encourage the gamblers during quieter times.

The houses were all charging a percentage of each game played, which had to be paid by each player. It did not matter to the house who won or lost as the club's share was based on the money being bet in each game. Under NSW law, it was not illegal for people to sit down privately and play for money, but if the organiser was taking a share it became a common gaming house and that was against the law. At times large sums of money were exchanged.

The clubs were usually located in shopping centres and copied many of the features of the illegal casinos, without their style and luxury. They were typically on the first floor, accessible only via a long stairway which made it easier to prevent or delay police intrusion, so gamblers could quit the tables and the gambling equipment could be hidden. Many added to their protection by using cockatoos to spot trouble coming, then sound the alarm.

As with the casinos, the cockatoos and barred doors proved no match for the determined and well-equipped Raiders.

Bill Allen had told Beck, when he was not long in the job, that the Government did not want pressure on the ethnic clubs. Allen said the Labor Party regarded the 'ethnics' as supporters and did not want to antagonise them. The gambling, he argued, provided the clubs with an income and without it, they might have to close, leaving their communities with nowhere t meet informally.

As far as Beck was concerned, the argument had no merit. It meant illegal gambling in some places was allowed, and in other places prohibited. This was just the situation that, Beck believed, he had been appointed to correct.

To check that he was being fair, Beck spoke to several leaders of the Greek and Italian communities. In contrast to Allen, they strongly supported his action and condemned the people who operated the gambling clubs, calling them "bludgers" and criminals. One of these leaders told Beck that in the United States, similar places were run by the mafia. Beck was not sure that similar connections had not been made in Sydney. Although several of the ethnic clubs appeared to be owned by the occupants, he received information from various quarters that they were actually financed by and owned by major Sydney criminal syndicates or their associates (Frank Hakim was one of the criminals who owned a club). In other cases, the clubs were not owned by crime bosses but had been forced to accommodate unlicensed poker machines or SP agents under criminal control.

From the sparse records available to him, Beck could see that complaints had been made about the ethnic clubs over a long period of time. A number of the more recent complaints were from journalist and City of Sydney councillor Tony Reeves, one of the few public figures who proclaimed his concerns about the growing grip of organised crime on King's Cross.

In defiance of Allen, Beck continued to target the clubs. But the pressure on him increased when several Labor Members of Parliament publicly condemned the raids. While Beck had seen from the inside that they existed purely for gambling, the MPs claimed they were important places for cultural and social gatherings.

A lot of money was being bet on okey, a fast paced Turkish game played with tiles and popular in Italian, Lebanese and Greek clubs. The game had a limit of four players plus the banker,

After Beck's team arrested four people for playing the game, a Labor MP publicly attacked them for picking on a small group of men having a quiet social game.

Beck disregarded the criticism, convinced the politicians in question were just looking for excuses to stop him going into these sorts of premises. But the political backlash had been heard in high places.

On Thursday 20 September Beck had his regular meeting with Lees. There had been some speculation in the newspapers about a rift between Lees and Premier Wran over the gaming and betting squad's crackdown on SPs, and Beck asked Lees if it was true.

"There's no rift. I spoke to the Premier earlier. He said he heard the same rumour repeated by one of his ministers, and told him it wasn't true.

"Wran said he was completely happy with the job you're doing."

Beck was relieved until Lees continued. "With one qualification."

Wran was pleased that the squad's diligence and obvious honesty was dispelling notions of police corruption, which was reflecting well on the Government.

But, he said: "They have put the lid on it. Do not screw the lid too tightly."

Targeting the ethnic clubs, Wran suggested, was a turn too much.

"The Government looks to these people to support them in elections. When they complained about arrests, they got a good hearing from Wran," Lee said.

"So you are not to make any more arrests that could embarrass the Government. The rule is, you take no action unless there are eight or more people playing in the game."

Beck was extremely disappointed to hear this from the Acting Commissioner.

"This eight rule is ridiculous, it will stop us targeting the ethnic clubs at all," he protested.

"I can't expect my men to plan a raid and carry it out with all the difficulties that involves, and then just say 'sorry' and leave because there were less than eight people found at that moment in a game.

"As soon as they hear us coming they will just split up.

"As far as I'm concerned, political requests about arrests have no part in police work!

"The Premier was a barrister, does he really think someone should get different treatment before the law because they vote Labor?"

Lees knew Beck was right. But he also wanted to be confirmed as commissioner. He stood by his directive.

Beck considered the 'eight rule' a farce. It failed to take into account the nature of some of the games being played in the clubs, or their social impact. He was also correct about its impact on the Raiders' work.

The eight rule was publicly announced. The gambling operators knew exactly how to exploit it. The first time after this that the Raiders broke into an ethnic club, the found the players scattered across the room. There were less than eight players at every table. The police could take no action, even though all of the people had been gambling in the same room.

When the police realised they were defeated, the gamblers laughed at them. A couple of them boasted that the team had been hobbled because of "their" Members of Parliament, which they said as though they owned the MPs..

After the failed raid, the team emerged empty handed. They were surrounded by ethnic women who had seen the police truck. They demanded to know why no gamblers had ben brought out by the police.

Beck explained with embarrassment that they had not been able to make any arrests under a new rule.

The women were unhappy to hear this.

"You should stop them," one woman spoke up. "I work in the factory, I work hard, all the time.

"My husband and my son, they no work. They come here, they play games, they only come home on Friday 'cause I bin paid.

"They take the money and come back here and all-a time they losing! Losing my money for the food!

"You are police, why you no stop this? Please, stop this gambling!"

The other women all agreed, as they had similar stories. They wanted the police to help them by closing the gambling premises, and were not happy that they had taken no action.

The secretary of the New Settlers Federation, Saba Baltinos, went public with a call for the police to close the migrant clubs. He said there were about 300 privately owned clubs operating in Sydney's inner western suburbs and other areas with high migrant populations. The clubs were fronts for illegal gambling, drugs dealing and exchange of stolen goods, he claimed.

"It's just migrant robbing migrant," he told a newspaper. "The socalled ethnic clubs are flourishing and have become a bloody nuisance. We get many complaints from women whose husbands are throwing their money away gambling.

"These places are being run by criminals and deserve to be raided (by police) more than they have. Only recently a club opened in Redfern which has poker and card machines and well as running an SP bookie agency.

"We must stop the spread of these activities which are causing hardship among migrants."

The public support encouraged Beck and the squad to continue to visit ethnic clubs and do their best. When they raided a club at Hurlstone Park, 15 people were caught playing the illegal game of manila. A man who appeared to be the organiser could not believe he was being arrested.

He told Beck games had been played at the club for 18 years and had never had a visit from police, let alone arrests.

Beck asked why he thought that was the case.

"Things were different, where you are now," he replied.

Despite some successes, the squad found it very difficult to control the ethnic gambling with the eight rule in force. After Lees was finally appointed as commissioner on 17 October, Beck asked him to withdraw the eight rule.

Again, he got short shrift.

"Well, you can't do much about it, you have got to remember that it's a political thing," Lees said. Beck thought this was weak.

"No, Jim, I'm not in this for politicians," said Beck, ignoring the contrast he was drawing with his superior. "I do the job properly, or I don't want it."

Lees said nothing more about the rule and turned the conversation elsewhere. Beck left his office unimpressed. He decided to ignore the new rule, regardless of the cost.

"I just took it upon myself to just make the arrests as they should have been, there was nothing in the law about numbers," he recalled.

* * * *

A few months after Allen's request that he avoid Chinatown, Beck found himself there at the end of one night. He and a team had already made a number of arrests in the Newtown and Marrickville area and by chance had swung back through Chinatown about 3am before going off duty. Beck, accompanied by several male police and one policewoman, stopped near 71 Dixon St. As was typical of Chinatown gambling premises, they were able to walk straight in.

Gambling was under way in plain view. When they saw the police, a dozen Chinese players grabbed the money from the table and shoved it into their pockets, where it was mixed up with their other belongings and could not be identified by the police. Beck spoke to the principal, whom the squad had arrested before, and made notes of the conversation. Once they had been arrested the players were calm and not hostile, and the police treated them well. They were taken to Central police station and charged.

It had all seemed run of the mill but a surprise was in store. When the charges came to court, the Chinese gamblers and the principal all pleaded not guilty. This was very unusual, as nearly all the people arrested by Beck's squad had pleaded guilty, and the Chinese in particular seemed to accept their fate, once they were caught.

The cases were adjourned and the Chinese hired a solicitor and barrister to defend them as a group. On the day of the hearing the defence barrister approached the police prosecutor and asked to have a word with him.

"Look, I have an interesting problem," he said. "My clients have all told me they want to plead guilty, but they haven't because they're afraid to. There's something adrift."

The barrister continued, "So I instructed them that, in the circumstances, if they believe they are guilty, that is now they should plead. But then they told me that couldn't do that because the police from 21 Division won't let us."

The police prosecutor agreed this was very strange. He knew the police who had laid the charges were from 21 Division, and they would definitely want the matter to go through quickly with pleas of guilty.

The defence barrister suggested they move the matter to later in the day, so he could have another talk to his clients. A few hours later he approached the prosecutor again.

"This is going to amaze you," he said. "I had a talk to my clients and told them they should plead guilty, it's a straightforward matter with small penalties and they'd save money by getting it over and done with. They listened to me but then one of them made a phone call to police headquarters to a very senior member of your police and asked him if it was alright for them to plead guilty as I had advised them. And his instruction to them was, 'No!'"

When Beck heard this he was furious. He knew that senior police were working against him, but had not expected such direct interference with the legal process.

The defence lawyer had no choice but to accept this clients' wishes. The case proceeded with the defendants arguing their innocence, despite the evidence. The hearing went for three days: Beck and several squad members had to stay for the duration, which prevented hem doing other work.

The majority of the Chinese were convicted, but the magistrate gave the benefit of the doubt to a few who claimed they had just arrived at the club and were not part of the game. They were let off.

More than a year later, Beck received a message from a drug squad detective who had been working in the Chinatown area. The detective passed on an apology from the Chinese arrested that night for the trouble they had caused Beck by pleading not guilty. They said they "could not do anything about it" because the instruction given to them had come from Bill Allen. The detective told Beck he would not go on the record about the incident. "I wouldn't be allowed to exist in Chinatown," he said, if word got out that he had spilled the beans on Allen.

Beck wrote in his notes.

"The 71 Dixon St affair is one of intrigue, disloyalty and prostitution of those within the police service, (who) have given their all to defeat the prosecution. Why?

"1) Being in the pay of such people (the gambling operators and criminals) every effort must be made to impress on those paying that their servants are doing their bidding and utmost to help.

"2) On conviction, the premises could be declared common gaming houses, which would put them out of business. (In fact this was unlikely at the time.)

"3) To assist in shielding the efforts of the Chinese gaming houses from the public eye and allow them to continue in false respectability.

"4) To prevent any suggestion of an open inquiry into the activities of the Chinese mafia.

"5) To prevent adverse publicity to Chinatown, for there have been murders down there and there is information on tapes at the coroner's court where a break and enter and steal attempt was made to get the tapes."

Beck had heard from another police prosecutor that detectives had been pulled off inquiries in Chinatown, and was given two names. But there was little he could do except keep his eyes and ears open and continue to do his best to enforce the laws under his responsibility. That, he hoped, might at least disrupt the activities of the Chinese mafia (later commonly termed the triads).

Limited as it was, Beck's disruption was not welcome, in Chinatown or anywhere else. Beck's work was impacting on ruthless organised criminals with a lot of power, and a lot of money at stake.

It made sense that even some of his supporters, like Jim Lees, preferred not to take his side in case they were caught up in the backlash— even though Beck was simply enforcing the law as he had sworn to do. Often Beck thought the gambling phrase, 'one against the house' applied to him.

Members of the public and even a priest contacted Beck to warn him. A NSW Member of Parliament said he had heard of possible 'setups' being arranged to try to discredit the squad. Then a senior public servant from Police Headquarters came and saw Beck to tell him that he was most concerned for Beck's life. The public servant implored Beck, as a favour to him, to take steps to protect himself at all times.

It seemed those most likely to take action against Beck were not the crime bosses themselves, but the former and even serving police who were helping them.

"So many people warned us about police that it was just a shame. The warnings came from some of my senior police, and one senior officer told me straight out that he was of the opinion that I would be lucky if I survived one way or another, if they entrapped me or set me up or carried out some act of violence against me or my family," said Beck.

"There was a time that I considered I would be lucky if I did survive.

"But I felt, no way was I going to give in to those people or those they represented. And it was with that determination that I carried on to do the job that was given me."

Beck had been in the job just under three months when, on Friday 5 October, he learned in detail about some of the powerful figures scheming against him.

A businessman, who had been arrested by Beck, had received information that corrupt former police and gambling operators intended to take action against Beck, He called Beck to tell him he was in great danger, and "anything could happen".

The caller said he had attended a meeting of the so-called 'police barbecue set' the previous weekend at the Kensington home of Frank Hakim, a Lebanese businessman whose interests including a gambling club and an ethnic club.

Beck already knew of the existence of 'the police barbecue set'. It was made up mainly of former 21 Division officers and sergeants, who would meet in the eastern suburbs at various times, usually on Sundays, for a barbecue and discussion about their mutual interests. The group was formed before Beck's time, for different motives, but during Beck's period it became increasingly a forum for complaining about him and plotting to get rid of him. Hakim was the regular convenor.

According to the informant, CIB Chief Ray Goldsworthy was an invited guest at the barbecue at Hakim's house that day. Others in attendance included Crocodile Palmer, who had every reason to be angry with Beck, poker machine supplier Les Jones, former NSW Commissioner of Police, Merv Wood, former 21 Division head Pat Watson, and Richard (Dick) Cox, a former member of 21 Division. Two politicians who often attended the meetings, one of whom was the Labor MP for Balmain, Roger Deegan, were not present.

Hakim, by then known as 'the Lebanese godfather', had started his criminal empire under Lennie McPherson, then started providing his own protection to ethnic gambling clubs before expanding into other areas. He had also become a Justice of the Peace and had leased a shop close in Cleveland St Redfern[17]. When the gaming and betting squad needed a warrant they inevitably went to Hakim. The last warrant he signed was on 26 June 1979—a week before Merv Beck took over the squad[18].

Before Beck, Hakim had also been a regular visitor to 21 Division. He would turn up on the morning of Saturday race days, with a basket of food and drink for the gaming and betting police, and was photographed during one of these visits by Bob Bottom.

(Hakim was charged in 1984 and subsequently jailed as one of the conspirators who had organised for money to be paid to NSW Corrective Services Minister Rex Jackson, in exchange for the early release of certain prisoners from 1982 to 1983. Neville Wran was still Premier at the time of the corrupt payments.)

At the barbecue set meeting in the last weekend of September, discussion was held to the effect that Beck was causing havoc to the gambling 'industries', and something had to be done. The group looked to the police in their midst for ideas on what this something could be, and how to do it. The majority did not care what was done, as long as it was effective.

What they came up with was a plot to intercept Beck while he was driving to or from work. It was known that he drove himself, and he always followed the same route. It would be a simple matter, it was claimed, to get to Beck while he stopped at traffic lights, such as throwing a petrol bomb in the car, or setting up a fatal accident. Another of those present built on this idea: they could find a drug addict, give him a loaded gun and point out Beck as the target. The reward for shooting Beck would be a supply of free heroin. If the 'druggie' was identified as the shooter, no one would believe his story.

Not all of those present at the meeting liked this sort of talk. They may have been running illegal businesses, but they knew Beck was just doing his job and, unlike some they were mingling with, murder was neither their style nor their intention. No decision was made, but the anger at Beck remained.

Beck was grateful to his informant and accepted his advice to take the threat seriously. From that time, he was very careful to vary the way he drove to and from the office.

---

[17] https://www.sydneycrimemuseum.com/crime-stories/frank-hakim/
[18] Sydney Morning Herald 9 February 2005 "The Man Who Knew a Man Who Could"

Beck passed on the information he had received to Acting Commissioner Lees. Lees as usual had no solutions, but asked to be kept informed.

Beck also asked a good contact to get whatever inside information he could about further meetings of the barbecue set. This was his brotherin-law Neville Bell, a former policeman who was by then retired. Bell had worked in 21 Division in the past and also on the Police Licensing Branch dealing with hotels, liquor outlets and illegal sales. Neville was a very friendly, happy fellow, well-liked by most people.

Like most police, Bell had informants or 'fizzgigs' as they were known, one of which was was Frank Hakim.

With Beck's operations severely affecting his gambling operations, Hakim had already contacted Bell and asked him to do something to get Beck off Hakim's back. Bell said he could not oblige.

"Look, if I was to mention that you had spoken to me and requested that I help you or anyone else, it would only make it so much harder for you, it would be like waving a red rag at a bull!" he said earnestly. "So I'm going to do you a good turn and not even mention any requests from you."

In fact Bell did tell Beck about Hakim's approach, which gave Beck some satisfaction. Now Beck asked Bell to get whatever information he could from Hakim about barbecue set discussions about getting at him.

Around this time Beck was also plagued by another problem. He developed a major infection, which turned a difficult period into an even worse one.

The fact that he was working extremely long hours undoubtedly contributed. Beck was confident that he only needed four or five hours of sleep a night, and almost all of the rest of his 24 hours was occupied with work.

One Friday afternoon, at about 2 pm Beck was preparing to go to work; he had been out all the previous night and had a few hours' sleep. Elsie was away and no one else was at home. Elsie or one of their girls must have been sewing and had dropped a needle into the carpet, which was then hidden. Beck trod heavily on it with the ball of his bare foot.

He pulled it out, which took some effort, and without looking at it threw it into a bin. In a hurry to get to work, he squeezed his foot to make it bleed so he could assess the damage. There was very little blood so Beck continued dressing and went to work.

About six hours later, at 8pm, he was at the CIB, walking to a meeting when he felt a tremendous pain in his foot. Within moments the pain was shooting up his leg and into his groin. Beck continued walking, with some difficulty. Soon after he was joined by Superintendent Barney Ross, who noticed that he was limping and asked what the problem was. Beck mentioned the needle, and Ross asked if he had had any treatment.

When Beck admitted he had not, Ross realised an infection had developed in the foot and was rapidly spreading up the leg. He immediately made arrangements for Beck to go to the Mater Hospital at North Sydney.

An X-ray disclosed the eye of the needle, almost half a centimetre long, had broken off and was deeply embedded in Beck's foot. Beck was advised to go home to bed and get some rest, then return to the hospital at 9am in the morning when one of the visiting doctors from St Vincent's Hospital would be called. It was expected that the operation would be done that day.

Beck had a heavy night planned with several places to raid, and his men were ready. Being as stubborn as he was, instead of going home to rest, he returned to the squad and carried out all the tasks he had planned.

By the time he finished at 4 am, and drove himself home, his foot was a mess. He duly turned up at the hospital and was prepared for the operation, but when the visiting doctor examined the foot he shook his head.

"I am sorry Mr Beck, there's no way I could possibly operate on your foot today," he told Beck. "It's very infected and in a bad way and if I were to open it now, the infection would spread rapidly. My advice to you is to stay in hospital or if you give me an undertaking you'll rest at home, you can come back on Tuesday."

Beck knew that this time, he had to do as the doctor ordered, or face a serious medical problem. He went home and stayed there, monitoring his squad as best he could via telephone. There were no mobile phones so he had to wait until a raiding party arrived back at their offices to hear what had happened. Staying away from his job was akin to torture, and the pain in his foot was not much better.

The following Tuesday morning he caught a taxi to the Mater. He was keen to get the broken needle out, but he was also worried. He had received a warning that he could be 'got at' in hospital by a determined assassin, while he was bedridden or, worse, unconscious. After undressing, he lay on his hospital bed waiting to go to the operating theatre with his police service revolver under the pillow, just in case. Firing a gun in a hospital would not be a great idea, but Beck was serious about defending himself as far as possible, if any attempt was made on his life.

When Beck awoke from his anaesthetic, he was safe and alone. But soon the doctor appeared, with bad news. The operation had not gone as planned. The surgeon had opened up the foot and searched for about 80 minutes, but could not find the piece of needle. Although it was clearly identifiable on the X-ray, it was hidden in the complexity of fibres in the foot. The surgeon said Beck would have to undergo a further operation at a later date, if he wanted to get the needle out.

Beck was accustomed to being on the go for up to 20 hours a day and could not contemplate being lame or bed-bound for any further period of time. He immediately arranged to get to Mona Vale hospital, where he had a friend, to get a second opinion, but the news was the same. The foot could not be operated on again until it was rid of the infection and the muscles had healed from the previous probing.

Word spread very rapidly that Beck was hurt and out of action. Rumours came back to the squad that operators who had given up because of Beck, were now thinking of starting up again. Beck decided to head off this speculation and got his men to send messages to several operators that he wanted to meet them at certain times. Beck could not keep the appointments, but the messages kept the gambling operators guessing.

After a few days off work, which seemed like an eternity to him, Beck was determined to go back regardless. He could barely put his foot to the ground, but managed to force a shoe on and organised for a squad member to drive him to and from work.

The CIB where 21 Division was based was in Liverpool Street, about 150 metres from Police Headquarters where Beck would make his daily reports. It was no longer an easy walk.

"It was just hell to walk across that road," recalled Beck. "I couldn't place the sole of my foot on the ground, I put my weight on my heel, and it would take me about a quarter of an hour to cover that territory.

"I put up with that for the sake of the job because I didn't want to lose ground at this particular time. We were holding them at bay, but on the other hand they had accepted the challenge of my crackdown and given half an opportunity they would open up again."

From his desk he was still able to organise raids and keep the pressure on the illegal gambling operations. He also had a driver take him around in his car just to be seen, to let it be known he was still on the job.

When he was driven to King's Cross one night, two of Beck's men entered an illegal gambling place while Beck waited, standing beside his car. Inside, the man in charge of the premises, a well-known operator was asking about Beck's health. "Is it true that your boss is away sick?" he asked the two gaming and betting police. "No," one of the sergeants replied, "he's downstairs outside at the car."

Disbelieving, the operator demanded to see Beck himself, so the police showed him down the stairs and to the car where Beck was indeed standing.

"Word is you're not well enough to be on the job," the operator said to Beck, obviously disappointed that this was not the case.

"Just a rumour. Don't believe everything you hear, ass you can see I'm on duty!" replied Beck, pleased he had made the effort to appear.

When the offender had left, Beck waited a few minutes then eased himself back into the car, his foot throbbing, and they continued their patrol.

Being physically disabled was a new and very difficult experience for Beck. For several painful weeks he continued to hobble around, in extreme pain, until he could arrange a second operation. Each day when he returned home after working day and night, the foot would be swollen and even more painful. Finally, Beck he was able to arrange for his own doctor to carry out a second operation.

Even then, there was a problem. The day scheduled for the operation, Monday 20 August, coincided with a court hearing in which Beck was one of the police witnesses, but not the main witness. Beck consulted the Chief Prosecutor, a Mr Redhead, on what to do and was advised that the prosecution would make their case 'part heard'. Beck should produce a medical certificate that he would not be at the court, which he was assured was a routine procedure.

The Senior Police Medical Officer, Dr Pedersen, strongly advised him to have the operation and forego the court appearance.

"You won't be doing anything otherwise," Pedersen told him firmly. "I will help you along—I am directing you to undergo the operation as scheduled." Pederson then provided him with the medical certificate stating that he could not be in court because he was undergoing an operation.

Despite this, Beck had it in the back of his mind that perhaps he could do both. He half planned to leave hospital as soon as he was conscious and head to the court to give his evidence.

The operation at Mona Vale was a success and the needle was recovered after the surgeon opened up the foot from the top, rather than the bottom. But when Beck regained consciousness the pain was intense. He could not stand on the foot and realised that if he went to court, he would be subjected to hostile cross examination and might not be able to respond well. Wisely, he decided not to go and let the prosecutor rely on his written report.

The defendant in the case was Harry Eden, a well-known former first grade footballer. He had been arrested on 21 July at his own home in Sans Souci for conducting telephone betting, and remanded until the hearing on $100 bail. After Sergeant Fred McHardy and another constable had given their evidence against him, the police prosecutor asked for a part hearing and adjournment because of Beck's injury and the operation he had just undergone. Beck's medical certificate was tendered in accordance with proper procedure.

But hearing the case was a Magistrate Quinn, one of a pair of brothers, both magistrates, who were often considered unfriendly to the gaming and betting squad. In this instance, the magistrate was not impressed by Beck's request for leave.

Quinn immediately told the court he knew nothing about Beck's operation, and suggested that Beck should have organised the operation for some other time. Over the prosecutor's objections, Quinn refused the request for adjournment and promptly dismissed the police case.

Beck, who had obeyed police procedures and acted on the advice of the senior police prosecutor, was disgusted. Literally adding insult to injury, the lawyers for Eden promptly issued a writ for false prosecution against Beck and Commissioner Lees. The writ should have been addressed to the arresting officer, who was McHardy, but by this time he was no longer in the force so it fell back on to Beck and Lees. The writ lay on the books for nine years without being acted on, before being quietly withdrawn.

* * * *

There were 32 officers in 21 Division but in Beck's estimation they did the work of twice that number in long hours and double shifts. In doing so they were following their leader, as Beck's own schedule was gruelling.

Beck often asked for more men but Bill Allen refused. He made no attempt to give them extra resources and after several months he reversed one of his initial instructions, effectively increasing their workload.

When Paull and Beck were setting up the new Squad, with Allen, Paull had suggested that two police from each district be detailed in plain clothes to SP betting duties, to assist 21 Division. Allen agreed and issued a direction to all district superintendents to do this and to report on SP arrests to him direct, by telephone after each mid-week and Saturday race meetings, so that he was kept fully abreast of their progress.

Two months later, Allen changed his mind. He rang Keith Paull at D District to ask whether he still had two police rostered on to betting suppression, which Paull affirmed. Allen then suggested that the officers be put back on normal duties as they were no longer needed on gaming matters as SP betting had been controlled.

"I said I considered they were necessary and asked whether it was my prerogative as to whether to two police were taken off or not," recalled Paull. "He said yes; so I left them on." But Paull was one of the few who was prepared to stand up against Allen. Over the following months, Allen rang him three times to raise the issue, and told Paull that all the other district superintendents had taken their police off betting. Paull thanked Allen for his interest, but reaffirmed his own belief that the Chatswood police were doing a good job on gaming and would stay.

Allen also found other ways to slow the squad down. He imposed administrative orders which were time consuming and produced no benefits in terms of their performance. Beck complained about this nit-picking to a senior officer then in Internal Affairs, Ralph Masters. Masters said he was not surprised as he had been told a politician had instructed Bill Allen to "give them hell". Tying the squad up with paperwork was one way of doing that.

With a shortage of men, the inevitable episodes of sickness and leave and more paperwork, there were times when Beck only had small numbers of men available to go out in the field. But their energy and planning meant that they generated the impression of much larger numbers among those involved in illegal gambling. Beck was also relieved when he asked for and received permission to use CIB observers to work undercover with 21 Division on bigger cases, which was most successful.

Beck took the opportunity to warn offenders about the scale of his team and of their enforcement efforts. In reality, sometimes members of the squad who had worked during the race day would back up for gaming raids during the night, without complaint, because there was no one else to do it. Beck was proud and also unabashed about letting them know his gratitude.

The niggling issue remained that those arrested, with a few exceptions, were mere employees. The 'big fish' who controlled the gambling enterprises were much harder to locate and bus, ad all wielded considerable influence in their own way. Chief among them were the major criminals but there were also sporting personalities and well-known on course bookmakers who had branched out. Knowing that Beck's raids were no sham, these people made sure that they were well clear of the action, as they did not want to be arrested.

According to Beck, one of these sporting identities was high profile rugby league coach and former player, Jack Gibson. Gibson had worked in the 1950s as a 'spinner' and doorman at Thommo's Two-Up establishment near Central Railway Station, but had never been publicly linked to illegal gambling later in life.. In contrast, Australian Rugby League (ARL) chairman Kevin Humphreys was a known associate of George Freeman and a heavy gambler. Kevin Humphreys and Ken Arthurson, who succeeded him as head of the ARL, were also publicly accused of running a two-up school in Brookvale.

"It was well-known in police circles that Jack Gibson was running an unknown number of SP operations. He also employed a number of rugby league players in his illegal operations," Beck recalled.

"But he was never sighted at an illegal enterprise. On Saturdays when raids were most likely, he would be at the football or at Randwick Racecourse, where the betting was completely legal, and far from his SP interests.

"The coach and his wife owned a hotel at Redfern, at which there were constant reports of SP bookmaking. I would send police out and they would drink with the crowd, but could not find anything. Then one of the team discovered a false wall along the back of the pub, and inside was the betting shop.

"The day the pinch was made, the squad found a number of people laying bets, including some off duty police. The coach was far away at the time, but not so his wife.

"She was arrested along with the other staff.

"Another of his employees was footballer Harry Eden, who was also arrested by me."

Some other sporting identities who were involved in SP bookmaking would pay other people to pick up bets for them, and if they were arrested, the identities would bail them out. Some of the pick-up people were pensioners, others were barmaids, who were keen enough for extra money to take the risk.

Several big on-course bookmakers were also running SP operations as a profitable sideline while they themselves were visible at the racetrack, well clear of the Raiders' attention. One of them was Bill 'Big Bill' Waterhouse, who admitted in his 2009 biography[19] to taking SP bets from media mogul Kerry Packer in 1976 (just three years before Beck came on the scene). Packer lost more than $1 million on one day and according to Waterhouse, never settled.

While the big fish managed to escape arrest, their premises were raided on numerous occasions. George Freeman's SP premises in Glebe Rd, Glebe were among the first to be targeted by Beck after he joined 21 Division. As well as arresting a number of people, they also seized telephones that were being used to accept bets.

Beck also instructed his team to keep a watch on the manager of the Glebe Rd operation, a man called Johnson, after the arrest. On race days for a period of weeks after the raid, he was shadowed to see if he would lead the squad to other SP locations.

But Freeman was apparently cunning enough to know his man could be a danger and the former manager appeared to have a lot of time on his hands. He was followed to Clovelly Beach and spent most of the day there, a pattern that was repeated until Beck was satisfied that he was no longer involved in the SP operation.

Freeman and Lennie McPherson were among the major criminals who were selling their 'insurance' to independently run illegal gaming houses, mainly ethnic clubs. If not accepted, forceful means such as fires to their premises, damage, assaults and threats to their customers would be arranged, to put them out of business.

Most people who had been involved with SP bookmaking for a long time were unhappy about organised crime moving in. Beck spoke to several people who complained they were being threatened or stood over by much heavier criminals who wanted to take over their business. Ironically, one man who ran a small club and had allowed an SP to

---

[19] Waterhouse, Bill (2009). What Are the Odds? The Bill Waterhouse Story North Sydney: Knoff. ISBN 978-1-74166-630-4

operate there claimed the organised criminals had moved in after a raid by Beck's squad.

"It was all fine until you fellows came and arrested him (the SP)," the club owner said. "Since then some of the heavies came along.

'They told me, 'get rid of your SP, our SP is going to take over your business next week, you'll get a percentage but it will be our man.'"

The club owner protested that he was quite happy with his set up, but the big operator would not take no for an answer.

"I've made a generous offer. You take the offer, you'll be looked after. Either it will be that way or you won't be in business," he said.

As organised crime was already running the great majority of SP outlets, Beck hoped and believed this was a rare turn of events. He also made sure to keep an eye on the club with a view to raiding it again if one SP or another opened for business.

* * * *

In early October, senior police were talking to Beck about the likelihood that he would be promoted to Superintendent. Beck was very pleased by this prospect, not least because it would make him the first ex-serviceman who had joined the NSW Police Force after World War 2, to reach that rank.

The promotion was dependent on performance assessment by several superior officers. Each member of the force had to undergo an annual assessment by more senior officers. For Beck, this meant being rated on response to pressure, leadership, training and development of subordinates, management of subordinates, delegation, planning and organisation. There was also an interview in which officers were rated on their knowledge of work, appearance, paperwork, speaking skills, and judgement.

Beck's assessments had always been excellent. Given the huge and difficult job he had been doing, he had every reason to expect a glowing report on this occasion too. He had done everything Jim Lees had asked of him, and more than would have been expected of anyone else.

Even Bill Allen had ranked Beck highly in the past and in the first week of October, Allen told Beck in passing that he would improve on his previous rating. Beck was pleased. But when he received the assessment on 11 October, it was well below his usual score. The reason was a very poor rating from one assessor: Bill Allen had marked him down on all grounds.

While Allen's ratings were unfair, he did not have to provide any evidence to support them. Beck knew Allen was paying him back for his refusal to accept Allen's orders. He should not have been surprised, but he was disappointed with Allen's mean-spirited, paltry attitude. For a moment Beck had hoped that even Allen would do the right thing for the Police Force and an officer who was doing his duty, as requested by the commissioner.

The other assessors disagreed with Allen. Beck knew that he had a right of appeal and immediately used it. In time the assessment was adjusted. Many years later, the issue was raised before the 1990s Wood royal commission into police corruption. A lawyer for the royal commission asked Beck, who was giving evidence, whether he had been angry over the assessment. Beck said no, he was more disappointed, because he knew the poor assessment would be overturned.

While Beck had to fight to overturn the assessment, he was becoming ever more popular among the media and the public. Finally, they applauded, the police were doing their job against illegal gambling and organised crime, after years of evidence (despite the suppression caused by the defamation law) and complaints about corruption.

The nickname, "Beck's Raiders", was used in an article in *the Sun-Herald* newspaper by Kevin Perkins when Beck had been on the job for three months. It stuck.

Perkins' detailed piece on the gaming and betting crackdown appeared on 14 October, spelling out not only the achievements under Beck's control, but the opposition Beck was facing from within sections of the Police Force and the NSW Government.

"It's a hard life in Beck's Raiders", was the headline, with a subheading: "Honest Cops proud of Untouchables".

"To Senior Inspector Merv Beck it's just a job. But his devotion to duty has caused a revolution, setting off a violent reaction among criminals, certain politicians, and even his own police colleagues," Perkins wrote.

"In recent months he's been vilified, threatened and sabotaged, constantly working under the shadow of political pressure to put a stop to his activities.

"Some senior police officers, once friendly, have cold-shouldered him. His telephone lines have been tapped, his men have had to watch themselves carefully for fear they don't commit even the most minor misdemeanour that could be pounced on.

"His enemy has been as much within the Police Department as without.

"Indeed, the pressure to have him called off has been daunting enough to induce most men to take the easy way out. But as the officer in charge of 21 Division— and leader of the feared "Beck's Raiders"— he has steadfastly stayed on course to clean up the State's SP betting mess.

"And since last (July), backed by a team of about 100 conscientious policemen (see below), he has been able to achieve what a long line of State governments, police forces and royal commissions have been unable to do.

"Merv Beck has thrown SP betting operations running into hundreds of millions of dollars into confusion and wiped out a big percentage of SP betting.

"His raiders, sometimes chopping their way in with axes and sledge hammers, have arrested more than 2000 SP people since April 2 – about 1500 in the city and suburbs, the rest in the country. More than 20 gaming houses have been closed.

"About 700 of those arrested have been SP bookies, the remainder staff. More than 200 telephones have been seized.

"Many of the 40 or 50 big syndicates that control most SP operations have been disrupted and now find difficulty in laying off money just before races start.

"Hardly a bookie remains in the pubs, and most of the big operators have gone underground. Others move around week by week, changing from one friend's place to another. Hundreds operate by telephone from other States, especially Queensland.

"Although the big money men of the SP world are still in there pitching, extreme nervousness exists. Nobody can be sure when Beck and his men will hit, despite the (police) informers. Raids are no longer by appointment."

Perkins referred to Beck's "100 conscientious policemen", but in fact the gaming and betting squad had just 32 police, most of them trained during actual raids. The squad also had only two officers, rather than three it had been assigned prior to Beck. But Perkins was spot on in his description and the team now became widely known as Beck's Raiders.

Perkins was also right that some well-known casinos had closed down, rather than be raided again. These included the Kellett Club, 28 Kellett Street, Potts Point (on the cusp with Kings Cross); the Palace

Club in Rockwell Crescent, Kings Cross; the Double Bay Bridge Club at 455 New South Head Road; the Carlyle Club at Bondi Junction; the Telford Club in Telford Towers (as it was then known), 79-85 Oxford Street Bondi Junction; and Brown's Two-Up at Ryde.

On the same day as Perkins' article appeared, an equally large article applauding Beck and his squad was published in the other huge circulation Sydney newspaper, *The Sunday Telegraph*.

Written by Professor Alfred W McCoy, it was headed: "A $1420m SP Racket At Stake: Police and Politicians under pressure from crime bosses."

"Flushed with cash by the late 1970s, Sydney's SP parlours leased computers to manage the flood of phone accounts that required up to 40 telephones and up to 100 employees. But by far the most important change was the growing influence of organised crime in the SP industries of the 1970s," McCoy wrote.

"On Wednesday of this week amidst ministerial speeches and rounds of free drinks for the press, NSW TAB hosted a ribbon cutting ceremony for the opening of its new $2.5 million telephone betting branch.

"Awash in an unexpected flood of cash and custom, the TAB has watched its revenue soar by over $1 million per week since the NSW Police launched its aggressive blitz on illegal SP bookmakers...

"Thanks largely to the efforts of the new Police Commissioner James Lees and the fresh faces in 21 Special Squad, the unit with special responsibility over illegal gambling, the TAB is making great profits, paying more state taxes and creating new jobs by taking on more staff.

"With this kind of success to their credit, one would expect a grateful NSW Government to reward acting Commissioner Lees with an immediate confirmation of his appointment, and to lavish praise upon the new aggressive head of the 21 Squad, Inspector Mervyn Beck, for his good work," McCoy wrote.

"Yet Commissioner Lees remains unconfirmed in his post, the 21 Squad is under attack, and projected reforms of the Police Drug Squad and other CIB units have been halted on direct orders of Premier Neville Wran. Why?

"The simple fact remains that in the world of NSW betting, the TAB's gain is the SP syndicate's loss. As the anti-betting campaign gathered steam in July and August, police raiders from the revitalised 21 Squad smashed in doors to SP centres, discovered a modern computer operation with an illegal line to the TAB, and drove the bookmakers out of the pubs. Projecting the TAB's $1 million weekly gain over a year, the loss to the illegal SP operators is some $52 million.

"Taking the figure of $1420 million as a conservative estimate of the SPs annual turnover in NSW, the police anti-betting campaign has cost he illegal bookmakers a substantia part of their business.

"The illegal SP operators, many closely linked to organised crime, are not taking their losses gracefully. Working through contacts in the State police and political parties, the bookmakers have mounted a strong lobbying effort to stop the police crackdown.

"There are reports of cash gifts, contributions, blackmail and pressure—all the mother's milk of any political lobbying campaign—being brought to bear on the NSW Government.

"Working largely through the byzantine bureaucracy of the NSW Labor Party, the illegal bookmakers are trying desperately to swing the State Government away from its support for the police anti-betting campaign.

"Never before in the State's history has a political battle been fought with such intensity for so much money with so little publicity or public awareness."

On the back of the newspaper reports, Beck decided to push his luck. The day after the articles appeared he went to Police Headquarters to see Bill Allen. Beck wanted the Government to agree to declare casino premises as common gaming houses, in line with police instructions. To have such a declaration issued, the police had to submit a lengthy report on all aspects of the evidence, to the NSW Attorney-General. If the declaration was made, the premises were effectively banned and any persons found there could be arrested without requiring any further evidence of gambling.

While Allen had previous insisted the Government would not issue declarations, Beck told Allen he intended to start using this aspect of the law because it was the most effective way to close casinos and keep them closed. The squad would prepare the required paperwork and submit it up the line, putting pressure on the Government to provide the required signature.

Allen was unmoved.

"I told you before, declarations are not required," he said.

"Why not?" Beck demanded. "It's the correct procedure."

Allen became angry and told him the Government did not want the premises declared.

"Did the Government tell you why not?" Beck demanded.

"Who knows? They might be going to legalise casinos!" Allen snapped angrily.

"Well that would take a long while to implement," Beck insisted. "Meanwhile these illegal places should be put out of business!"

Allen did not want to be quizzed by Beck any more. He walked away, and Beck could only shake his head in annoyance.

On the same day Beck received a number of complimentary calls from police and members of the public about the Sunday newspaper articles. Such calls helped him to stay focused and highly motivated. Knowing the importance of morale, he regarded the positive press coverage of his team as a boost for the NSW Police Force as a whole. The many honest police who read the glowing articles would, Beck hoped, regard the squad's work as the start of a fight back against corruption and a sign of a healthier future.

The following day, Tuesday October 16, Jim Lees was finally confirmed as NSW Police Commissioner, effective the following day. Bob Bottom in his book *Without Fear or Favour* claimed Lees' long delayed appointment only occurred after the Government's preferred candidate was caught out by the Federal Police. According to Bottom, this officer and two other senior police were photographed by the Federal Police in company with Abe Saffron. Bottom ensured that senior members of the NSW Labor Party knew about the photograph., and the other contender for the top job left the Police not long afterwards.

Beck, who knew Lees well enough to call him Jim, dropped by his office to congratulate him, and to discuss the squad's successes and the high number of recent arrests.

"Merv you are doing a great job and I really appreciate it," Lees said sincerely. "I know it's tough.

"But I am sure what you are doing, helping to clean up this city and across the state, is one of the reasons I have now finally got this job." Beck was even more delighted when Lees added: "and that ban on Chinatown now longer applies".

Beck then told Lees about Allen's advice that declarations of common gaming houses were "not required". Lees told Beck to wait for a while, promising to go and see Premier Wran and clarify the Government's position. Lees said he would also ask Wran if it was true that he intended to legalise casinos.

Lees' appointment after many months acting in the position was regarded as a good sign. Beck wrote in his diary, "I and a number of others now hope Mr Lees appointment to Commissioner of Police will herald in a new era and our service will be able to go ahead in leaps and bounds, as is required."

This proved to be overly optimistic, as Lees did not exhibit the independence and willpower which Beck expected. But without doubt, he was better than the proposed alternative.

Confirming Jim Lees in the top police job was a wise move by Premier Wran. Lees was widely regarded as a man of integrity, just what was needed to reduce heat on the Government over police failures and corruption allegations. This was essential as the NSW Royal Commission into Drug Trafficking was about to hand down its final report.

Justice Philip Woodward had been appointed to conduct an inquiry in August 1977, soon after the disappearance of anti-drug campaigner, Donald Mackay. The terms of reference of the royal commission were focused closely on "the cultivation, production, manufacture, distribution or supply" of marijuana and other illegal drugs of addiction in NSW, and the identity of persons involved in those activities.

After more than two years, Justice Woodward finally delivered his report on 31 October, exactly two weeks after Lees' appointment, He found that the six prime suspects to the murder all had convenient alibis. Principal suspects Tony and Domenic Sergi, for example, were on a 'pub crawl' in Griffith on the night of the murder, conveniently accompanied by a number of local police.

Despite the alibis, Woodward found that Mackay had been murdered by a hitman acting on instructions from the 'Honoured Society', a Griffith-based cell of an Italian mafia based in Calabria. He named Tony and Domenic Sergi among members of this organisation involved in the organisation as well as Francesco Barbero (who was related to the Sergi family by marriage) and the mafia kingpin, Robert Trimbole, who had previously made death threats against Mackay[20].

No charges were laid as a result of the inquiry. It was not until seven years later in 1986, after a belated inquest, that hitman James Frederick Bazley, also known as The Iceman or Machine Gun, was sentenced to nine years for conspiring with Gianfranco Tizzone, Robert Trimbole, George Joseph and unknown other persons to murder Mackay. Bazley was also given life imprisonment for the murders of drug couriers Douglas and Isabel Wilson.

---

[20] See Bob Bottom *Shadow of Shame*, 1988p. 46

Bazley was never tried for killing Mackay, and denied this until his old age. He died in November 2018 without ever revealing the truth, despite a $200,000 reward for information about Mackay, offered in 2013[21].

Despite its tight focus on the drug trade, the Woodward report touched on the importance of gambling as a means for the international drug syndicates to 'launder' or explain their profits.

"Money can be laundered at a race meeting and race meetings are of considerable value to persons seeking such a facility," the Royal Commission report stated. "By way of illustration, a person possessing $1000 in cash which has been obtained illegally, may launder it by producing evidence of an acceptable nature to show that he had won it at a race meeting. The only certain way of doing this is by producing either a betting ticket on the horse that won or a cheque from the bookmaker.

"With the cooperation of the bookmaker, a winning ticket may be obtained in several ways. One way is to approach the bookmaker after the race has run and place with him a purported bet on the winning horse. In such an event, the bookmaker may write a ticket in the right order and enter it on the betting sheet as either a cash or credit bet. In either way it will appear as the last bet on the horse in the race. With further assistance from the bookmaker, an additional ticket may be issued for a very small bet so that bet becomes the last bet in the race. The suspect bet is then second last.

"Such a procedure however may represent difficulty if the turnover tax figure has already been entered in the betting sheet. In that event it becomes necessary to alter the tax figure by substituting for the former entry and entry which includes the new stake. Where a series of such errors appear, where the bet is the last or second last on the race, and where the person making the bet is suspected of or known to be laundering money, the individual transaction becomes highly suspect."

* * * *

Beck was pleased to have Lees' approval to target illegal gambling in Chinatown. He was particularly keen to raid the Fuk Lee Club at 70 Dixon St.

---

[21] https://www.abc.net.au/news/2018-11-02/donald-mackay-murder-james-bazleydead/10458946

Bill Allen had other ideas. The issue caused a major confrontation.

"Keep out of it (Chinatown), I am telling you! I am the boss and you will only take orders from me! And you can leave the ethnic clubs alone too, those migrants are Labor supporters and their clubs are off limits." Beck was astonished by Allen's audacious claim.

"How can I comply with that when Lees has told me to go there and he is the commissioner?" he replied. "He is your boss! What do you want me to do if he sends for me?"

"In that case you see him, but I am in charge of you and I am ordering you to give me copies of all reports you submit to him," Allen demanded.

"How can I do that when all files are confidential?" Beck responded.

"You heard what I have said!" Allen thought for a moment.

"What's more, I want to see your diaries. I want them today and you can drop them at my office.

"And another thing. You have leave due. I am directing you to take that leave, immediately."

The diaries contained detailed information about evidence which would be used in court in support of charges, and were normally only inspected by a senior officer in the presence of the officers who owned them.

Beck had heard stories from other police at the time that their diaries had been inspected and they believed information had been leaked to defence lawyers, at a price, to enable them to twist the case.

Now Allen was insisting that Beck give him unfettered access to his books. Hoping for a compromise, Beck offered to leave his previous diary and retrieve it the following day as he needed it for court cases. He said he could stay and wait while Allen looked at his current diary, which he needed to carry out his duties.

"No way Beck. I told you to bring the diaries here and leave them. Do you think I'm going to put myself out for you? If you do, you are wrong. I'll take them both and you'll have them back when I am ready," Allen snarled.

Beck reluctantly handed his books over, and it was another two days before they were returned to him.

The next day a gaming and betting case was going to court and the charge was upheld. When it went to appeal many months later, however, the defendant won. The defence lawyer read out details which could only have come from Beck's diaries. Beck was furious. He waited outside the court for the magistrate, although he was uncertain about talking to him. The judge noticed him loitering. "You want to see me?" he asked. "Come up to my office."

Beck told him that he was not satisfied with the way the case had gone as the defence clearly had information taken from his private diaries. The magistrate dismissed his concerns and claimed that that evidence had not swung the case, but Beck was not convinced. Not long afterwards, that magistrate was removed from the bench.

Many of the judicial decisions witnessed by Beck and his police colleagues over the years left them more than sceptical about the independence of the bench. It was not until April 1983, after a major investigation by the ABC's *Four Corners* program, that detailed allegations surfaced about interference by Premier Wran and the Chief Magistrate Murray Farquhar in the 1977 prosecution of ARL chairman Kevin Humphreys over fraudulent loans he had taken from the ARL. The claims were no surprise to Beck and others who had observed the workings of the magistrates court close up.

After Allen took his diaries, Beck returned to his office and told his assistant officer, Ron Flood, what had happened. Beck said he could not work under the conditions Allen had set. He then rang Lees, who agreed to see him immediately.

Still seething, Beck told Lees how Allen had treated him, and of his orders regarding Dixon Street and ethnic clubs.

"I'm sorry Jim but my position is untenable. Allen is eroding my control and contradicting my commissioner, it's just not acceptable, I can't do the job like this. I would like an immediate transfer to general duties." Beck said he was aware that his transfer would be greeted by an outcry from the TAB, Opposition MPs and the press, and he regretted this as he did not want to harm Lees or the police service.

Lees agreed. He had just been appointed and losing one of his most high profile crime fighters would reflect badly on him.

"Look Merv, I understand what you're saying but I really need you to stay in gaming and betting.

"I am aware, if you moved now, it would be damaging for everyone. I agree Bill Allen has a bad manner and frankly I wish neither of us had to work with him. But he was appointed by the Premier.

"I ask you as a friend not to leave now. Also, you absolutely deserve a promotion and resigning now won't go down well.

"I want you to bite the bullet and although it's hard, don't say anything to him (Allen) that could be held against you and stop your promotion.

"I will tell the Government I have in mind making you 4th superintendent at the CIB."

Lees added that he had already told Allen the Dixon St gaming places were fair game, and were to be targeted by 21 Division. But he declined to tackle Allen over his administrative orders to Beck.

It was clear that Lees was not completely confident that he would win a showdown with Alen, and he was not prepared to sacrifice his position.

"You put a lot into your work, Merv. Honestly, it's not worth it," Lees counselled Beck. "Should you or I die, we would be replaced overnight."

It was not a message that Beck wanted to hear.

"Yes, I agree with your theory," Beck replied. "However, neither of us are yet dead.

"I've told you before, I'm very tempted at times to punch Allen in the mouth."

Lees shook his head. "I know you're a fighter, but Allen isn't your only problem."

Lees then confirmed to Beck that there was still a bad leak in his office, without revealing how he knew this. He asked who might be responsible.

Beck named the two men who had been put in the squad on Bill Allen's personal direction, Bradbury and Hermes. While Bradbury had recently been removed, Hermes remained. It was almost impossible to keep the squad's targets secret, with Hermes in their midst.

Nonetheless, after Lees' warning Beck instituted regular checks for bugs in his office, and even tighter security around all planning for raids. He considered the phones to be unsafe, and for all important planning spoke only to a few men, in private.

Soon after this, Allen told Beck that Sergeant Bruce Trees would be transferred out of gaming and betting. Beck regarded Trees as one of his best workers, and told Allen he was strongly opposed to moving him.

When he asked for a reason, Allen was typically sullen.

"I have my reasons, and he is going," is all he would say.

The next day Beck asked the same question. Allen claimed he was not satisfied with Trees' work, although Beck knew that Trees was enthusiastic, efficient and very effective.

Allen then claimed that Trees had made a comment which was unacceptable. Beck knew nothing about the comment, but was sceptical. He knew that Allen would have received the information from Hermes, and suspected this was a payback for him removing Bradbury.

Lees again refused to overrule Allen on an administrative matter, even when Beck appealed to him as a friend. Their conversation about Allen's power was still fresh.. Once again, Beck reluctantly accepted defeat.

It was Sergeant Trees who had assisted Beck to arrest armed offenders at Kirribilli in 1974, when they were both commended for courage and dedicated duty. Although Allen succeeded in ousting Trees, Beck was able to bring him back to gaming and betting during Beck's second stint, in 1981.

CHAPTER EIGHT

Rats in the Ranks

The attention from the Raiders caused a commotion and in some instances, a hostile reaction from local police.

As with Sydney raids, a pair of squad members would go ahead to observe the premises in question and confirm that gambling was underway. Then Beck would organise a warrant, gather the team and set off by car to lead the raid in person. These out of town raids made work hours even longer for the night shift, as often the raiding party would not be back at the office for their debrief until long after dawn.

All of the anecdotal evidence that came to Beck indicated gaming and betting in country areas had received very soft policing, with most offenders let off with a warning. A uniformed policeman told Beck about a raid he had attended in Dubbo a few years earlier, on an SP bookmaker.

When the police arrived, the SP was busy packing up, as he had been warned by a phone call three hours earlier that they were coming, but was late closing up. He was so busy that he asked the police if they could help out by arresting his wife, instead of him. The police agreed and arrested her— but no charges were laid.

Under Beck's command it was very different. Some of the country cops were delighted to see the law finally enforced, while many others became 'rats in the ranks', doing their best to stymie Beck.

This was especially an issue with Newcastle. After members of the squad undertook reconnaissance, the extensive Newcastle SP operations went underground en masse. They changed their telephone numbers and addresses, at considerable expense, in the hope of avoiding detection.

When this failed, and the squad hit a big SP operator in the city, the manager reacted with arrogant jeers.

He made it clear he was well connected with the Newcastle police.

"Nothing you lay on me is going to stick," he declared to Beck. "My mate in the cops will make sure of that, your charges don't mean a thing."

It was a boast Beck had heard before and he did not hesitate to arrest the man and the other workers and lay charges. But Beck also knew that the charges would have little impact if they were not properly prosecuted and to some extent, he had to rely on local Newcastle police.

Word soon came back that some had no intention of cooperating with Beck. The resistance was so blatant that a senior Newcastle police officer called a meeting of detectives to raise 'a serious concern' with them.

Someone within the Newcastle police, he said, was passing information to Beck about the location of SPs. This was a betrayal of their control, this officer claimed, It was wrong. and it had to stop.

He ordered the detective sergeants to track down whoever was in contact with 21 Division and when identified, he threatened, the "culprits" would be transferred and put back into uniform in punishment.

Within half an hour of tis threat, one of the detectives in the meeting had called 21 Division and spoken to Beck, telling him not only what was said but the name of the officer concerned. Beck was extremely grateful and quickly reported what had happened to Bill Allen (as he was his supervising officer) and Jim Lees.

As far as Beck knew, no action was ever taken against the Newcastle officer. On the other hand, despite the threat to themselves, the honest detectives in Newcastle continued to supply him with information.

Keith Paull later told Beck he had been to Newcastle to investigate a murder around this time, and heard about the order not to assist Beck. He also told Beck that senior police were involved with gambling operations in the city. Paull said other senior police in Newcastle were aware of what was going on, but felt powerless to do anything about it.

Given these reports, Beck was not shocked to hear that someone in the Police Force was providing tip-offs to operators in Newcastle and other country centres.

On a number of occasions, the Raiders executed well-researched plans, only to find the target building empty or an innocent social gathering underway. While there might be evidence of betting, there was nothing they could act on.

An SP operator later told Beck that certain police had inside information which premises were going to be raided. He claimed these police would go to the SP operators and demand extra cash to head off the raids. In some cases they were already paying sizable protection money.

The SP who told Beck this refused to name the police involved, in fear for his life. But as 'insurance', he had recorded the names and securely stored them with instructions on where the document could be found, if he died suddenly.

Beck also heard that a well-known sporting identity involved in SP bookmaking in Newcastle would receive phone calls from a police officer when the gaming squad was going to Newcastle.

There was no doubt within Beck's squad about who was giving the tip-offs. Once again, Lees said there was nothing he could do.

Beck's flying visits to Newcastle and other regional centres such as Grafton also raised objections from a senior officer in Police headquarters, Alec Burnie, who was responsible for country districts. Burnie thought Beck was interfering in 'his' jurisdiction, after raids in places such as Grafton and Newcastle. When others explained to Burnie that senior police at Newcastle were associating with SP operators Burnie changed his mind and made no objection to Beck's operations.

The country raids involved a new level of secrecy for the squad, as word went around the countryside like wildfire if they were spotted.

Country police could not be trusted either. When travelling long distances to the Queensland border or down This to the Victorian border, sometimes in their haste Beck's team exceeded the speed limit and found themselves being stopped for speeding. Then they would explain they were police but claim to be from the drug squad or some other special squad, anything other than gaming and betting, so they did not blow their cover.

Despite these measures, to their disgust they sometimes found the country casino they were targeting had been tipped off before they arrived, and there was no evidence of gambling to be found.

Calls to many country areas at that time had to be connected through an exchange rather than the direct dialling which is now standard. These exchanges could also be easily tapped. Beck warned his men to avoid them wherever possible.

It was not always possible. Not long after the warning, one of Beck's sergeants phoned him from a country town, using a public phone, to advise that the team was ready to take action the following day on the illegal gambling premises they were targeting. To make the call, the sergeant had to provide the operator with Beck's office phone number.

When the operator put the call through, Beck realised what had happened and correctly predicted that the planned raid would be a failure.

It turned out that the telephonist was the wife of a local policeman. She recognised Beck's number and spread the word. By the time Beck's men arrived at the casino, it had shut up shop. Although there were suspicions about the woman, no charges were laid against her because of insufficient evidence.

After this, Beck realised he could use the 'grapevine' of country exchanges to his own advantage.

He was finding it difficult to crack gambling in one town, so rang the local police station and told the officer there that he intended to be in the town for the following Saturday race meeting, and given the number of likely arrests, would need extra police rostered on. The local officer said they would cope with the police they had, and Beck left it at that.

When the weekend came, an informant in the town rang and told him that the whole town had gone quiet, with not an SP in sight. When the informant asked what was happening he was told, "No betting today, the heat's on!" This confirmed to Beck that someone had been listening to his call. Two weeks later, without any advance warning, he and a team descended on the town and caught three large SPs re-handed.

SP operators were found in all sorts of premises in country towns. To Beck's amusement, some SPs when arrested, would volunteer information about their rivals and where they could be found. Presumably, they did not want their clientele to have other places to go.

On one occasion Beck sent two of his men to Moree. A local policeman saw them and moved quickly about the town alerting people who were carrying out SP activities. The same policeman let down the tyres of the police vehicle, to slow down the gaming police.

The Raiders did not take this lightly and reported what had happened to Beck, who lodged a formal complaint. The matter was investigated and the results given to the Commissioner of Police. For once, the matter as followed through with disciplinary action taken against the Moree officer.

On another occasion while the raiding party was driving towards a town, they heard someone on the police radio warning colleagues that a police car from out of town had been seen heading that way.

Beck ratcheted up the security another notch. He told his men to be extremely careful when they were driving, not to be caught by highway patrols. The observers sent ahead to watch the gambling premises would pretend to be tourists in town for a day, chatting to locals and asking casual questions about the local gaming and betting venues.

The Raiders would use either hired or unmarked cars, and bought petrol at petrol stations like ordinary motorists, with cash, instead of refuelling at the stations used by the local police where it could be put on the Police Department tab.

But the opposing forces were also sophisticated. Country gambling operators would pay locals to tip to sit in their cars outside town, as sentries, and raise the alarm at any car that might contain Beck's Raiders.

Illegal gambling in Albury on the Victorian border was flourishing, fuelled by Victorian trade. There were three illegal casinos in Albury at the time and Beck had them in his sights.

Beck was informed by Deputy Commissioner Roy Whitelaw that one of these casinos was part owned by Abe Saffron, who had a deserved reputation as a leader of Sydney's organised crime world. Beck had suspected Saffron's involvement in illegal gambling as he had noticed some of Saffron's doorkeepers and minders at Chinatown gaming houses.

The links between illegal gambling and organised crime were one of the most compelling reasons, in Beck's opinion, to close the casinos and SPs. Saffron's involvement made him all the more keen to 'knock off' the Albury operations.

Roy Whitelaw agreed and gave Beck his complete support.

Beck sent three police down to the town to make observations on the three casinos and find out their operating routines and the best times to catch games under way.

When this information had been obtained, they waited until the next suitable night. When the observation team had called to confirm games were on, a squad member was sent to get the necessary warrant. Then Beck joined his chosen team of three men and drove to Albury as fast as possible, without speeding. They arrived in the early morning. After a quick rendezvous with the observers, the raid was on.

This Albury raid trip in September 1979 and was memorable for the experience of one of the young constables, Dean McGuire, who was one of the most adventurous squad members.

As was often the case, the gaming premises were on the first and top floor of a large building. On the ground floor was a very heavy wooden door which the observers had assessed could not be penetrated, even with the sledgehammer, without giving the gamblers plenty of warning that trouble was on the way.

McGuire volunteered to try to bypass the door by getting in on the first floor. There was a balcony, and adjacent to it was the rainwater down pipe. McGuire ran fast at the building and managed to launch himself far enough up to get a foot on the downpipe bracket and from there, launch at the rail on the balcony. He quickly swung himself over and crouched on the balcony in the dark to get his bearings.

There were open windows along the balcony. Some light spilled out from the room where gambling was taking place.

McGuire waited for a few moments to make sure no one had seen or heard him. Then he crawled along the balcony, passing under the windows and lifting his head occasionally to get a glimpse of what was happening inside.

He was just passing one window when he heard footsteps approaching the window. He froze and lay as still as he could, listening intently.

One of the players came over to the window and stood there while McGuire lay on the balcony floor less than a metre below. The player was smoking a cigarette and looked out onto the street, getting some fresh air. When he had had enough, he carelessly dropped the burning butt out the window, but stayed for a moment to enjoy the fresh air.

It was just McGuire's luck that the smouldering butt went straight into his clothing. McGuire did not dare move, but his clothes were starting to burn! With adrenalin pumping, he stayed motionless until to his great relief he heard footsteps as the man finally returned to the tables.

McGuire jumped up, brushing the butt to the floor and anxiously patting his smouldering clothes. Then, regaining his composure, he climbed through the window and dramatically announced "Police! Stay where you are!" The startled gamblers did as directed and McGuire ordered the staff to go and open the front door.

As the team had no expected McGuire to get in to fast there were only two other Raiders there at the time. Beck arrived with the car crew a few minutes later and supported McGuire in arresting 21 people. When the charges had been sorted, the Raiders had a short rest at the police station and a good laugh at McGuire's burnt clothes, before making the long journey back to Sydney.

Beck and his Raiders made two more trips to Albury over the following nine months, to raid the other known casinos there. Each casino was found to have a connection with a Sydney or Wollongong criminal identity.

(It was only years later that secret NSW police tapes emerged, recording illegally intercepted phone conversations between various people linked to organised crime, leading criminals themselves, and public figures. Several tapes were made of conversations with Abe Saffron in April 1979, dealing with casinos in Albury.

On the tapes, Saffron advised that a meeting was to be held to discuss a proposal for two feuding casinos in Albury to amalgamate on a 50-50 basis. Saffron asked which premises the merged casino should operate from, and the associate suggested that 'the Cue' was the best address, but either would do.

The next day, 12 April 1979, the associate received a guarded call from Saffron seeking an urgent talk, but not on the phone. It appeared that someone had tipped Saffron off about the police tapping operation as he knew the previous conversation had been recorded.)

Not everyone was as adept at negotiating rooftops and balconies as Beck's men, While McGuire's adventure ended well, this was not the case for a man who fled to the rooftop during a raid by Beck's team in Wollongong.

The gambling premises in that case was on the second floor. When the Raiders appeared, this gambler ran to the toilet and locked himself in to avoid arrest. Beck followed him and demanded he come out but he refused, so Beck left him there while the squad collected the evidence and arrested the other players and staff.

The toilet window was made of glass louvres, and it was not hard for the gambler to remove two of these to create a space. Outside the window was the roof of the first floor, as the second floor was a smaller space. The man squeezed through and tumbled onto the roof then picked himself up and went as fast as he could across the roof, looking for a way down.

It was very dark on that side of the building. The man could see the police truck down on the street. Distracted, he put his foot into a deep shadow and realised too late he had crossed the edge of the roof and the shadow was actually a gap between the and the next building. There was nothing to take his weight and he crashed down. He was very lucky to land on a bush, or the result may have been even worse, As it was, he lay there injured until Beck's men found him after hearing his groans. They took him to hospital, but also made sure he was charged.

Beck had initially complied with Allen's order that he be advised before any raids outside Sydney. But after Lees was confirmed as Commissioner in mid-October, he refused to continue the practice. Beck told Allen in future he would tell him after the squad had made a country raid. This was more appropriate and protected the confidentiality of their plans; if any leaks did occur, it would make it easier to track them down.

When Allen objected, Beck pointed out that he was following Commissioner Lees' orders. Lees had told him not to tell anyone in advance about impending raids, including himself. This time, Allen had no comeback.

* * * *

Keith Paull was a close friend of Beck's since they had worked together as sergeants. Paull had a sound head, a steady manner and was good at keeping a confidence. As a result he was often used by other police as a sounding board and a source of advice. Bill Allen was one of them, which is why he had asked Allen about Beck's appointment to 21 Division. This gave Paull an insight into Allen's thinking.

Paull, then a superintendent in D District, recalled that towards the end of 1979 he saw Allen at a superintendents' conference. Allen told Paull openly that he was not happy with Beck and neither, he claimed, was the Premier.

"I am f...ing cranky with Merv Beck, he's gone power mad," Allen told Paull. "That Merv Beck is embarrassing me with the Premier, I cannot control him".

Allen said Beck was overdoing it, arresting groups from ethnic clubs, sometimes three or four men, despite Allen's order that he follow the eight rule and . He claimed Neville Wran was "ropable" and he (Allen) had to be loyal to the Premier because Wran had appointed him.

Allen then said he was sorry he had ever appointed Merv Beck.

"I thought Merv Beck could be controlled!" he complained bitterly.

Keith Paull replied that he thought Merv Beck was doing an excellent job. Allen did not like to hear this.

"He's your f....ng mate, not mine, Keith," retorted Allen angrily. "You talk to Merv Beck, I can't tell him to wake up, there is no need to carry on like he is.

"The gaming and betting is controlled now, tell him to grow up! And calm down."

Paull passed on Allen's sentiments comment to Beck, but Beck was unrepentant. He was also incensed that Allen was trying to use Paull to steer him away from the ethnic clubs. He reminded Paull that when he had taken on the job, both Allen and Commissioner Lees led him to believe that he would have a free hand and would not be hobbled.

Beck again raised the prospect of quitting if limits were put on him.

"I meant it then and I mean it now Keith!" he said resolutely.

Paull reported back to Allen on Beck's reaction. He told the Chief Superintendent Beck believed he was doing the right thing, as there were "abundant and flagrant" breaches of the gaming and betting laws which had not previously been policed.

As Beck was immovable, Allen decided to try to use the media to pull him down. At a luncheon with journalists later that day he criticised Beck and repeated his views that Beck was 'power mad' and taking his job too far. Beck was told by a journalists who attended the lunch that Allen had been highly disparaging of him, and claimed anyone could do his job. He thought Allen was jealous of the publicity Beck was attracting, and questioned whether his word could be trusted. Beck's response was that he was sure others could do the job, but he was there because others had not and would not do it. As for his conflict with Allen, while jealousy may have fanned it, the dislike was much deeper.

While Allen claimed Wran was "ropable" about Beck's actions and especially in relation to the ethnic clubs, the Premier said nothing of the Sort. Officially, he supported Beck and in a letter to Commissioner Lees not long after his appointment he urged him to maintain the crackdown on illegal gambling.

The letter gave Wran a means of proving to the media and the State Opposition, if the need arose, that he was sincere about the crackdown. But when Lees showed it to Beck, it gave him the authority to continue to resist Bill Allen.

As his conflict with Beck became more open, Allen's tactics became more bizarre. One day, Beck had led his team on raids on a number of SP operators across the city. Beck headed home at a reasonable hour, leaving two of his squad on night shift.

After he had left, Hermes rang the two police on duty and told them they were going on a raid, on direction from Bill Allen. Their destination was the Chinese club at 33 Dixon St.

Despite their protests that they should contact Beck, Hermes insisted they had to leave immediately to meet him and Allen at St Mary's Cathedral, as the raid would take place at 9.30 pm.

When they arrived at the rendezvous point the two squad members found not only Hermes and Allen but Bradbury. They drove the short distance to Chinatown in silence.

When they arrived at 33 Dixon St, there was a crowd on the street. A doorman greeted the police

It was 9.30pm. "Well, you are on time!" remarked the doorman. Allen instructed the four police to go inside and make arrests, while he stayed outside.

There were very few people inside. A few people seated at gaming tables were arrested, along with the manager, and taken to Central Police Station. While this was being done, Allen remarked to one of the station sergeants, "This'll show Beck I can do it too!"

One of the squad members had a relative who knew a man who was a regular gambler. This gambler often spoke to the relative about his experiences, providing a good source of information for the squad. As it transpired, this gambler had been at 33 Dixon St during the raid led by Allen, and passed on the story of what had happened.

"You try and tell me the police are fair dinkum?" the gambler told the relative. "I was down in Dixon St last night, and the chows told us that there would be a raid at 9.30, and most of us had to go out and stand around the street at that time while the police came. So I stood around in the street and I watched the performance. The police came down right on time, and after they had gone, we went back in and gambled for the rest of the night."

On the same night, after the Chinatown 'raid', Allen took the men to a Strathfield two-up club where the reception was similar. The door was shut, but there was no need for a sledgehammer. As Bradbury went to open the door, it was opened from the inside, and the police walked in.

When Beck found out his men had been used on what he deduced were fake raids, he was furious. He confided in Deputy Commissioner Whitelaw, who agreed. "The fellow must have some mental troubles," he said, referring to Allen.

Beck was not sure what could have motivated Allen to undertake the raids. It could have been a simple matter of showing off, having a dig at Beck, or perhaps showing the gambling establishment that he,

Allen, was in charge. Beck had no doubt the people arrested in the raids preferred Allen's methods to his own and were not worried about being found guilty and hit with minor fines.

With all pretence of cordiality between Allen and Beck gone, they seldom spoke to each other, and only when necessary. Beck had had enough of Allen's demands that he keep away from certain places and did not buy any of the excuses. The only motive, he believed, was to protect the proprietors, a belief which was supported as time passed.

But Beck had no way of escaping Allen's interference. On 14 November 1979, Wran announced the appointment of two new assistant commissioners—Bill Allen, and Cec Abbott, both appointed ahead of many more senior police.

Beck was convinced that Bill Allen's promotion would prove to be an embarrassment to Premier Wran. Beck did not want to work under Allen any longer and neither did his men. Once again, Beck was ready to leave then and there, and had to be implored by Lees to stay on in the job.

A few days after Allen's promotion, Beck was called by Andrew Watson, a lawyer and journalist. They met that evening at the Hyde Park Hotel.

Watson told him that certain crooked police, whom he would not name, were in league with organised crime figures involved in SP and gaming, and were intent on smearing Beck's character. He urged Beck never to trust Bill Allen who, he claimed "will destroy all who get in his way". Beck felt it prudent to pass on this advice to Lees, who said Watson had also spoken to him.

Beck received more warnings from police and others that Allen was working against 21 Division, than about any other issue. It was galling to him to have to work with Hermes on this squad when he knew that Hermes was disloyal and working for Allen, not for him.

While Beck was dealing with these internal issues, interstate police forces saw only that NSW was succeeding in dramatically reducing illegal gambling, and boosting its TAB revenue, while they seemed powerless. Many of the syndicates that Beck was combatting, also operated in other states.

The Victorian Government was particularly interested in what was happening in NSW, including in Albury on the border. On 20 November 1979 Beck reported to Commissioner Lees that he had been phoned that morning by Inspector Cartwright of the Victorian Gaming and Licensing Squad.

Cartwright had been recalled from annual leave to prepare information for a meeting of Victorian Government Ministers, police and gaming officials the following Monday, to discuss the poor performance of the Victorian TAB compared to its NSW counterpart.

Cartwright innocently asked Beck why the NSW TAB takings had jumped so markedly in recent months, and whether there was any "secret weapon" which Victoria could also employ. He said he and the Deputy Commissioner would be asked, at the meeting to explain Victoria's poor performance from a police point of view.

The only secret weapon was Beck. Beck told Cartwright that the TAB takings had escalated since he had begun the crackdown on illegal gambling: the TAB turnover in the 12 months to October 1979 was in fact about $17 million greater than over the year to October 1978.

After talking to Cartwright, Beck contacted the NSW TAB executive officer, George Ralph, who said the TAB Board had discussed the very same issue a few days before.

"The Board has no hesitation in attributing the New South Wales escalation in takings as the direct results of the honest police now in charge of gaming and betting in NSW carrying out their duties in the efficient manner they are doing, thus bringing about the results achieved," Beck duly reported to Lees.

CHAPTER NINE

"Watch your back"

Some of the people opposed to Beck's crackdown were police colleagues he had known for many years. Some would make remarks to his face, others made comments to civilians who passed them on to Beck.

"Merv, what are you doing to these people, what have they done to you?" was a typical approach.

"Just doing my job. Why, is it upsetting you?" Beck would answer.

"Oh they're pretty decent people, they're not doing anything that hasn't been going on for years!" the apologists would reply.

One night, detectives from the CIB made some very forthright comments about Beck in a public restaurant. They were having a social occasion with their wives and were drinking and loudmouthed.

One of them, Merv Brazel remarked, in a voice that could be heard across the room, "I would like to hit Beck in the head with a hammer!"

"Why?" asked someone at his table, equally loudly.

"Because he knocked my SP off," Brazel replied, as his companions laughed equally loudly.

A businessman who was in the restaurant at the time, and whose dinner was disrupted by the rowdy detectives, knew Beck fairly well. He rang Beck and told him what had been said, and was able to identify Brazel.

Just a few days later, Beck met Brazel himself in a lift at the CIB building where they both worked. Beck did not let on what he had been told, but decided to have some fun.

Brazel was putting on his nicest manners.

"Good morning Mr Beck, by jeez sir you're giving it to those gaming and betting people, your men are doing a good job," said the detective.

"Oh that's interesting to hear," said Beck with feigned innocence.

"You know, some people don't appreciate what my fellows are doing.

"As a matter of fact some of them would like to hit me over the head with a hammer."

Beck then watched, amused, as a bright beetroot red flush emerged from the detective's neck and across his face. When the lift arrived at its destination, Brazel did not say a word but he hurried out, leaving Beck to laugh to himself.

* * * *

Around early November, a couple of people arrested during a raid complained that 21 Division was being unfair, as no action was ever taken against people making and taking SP bets on yacht races. By coincidence, a prominent businessman who had also been a highly ranked serviceman raised the same issue with Beck.

He said there was talk in some of the yacht clubs that police from 21 Division and some politicians were receiving money from the boat SPs, not to take action. Beck reacted predictably to this red rag.

Beck was very familiar with the betting boats. As a young constable on 21 Division in 1946, he had often been sent to raid bookies taking bets on yacht races and had nearly had is leg crushed while boarding a ferry full of gamblers.

As far as Beck (and the law) was concerned, gambling that was not either private or government sanctioned was illegal and where it was done was irrelevant.

On Sunday 2 December, six men from 21 Division took part in raids at two locations on Sydney Harbour. Three of them boarded the ferry MV Royale at Circular Quay. They mingled with the large crowd as the ferry sailed and, out on the water, arrested three SP operators who were accepting bets on 18-foot yacht races then under way.

The three SPs appeared in Sydney Court of Petty Sessions the following day and pleaded guilty. Each was fined the maximum fine of $200.

Another three squad members boarded MV Karingal at the Bay St, Double Bay wharf. Karingal was also carrying about 150 passengers and during the trip the police were able to locate and then arrest seven SP bookmakers. Five of the SPs appeared at the Waverley Court of Petty Sessions on 5 December and also pleaded guilty. They were fined $50. The other two failed to appear and their bail of $100 was forfeited. Warrants were issued for those people.

Although the raids were a success, they attracted media criticism. The following Saturday's *Sydney Morning Herald* quoted Premier Neville Wran implying that the raids were a mistake and a waste of taxpayers' money. It emerged later that Wran himself had, as a young man, had a job as a penciller for an SP bookmaker working on a boats.

Beck was furious and wrote a note to himself in uncharacteristic red ink to reflect his exasperation.

"If quoted correctly in Saturday's *Herald,* the Premier stated police would be better deployed in raiding much more important gambling places than boats on Sydney Harbour," he wrote indignantly.

"He has not told us of his knowledge of the location of important gambling dens which we would police. As far as I am concerned all gambling dens are important, including boats containing 10 SP operators."

While the Premier found it trifling, the TAB was impressed by the extent of the gambling on boats detected by Beck's police. The TAB chief, George Ralph, contacted Beck on the Friday after the raid suggesting the TAB might set up its own agencies on the ferries.

Lees had asked Beck for a written report on the boat raids in case he was asked about them by the Minister. Beck provided this in a memo on Monday 10 December. As usual, he found it hard to disguise his indignation.

"Police have been taking action against SP operators on boat races for over 40 years," he wrote. "In addition, action in the past has been taken at hotels where crowds have been gathered and SP betting taking place. Having regard to the fact that I had no reason for not taking action, plus the adverse criticism of police and others (for taking no action), I made the decision to take the action resulting in the arrests made.

"Should the Premier have **not** wanted Police action to be taken surely he would have spoken to you (Lees) before speaking to the press. In the past we have been requested, on behalf of the Government, to refrain from taking action against the Rozelle Casino, the ethnic clubs, the Chinatown area, and even told to leave Newcastle alone.

"As for the Premier saying that police would be better deployed raiding other gambling dens, gamblers in all known gambling places are being arrested."

To counter the Premier's claim that the raids had been a waste of money, Beck also detailed he cost of the raids. They had involved no expensive equipment and very few men. They had each been given $7 to cover their expenses, $3 of which went on their boat tickets and the remainder for general expenses such as buying a soft drink or beer. This brought the total cost to $42 for the day's raids, while the total of fines imposed and forfeited bail was $1050. The squad members told Beck that at one point there were more than a dozen people taking SP bets on the Karingal, and that they could easily have made more arrests if they had had more police.

It was certainly true that the fines handed out by the magistrates on the Karingal SPs were disappointing. The maximum of $200 was paltry, but the reduced fine of $50 was not so much a penalty on the SPs as an insult to the police. It was widely rumoured that a magistrate in the court concerned was a member of the same yacht club as the bookies.

Given the Premier's unhelpful comments, Beck knew pressure was growing within the Labor Party to have his assignment in gaming and betting terminated. Journalists and others provided him with a steady stream of information about what various politicians, whom they named, were saying about him. Some, like Merv Brazel, were two-faced, supporting him in public and lobbying to remove him in private. Some of these MPs remained in the NSW Parliament and were still in power when Bob Carr was Premier in the late 1990s.

The question of how long Beck would remain in 21 Division was also being raised in the media, amid speculation that he would be moved to another position.

Journalist Kevin Perkins, one of Beck's friends in the media, told Beck that he had personally raised the issue with Neville Wran, who assured Perkins that Beck would not be moved sideways. Wran said he would personally tell Commissioner Lees that Beck should stay where he was and the clampdown on illegal gambling should continue.

Despite this assurance, the hostility to 21 Division from some sections of the police was palpable. Morale on the squad was not helped when the Premier again criticised the squad for being too zealous in its duties.

A journalist had asked Wran what he thought of the performance of the gaming squad.

"I thought they were doing alright, but they must be mad to arrest a 75 year old woman, as they did, for SP bookmaking," he said.

In fact the old woman in question was 84 not 75. But she had not been arrested by Beck's squad.. She had been arrested in Leichhardt by a uniformed sergeant named Newton from Balmain, because she was SP bookmaking. The policeman concerned was only doing his duty, and age was never a defence under the law. Yet it was not only held against him but against Beck, who had nothing to do with it.

Wran also criticised Beck for arresting two Lebanese cooks for playing cards. Beck had actually arrested four of them, they all pleaded guilty to illegal gaming and were fined. But Beck could not contradict his Minister and Premier in public.

Immediately after this criticism, Beck finally got to meet Wran face to face. On Wednesday 5 December, Wran attended the CIB and addressed the police. Before the event, Jim Lees contacted Beck and invited him to attend as Wran had asked to be introduced to him. When Beck arrived at the meeting room at the CIB with Lees, tea cups and saucers were all out ready for the Premier.

Beck could see from the faces of some of the senior CIB officers that they were far from happy to have him in their midst, and CIB Chief Ray Goldsworthy spoke up.

"Who asked you here?" he demanded.

"The Premier," responded Beck. "Why don't you ask Lees if you doubt me". Beck guessed that some CIB detectives were feeling the pressure that his activities was putting on their 'clients' in the gaming business. Just then Wran arrived, forcing Goldsworthy and the others to put on their best behaviour.

While some of his colleagues were scowling, Premier Wran had nothing but praise for Beck, and made a point of shaking his hand.

"You are doing an excellent job, keep up the good work," smiled Wran, adding, "and watch your back." Beck accepted the compliment without comment, but his mind was full of questions afterwards. Why was he being told to keep away from the Rozelle casino, the ethnic clubs, Chinatown and even Newcastle, if the Premier thought he was doing a good job?

Like their leader, the squad members were getting tired of political interference, and harping by senior officers when the Division was getting great results.

Beck's stock of faith was running low. "I am sorry to say I feel Mr Lees is being used by the Government, he is surrounded by officers not loyal to him and I predict he will throw the towel in before he will be moved out," a disturbed Beck wrote at that time. "At this stage there is little doubt it pays to be one of the mob, don't try too hard etc. I find this might be what the great majority think, it is not my cup of tea nor any of my men."

Just a few days after Wran's visit, one of Beck's most valued squad members, Detective Sergeant First Class Fred McHardy, asked to be moved to other duties. McHardy said he was uncomfortable with the criticism and political interference the division was experiencing. Beck knew his men were under great pressure and wished he could offer them a better and more supportive environment.

He wrote at the time: "It is very strange how our Police Minister, the Premier, as astute as he is, is prepared to be critical of his police via the media, when the Commissioner of Police and all other police are available at all times where he could speak direct to them instead of going to the media."

McHardy's resignation followed a difficult period where McHardy was accused of stealing cases of alcohol from a gambling premises, after a raid. The investigation cleared McHardy and Beck of any wrongdoing but it had caused lasting damage. McHardy had reported off sick when the complaint was lodged. Then he had returned and worked solidly for the next four months until, without warning, he announced he was leaving.

Not only was McHardy resigning from the squad, he was leaving the Police Force entirely. He put in his resignation by letter, effective immediately and would not even come into the office to have a farewell with his colleagues.

McHardy, who was then 42, had had previous dealings with corrupt police which may have had something to do with his sudden departure. While working in Newcastle he had called out other police for their corrupt behaviour, and had suffered as a result. He was stripped of his detective's designation and reverted to uniform.

When Beck was re-forming the gaming and betting squad, being short of police, he had used whoever was available, and McHardy was one of them. Beck had quickly formed a bond with him and valued him highly as a member of the squad. Before long, Beck had moved to have his detective status restored.

McHardy had proved to be as tough as Beck himself, able to work all day and night, sometimes driving hundreds of kilometres, without ever complaining or seeming to flag, and his results were impressive. On one of the squad's raids on Albury, McHardy was part of the team which raced down there and made the raid the same night. The team was exhausted after working all night so Beck put them into a motel for four hours, then they had to drive back. Fred McHardy was the driver, as the other police were all falling asleep.

Recently, Beck had flagged sending McHardy on a special assignment. He wanted McHardy to leave a team to tackle the entrenched corruption and gambling in Newcastle. Beck had already discussed this project with Commissioner Lees and Lees had given his permission.

Shocked by the resignation, Beck went to McHardy's house to try to talk him out of his hasty move. But McHardy refused to even see him.

It seemed no coincidence that McHardy resigned in such extreme circumstances before he was able to carry out this mission. Beck was convinced that the gambling interests and their crooked police had made sure McHardy did not come to turn over their nest. Whatever threats had been made to McHardy or his family, the sergeant had taken them very seriously.

As he could not speak to McHardy himself, Beck asked his wife to pass on a simple message. "In my opinion, he is a real good bloke".

McHardy's exit meant the planned deep dive into Newcastle corruption would not go ahead. It was a victory for the gamblers and corrupt police, and with no move in sight by the Government to shift Beck the opponents tried to use the same tactics on him.

Bob Bottom, who had become a friend and adviser to Beck, told him that the tactics were very similar to those employed by the mafia in America against honest police and legal officials. The first step in any campaign was to urge their friendly politicians to take action. against the individual in question. The second step was to try bribery. The third step was threats to the official and his family in an effort to drive him out.

In Beck's case, the telephone threats had started very early after he took over gaming and betting. Now they increased in frequency and intensity, coming to both his office and at home. Usually the caller would start off as though it was a normal call, to keep Beck from hanging up, and then launch into abuse, threats and insults, "we'll get you, you bastard".

Often the callers accused Beck of betraying his colleagues: "What are you doing this to your mates for?" Beck was bemused by the misplaced notion that he would be mates with any cop who was receiving bribes to protect illegal gambling.

The callers would also attempt to appeal to Beck's self-interest. "You will be gone and forgotten and what will you get out of it? Everything you do will be undone quick smart, no one wants the gambling gone! You're the only one who thinks you're doing a genuine job!"

Reliable sources told Beck that crime boss Lennie McPherson had organised the threats, on behalf of the barbecue set.

While Beck refused to give in to the bullying, and was reconciled to accept whatever danger he was in, he did not feel the same way about his family. Now many of the calls were being taken by Elsie. She had seen a lot over the years, thanks to Beck's career, but nothing had prepared her for the abuse and threats now turned against her and her family.

Outwardly Elsie remained strong and resolute, Back knew she was frightened for herself and for him.

"My wife was getting indecent phone calls and threats that things were going to happen to me 'if you don't get that bastard out of this job'," Beck recalled. "I would work long hours at that time, I would work 18 to 20 hours a day, I'd get home about 4 in the morning and get about 4 hours sleep and be back in the office because I had to report every morning to the commissioner. And the moment I'd get home the phone would start ringing, which I couldn't turn off because I had police everywhere and if I wasn't there they would ring me at home; and the threats would start there.

"Now my wife was so much on her own, we had two children at home and two others who were grown up and married; but my answer to these threatening calls was, 'Do your worst you mongrels!' and 'you don't bluff me'."

Beck had the option of switching to a silent number, but he had no faith in them, having seen many instances where the number had got out to unauthorised people. He and Elsie refused to make any concessions to the dishonourable and unethical crooks and scoundrels who were persecuting them. They preferred to take the calls and treat them with disdain, as far as possible.

But as 1979 drew to a close the threat of physical violence became more real.

One of the Becks' neighbours worked for the Electricity Commission. He would be called out at odd hours. On two different occasions when he came home very late at night, he saw a car parked close by Beck's home, with the plate covered. As soon as the neighbour approached in his car, the other vehicle roared off.

On another occasion the power went off at Beck's home and on investigation he found that it had been turned off at a power box at side of the house. Unfortunately, the power also served the house next door which was occupied by a couple in their 80s.

This was both irritating and intimidating, as it was proof that someone with evil intent had been just outside the house.

The issue of police protection had been raised when Beck first took the job. Beck and his family again considered whether they should ask for a police watch on their home.

They also knew that not all police patrols were thorough. While Beck was in Cyprus, the family had joined him there for a while. For that period, Keith Paull organised for police on patrol in is suburb to check his home and make sure it had not been broken into. This kind of check was available to any member of the public at that time, as police routinely patrolled streets. A book was kept at each police station where residents could record that they were going away, with the dates, and a contact to be informed if anything happened.

It came back to Beck that some police who were given this job found it very boring and did not like having to get out of their cars to make any sort of inspection. There was also the issue of making sure police assigned to protection were on Beck's side, not against him.

Knowing this, Elsie did not believe that the family could necessarily rely on police.

"We discussed this at a family level about what we should do, and it came up about police protection," said Beck.

"None of us wanted that because we didn't know who we could trust, and for all we knew it might be somebody in league with the people who were making the threats.

"Our children knew some of these police that were around, and they weren't very impressed with them.

"It's pathetic that we had to think along those lines."

The potential was there for the threats to be carried out, if Beck's opponents had chosen. But Beck never blinked and his family were staunchly behind him. Beck and Elsie's friends and family were also very supportive, and gave them great encouragement and helped them to feel less alone.

Elsie Beck later confided to Kevin Perkins about how difficult the period was for her. "All the time I wished Mervyn wasn't doing that kind of work," she said. "I wasn't happy about it at all. The children were my main worry—the suggestion that their lives were threatened for something their father was doing.

"There was a whole series of threats. Mervyn knew more about them than I did. I guess I like to be a bit of an ostrich and put my head in the sand. (Still), it affected me a great deal. I became irritable and depressed.

"I was home alone most of the time as Mervyn was out on raids and rarely came home before the early hours, He'd always ring in to check if I was all right. One afternoon, after leaving work, I decided to go shopping. He'd been trying to ring me at home and could not reach me.

"After I arrived home, he came charging in to see if everything was all right.

"There were several incidents like that. He worried about his family."

Elsie revealed that there was one threat which Beck took particularly seriously. "On that occasion he gave me written instructions on what to do in case something happened to him," she said. "He didn't tell me who made the threat, but I felt he knew who it was and the instructions he left me would have culminated in the person being brought to justice. I still have those instructions.

"It got to the stage where I asked Mervyn, not once but several times, if he'd let the whole thing drop and stop doing that work for all our sakes.

"But he's a very determined man. Nobody can frighten Mervyn out of doing anything he feels he must do.

"I know his job's always come first. Not that his family came second because he was always there if we needed him."

* * * *

Shortly before Christmas 1979 Bill Allen, now Assistant Commissioner, rang Beck to tell him he had accumulated ten rest days, and ordered him to take them, starting the following Monday. This plus the public holidays would keep Beck out of the squad for a lengthy period.

Beck had been given permission by Lees to work whatever hours he considered necessary. He did not want to take holidays and lose momentum or control of the squad. There were targets lined up, and informants from other towns who were booked to come to Sydney.

Most of all, he knew that the illegal operators would soon take advantage if the pressure on them was eased in any way.

Usually, no one in the executive offices cared how long he worked or how much leave was due to him. This order seemed more designed to get rid of him than to give him a break. However, Allen refused to back down and Beck realised that a bit of time at home would be good for him, Elsie and the family.

As usual Beck worked throughout the weekend, but he came to work early on Monday 17 December to prepare a short report to Lees about the management of 21 Division, before he took leave. Beck wanted greater control over who was working under his command, but to achieve this, he argued for a change in the chain of command above him.

Over the years 21 Division had always been answerable directly to the commissioner. Neville Wran had changed that, handing responsibility for the division to Bill Allen personally, initially as Chief Superintendent and now as Assistant Commissioner.

In a carefully worded submission, Beck argued respectfully that the division should be returned to the direct control of the Commissioner, because of its special nature. If that happened, the division leader would also have more control and more time, as he would only have to report to one supervisor.

After sending off the report, Beck had a word to his deputy, Ron Flood, who would lead the squad in Beck's absence. Beck made it clear that although he would not be coming to work, he wanted to be kept informed of any major developments and was only as far away as his phone (mobile phones were not invented but Beck resolved to stay home, close to his landline, as much as possible.)

In fact Beck found it very hard to put any distance between himself and his work. On his first day off, he spoke to a contact who told him about SP operations at Charmhaven on the NSW Central Coast and Bowral in the Southern Highlands. Beck promptly rang Flood and told him to send teams to those places, resulting in the arrest of five principals at Charmhaven for SP bookmaking.

Despite his fretting, Beck enjoyed the time with Elsie and their children. The festive season passed without incident but as the new year ticked over, he was keen to get back to work.

When he rang Flood for an update on 4 January, he received unwelcome news about orders from Allen.

The first order related to an upcoming by-election. The NSW Treasurer, longstanding Labor MP Jack (John) Renshaw had announced his retirement from Parliament. A by-election was to be held in his electorate, Castlereagh, on January 29.

Renshaw had held the seat for Labor since 1941. It was a country electorate to the northeast of Dubbo. Although it had attracted little attention from Beck to date, Bill Allen had issued an instruction to

Flood that no gaming and betting police could be send into the area until the election was over.

The seat was being closely fought between Labor and the then Country Party (later the Nationals). According to Allen, the Labor Party and the Wran Government believed that a raid from Beck's squad could antagonise voters and affect their chances of retaining the seat, especially if a raid was held on polling day, which was also a race day.

Flood was not happy about this and neither was Beck when he found out. Beck saw it as the latest in the string of restrictions Allen had imposed on the squad.

The second order was even more incendiary. Almost as soon as Beck had gone on leave, Allen had told Flood that the squad was no longer permitted to undertake any raids in Newcastle.

Although he was still on holiday, Beck rang Allen and told him that as far as he was concerned, neither order was acceptable. The squad had a job to do regardless of politics, and it had the legal authority to go to Newcastle. Allen said he was not interested in Beck's opinion and refused to discuss the orders further, as Beck was on leave.

In the event, no raids were conducted within the Castlereagh electorate during the election period. But Beck was incensed that, once again, limits were being put on his police. The order regarding the by-election was in breach of a strict rule that police, judges and public servants should never play politics and assist one political party over another. As he noted at the time. it was highly unlikely that any other police duties were put on hold in the by-election area, although it was possible that police patrols had been increased to convince the voters that laws were being properly enforced.

As for Allen's instruction to stay away from Newcastle, Beck could only assume that, once again, the Raiders were doing their job too thoroughly for the liking of some.

When Beck got back to work the following Monday, he discovered even more meddling from Allen.

In December, Allen had directed that the gaming and betting squad assist with armed hold-up duties as required. Beck did not object, as he understood that workloads could vary and was happy for his men to take part in criminal work. On his return, he found this assistance had been expanded so that the gaming and betting staff were diverted to armed hold-up duties for two full days of the week.

Given the amount of work in their own area, the order could not be seen as anything less than an attempt to reduce the number of raids on illegal gambling operations.

Jim Lees was on holiday. Beck appealed to Acting Commissioner, Roy Whitelaw, who asked Beck for a full report, which he provided before the end of the week.

"Mr Whitelaw,

"Enclosed is the gaming and betting roster showing on Thursdays and Fridays at Mr Allen's direction gaming and betting police are mainly confined to armed hold-up patrols. Wednesday being a race day is generally one when information comes to hand about SP betting on Friday nights, Saturdays and Sunday nights. When on armed hold-up duties on Thursdays and Fridays the gaming and betting staff are not able to seek the information and have insufficient time to follow up what information they gain on the Wednesday.

"Thursday, Friday, Saturday and Sunday nights are the main gaming and betting nights and in fact this can be said about any night of the week when we consider last Tuesday night when 46 people were arrested for illegal gaming..."

"Trainees are added to the 6 am shifts, bringing those on gaming and betting at the present time to six and five on Saturday nights. In a city as large as Sydney, a staff such as this in my opinion is most inadequate to control gaming and betting. At the present time two men only are engaged on the 6 pm shift to cover the city on Sunday nights."

Whitelaw, a Deputy Commissioner, did not have the same difficulty standing up to Allen as Lees. As soon as he received Beck's report, he ordered the gaming and betting squad back to its primary duties.

Beck also took the opportunity to talk to Whitelaw about Allen's order to stay out of Newcastle, where Beck believed entrenched police corruption was closely linked to the illegal gambling scene.

As Acting Commissioner, Whitelaw immediately overturned Allen's order. He told Beck he could go to Newcastle and take whatever action was necessary. Relieved and grateful, Beck did not hesitate in lining up new targets in the city.

When Beck told Allen he had new orders, Allen took some time before responding. It appeared he did not think lightly about standing up to Whitelaw.

Instead, he attempted to appease Beck.

"Look, I don't mind where you go, provided you tell me in advance where you are sending people," he said.

Beck refrained from laughing at the suggestion that this would be a good deal.

"Commissioner Lees told me not to give out advance notice to anyone. Those are my orders."

"Well MY orders are that you can't go to Newcastle unless I am told in advance, and give my approval," Allen replied forcefully.

Beck could see they were at a standstill. He decided to defer the conversation until Lees was back. He had no intention of conducting raids which were likely to end in failure. Newcastle was a hotbed of illegal gambling, but he had plenty of other targets to keep him occupied.

"I'll keep you informed," he said, closing the conversation without promising anything about advance warning.

As it turned out, when Lees returned to work and Beck raised the Newcastle ban, his support for Beck was lukewarm. Lees agreed that the squad had the right to go to Newcastle, but he was not prepared to directly counter Allen's demand for advance warning.

Beck protested that providing advance information would inevitably results in failures, but Lee was adamant that he could not overturn Allen's order without a strong reason.

"You'll have to see how it goes, Merv. Let me know."

Beck agreed but he left disheartened. He had already decided there would be no further raids in Newcastle until Allen's order was lifted.

There was one more unwelcome intervention by Allen during Beck's enforced absence. When Ron Flood suggested that he watch his correspondence in future, Beck asked what he meant.

"I don't know much about it," Flood said nervously, "but I think there might have been some mischief going on while you were away."

"I left you in charge, you tell me what the mischief is," replied Beck.

Flood then revealed that he believed Bill Allen had read Beck's report to Lees about restoring the Commissioner's direct control of 21 Division. He did not want to get involved and would not elaborate, saying only that he thought there was a problem.

The report had been typed up by Beck's secretary-stenographer. Beck dictated all his letters; she would take them down in shorthand, before typing them up. This was done with the special report on the Division's management, and Beck had sent it off through the internal mail system to Lees.

It was marked confidential, but someone—later established to be Hermes—had tipped Allen off that Beck had made a special report to the Commissioner.

Beck asked the secretary if anything unusual had happened.

"Yes, it did," she said. "Mr Allen came over and asked me for my shorthand books, and he took them away."

"He didn't bring them back until the next day."

Beck was fuming. He was sorry that his secretary had been dragged into the tussle between himself and Allen. As she was employed by the Police Department as a public servant, not by the Police Force, Beck went to Police Headquarters to get advice.

He demanded to see a member of the departmental executive. One of the senior executives, with the initials NS, took him into his office When he heard the story, he confirmed that Allen had no legal right to take the notes, which were considered to be Beck's property as they recorded his dictation.

Beck wanted to lodge a formal complaint, but the official thought this was a bad idea. Allen might be in the wrong, he suggested, but he had also just been appointed Assistant Commissioner by the Premier.

Beck found this interesting advice from the apolitical public service, but accepted it. When Lees returned from holiday he gave Beck the same advice. Whether Allen found out that Beck knew or not, he never said a word to Beck about the notebooks or the report to Lees.

As time went on, Beck realised Lees was not going to provide a formal response to his report. It seemed to have fallen into an abyss, and he was left to continue his crackdown under command of an increasing hostile superior officer.

In early January, however, Beck was delighted to have the full backing of Acting Commissioner Whitelaw. The support inspired him and the men to take on one of the biggest targets they had so far failed to knock off, the famous and notorious Goulburn Club in the street of that name in Sydney city.

The casino, conducted by George Walker, was very well fortified.

It was on the first floor, with a large man as the doorkeeper. In addition to the locked steel doors, there was an electric beam across the stairway which would sound a warning if a person was coming up. The doorman would see who was coming and if it was police, the doors were locked immediately and securely.

Looking up at the building, however, Beck saw a small window high up on the side of the building. The window was unbarred, and open, but it was about 40 metres above ground. From their experience, the team believed this window very likely led to a small room off the gaming room and was the key to a raid.

Beck pondered what to do. After the Kirrawee raid he had been banned from using the Rescue Squad, but he clearly needed a very long ladder. Borrowing, buying or hiring one were options, none of them attractive or very practical. But there might be another way if he was very careful.

While the Rescue Squad were not to take part in any raids, the decree did not apply to their equipment. Beck went to the Rescue Squad base at midnight and asked to see what large ladders they had. They showed him a long metal ladder which was just what he needed.

The only way to move the big ladder, which was extremely heavy, was on the purpose-built truck. The Rescue Squad members agreed to transport the ladder to Campbell St in Haymarket.

There Beck, with two of his men, Detective Tomic and Constable Dean McGuire, took possession of the ladder. Struggling under its bulk and weight, they lifted it up to their shoulders and staggered around the corner and for three long blocks. It was about 2.30 am so there was not a lot of traffic which was just as well as they made quite a sight, especially as there was no sign of a fire nearby.

Raising the ladder was even more difficult than carrying it. The whole raiding party gathered around and, with much grunting and groaning, succeeded in propping it up high against the brick building side, as close as they could to the little window.

Then one of the intrepid young police climbed high up the ladder and reached the window. While the team below watched with bated breath, he prised it open and then fell through to the inside.

He found himself in an office which doubled as a bedroom. To his astonishment, immediately under the window was a bed and in it was a woman sleeping, whom they thought to be the wife of the casino proprietor.

The young policeman climbed over her and stood up next to the bed to make sure she was still asleep. Then he walked very softly across the room and opened the door. On the other side of a corridor he could see into a large room. There were half a dozen tables, each with a group of people gathered around and games under way.

The policeman walked straight out into it and declared who he was, to the shock and displeasure of everyone present. The constable demanded that they open the door, and so Beck and the other team members were able to get in.

They arrested the manager, who turned out to be George Walker's son, and another man for conducting the illegal games, and 16 other people for taking part, while the cards, tables and other paraphernalia were seized as evidence.

The arrested people were taken to Central Police Station, but Beck's job was not done. He and his weary men had to make sure the ladder was safely returned. Getting it down from the side of the building was a highly risky affair, but thankfully with the help of the solid brick wall and the empty street they were able to slide it down to the ground without a crash. Then Beck and two team members lifted it again and carried it back down the street, from where it was collected by the Rescue Squad with their truck.

It was 5 am and dawn when Beck finished for the night. He was back at work at 9am to see Whitelaw, who was delighted with the night's results.

(Later, Beck discovered that George Walker was a friend of the former Police Commissioner, Mervyn Wood. The Goulburn Club had been 'off limits' for police for many years, and the raid was a major symbolic blow against illegal gambling.)

With Whitelaw's encouragement, Beck determined to back up from his big success by attempting to snatch another major prize that same evening—a hit on Bruce Hardin's previously off limits casino in Rozelle.

It was Friday 11 January, Beck deployed a small team of observers to gather more information about 680 Darling St. In the late afternoon they returned to the office to brief Beck, who resolved to take action that very night.

At 12 midnight two of the squad arrived at the rear of the building. They found a vantage point and with binoculars, were able to confirm that gambling was taking place in the casino. After they phoned this information back to Beck, he sent an officer for a warrant and tbe squad swung into action.

The casino was located in a building on the corner of Victoria Rd and Darling St. Downstairs was a shoe shop entered off Victoria Rd, while the casino had the whole first floor, comprising three rooms, and was entered through a plain wooden door next to a vacant shop in Darling St. The only sign for customers said, "Press buzzer please".

Beck's preferred option was to get one of his police officers inside the casino, in disguise and without force, by entering with some of the real clients. Luck was with them, and in this way the first police succeeded in getting entry at 3.15 am.

Inside, there were games of two-up and blackjack in progress. Blue lights and a buffet of meat rissoles and various salads added atmosphere. The clientele was mainly Italian and Greek men in casual clothes, not the wealthy crowd seen elsewhere.

When Beck's police revealed themselves there were two staff and 19 people gambling. When the rest of the raiding party was let in, they seized money, cards and tables.

One of the staff made a comment. "You fellows are not what I expected."

"What do you mean by that?" responded Beck.

"I expected you to come in and walk all over us, we've heard you're pretty tough and you do these things."

"No, you've been given the wrong information. That's not the way we work at all," was Beck's honest reply.

Hardin was not there; but Beck soon found him, hiding behind a door in the ladies' toilet. He was crouched down with his head tucked into his chest. Beck arrested him.

Although the club premises were expensively decorated, with statues and paintings on the wall, little attention had been paid to safety. All of the effort had been devoted to ensuring that people could not get in, with no attention to the ability of people to get out in an emergency. The windows were barred and the only exit was through the steel door onto the stairway, Beck regarded the place as a serious potential fire trap.

While the arrested people were taken to Balmain police station to be charged., Beck remained behind waiting for the police scientific officer. In case there were allegations of the kind that arose from the Kirrawee casino raid, he wanted to ensure he had detailed photographs of the casino after the squad had left.

He instructed his squad members to return when the charging was finished.

Beck was pleased to be able to charge Hardin with conducting a common gaming house. Two others, John Radcliffe and Ross Escott, were charged with assisting to conduct a gaming house and the others were charged with being found there.

When his men returned, Beck asked for a copy of the police occurrence records from Balmain station for the evening. He looked them over and noted that all the relevant details were correct.

It was later discovered, however, that in the actual charge book Hardin was written as 'Harting', despite his correct name being entered on the occurrence sheet. This was the name he was subsequently charged under, at Balmain Magistrates Court on 15 January. 'Harting' pleaded guilty and was fined $400 by Mr G Gorman SM.

The Balmain police—whether by accident or not—also got Hardin's address wrong, recording it as 56 Kingston St Haberfield, when he actually lived at 127 Homebush Road Strathfield— described at the time as "a $1.5 million home".

Hardin was an associate of George Freeman and Graham Palmer, both of whom had previously been hit by Beck, and well known to the media. It was also rumoured that his sister was married to a detective at a city police station, although this was not confirmed.

Although the mistake over his name was corrected on the court charge sheets the following day, it was picked up by *the Sun-Herald* newspaper in early March, leading to questions in NSW Parliament.

In a follow-up article, *the Sun-Herald* reported that Attorney General Frank Walker had told Parliament that Commissioner Jim Lees had ordered an urgent inquiry into how the wrong details were recorded for Hardin. The inquiry was conducted by Senor Commissioner, Roy Whitelaw, and resulted in disciplinary action against the Balmain police officer who made the error.

Beck was annoyed by the mistake. But if the intention was to let Hardin escape the law, it was a failure. Hardin was formally identified by his fingerprints, and the incorrect name was added to the record as a known alias.

An English croupier, Jane Bathurst, who worked at the Rozelle casino later went public with revelations about its attitude to clients. She told *People* magazine that staff were told customers at the casino were "to be watched, fought and robbed".

"The odds were biased heavily in favour of the house, and tables were closed when they were winning to ensure high profits," Bathurst claimed. She also claimed that prostitutes were provided free of charge as "bait" for the customers.

After raiding Hardin's club, Beck's team finished up quite late in the morning. Beck was on a high after finally being able to crack the Rozelle casino. He decided not to go home to sleep but just continue for the rest of the day.

He was very happy to tell Roy Whitelaw about the second successful casino raid, and Whitelaw was full of praise. Whitelaw thought Beck might like to share the news with Superintendent Brotherson, the district commander for Number One Division, or Central as it was known.

This was the division Beck had previously commanded which covered a large part of the inner city from Balmain ad Rozelle to Chinatown up to King Street. Whitelaw said Brotherson might like to know that 88 people had been arrested for gaming and betting within his district in the previous week.

It was well known that Hardin had a large yacht moored on the harbour, where he would often entertain important people including politicians and senior police.

One of them was the head of the CIB who had told Beck in person that he and his wife had been guests of Bruce Hardin on his boat. Beck knew that the CIB chief would have known full well about Hardin's gambling interests.

It saddened Beck to know that senior police were consorting with criminals, apparently with no shame. Their disregard for the ideals of the Police Force was highlighted by an interesting postscript to the Rozelle casino raid, many years later.

It was the 1990s and Beck was long retired when a man approached him on the street and asked if Beck remembered him. Beck replied that he did, but only vaguely.

The man explained that he had been a doorkeeper at the Rozelle casino when Beck's team raided it the first time following the green light from Allen. The raid was a letdown, with no one but two cleaners on the premises. This man claimed that if the Raiders had come 10 minutes earlier on that night they would have found gambling in full swing. Moreover, among the clientele was one of Australia's most powerful men.

When Beck pressed him, the man said it was media mogul Kerry Packer, owner at the time of the Nine Network among other assets. He became Australia's richest man in the late 1990s.

"What would you have done if you had found Packer there in the casino?" the man asked Beck.

Beck did not hesitate. "He would have been charged, like anyone else."

"Don't you reckon, if you'd done that, you would have been moved overnight from your position?" asked the man.

"Anything can happen," Beck agree. "But I doubt it. Who would be prepared to stand up publicly and argue that Packer should be exempt from the law just because he's rich and powerful?"

The man then mused on whether the media would have picked up the story, if Packer had been arrested. Again, Beck had no doubts: the Fairfax and Murdoch media were direct rivals of Packer and unlikely to offer him any favours.

"That's good to know," the man said. "It's often been a talking point amongst us fellows as to what would have happened; and in a way it's a pity that you didn't arrest him!" He shook Beck's hand and they parted.

(The Packer family continued its association with gambling. In 1999 it bought Crown casino in Melbourne and Kerry's son James became a major player in the international casino industry, before a sudden change of heart and a major divestment from around 2016.)

CHAPTER TEN

Loyalty comes in all forms

Beck and his Raiders had become household names, thanks to the attention of the media. Some of Beck's superiors including the executive could not bear to deal with journalists and would not give interviews or even make statements. They also sent out the message to their officers that journalists were not to be trusted.

This was never Beck's attitude. He could also see that the resistance of some police to media attention was counterproductive, creating mistrust and often resulting in adverse publicity. He also believed that he had nothing to fear from exposure and supported the right of the public to know what was happening, and the media reporting could be useful. As in all of his endeavours, throughout his career he dealt with journalists straight and square and expected the same in return.

In general the media coverage of the Raiders was very positive, and individual journalists were privately and publicly supportive. The police reporters for newspapers, radio and television were keen to cover the gaming and betting squad's activities, and some would turn up at the scene shortly after a raid had been carried out. Sometimes Beck asked, and received, the assistance of senior reporters and editors in refraining from disclosing details that might spoil further investigations.

Beck regarded their support as an important indicator of public sentiment. In addition, the publicity encouraged members of the public to come forward with new information, often seeking out Beck in person.

On the other hand, some reporters made it clear in their writing and their manner they disagreed with what Beck was doing. Beck was warned by several media figures whom he trusted to be wary of others who were regular gamblers and one high profile television journalist who, it was claimed, was used by crime figures to lay off bets.

Despite this warning, Beck was stung by a rare spate of criticism in two articles in *the Daily Telegraph* immediately after the squad's huge successes against the casinos in mid-January 1980.

Beck was sure the stories were based on information fed from within the Police Force. Whitelaw's sensible advice was to ignore them, but Beck found this hard. He knew bad publicity undermined the morale of the squad, which was hard enough to maintain.

Then he had another setback. All he wanted was to be able to get on with the job, but Commissioner Lees had come back to work and almost immediately told Beck he had to take a break from normal duties to carry out a mandatory training course.

Together with other senior police, he was required to attend a three-week management course at the Shore Motel in Artarmon, from 23 January to 11 February.

Three weeks seemed like an eternity to Beck, especially as it was a residential course. No matter how good the training, he argued, his duties should come first. To add to Beck's misgivings, he was rung at this time by a contact in State Parliament, who told him he believed the timing was no accident, and that Beck was deliberately being sent away following complaints from gambling operators. Ron Flood could lead the team but Beck knew Bill Allen would take advantage of his absence, if possible, to hobble the team.

Beck resolved to keep his hands on the reins at 21 Division as much as possible, even while he was attending the course. He arranged for selected members of his squad to meet him each day to brief him on the latest information they had received about illegal gambling premises, and receive his suggestions on targets, times and personnel.

Every night while on the course, Beck would also ring home and speak to Elsie. But one night there was no answer. Already agitated by his forced absence from the squad, he feared the worst in view of the threats that had been received.

As soon as he hung up, Beck swung into action. He left his motel room in a rush and raced out to the carpark, driving straight home with his heart thumping. When he pulled up outside the house, he could see the curtains were open and a light was on. Elsie was as surprised to see him as he was to see her. She was safe and there had been no drama, she had just arrived home a bit later than usual, after visiting a friend who regularly played tennis with her.

During one of the management course lectures, Beck noticed Justice Edwin Lusher sitting in the room, listening in. Lusher had previously conducted the inquiry into legalisation of casinos for the Wran Government in 1976, research for which took him round the world. He had recommended that if legal casinos were to be introduced in NSW, they should be modelled on the up-market and privately run British gaming houses. His recommendations were not taken up, but Lusher was appointed to the NSW Supreme Court in September 1977.

At this time, he was on another assignment for Premier Wran, conducting an inquiry into police administration.

The inquiry had been triggered by the Cessna case and suppression of tapes made from phone taps on George Freeman's phone, which had led to Merv Wood's sudden resignation as Commissioner.

Lusher was the second choice for the job, after Justice Ronald Cross withdrew due to ill health on June 22, 1979. Although the inquiry was originally supposed to focus on corruption, Wran had switched the focus to administration and structure.

Lusher appeared at a second lecture, and on this occasion, he caught Beck's eye. He approached Beck and took him aside for a word.

"Mr Beck, I wish to talk to you while here and seek some of your advice," he said.

Beck was more than happy to oblige. "I look forward to meeting you. I have some important matters I would like to discuss with you too, that I think require your attention."

But although Beck saw Lusher several further times, sitting in on the lectures, he seemed to have changed his mind. He avoided Beck's gaze and did not make contact again.

Lusher had a long and quirky connection with Neville Wran, and with the NSW Police Force. As a barrister he was reported to have been ejected from the District Court by a Justice Prior for what the judge called "dumb insolence", forcing his junior—Neville Wran—to take over the case.

He also appeared for Police Association members at the Moffitt Royal Commission on organised crime where, according to Independent NSW MP John Hatton, Lusher claimed there was no organised crime in NSW.

* * * *

While Beck had keenly tackled many of the regional gambling centres, he was keenly aware that one had so far escaped his attention—Broken Hill.

When he had first taken over 21 Division, one of the first calls he had received was from a journalist in Adelaide drawing his attention to the illegal gambling in Broken Hill and asking whether he would do anything about it.

"Now that you've taken over 21 Division will you be going to Broken Hill, because nobody seems to be going there," the journalist said. He said the situation was a farce, as mainly working-class people from Adelaide were driving up the highway to Broken Hill, in about six hours, gambling all night and driving back.

"What's going on there," he said, "is nobody's business. It's spoken about in police circles that it's a protected area."

"As far as I'm concerned there's no place that I will not be able to go," replied Beck. Despite Allen's attempts to control him, that remained the case.

Beck had heard snippets about gambling at Broken Hill, apparently immune to police action, for decades. It was lore in the Police Force that when former Commissioner Fred Hanson was stationed there, early in his career, he made a habit of showing newcomers the two-up games on offer. As head of the gaming squad, Beck had further been told by one of his police, John Garnett, who was friends with Pro Hart, that the artist had been introduced to two-up by Hanson.

In 1970, Beck had been told by a senior detective that a few years earlier, he and another detective had been sent to Broken Hill to observe a two-up 'school'. They had no difficulty finding the place and infiltrating the game pretending to be tourists. They were surprised, however, to find the players included a local inspector of police. The pair of detectives reported this back to their supervisor in Sydney but heard no more about action being taken.

The story was corroborated by a superintendent who worked with Beck when he was stationed at Hornsby. The superintendent told Beck that during his posting in Broken Hill, three two-up games were played openly and all night at Broken Hill. The superintendent claimed police ranked as high as inspectors had been summarily removed from Broken Hill after complaining about the gambling, and illegal hotel hours, to police headquarters.

The Hornsby colleague also claimed that each week, money from Broken Hill was sent to Sydney to be distributed to senior police and politicians, at City Tattersall's club. It was delivered each Monday by a fellow referred to as Mr Big, who allegedly was a leading trade unionist. As a result of this cosy arrangement, the superintendent alleged, Broken Hill had long been a 'no go' area for 21 Division.

All of this made Beck very keen to break the deal. Bill Allen told him that the 'Silver City' was too remote to be policed by a Sydney-based squad. Beck argued that while it had been remote in his grandfather's day, that was no longer the case with regular plane fights available. Nonetheless he had not found time to focus on the issue when, in January 1980, he was contacted directly by a senior executive at the NSW TAB about his concerns about what was happening in the far west of the state.

Beck recorded in his book of notes at the time:

"On the 22 January 1980, I was contacted by George Ralph of the TAB who stated that there had been complaints by their district TAB officer at Broken Hill about the large-scale SP betting there and how it had badly affected the three TAB agencies there. According to Ralph their representative had visited a man named Keenan, President of the Barrier Council and complained to him that SP betting was rife in every hotel there and it was alleged that 52 SP bettors were there and something would have to be done about it.

"Keenan stated if any action were taken to curtail SP betting it would ...drive them to the telephone betting, thus depriving them of the ordinary SP operation. He further is alleged to have said, 'I told that silly Police Inspector here the same thing when he came and saw me about it'.

"George Ralph asked could 21 Division go and clean up the place and I told him I would gladly do so if given permission by the Commissioner of Police, as I felt that Broken Hill was in New South Wales and it should be on all fours with the rest of the State. It appears that SP operators are using the big stick of the unions to protect them. George Ralph told me the three TAB agencies at Broken Hill had the lowest bet take of any agencies in NSW."

Beck notified Assistant Commissioner Whitelaw of the TAB request. He wanted to act quickly and started making plans for the squad to fly to Broken Hill and use rental cars to conduct their raids.

But Whitelaw was no longer Acting Commissioner and when he got back to Beck the following day he was not as positive as usual. He had spoken to Lees and before any action was taken, Lees wanted Ralph to come into Police headquarters and discuss the problem.

When Beck rang Ralph, he did not like this idea. Ralph had hoped that the Police Force could take the cue from him and initiate action, without him getting involved. He did not want to be seen to be interfering or sidestepping his own Minister especially given the apparent political sensitivities.

Under pressure, from Beck and Whitelaw, Ralph reluctantly agreed that he and his senior officer would make an appointment with the Commissioner. Before this could happen, however, the TAB chief executive. Robinson became involved. He suggested they wait until the following day, 25 January, when another senior executive, Al Smith returned to work. Smith was more familiar with the Broken Hill situation and in the past had brokered an agreement between the TAB and the Barrier Council, the council of trade unions which had effective control of Broken Hill.

As this dialogue unfolded, Beck put his plans on hold.

"It appears there exists a big difficulty in this area, hence the caution displayed by all concerned," he wrote. "Further developments will prove interesting. I am prepared to lead the men there as soon as I am given the word."

When Al Smith returned to work, he confirmed there as indeed a "big difficulty". He was adamant that the TAB did not want police action taken at Broken Hill, and Ralph and Robinson immediately backed down.

Lees then passed instructions to Beck that he did not have permission to fly to the town and to abandon his plans. Lees used the same argument as Bill Allen, that Broken Hill was 'so remote' and getting there would cost a lot of money and time.

Apparently, the official police view was that Broken Hill could be a law unto itself as far as gaming and betting was concerned. Beck wondered if any other law was able to be broken without penalty in remote areas of NSW, but Lees' position was a barrier that not even his sledgehammer could remove.

* * * *

In January and February 1980, rumours were swirling that Beck would soon be transferred out of 21 Division, and Beck himself knew this was possible.

For some of his opponents it could not happen soon enough. Through acquaintances in the business world, Beck would hear snippets of what was being said about him behind closed doors. On the other hand, given his huge public profile any attempt to injure or kill Beck would have generated massive publicity and public outrage.

It would almost certainly have made it impossible for the Wran Government, or its successors, to go ahead with establishment of a legal casino industry.

While Beck's future on the squad was debated, one of those arguing strongly that he should be retained was Professor Alfred McCoy.

"Instead of (focussing on) the migrant gambling houses and small pub SPs as in the past police crackdowns, Inspector Beck's blitz was a frontal assault on the big syndicate operators," McCoy wrote.

"Under Beck's leadership, 21 Squad zealots (sic) raided a Tweed Heads SP operation with a $100m turnover, smashed down the door of a Sydney shop with 40 phones and discovered an SP computer centre in Ultimo with 10,000 phone accounts.

"These raids produced impressive results but they are only the first steps. Despite enormous losses and disruption of some of their network, the big SP syndicates can easily recover if the pressure stops now.

"If in fact the crackdown stops soon the five major SPs will bounce back bigger than ever. The surviving medium and small operators swept away in the blitz do not have the resources to resume operations in the time of strict enforcement.

"Unable to hire the support of police and politicians, the few remaining independent SP bookmakers will be forced out of business, leaving the field clear for the multi-million-dollar syndicates.

"If Commissioner Lees and Inspector Beck are allowed to continue their campaign, it will be possible to bring the great majority of the state's betters within the fold of the TAB within the next few years.

"The continued success of the anti-betting campaign is, in a very real sense, vital to the future well-being of this state. Police have gathered strong evidence to show that the top SP men have shifted their capital and contracts into financial bulk shipments of high-grade heroin from South East Asia.

"No longer an innocent Saturday pastime for the State's working class, SP bookmaking has become merchant banking for organised crime, providing both a front and finance for Sydney's booming heroin trade. The successful eradication of the SP business will destroy a support system vital for the growth of the narcotics traffic.

"The survival of syndicated SP bookmaking will make the solution of the city's drug problem far more difficult.

"Next time you step up to the bar of your hotel to talk to Fred your friendly bookmaker or pick up your phone SP to place a small bet, just think about it for a minute.

"Remember you could be financing your own child's first shot of heroin."

McCoy was a very credible source on the drug trade. His views confirmed Beck's belief that the job he was doing was worthwhile.

He was shutting down the illegal gaming and betting because it was against the law, and the more he saw of those involved, the more convinced he became that the law was correct and that the SPs and casinos were supporting much greater evils. He lamented that many in the NSW Government, including the Premier, did not share this view, for whatever reasons.

"If the governments were genuine in wanting to stamp out SP betting and illegal gaming for the very reasons explained by Professor McCoy, the police effort could be supported by strong legislation," he wrote.

"However, in NSW there is no penal clause regarding SP betting and that is where the great weakness comes.

"It is to be hoped that with (a) change of government this will be seen and stronger efforts taken.

"It has been my experience there is a strong tie up between politicians, police, SP betting and illegal gaming operators, and this will always be until such time as the Government becomes—to use the old Australian colloquialism—fair dinkum."

These doubts about the Wran Government/s real motives for appointing him were enough to dent even Beck's optimism. There were times when exhaustion, constant pressure, lack of support from his senior officers and dislike from many other police generated the melancholy he did his best to shelter his men from.

When he tried to rationalise this, Beck saw the opposition to the work he and the squad were doing as a symptom of deep and wide corruption within the Police Force.

The silent majority of police appeared to admire the squad's work, and the number of applicants hoping to join the squad seemed to suggest this. Yet often Beck found that practical support from the senior ranks was often lacking.

The police colleagues he discussed his situation with agreed that the illegal gambling industry and the corruption it bred were an embarrassment and a discredit to the force as a whole. But there were many who were happy for Beck to carry the sword but would not pick up arms to fight with him.

In a despondent moment, Beck typed up his thoughts on paper.

"Mr Allen has undermined the morale of the staff at 21 Division by his general attitude of picking on matters within the Division which are obvious points taken to erode the authority of the OIC (officer in charge).

"First, he wanted rosters changed and when changed, wanted them back to what they were. He has introduced duty pads for all police in this division, not previously required, (and) lengthy reports on all occasions SP bookmakers are arrested in hotels.

"This is understood by the men, however the time it takes prevents them from gaming and betting duties.

"He has interfered with detectives' duties without reference to the assistant commissioner for crime, called for their diaries, made remarks they would not be there long, and adversely affected their outlook to their duties.

"The reality is he has a spy system within the division which (I) proved by allowing those police he has informing him (a reference to Hermes) to hear things I made up, which Allen has repeated back to me in his conversations.

"(He) has adversely made reports to the government re gaming not being out of the ordinary when 21 Division was revamped, yet everyone knows it was and arrests proved this."

Beck then referred to the two month ban on raiding the Rozelle casino, Allen's insistence that Bradbury be given a car and men from the Division; his direction that he be advised in advance of any raids on country towns; the ban on raids in Newcastle; and his uncooperative attitude after Beck refused to comply with his request to stay out of Chinatown.

"Newspaper correspondents have informed me he rubbishes me about the town, claims anyone could do my job," Beck continued. "They believe ... he is jealous. They consider he is a liar.

"He required I tell him of all premises I intended to raid in advance which I have not always complied with, He resents Mr Lees and Whitelaw even talking to me....

"I have reached the stage I do not trust Mr Allen, I believe he will embarrass Neville Wran. I do not desire to work under his control as the men do not and if the (Commissioner) had not prevailed upon me to stay, I would have left the Division in November of '79. I receive more advice about being careful of his anti-21 Division actions than I do about any other person."

Beck had other reasons to be concerned about Allen's motives, which he kept to himself. A senior detective at the CIB had gone out of his way to tell Beck that Allen had held a meeting with Dixon St identities and 'big time' gambling operators from Kings Cross. Beck could not dismiss the report.

He knew that the campaign against him, attempting to spread rumours, lies and character assassination, was motivated by greed. His predecessors in gaming and betting had created an environment where the ill-gotten gains of graft and corruption were accepted by many as a 'bonus' on top of their Police Force salary.

Rumours and allegations were also levelled at other members of the Raiders.

Former 21 Division head Pat Watson was known to have attended the Kensington barbecue set meeting where moves against Beck were discussed, and he was intent on doing whatever he could to foil Beck's squad. Knowing the system, Watson thought he could throw the squad off balance by forcing it on the defensive by making a false allegation.

Watson phoned one of the sergeants on Beck's squad to tell him that two other squad members were organising collection of corruption money and were being watched. The sergeant concerned passed this on to Beck at the first opportunity.

Beck thought the tip was interesting, but also suspicious. He had been told that corrupt members of 21 Division had spread rumours about honest members of the squad in the past, as a way to reduce their credibility and encourage them to leave. This looked like the same tactic, as the two men named were very good workers and Beck considered them both very loyal. The tip just did not ring true, and Watson offered no evidence.

Despite this, Beck referred the claim to Internal Affairs, and also discussed it with Commissioner Lees. Although he trusted the two men involved, he watched them very closely. He was relieved that the observations showed them to be loyal, and that they rejected opportunities for corruption.

Internal Affairs came to the same conclusion. Beck believed Watson's intervention was entirely mischievous, just another of the many attempts to discredit Beck and his team and slow down their continuing blitz on illegal gambling.

As talk of Beck moving on increased, the squad members felt the weight of the forces lined up against them.

After acting for Beck during his absences, Ron Flood told Beck in February 1980 he had had enough of Allen's interference and the stress was making him sick. Other squad members approached Beck and told him openly that they would have to think of going to other duties if Beck was moved.

Flood and Beck were the only two officers on the division, and often that left just one of them doing the work of three. They had been promised a third officer eight months earlier, when they had started off in 21 Division, but still there was no indication that this promise would be kept.

Flood hoped that things would improve but Beck could sense that he was not coping. Beck hoped he could arrange a relieving officer or for extra sergeants to support Flood, but he was not optimistic.

Even Beck admitted the circumstances to be "challenging".

"I am at this stage concerned that pressures being applied on Flood and staff are affecting the division," he wrote then. "The other men feel and state that if I leave, that they would want to leave with me. And that's a sorry state of affairs."

Beck went to great lengths to try to change their minds, insisting that it would be undisciplined for them to leave their positions if he was no longer their leader. He appealed to them to stay and do their duty no matter what happened to him or any other officer.

He also insisted there was nothing unique about his abilities and others from his team would be able to do the same job. But as Flood's experience suggested this was probably wildly optimistic: Beck's unrivalled courage, determination and physical stamina were pivotal to the squad's success.

He was touched when one of the men drew a diagram summarising their position.

The Gaming and Betting squad was a wheel. Each spoke represented one of the elements pitted against it: political pressures; Bill Allen's pressures; the outside police who were obstructing and working against them; the SP betting and the gaming syndicates, and tangled up with them, the organised crime figures.

Finally on the outside were the general public, whom the squad was trying to serve but whose opinions could go for or against them.

Another factor which could have been added was the lack of support for Beck in the highest echelons of the Police Force and the NSW Government. This was emphasised to him just as he was getting back into the swing of things after the management course.

For some months before this, Beck's promotion to superintendent had been discussed. After Bill Allen had marked him down, his ratings were all returned to excellent. There was no barrier to his promotion, but it had not been processed.

The promotion would have raised a procedural issue. The special gaming and betting squad, 21 Division was not a senior enough post for a superintendent. There was, however, a precedent for someone of that rank to lead it. The infamous former head of 21 Division, Pat Watson had remained in charge of the division for several months after becoming a superintendent. Beck had canvassed the possibilities with his senior officers and was assured that he could stay on and complete the task as he saw it, when his promotion came through.

On January 23, just before he began the management course, Beck had seen Superintendent Barney Ross, who was president of the Police Officers Association, to ask about his promotion. Ross promised to look into why it was taking so long, as it had been waiting for signature from Premier Wran, as the Minister responsible for the Police Force. Lees and other senior police had repeatedly promised to speak to the Premier to see what was holding it up, but the days went on with no result.

Three days after the management course finished, Thursday 14 February, was Beck's 58th birthday. On what would normally be a happy occasion he had reason to be sad as the day came to an end. Under the police regulations, the promotion to superintendent had to be received before the officer's 58th birthday, because it could not occur less than two years before compulsory retirement at 60.

With the deadline passed and no promotion letter, although Merv said nothing, Elsie could feel his hurt and disappointment. He put his hopes of promotion behind him.

On the following Saturday, 16 February, Beck received a call from a fellow who wanted to see him urgently. The man was very upset and claimed he had been threatened by Lennie McPherson. Beck agreed to meet him the following Sunday morning.

At 10 am Beck met the man as arranged. He was Tim Bristow[22], a 'private eye', club bouncer, former footballer and standover man. Bristow had been convicted in 1976 of assault and sentenced to 18 months in Berrima jail (and was also sentenced to five years in the 1980s for supplying marijuana), but he was also a useful informant.

With Bristow was a well-known journalist. The three got into a car and drove to the car park of Mona Vale Hospital where they could talk.

---

[22] Bristow died in December 2003

Bristow knew a lot of Sydney's leading personalities on both sides of the law. It transpired that he had helped the journalist with a crime series he had been writing, and this had raised McPherson's ire. McPherson had also warned Bristow, he claimed, that if he gave any help to Beck, he would be 'rubbed out'.

Bristow said George Freeman was also on the warpath against 21 Division and was making plans to find someone who wanted to make a name as a hitman, to get rid of Beck, permanently.

Beck had heard this all before. He did not take the threats seriously, although there were clearly people with serious grievances against him. It was not in his nature to think too hard about risk, and he was accustomed to a level of physical danger in his work.

But what Bristow said next was far more worrying. Mention had also been made of something being done to Beck's children, and Freeman had named them and given their ages.

The elder daughters, Elizabeth and Pauline were married and living with their husbands and children. The son Mitchell, then 21, was away working in the country. But 19-year-old Charlene, the youngest, was still living at home. It appeared that Freeman had had someone following Charlene, who reported where she had been with her boyfriend.

The threat to his daughter was something different. Even though he knew criminals often referred to the family when they wanted to intimidate a person, Beck also knew that sometimes the threats were carried out.

"At the time and with the heat of the activities going on, I just accepted threats to myself as gossip and talk and idol threats, being made in the hope of frightening me out of the position," said Beck.

"The only thing that affected me was when they turned on my family. I think that was a natural reaction."

Beck knew that George Freeman had to be taken seriously. He was not only a ruthless and sharp criminal, but a remarkable political and social operator. On one hand, Freeman was friendly with many state politicians, police at both senior and lower ranks, legal figures, and highly placed people in the racing industry, media and business. On the other hand he was a hardened criminal involved in many areas of crime and did not hold back from carrying out threats or revenge when he felt it was needed.

Freeman was at his most dangerous when he was cornered or afraid. Like most criminals he had started as a brutal thug and thief before graduating to wheeling and dealing in organised crime gangs here and overseas. He was also during Beck's time on gaming and betting known as a 'fixer' of trotting and galloping racehorses and races. He could arrange to have a horse doped or a jockey paid to ensure his horses won. People in the know, many of them wealthy businessmen, were believed to have made fortunes over a period of years by following Freeman's racing 'tips'.

Freeman was able to obtain meetings with politicians, judges, magistrates and police where other people had to wait for weeks. He was often featured in the social pages of the Sydney newspapers, while stories about his criminal operations were heavily censored. The editor of a major newspaper told Beck that when a story about Freeman was being prepared, Freeman would get straight onto his legal advisers who would use the threat of defamation to his full advantage. When stories were published, Freeman was always ready with a response before the papers had rolled off the presses.

Beck had hit one of Freeman's SP operations in Glebe as one of his first raids when he took over gaming and betting in 1979. Freeman was not there but his staff were arrested and charged, the phones were seized and the operation was put out of action, at least temporarily. Another premises run by Freeman at Rockdale was also raided by Beck, after which Freeman made sure he was not present at any of the SP operations while Beck remained on the job.

Nonetheless, Beck had to question Bristow's motives for approaching him with this story. Bristow was good at playing both sides. (Bristow was later reported to have stated: "I bribed police for 40 years. I found that the higher I went in society the lower the morals became." In his trial in the mid-1980s, Bristow gave evidence that a number of police at the Chatswood station had thrown 49 packets of marijuana from a window of the detectives' office, and that he had caught them with a towel before loading them into his Mercedes.)

It was quite possible that Bristow had been sent by Freeman to scare Beck off. Beck decided to warn his family to be on heightened alert and take whatever action they could to protect them, but to otherwise carry on as usual.

* * * *

At the end of February 1980, the NSW Police Force got a new minister. Premier Neville Wran finally gave up his second portfolio, giving it to Bill Crabtree.

Soon after this, Beck again turned his attention to Thommo's Two Up School.

After his initial successful raid, the operation had moved to 179 Little Oxford St, which was not much more than a laneway. Security was also tightened.

When the gaming operators realised that taxi drivers were leading police to them, inadvertently, they introduced new rules. Some issued membership cards to their regular clients and only those with a card were allowed in. New players were not allowed unless an existing member introduced the newcomer and vouched for his or her details. Any attempt to get around the rules or otherwise fool the management was dealt with severely. These arrangements made it a lot more difficult for police to simply walk into games and the old air of confidence returned to the two-up premises.

The front of the building used by Thommo's was hidden behind a high, galvanised iron fence, with entry through a big steel gate with an electronic lock. Above the gate was a cockatoo's observation post with views to both ends of the lane.

The cockatoo could unlock the gate electronically, if the approaching person was recognised as a regular customer. The customer then entered the yard and had to walk upstairs to another cockatoo, who had a buzzer to warn players inside if there was trouble.

Beck's squad had visited the new Thommo's location, armed with warrants, without success. As soon as they entered the lane, the alarm was given.

Now Beck attended the raid himself. When he and his group of men arrived at the steel gate, the lookout asked what they wanted. Beck pulled out his identity card and demanded, "Police here, open the gate!"

Unfussed, the lookout replied, "Sure thing. I'll come down and let you in."

Then he got down from his perch, walked over to the door of the gaming premises and pressed a buzzer. It was clear to Beck that the buzzer rang an alarm upstairs, where people were gambling, which was the signal for them to quickly gather up the gambling materials and hide them.

After sounding the alarm, the lookout went calmly back to the gate, taking a minute and a half for the round trip, and finally opened it.

By the time Beck and his team got upstairs and into the large room, there was no sign of any gambling equipment. Instead, what appeared to be a rather sloppy game of indoor bowls was underway. A notice proclaimed, "the Oxford Club—indoor bowling and social".

A large and lengthy piece of worn-out carpet covered part of the poorly kept wooden floor. The carpet was once green but now a mess of cigarette burns and stains. It was also full of dips and hollows, as some of the boards underneath it were broken and missing in part. As the police walked in, one of the men sent a bowl rolling down the green. It went in and out of the holes while the crowd, smiling at his cheek, followed its progress with cheers, "Oh good shot Tom!"

"Who's running this place?" asked Beck. Several people responded on cue, "We're having a bowls tournament!"

Beck and his men searched but could find no evidence of betting. They left empty handed and could hear the two-up game starting up as soon as he and his men had left. Jeers, swearing and insults followed them down the stairs.

To Beck, the raid was not a failure, just a fact-finding mission. A few nights later, on Friday 14 March 1980, he returned with seven or eight men.

They followed the same procedure, with the same result. Once inside the 'bowling club', the police scattered around looking for the pennies and kips. They could not find them.

"I guess we will have to give you the benefit of the doubt," Beck announced, to smirks and sniggers from the crowd, and the police exited to more jeers.

About 45 minutes later, Beck and his team were back in the lane. The cockatoo was surprised, but not alarmed. He followed the same procedure, and after the required delay, Beck and his men went upstairs again.

The game of 'lawn' bowls was again under way, with even more raucous applause. The players were even more cocky and flippant.

One of them jeered, "Give the inspector a bowl, he looks like a bowler!" There was much laughter.

Then another who seemed to be the leader asked coolly, "I'm surprised to see you back so soon. What can we do for you, inspector?"

"Well you can all get yourselves together because you're coming with me," replied Beck.

"What have we done? We've done nothing," the principal protested. Then Beck laid down his trump.

"Constable, please come forward," he said, and the policeman stepped out of the back of the group.

The laughter immediately turned to dismay as a man stepped forward.

Unbeknownst to the crowd of about 60 players, Beck had prearranged for one of his men to slip out of view when the rest of the team left the previous time. Once they were safely gone, he left his hiding place and joined in the mocking of the police. When that settled, he merged into the back row of watchers as the two-up game was set up again.

"Who's conducting these premises?" Beck asked his constable, the constable pointed to the principal.

"Where are the implements of gaming, the pennies and the kip?"

(The kip is a wooden instrument at least 12 cms long used to hold the pennies for the purpose of tossing them into the air. Bets were laid on whether the coins landed heads or tails.)

The constable pointed to a weighty Aboriginal woman with very large breasts.

"She's put the kip down the front," said the constable.

Beck went over to the woman. There was certainly enough room, even for a long kip, in her ample bosom.

"I understand you've got the kip, and I want you to hand it to me," he said.

"If you think I've got it, you'll have to search me!" she retorted.

"No, if you don't produce it, I will send for a policewoman from Darlinghurst and she can come down and search you. And we'll be telling the court the way you were obstructing us," said Beck.

"Look, no bloody policewoman's gonna search me," replied the woman loudly, "if I'm going to be searched, I want to be searched by a MAN!"

When he and his men had stopped laughing, Beck made a suggestion.

"Well do yourself a turn, jump up and down," he said. The woman gave in, and when she jumped the kip fell through and onto the floor.

A lively argument then developed as the cockatoos blamed each other for letting in the undercover man. The organisers stepped forward, but also blamed the cockatoos.

Amid their continuing successes, the Raiders found themselves targeted by a growing number of ugly accusations which were both time consuming and bad for their morale.

As they had been at Thommo's, the Raiders were under strict instructions from Beck to always be polite and to use as little force as possible. Usually, arrests made by Beck's team without any trouble, but there were times when the offenders resisted and had to be dealt with firmly but fairly.

Very rarely, complaints had been laid about the behaviour of the Raiders which were invariably found to be motivated by the desire to make trouble rather than a genuine grievance.

But now Beck and his team face a stream of damaging allegations, over several months which distracted them from their policing duties and sapped their optimism.

The first of these was more shocking as it made by a senior serving police officer.

The squad had made a successful raid at an Italian club. Despite the limitations imposed by the eight rule, they were able to charge the operators with supplying liquor without a licence. The Italian manager and a staff member had been arrested and 11 bottles of whisky had been seized.

The Italians were taken to the local police station and charges laid as usual. Later that day, the trouble began. An inspector of police made a complaint to internal affairs about the conduct of Beck's squad. This inspector said he had been told by a sergeant at the station where the charges were laid, that member of the Raiders had belted one of the Italians across the mouth. The inspector also claimed that when the whisky was seized, the arresting police opened a bottle and drank it all, at the police station.

The inspector's complaint was given to Beck's friend, Keith Paull, who was now in charge of internal affairs. As unlikely as it was, especially the claim that an officer had drunk a whole bottle of whisky, Paull treated it very seriously. He went in person to the police station involved and interviewed the three senior sergeants who were on duty at the time the Italians were charged.

Each of them said there had been no problems at all. Specifically, there was no violence, and all of the whisky seized in the raid was accounted for.

Further undermining the allegation, no claims of mistreatment or police misbehaviour were made by the Italians when they appeared at the courts on remand, which occurred several times.

Beck himself spoke to one of the Italians when he called at Beck's office to discuss other matters, and he made no complaint about his treatment.

Keith Paull then re-interviewed the inspector who had reported the allegations. At first he said he could not name the sergeant who had reported the misconduct to him, but when pressed, provided a name.

Questioned by Paull, this sergeant strongly denied saying anything to the inspector. Paull went back to the inspector, who then said it might have been another sergeant, and gave a different name; but that sergeant also denied any direct knowledge of it.

The inspector then said he "could not recall" who told him.

Paull also questioned Beck's men who had been on that raid and all said they had encountered no problems and the arrests and laying of charges had gone smoothly. No whisky was missing. Paull concluded that the whole thing was a lie.

Beck had no doubt why the allegation had been invented. Given that a high ranked policeman was responsible, he raised it in a private report to Lees. Although Beck could have said that the senior police officer was a liar, he was too careful to put that in writing.

"This is an unusual and serious allegation made by a senior police officer who cannot recall the name of the member of the service who supplied him with the information in the first instance," Beck told Lees.

"The alarming part that concerns me is that this officer is prepared to pass on unfounded allegations without any investigation on his behalf. I feel this is part of the overall resistance this particular squad has been receiving."

Beck also had to deal with a angry criticisms made by a Labor Member of Parliament. In a terse letter to the Police Commissioner. Member for Bathurst Mick Clough denounced the gaming and betting squad for going to his area and arresting two railway workers for SP bookmaking.

The railway workers, he claimed, had been doing no harm. He and questioned the cost of sending the gaming squad team out to his area, suggesting they surely had something better to do than arrest two unionists.

The suggestion that people breaking the law should not be arrested because they were unionists was a new one for Beck, but was forced to look into the claim and make a formal response.

When he did, he found that Clough had got his facts completely wrong. The men had been arrested by two local policemen from Bathurst, not by the Raiders.

Beck wrote Clough a strongly worded reply pointing out the facts, and also noting that it was his job to police the whole of NSW, notwithstanding the restrictions put on him by others. Whatever cost was involved was completely justified, he argued.

Beck heard nothing more about it. He was still annoyed that a member of the Government which had given him his task had berated him in writing without checking a single fact. If there was a waste of police resources, he thought, it was the time he had to spend replying to unfounded allegations.

The time spent on Clough's claims and the annoyance they caused wee soon vastly eclipsed, however, as Beck and the squad became the subject of a nasty and well organised anonymous letter campaign from within the Police Force.

Copies of the letter were written and despatched to every police station in the metropolitan area in the last week of March. They were also sent to the Sydney Sunday newspapers, *The Sun-Herald* and *The Sunday Telegraph,* radio and television stations, both conservative and Labor State politicians, the courts, and Premier Wran.

As reported in the *Sun-Herald* on 30 March, a letter addressed to the Premier at State Parliament House began, "Dear Sir, I am writing this letter to you as a concerned member of the NSW Police Force and a member of No. 21 Mobile Division."

The report by Andrew Watson said the letter was indicative of lobbying against the Commissioner, Jim Lees and "his right-hand man, Inspector Merv Beck…"

"It contains a number of apparently unfounded allegations against Detective Inspector Beck, the tough head of 90-plus members of 21 Special Mobile Squad.

"The new Minister for Police, Bill Crabtree, has refused to discuss the document and its allegations with the *Sun-Herald*."

The letter attacked Beck's methods and integrity. It alleged that he was "picking on" Chinese people and other ethnics, and that he was "out of control".

It referred to an actual arrest that the squad had made, which was only out of the ordinary because the gambling principal and the others arrested had pleaded not guilty despite the clear evidence against them.

A bizarre claim was that Beck had ordered the Sydney City Council to dig up the streets, because he believed the Chinese had "gone underground".

Another of the allegations was that Beck was 'verballing', or falsifying witness statements, and threatening people after they were arrested. Verballing was a serious allegation, as it was a known and scandalous practice by NSW police. At that time there was a strike by prisoners at

Long Bay jail alleging that they had been verballed and their confessions were false.

The anonymous writer urged that Beck be removed from his duties immediately.

Some of the letters had been sent through the police internal mail system. Given this, and the information they contained, it seemed obvious to Beck that they had indeed been created by a person or persons inside the Police Force.

When the letters arrived at their destinations, Beck received a string of phone calls from the recipients denouncing what they believed were disloyal police. The calls came from other police, journalists including Bob Bottom, media executives, and others, often using colourful language about those responsible, dismissing the claims and urging Beck to ignore the cowardly attack on his reputation.

Notwithstanding the strong show of support, the letters were annoying and disturbing for Beck, and even more so when the new Police Minister, William (Bill) Crabtree (appointed on 29 February) became involved.

Although some of the claims were laughable, Crabtree insisted the letter warranted investigation. He told Commissioner Lees to get a written report from Beck answering the allegations. Lees in turn asked Keith Paull, as the head of internal affairs, to ask Beck to provide the report.

Beck was not impressed. He told Paull, "Tell Mr Lees that I have no intention of reporting on these farcical and corrupt letters that Blind Freddy knows are from police and I don't think I should be required to do so."

Paull passed this on to Lees, but the message came back that Lees still wanted the report "as a favour". Beck decided if he had to respond to the insulting claims he would add some truth about real difficulties he had to contend with in carrying out his duties.

After he had submitted the report, he got a call back from Lees. After thanking him for the report, Lees asked him to make some edits.

"I don't think you should include the part about the threats to yourself and your family Merv," Lees said. "I would rather the Premier didn't know that sort of filth had taken place."

Beck was astonished.

"But that's why it's in there Jim," he protested. "I want Wran to know it all, so he understands what my men and I are contending with.

"I am fighting against the odds and there's a lot at stake and my family are under pressure every day, just as I am!"

Still Lees disagreed, and the sections of the report which he felt might disturb the Premier and Police Minister were removed.

The letters were also treated seriously by reporter (later television presenter) Steve Liebman, who waited outside NSW Parliament House for Premier Wran armed with a copy of the letter and a cameraman at the ready.

When Wran appeared, Liebman stopped him, holding out a copy of the letter for the camera and stating that it contained "very serious allegations".

The Premier appeared to look at the letter Liebman was offering to him. Then he pronounced, in his famously grave and gravelly voice: "Anonymous letters— the best place for them is in the garbage bin."

Wran's response, which was televised, gave Beck a smile. For once, he and the Premier were totally in accord.

A few days later, however, on 19 March 1980, another anonymous letter appeared. This one was about the Kirrawee casino raid and again claimed that people charged with offences had been not guilty but had appeared before the courts with "guilty" pleas after being verballed by the Raiders.

The verballing accusation made no sense when the squad's record was examined. Of the 3500 offenders arrested by Beck's squad when the first round of letters appeared, just five had pleaded not guilty. Those five, Beck was satisfied, had fought the charges purely for form because they were instructed to do so.

Even some people involved in SP and gaming who were arrested by Beck or dealing with him in the courts over the days following the release of the scandalous letters expressed their sympathy. One assured Beck 'bad police' were behind the letters.

The evidence certainly pointed in that direction. Both anonymous letters were typed on an electric typewriter of the kind used in the Police Force, on Police Department issue paper, placed in Police Department envelopes and forwarded through the special police mailing system.

The second letter contained references to an entry in the exhibit book used by the Raiders and used police terminology. As claimed in the first letter, it was clearly the work of someone not just inside the Police Force, but on the squad.

Beck went to see Lees and asked that he be allowed to carry out his own investigation into those responsible. But Lees took the view that

Beck had enough on his hands and said he would give the inquiry to Keith Paull and internal affairs.

Despite his close relationship with Paull, Beck heard nothing more about the inquiry. The NSW Police Association was also reluctant to take up Beck's cause. Clearly nothing was going to be done, although there were ample clues as to where the perpetrators might be found.

Beck was extremely disappointed. It seemed the Police Force felt the letters were of no consequence, despite the mental pain they had caused Beck. He felt whoever was responsible for the letters should be called to account and punished and he was convinced Allen's spy on the squad, Hermes, was at least partly responsible. Allen continued to use Hermes as a conduit to the squad's internal workings.

In exasperation one day, Beck went to see Paull. He found him talking to another officer, Bob Blissett.

Beck told Paull and Blissett he was "absolutely fed up" about the anonymous letters and wanted a proper investigation.

"As a matter of fact I am so fed up I am going to call for a royal commission into the Police Force. This sort of rubbish is just the tip of the iceberg!

"It's time dishonesty, corruption and despicable behaviour are rooted out and perpetrators are punished," he announced.

Blissett's demeanour changed immediately. "Hang on, Merv. You don't want to do anything rash."

Before Beck could reply, Blissett jumped in again.

"Don't bother Keith any more about this. Let me get onto this. I'll look into it, and I'll let you know very soon!"

Blissett left in a hurry, leaving Beck and Paull looking after him in surprise. Beck did not hear any more from him, but no more anonymous letters arrived.

Sometime later, Beck sought Blissett out and asked what happened. Blissett said he had spoken to a deputy commissioner, but no official inquiry had been launched.

His annoyance unappeased, Beck complained again to Lees, who did not dispute that police were involved. But he advised Beck to simply ignore the letters, which he said had done no damage.

When Beck again suggested a royal commission into police corruption, Lees reacted as sharply as Blissett.

"No, that is a bad idea Merv, I want you to drop that right now. We do not need a royal commission. What good would it do? It would just stir everything up and the publicity would set the Police Force back 30 years," Lees suggested. (Ironically, many years later, Beck also told this story to the Royal Commission into Police Corruption in NSW.)

Most senior NSW police shared the same view and were opposed to any serious inquiry, despite the strong evidence of widespread rot in the force. Beck could not agree. He thought of the senior police and politicians who had been raking in graft money and were now keen to remove or discredit him purely because they were losing money that never should have been theirs in the first place.

Truth could be hurtful; but it was better than allowing scoundrels to continue in positions of power and influence, he believed.

Changing the subject, Beck asked how his promotion was going. Lees said he would chase it up and it should come through "very soon". Beck had heard this before. When Beck asked if an extra officer would be provided for the Division, Lees was also non-committal.

Beck left the meeting feeling despondent. For perhaps for the first time, he realised that Lees was never going to give him the backing he wanted and needed. It was surprising that it had taken him so long to reach this conclusion. He had not forgotten how his previous special assignment, in Darlinghurst had ended.

Disillusioned, he wrote himself a note.

"I feel our officers are a poor lot and they should be made do the job. To be told when I went to Darlinghurst, I was the only officer they could find that could give the proper discipline—what an indictment.

"The mistrust in our service is because there are too few officers who are reputable. The honest rank and file men are poorly supported. Discipline has fallen away, generally, and it is most difficult to obtain a trustworthy team. Those loyal police are knocked and criticised by senior officers, and a lot of this is in the hands of Pat Watson, who ended up a Superintendent on the gaming and betting and then he went to the CIB.

"None of those people would have survived an inquiry. Statements from SP operators, gaming people and ethnic club owners all say that they paid money (to gaming police). It wouldn't have been hard (for an inquiry) to get that information at all, or in other cases.

"All you have to do is give immunity to vital people and they'll tell all, but there doesn't seem to be any authority prepared to take that on.

"I think they're more afraid of being told too much, which would not suit the police or the Government."

At this point Beck began to consider quitting 21 Division. He did not want to give up on the fight against illegal gambling, as the job was not finished; but he could not help thinking about working in other duties where he might not be banging his head against a brick wall.

He had been told by senior officers, including Superintendent Ross, that the force was looking for someone with drive and determination to lead a taskforce on a project yet to be approved, on special drug investigations.

The thought appealed to Beck, whose strong ethics and sense of community responsibility, as well as his knowledge of the operation of the crime syndicates, made him passionately opposed to the illegal drug trade. He decided to make a submission to Commissioner Lees offering his services in the drug squad and see what happened.

In the meantime, his squad continued to attract the attention of the NSW Opposition, and the media. On 20 April, the *Sun-Herald* reported that 21 Mobile Division had "been directed to keep out of Newcastle—one of the hottest SP areas un the State".

"The squad has not been allowed to operate in the Newcastle area for about four months," the paper said. "Some police have speculated that there may have been pressure to go easy on the area.

"Following a crackdown in Newcastle by 21 Division late last year, which sent SP operators further underground or out of business, big SP operators are again in full swing there.

"A direction was given to 21 Mobile Division three or four months ago to stay away from Newcastle.

"The local gaming police would handle the situation, a senior official said.

"However, police sources say the local gaming section, comprising a sergeant and two or three young constables, cannot cope with the SP problem."

The article then quoted Liberal MLA John Dowd repeating the claim and demanding that the directive be lifted.

Beck was never averse to publicity, and believed the public had a right to know what was happening. But the article was undoubtedly irritating to the Government, and he was likely to get the blame. Shortly after this, Beck discovered that the media spotlight could also be damaging, if it was misdirected.

In early April 1980, Commissioner Lees had selected Beck to lead the police contingent in the annual ANZAC Day march in Sydney. Beck was honoured, especially as it was a rare occasion when he would appear in full uniform.

As Anzac Day, 25 April, approached, however, his pride turned to dismay. Beck was walking along a city street when he was astonished to see his name on *the Daily Mirror* banner: "Beck declares war on Diggers".

The screaming headline pointed to a report which quoted an unnamed police sergeant. This person claimed that Beck had issued instructions that all people playing two-up on ANZAC Day, would be arrested.

It was completely false, but Beck knew the claim would cause immense damage to his public image. Once again, he was disheartened at the mischievous lies being spread to damage him, in this case to turn public opinion against him.

As a war veteran himself, Beck had already spoken to Lees about ANZAC Day and how the traditional two-up games among diggers should be approached. It had always been the practice that police took no action against these games. Beck thought this should remain the case.

However, he suggested that—as they had in the past—the consorting squad and other police who were on patrol should be directed to make sure that the criminal element did not join in the games and disrupt them.

Lees had agreed. "We won't change that, that's been going on for years," he said.

But the impression created by the article in the mass circulation afternoon tabloid was hard to correct. People called him at home and at his office to protest, while people who knew them were stopping Elsie on the street to also ask, "does Merv really want to arrest the diggers?"

For the first time, already roused by the anonymous letters, Beck decided to sue for defamation. He sought legal advice and was told that he could certainly take action; but if the jury decided his reputation had not been damaged, it could cost him $15,000.

That was a lot of money. Beck did not have $15,000. After several weeks while he attempted to raise the money to finance the action, he dropped the matter.

When ANZAC Day came, Beck went ahead and led the police march, without incident, but as he marched along the streets leading the NSW Police contingent, he could hear calls from police and members of the public as he passed, "That's the bloke who's going to arrest the fellows for playing two-up!"

While he kept smiling, he was sad. The occasion was ruined for him.

Beck in fact had two roles to play in the Anzac Day march, as he had also given an undertaking to lead the United Nations group, including a group from the British Army, as he was the senior officer among them.

After leading the NSW police on the march, Beck took off his police hat and donned the blue beret of the UN and did it all again. In this new outfit, it seemed that the crowd did not recognise him, and Beck was able to relax and enjoy the ceremony after all.

* * * *

After 10 months of Beck's assault on illegal gambling, most of the casinos were closed and SP bookmaking, while not dead, had been badly mauled.

Beck was keen to tackle other forms of illegal gambling, including the emerging betting fashion, rugby league cards. The cards, reportedly a million-dollar industry in Sydney, came in a number of brands including Reliable Football Card. Players had to pick six winners from the weekend round of matches.

They commonly offered odds of 33-1 for picking six winners, with a points handicap for less favoured teams, but other cards offered different odds for different winning combinations. Cards were sold freely in hotels, clubs, offices and even on street corners.

The Sunday Telegraph had reported on the football cards on March 30, 1980.

"The betting is so blatant some cards even carry advertising. They are available at almost every pub or sporting club in Sydney. Daily papers catering to gambling fans carry the points start, quoting them as having come from betting cards operators…

"So far no one has been charged with operating a card (game) even though some operators have been in business for years.

"There are about 14 major betting card operators in Sydney including a former League test footballer. Last year, one of Australia's current test heroes was involved.

"There have been moves to make rugby league betting legalised and taken over by the TAB. At one stage a form of pools betting incorporating league and VFL games was proposed.

"Many people feel betting cards and doubles are a harmless entertainment, but others feel they could lead to corruption if allowed to continue."

The article annoyed Beck. The statement that no one had been charged was untrue and implied that his squad was ignoring the league cards. In fact, a number of people had been arrested for dealing in them.

It was true that none of the current and former football players involved in promoting the cards had been arrested, but it was not for lack of will. They were involved at the top end of the business, not out in the public where they could get caught. Like the SP bosses, they paid pensioners, bar maids and other people looking for extra cash to distribute the cards. If these were arrested, the footballer behind them would pay their fines and give them $100 for their trouble.

Beck was keen to move on to the logical next phase of his crackdown anyway, and the newspaper article gave him the impetus. He approached Commissioner Lees and proposed that the squad now investigate the principals behind the rackets, rather than just the staff and clientele, and expose them by placing them before the courts.

The squad had information that many so-called ethnic clubs were now owned by the same major criminals who ran the casinos and SP—Lennie McPherson, George Freeman and others. Usually they had taken over the clubs much as they had taken over SP territories, offering protection on a no-refusal basis. Those who resisted discovered why the crime syndicates had become so powerful.

A more profound investigation by the untouchable Merv Beck and his squad would have caused huge problems for many powerful Sydney identities. It would also target the sports personalities and others behind the league cards.

Lees did not respond immediately to Beck's proposal. But around this time, in late April, speculation began to circulate openly that Beck would be promoted, despite missing the traditional cut-off date, his birthday.

Talkative SP operators arrested by the squad confidently predicted that Beck would shortly become a superintendent. Moreover, they were confident the promotion would mean he was moved out of gaming and betting.

One bookmaker told Beck cheerfully, "You'll be promoted to superintendent and you can go and ride off into the sunset. You won't have to bother us anymore."

Beck asked the SP where he had got this information, he said it came from a State politician.

"I spoke to my pollie, a couple of days ago. He said not to worry about you, because you'll be gone soon.

"I wasn't sure, 'cause we heard this before, but my pollie was very confident this time and said it would be soon. Sounds good to me."

Beck said nothing. He had to consider the possibility that the SP was right, but it was embarrassing to think an illegal gambling operator knew more about his career than he did himself.

The speculation was also reported in the media. *The Sun-Herald* journalist Kevin Perkins was confident that Beck would be promoted, but his squad would continue to crack down on illegal gambling.

"The promotion will probably mean his (Beck's) transfer to other police duties," wrote Perkins. "But, according to top police officers, it won't mean the end of Beck's Raiders ...

"Senior officials in the police department said this week a superintendent's vacancy existed and Inspector Beck had the qualifications to fill it.

"One senior officer said this week: 'There is not the slightest intention in the department to promote Inspector Beck simply to move him from the area of illegal gambling....If Mr Beck were to be transferred, his successor would simply have to follow the guidelines provided by Mr Beck.'"

Just days later, Beck learned that the rumours of his promotion were true. While this was good, he was especially pleased when Roy Whitelaw assured him he would not be moved from 21 Division.

On Monday 5 May 1980, Beck issued a memo to his staff to quell the rumours.

"I have been instructed by Senior Assistant Commissioner Whitelaw that I will be remaining at 21 Division as officer in charge for an indefinite period.

"Even though my promotion to superintendent is anticipated within the next few weeks, I was informed by Mr Whitelaw that the running of 21 Division will be my responsibility and that of the other officers of this division.

"Detectives' duties will in future be a matter to be determined by the Assistant Commissioner of Crime, Mr Abbott, and in that regard I am arranging for Detective Sergeant Grace and I to discuss with Mr Abbott the future duties of the detectives of this division.

"All duties to be performed by this division in future will be at my direction or by an officer delegated by me. This division will be responsible for organising future raids under my direction, changes will be made in area of supervision, security and each man's performance of duties.

"I want it to be clear that I want to see a big improvement in areas of exhibit handling, recording, disposal and special warrant recording. We have experienced some difficulties in recent times and a lot of it has been brought about by people delegated to do certain duties and not carrying out those functions.

"In future, any member of this division who does not do what he is told will not remain at this division, for I want you all to understand that this is a particular position that requires full alert in regard to security at all times.

"Loyalty comes in all forms, from a very poor standard to a standard of high degree.

"Self-preservation in regard to the care and security of your diaries, your personal behaviour, drinking and driving and placing yourselves in vulnerable positions is to be given your utmost attention at all times."

The promotion came through on the Wednesday. Two days later, on Friday 9 May, the Wran Government announced that it would indefinitely postpone introduction of legal casinos. Opposition Leader John Mason described this as a "significant and curious" backdown.

"If the Premier's announcement is taken as a signal for a return to all the old illegalities and graft, there will be a massive outcry right across the state," Mason told the media the following day

"The public in particular will want an assurance from Mr Wran, as Police Minister (sic), that he will not transfer Inspector Merv Beck from the police force's 21 Division."[23]

Mason called Beck "the state's $58 million man" because in the nine months since Beck took on gambling, TAB revenue had lifted by $1 million per week, and Beck had also brought in about $6 million in gambling fines.

Country Party Leader, Leon Punch, echoed Mason's comments, saying he was "mystified" by Cabinet's decision. "It appears that Premier Wran has gone to water for some unknown reason. We will be monitoring the situation closely," Punch said.

While Beck was also puzzled, he was pleased to be able to continue his job.

It came out of the blue when on the following Thursday, 15 May, the Police Orders were issued. The orders were the public record of transfers

---

[23] *Sun-Herald* 11 May 1980"Casino Move Mystifies Mason".

and there, in black and white, it said that Mervyn Beck was moving to Police Headquarters.

Beck was genuinely shocked. He immediately went to see Commissioner Lees and demanded to know why he was being moved.

"What's going on here? I've just been promised that I won't be moved and it says here I am being moved. This went to print last week, so someone has been less than honest with me!"

Lees raised his hands in a gesture of helplessness. "This was not my idea, Merv. I had no choice."

As Beck stared at him, he continued, "I was instructed by Macquarie Street that you were needed elsewhere.

"This is not a punishment, far from it. You have done an excellent job on 21 Division and I know you are ready for a break. I want to congratulate you on your achievements, you've done more than anyone else in this job."

Lees also thanked Beck for his personal support, which he said helped him to finally gain the Commissioner's job,

Beck was momentarily stunned. Although the duties at 21 Division had been onerous and wearing in every way, the move was still a disappointment and he did not accept it.

'Thanks Jim but I'm not ready to go yet," he said. "I know I said I would take another position but I have been drawing up plans to get the big fish, I think that's the important next step.

"If it's about the promotion—I thought that was not going to happen. Anyway. I am quite prepared to forego the promotion if I can stay and finish the job."

Lees shook his head. He argued that knocking back the promotion would be a bad move not just for Beck, but for Elsie.

"You'll get a better superannuation payout if you take the promotion Merv. Think of Elsie! You will want to have a comfortable retirement for you and for her."

It was an argument that was difficult for Beck to counter, even though he sensed that Lees had ulterior motives for pushing him in that direction. Reluctantly, Beck agreed.

"I feel I am being moved sideways from the area I am in and no doubt excuses will be made such as 'for the good of my health,'" he wrote at the time. "In truth there are too many people upset by what I have done.

"From my point of view, the Opposition and those who have proved to be my supporters in the media, with Barney Ross and Keith Paull,

Whitelaw and Lees are the only ones who might be strong enough to ensure the job continues against illegal gambling and the criminals behind it."

His final day at 21 Division was to be Monday 19 May 1980. The day before, when he should have been relaxing, Beck expressed his mixed feelings in a diary note.

"I will miss my work at 21 Division and many of the good police officers with whom I have worked.

"Duties here have been carried out under unusual circumstances with many difficulties created by those who opposed the charter given me to close illegal casinos and curtail SP bookmaking.

"There were those on my staff who proved to be disloyal and acted as informants to Allen.

"My time on the gaming squad was not smooth running. Although my close friends and relatives were alarmed for our family welfare, I endured and persevered.

"After all I had a job to do and giving in would have been playing into the hands of my enemies and that is something I would never countenance."

Elsie Beck had no such qualms.

"It appears they have had enough of law enforcement in gaming and betting. I want you to go!" she had told Beck with certainty.

Elsie had put up with all the privations and stresses that the 21 Division job had caused, without complaining. But she had had enough and was keen to see the end of it. More than anyone, she knew that Merv Beck was a mere mortal, not a machine,

He had done his best. It was time to take himself and his family out of the firing line.

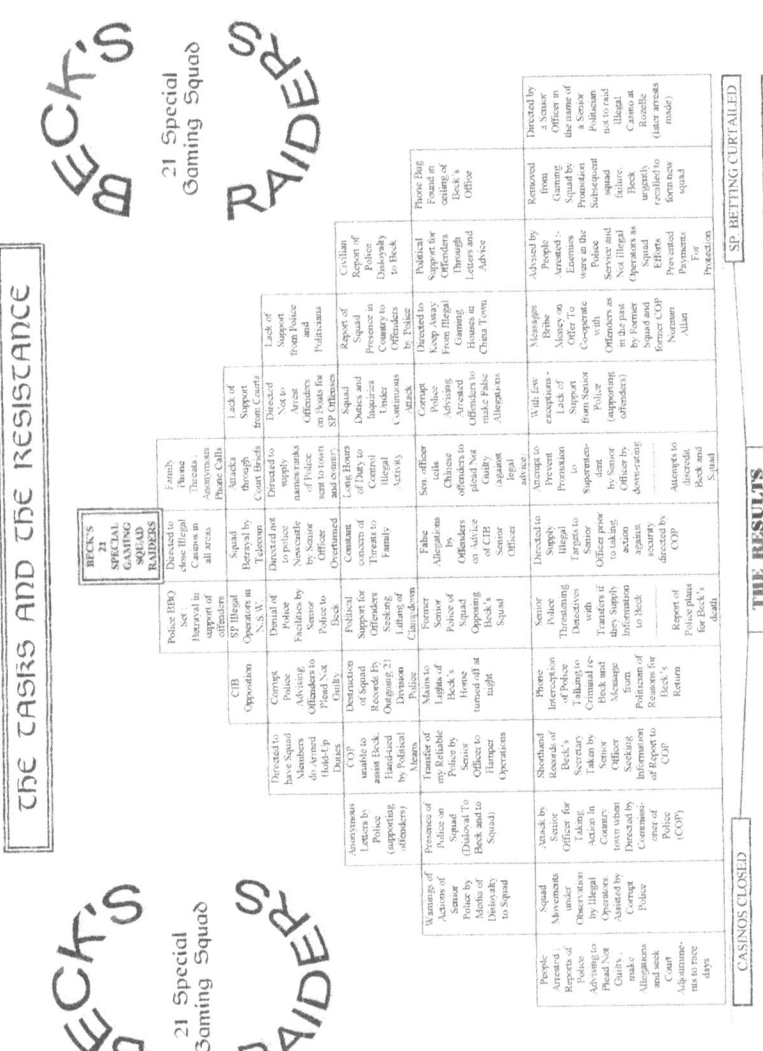

Diagram of the obstacles faced by Beck's Raiders, made by a squad member.

CHAPTER ELEVEN

The Gambling State

After leaving 21 Division, Beck was first sent to a section of Police Headquarters known as 'the corridors'.

Although Premier Wran and Bill Crabtree had told Commissioner Lees he was 'needed elsewhere', like the other officers in the corridors Beck had no specific duties. He was given whatever tasks came up, such as supervision duties, inspecting city police stations, department investigations, arranging police resources, and the foreign visitors' program. It was a far cry from the high pressure, action-packed 21 Division.

Beck kept some links with gaming and betting. Commissioner Jim Lees had tried to retain a semblance of Beck's forceful presence against illegal gambling by directing all superintendents to seek Beck's advice on gaming and betting matters, where help was required. Beck also remained an unofficial contact point for people, including police, who had information about gambling activities but did not entirely trust other police to act on it.

On his third day in his new position, 22 May 1980, while at Police Headquarters, Beck was contacted by a Sergeant First Class who had worked under him at Central Police Station. The sergeant told Beck word had gone out that gambling premises throughout the city, and SP and gaming operations at Cabramatta, were set to swing into action now that Beck was gone. Beck passed on the information to 21 Division.

A week later he got another tip-off from a very reliable detective on the vice squad about gambling premises in Dixon St. The detective also had a message for Beck from Eddy Yee, who had been arrested by Beck and who had pleaded not guilty in strange circumstances.

Yee wanted Beck to know that he had only pleaded not guilty on instruction from Bill Allen. It was a shocking but not surprising revelation. Beck was excited to think that perhaps he could make some mud stick to the despised Assistant Commissioner, and asked Yee if he would provide an interview. Yee was understandably not keen to take on such a powerful policeman and Beck had to let it go.

Then Bob Bottom, who had been advising the NSW Liberal Party on crime matters but was returning to full time journalism, told Beck he had a great deal of information and photographs of Newcastle police involved in SP operations. Beck passed this on to Lees on 5 June but received no feedback on whether it had been acted on. He suspected, given Allen's continued supervision of the gaming and betting squad, that Newcastle was still out of bounds.

The news reaching him quickly got worse. He had only been gone from 21 Division a few weeks when a member of the police intelligence unit told Beck that gaming and betting in Sydney was rapidly getting out of hand. The claim was supported by journalist Kevin Perkins, who told Beck that he had been informed by a group of gamblers that the casino at 660 Darling St Rozelle would reopen, pending 'tacit approval' from Neville Wran.

A regular informant told Beck George Walker had circulated word that he, too, was about to reopen his casino.

At this time, journalists from the major metropolitan daily newspapers were on an extended strike. They issued their own newspaper, *the Clarion,* on 6 June, which included a number of articles which were unlikely to have been published in the regular media because of defamation laws. Unlike the major media organisations, *the Clarion* had no assets or income, so here was no point suing it for damages.

One article claimed that gaming and betting was increasing after Beck's departure. It said the Double Bay Bridge Club, the Kellett Club and premises at 65 Darlinghurst Rd had reopened shortly after his departure. *The Clarion* also said Beck was not happy with his new job.

The article was publicly denied by both Commissioner Lees and Police Minister Bill Crabtree. But Lees asked Beck to call in to his office, and asked him if the article was right about him being unhappy.

Beck did not want to complain, but he could not pretend to be content. He felt isolated and was forced to stand by while the work he had done in gaming and betting was being unravelled now that the squad was firmly under the control of Bill Allen.

Ron Flood, who had taken over command of 21 Division, was a capable police officer. But he was no match for Beck in terms of courage, tenacity and strength of will. Bill Allen was a bully as well as his superior officer. Even before Beck had left, he could see that Flood was inclined to side with Allen to make his life easier.

"Flood is considered by the men to be weak and he will not accompany them out on the job. I have information he is a tool of Allen and loyal to him," Beck wrote in his personal notes.

Even with the gambling premises named in *the Clarion*, Beck did not trust Flood to be effective. The 21 Division records from before he arrived showed that complaints from the press as well as the public from 1970 on had been ignored or brushed aside. Although he had proven that the cockatoos and reinforced doors could be defeated, Beck knew other excuses would be made.

"It's garbage, but if ever the wool has been pulled over the eyes of anyone it is by 21 Division," Beck wrote cynically at the time. There was little he could do about it.

After five uninspiring months at head office, Beck was appointed as an assistant superintendent in Hornsby district. This covered an area stretching from Ryde in the south to the Central coast, including Gosford and Wyong.

He remained there as assistant to Superintendent Bill Marcroft well into 1981, carrying out the usual range of policing duties. Throughout this period there were many comments in the media about the return of the illegal casinos and calls from commentators for Beck to be brought back.

Beck did not get drawn into the public debate, but he was keenly interested. He continued to do ordinary police work, inspecting police stations on the Central Coast and Northern Suburbs and attending to departmental inquiries, but he also kept in touch with what was happening in gambling and with organised crime, through his many contacts in the police, media, business and the legal profession.

Loyal members of his former 21 Division team confided they were looking for other duties as the job satisfaction was no longer there. Their comments saddened Beck, but a particularly exasperating incident left him angry instead.

Beck was contacted out of the blue at the Hornsby police station by a man claimed he had run a long-established two-up school in the district. The premises had been closed by Beck and his Raiders.

"Now that you've gone, you're not on the Special Division anymore, is it alright to open up again?" he asked Beck.

Astonished, Beck asked, "Why would you think that I could let you open up?"

"Because since you left downtown, they have opened up there," the fellow responded. "I asked my mate, Sergeant Hermes in 21 Division if I could open up a two-up game, and he said to go and ask you."

Beck kept his temper. He arranged for the man to come and see Superintendent Marcroft, with Beck present. The answer he received was a definite "no".

The incident, laughable in some ways, made Beck fume once more over Hermes' presence on the gaming squad and Bill Allen's influence.

The resurgence in illegal gambling had become obvious, but Commissioner Lees did little to reassure the public that his police were in control. Unlike Beck, who had nothing to hide, Lees had always been reluctant to talk to the media, and this counted against him when *The Sunday Telegraph* broke the silence on 7 December 1980.

The article was a special investigation by Delamore McNicoll with assistance from Liberal MP John Dowd. The headline was spectacular: "Casinos Open Doors Again—Top Cops Silent, Wran says they're closed".

"Sydney's casinos are back in full swing. After a three-year break in operations (sic), the gambling joints are getting back to the standards of the early 70s—boom days, apparently free from police interference," it stated.

"So far only two of the eight once thriving casinos have fully reopened but they are doing turn-away business.

"This week the Police Commissioner Mr Lees refused to comment on the reopening of the casinos and the Premier, Mr Wran, maintained they were still closed.

"Mr Lees said information on any raids by the anti-gambling 21 Division Mobile Squad in the last three months was unavailable. And he refused to say if and when the two operating casinos were last raided.

"However entry is so easy that even Mr John Dowd the shadow Attorney-General managed to enter one casino this week.

"The two casinos operating are at Rozelle and Double Bay.

"The Rozelle casino is at 134 Victoria Rd Rozelle but is entered through a plain wooden door next to a disused delicatessen in Darling St (which backed on to the other premises).

"It has been operating in a low-key manner for almost a year and flat out for almost three months.

"The Double Bay Bridge Club operates in a building that housed an illegal casino in 1974. The new establishment is operating on the first floor, its predecessor in premises once used by the straight-forward Double Bay Bridge Club.

"The re-emergence of the illegal casinos follows dithering by Premier Wran over licensing of legal casinos in NSW."

The casino at Double Bay Bridge Club had been operating for many years and was owned by crime boss Perc Galea. It was closed during Beck's command of 21 Division. The article then described how to get entry to the Double Bay club past a cockatoo, who was usually sitting in a small car in a no standing zone outside the building.

"Yesterday Mr Wran said he did not approve of the law being openly breached," it continued.

"'My instructions to the police are clear and unequivocal and have been since I told the former Police Commissioner, Mr Wood, the casinos were to be suppressed,' Mr Wran said.

"Commenting on Mr Lees' refusal to give information about police raids on the casinos, Mr Wran said, 'It is often hard for police to give information because if they telegraph what they know it can make it more difficult for them to do the job.'

"A Police spokesman said yesterday the 21 Division Mobile Squad had made no raids on Friday night."

Beck read the article with barely suppressed anger. The Premier's argument that the media could not be told about gaming raids was specious: of course the media should not be told in advance, but Beck had proven that there was no harm, and considerable benefit, in informing the media after the event.

It was also galling to Beck to read that no raids had been conducted on a Friday night. The work he had done with so much effort and perspiration, was rapidly being undone. But if he wanted to stay within the Police Force—and ensure his retirement income—he had to obey the orders of his senior officers and just mind his own business. He was also mindful of his wife Elsie's views.

His spirits lifts considerably when, within a few days of the *Sunday Telegraph* article, Beck received very interesting information from two sources about Bill Allen.

Firstly, a reliable informant approached him on Wednesday 10 December. The informant said Assistant Commissioner Allen was in league with poker machine king, Jack Rooklyn and others promoting illegal pinball and gambling machines. According to the contact, Allen was receiving $5000 weekly from these interests.

The information was credible. Beck made arrangements for his informant to see Chief Superintendent Keith Paull at Police Headquarters. For once, there were no glitches and the interview went ahead. Paull later rang Beck and told him he had got the information, and it was "most useful".

More information about Bill Allen's activities came to Beck the following Monday night. He received a phone call at home from Liberal shadow Attorney General, John Dowd.

Dowd said he had interviewed a well-known criminal, Mr X who had interests in disco premises and gambling establishments. Mr X claimed he had been approached by Allen with a request relating to Dowd. A senior NSW politician had asked Allen to discredit Dowd, and if Mr X obliged, he would be given wide privileges in prostitution and gambling.

Beck thought he had better meet Dowd to find out more and organised to see him in the city early the next morning. As a precaution, he phoned Keith Paull and told him what had happened.

When they met the next morning, Dowd repeated what he had told Beck on the phone and added some extra information. Mr X had also claimed former detective sergeant, Fred Krahe, had been approached first about discrediting Dowd. Krahe (who died just a year later, in December 1981) had turned the job down as he did not want to get involved.

Mr X claimed he now felt under pressure as Allen had phoned him the previous weekend to see how he was going. Allen believed Lees was too weak to do anything if he discovered what Mr X had done, he claimed.

Even if only part of what he was told was true, it was enough to make Dowd worried that he was going to be set up. Krahe was notorious, even at that time. He was allegedly corrupt during his time in the force and was a close associate of other allegedly corrupt police, including detectives Roger Rogerson, Donald Fergusson, Ray Kelly, and former Commissioner Fred Hanson. Krahe also mentored detective Murray Riley, who became an international drug smuggler, had a long-standing relationship with powerful criminal Lenny McPherson, known as Mr Big, and was a close associate of former Police Commissioner Merv Wood.

Dowd was obviously afraid. At this stage it was just his reputation at stake, but with serious criminals involved, it could easily become a physical threat. He appealed to Beck to tell Paull and Lees that although Dowd had never publicly attacked the Police Force, if something was not done about Allen, he would.

Beck believed that Dowd was sincere and deserved his support. He promised to do his best.

The same day, Beck went to Internal Affairs and relayed Dowd's story to both Keith Paull and Sergeant Lionel Kellock. Beck then met with Commissioner Lees and told him. Lees promised that if Dowd came to see him and told him everything he knew, he would instruct two of his most trusted and senior officers, Paull and Assistant Commissioner Roy Whitelaw—both of whom would stand up to Allen—to investigate his complaint.

This was a big commitment from Lees. He was promising to investigate his own Assistant Commissioner who had been personally selected and appointed by the Premier. Beck dared to hope that this might be the start of major change to rid the force of its corrupt elements.

Lees was true to his word and at 3.30 pm that day, Beck received a phone call from Roy Whitelaw asking Beck to see him the next morning about Dowd's allegations.

Beck rang Dowd to pass on the good news. Instead of being relieved, Dowd was afraid that he would become more of a target. He did not want to be part of any official inquiry. Beck pressed him to go and see Lees, but he would not budge.

Beck recorded in his diaries: "At 4.10 pm today I phoned Mr Dowd and told him of me telling Mr Lees of his information. Dowd replied it would prove nothing to carry on with the matter as he would be done away (murdered).

"I suggested he should see Mr Lees in view of the seriousness of his information.

"He said, 'I am of the view that the Commissioner has every facility to conduct an inquiry into the actions of Allen.'"

Beck argued with Dowd that now was the time to strike. But the MP was panicky about what might be done to him.

"Lees has all the information I have, it's up to him to take the matter further without involving me," Dowd insisted.

Beck was disappointed by Dowd's lack of courage. He felt that accusations by a high ranked politician could have triggered a proper inquiry, which would have either cleared senior officers and politicians and proved that lies were being circulated about them, or uncovered corruption infecting the force.

At 9 am the next morning Beck went to Police Headquarters and saw Whitelaw and Paull. Both were keen to go ahead with an inquiry. But they agreed that without detailed evidence from Dowd, they had nothing but malicious hearsay, and no grounds for an investigation.

Despite this letdown, Commissioner Lees did his best to keep Beck's faith. He called Beck to his office for a private chat, and when Beck arrived, gestured to a small pile of documents on his desk.

"This goes back to Darlinghurst," Lees said. "You will find this interesting."

He picked up one of the papers and held it out to Beck. Beck leaned forward and could see it was a Victorian Police record of interview with a prominent NSW business figure.

"Here—take it," said Lees. But as Beck reached out his hand he changed his mind.

"No, hang on. I'll read it to you instead.

"I know you thought you were removed from Darlo for political reasons," Lee continued.

"According to this document, you were making a lot of people nervous."

Although they were alone in the office, Lees lowered his voice. "According to this person, and this is someone who knows a lot, you were removed at the direction of Merv Wood—and he was acting on a request from Abe Saffron."

Beck raised his eyebrows and folded his arms while he took this in.

Despite his high public profile in Sydney, Saffron was rarely mentioned in NSW Parliament. The protection afforded by parliamentary privilege only went so far.[24]

Lees read further from the document.

---

[24] Sydney Crime Museum website 2015 www.sydneycrimemuseum.com

The record of interview showed Wood and Saffron agreeing that Beck "couldn't be trusted" because he was "a man of the church".

"I couldn't be trusted! That's a bit of a laugh," Beck snorted.

Lees agreed that there was a large degree of irony in the description of Beck by a corrupt policeman and the leading criminal. Apparently, 'trust' had a different meaning to them, just as 'control' meant something different to Bill Allen. They were right: Beck could be trusted neither to do any corrupt deals, nor to turn a blind eye to them.

Lees' directive that Beck was available to advise superintendents on gambling matters still applied, and shortly after this Beck received a phone call from a visiting superintendent working in Parkes in the state's central west. He was not satisfied that enough was being done by local police to close down a gambling outlet there. After advising Lees of the tip off, Beck arranged for 21 Division to visit Parkes. This was done, and members of Beck's old team went to Parkes and arrested those responsible.

When Beck followed up with the visiting superintendent in Parkes, he was very happy that 26 men had been arrested playing two-up, plus the operator, John Moon. Police morale had lifted greatly because the police were no longer embarrassed by the failure of their own force, the visiting superintendent said. He was grateful for Beck's assistance.

A week later, however, on 23 December 1980, Beck received a phone call from Ted Quill (deceased), the Chief Superintendent in charge of country districts. Quill was a former member of 21 Division who had worked on gaming and betting and had a bad reputation.

"That you Beck? Quill here," opened Quill. "Are you the one that's been making waves in my area?"

"That depends what you are talking about for a start," replied Beck.

"Were you responsible for that raid up in my area (of responsibility)?" Quill bristled.

"Yes I was. Of course, you'd be au fait with the Commissioner's direction that I was to give police assistance in gaming and betting matters in any areas of concern."

"I'm not worried about any of that!" said Quill, agitated. "What are you making waves for me for?"

"The waves that I am making can be settled if you'd like to have a conversation with Jim Lees, because he's the fellow that directed me, he's the fellow I discussed it with and he's the fellow I planned it with," Beck returned.

Ignoring this, Quill demanded: "In future, you tell me what is happening in my area of command!"

"I cannot do that, my instructions are to report all such matters to Mr Lees, he arranged for 21 Division to attend Parkes," replied Beck.

"This is no good to me, and I will tell Lees that!" said Quill angrily.

"That's a matter for you," replied Beck. "What concerns me, is why you would be upset because these activities were cleaned up in an area where they shouldn't be happening!"

With that, Quill slammed down the phone.

When Beck was at Police Headquarters later that day, he made a point of informing both Keith Paull and Lees' executive assistant about his interesting conversation with Quill.

Some months later, Beck trod on Quill's toes again. Another country superintendent was on sick leave so Beck was sent to his region to fill in. While he was there, he took the time to make observations on several illegal gaming premises.

Local police saw him doing this and the response was quick. The night spots involved were closed, the sick superintendent was suddenly brought back to work at the direction of Ted Quill—and Beck was despatched back to Hornsby.

* * * *

While the demands of normal police life were not enough to fully occupy Beck. a bushfire crisis provided the opportunity for some hands on, physical work of the kind he had excelled in as a young policeman. Unpleasant as it was, the dangers of the fire were easier to contend with than the constant intrigue and deceptions that smouldered around gambling and corruption.

The fire has burnt into Brooklyn, surrounding a train and setting it alight. As night fell, Beck was in charge of the police action, part of which was clearing people out of houses in the path of the fires.

An elderly woman in one of the houses ignored his demand, insisting she was not going to leave for anyone. Beck left her to work with the fire brigade suppressing he fire, then went back.

"Look, if this fire comes up this valley and it looks like taking your house, I am going to lift you out of this house myself," he said firmly.

"I am not going to let you burn to death on my watch, even though you may be a stubborn woman!"

Fortunately the fire stopped just short of the house, even as Beck and his team were getting ready to capture the woman and take her away. So she stayed on, regardless. It seemed to Beck that for all her folly, the old woman had more intestinal strength than some of the senior figures with whom he had to deal as a policeman.

* * * *

The media continued to draw attention to the police failures in relation to illegal gambling and the contrast with Beck's success.

One example was a column by *The Sydney Morning Herald*'s esteemed State political reporter, Mike Steketee, headed "Crime, corruption, casinos: the big Cs".

Steketee referred to "the serious farce which is the casinos issue—a running sore for the Wran Government."

The saga of the illegal casinos would be comical is it were not such an indictment of law enforcement, Steketee wrote, including "the police special division under Mervyn Beck quickly closing the casinos, proving how easily it can be done and resulting in him being kicked upstairs to a desk job".

He concluded: "Until the Government takes some comprehensive step—such as establishing an Independent Crime Commission outside the control of the police, which at least can expose organised crime, and appointing a Director of Public Prosecutions, who would be able to initiate prosecutions where the police are reluctant to act—the cancer of organised crime will continue growing."

Despite being media shy, Commissioner Lees was forced to respond. In an interview with *Sydney Morning Herald* reporters he claimed allowing 'a certain number' of legal, licenses casinos would help police to stamp out illegal gambling and "give people somewhere to go to gamble".

He said the police had found it impossible to close all the illegal gambling casinos, because of their tight security. He also would not advocate tougher penalties for illegal operators and players, although he agreed this would slow the illegal casinos down.

Lees also claimed that transferring Beck out of 21 Division had not reduced policing of illegal casinos and other illegal gambling. While Beck had done "an excellent job", the division was still carrying on that tradition, he claimed.

Lees' comments looked foolish to anyone who was watching illegal gambling in Sydney and across NSW. He certainly did not fool journalists, and his attempts to hose down the issue following Steketee's article backfired.

On 18 January 1981, the big-selling *Sunday Telegraph* 'splashed' its front page with the banner headline: "Police Casino Revolt—They Want Beck Back".

"Top NSW police officers yesterday called for the return of Supt Merv Beck, the former head of the anti-gambling 21 Mobile Division, to stamp out Sydney's thriving illegal casinos and SP joints," wrote Andrew Watson.

"And they are supported by the State Opposition Leader Mr John Mason, who has called on the Government to either smash illegal casinos and SPs or legalise them.

"But the Police Commissioner, Mr Jim Lees, said yesterday there was 'no way' Supt Beck will be brought back.

"And he said Mr Mason 'doesn't know what he's talking about' in his call for Supt Beck to take on NSW's flourishing illegal casinos and SP joints.

"That statement is certain to create a major political controversy for the Police Commissioner. Senior NSW policemen contacted by *the Sunday Telegraph* say "it's obvious the current raids 21 Division aren't effective."

Beck continued to say nothing publicly. But he made a habit of catching up with his contacts every now and then, including Bob Bottom.

In mid-February 1981, Beck met Bob Bottom in Sydney city. Bottom was full of information and snippets about criminals and their connections which rang all true to Beck.

Beck was particularly interested in Bottom's claims about Tim Walker, a former Member of the NSW Parliament who had attended the Kirrawee casino opening. Walker had approached Bottom after he published an article about illegal casinos, asking him to lay off the casinos, especially the Goulburn Club, until after a certain date "so people can be fixed".

Bottom claimed Walker had in the past been a 'bagman' or money collector for Premier Askin, and was very close to George Walker (they were not related), the owner of the Goulburn Club casino (who was then facing charges laid by Beck's Raiders), as well as former Police Commissioner Merv Wood and former 21 Division head Pat Watson.

After Tim Walker's approach, Bottom told Beck, he had personally spoken to Premier Wran about George Walker. Wran had promised that even if casinos were legalised, Walker would not get one.

Soon after this there was other gloomy news about the progress of 21 Division. *Sydney Morning Herald* ran a two-part series, "Inside SP bookmaking". Part 2 described C and B as the biggest SP organisation, calling it a massive organisation which sent computerised statements to customers each month and took bets on every TAB meeting, races, trotting and greyhounds.

"Their annual turnover would be close to $100 million. Their set up includes a computer at Ultimo and numerous offices, the main ones being found in Rushcutters Bay and in the Haymarket area.

"Some premises with about 40 working phones are used as dummy offices in case of police raids … On race days, C and B employs 26 people, mostly poorly paid middle-aged or elderly women, to man their phones."

Beck had previously raided C and B, or Crowley and Buckley but it was clear things were now back to normal in the SP world.

In early April 1981 Beck had to go to the police prosecuting branch about some court briefs. While there, at 10 o'clock he met by chance another senior police officer who took him aside.

The policeman told Beck that he was very concerned that gaming and betting in all parts of Sydney and Newcastle was increasing and members of the public were complaining. This was not news to Beck.

"Have you contacted 21 Division?" he asked the other officer.

"No. I didn't think they could be trusted," he replied.

Beck did not know how to respond. He thanked the man and parted ways.

Privately he was annoyed that police were taking their concerns to him and not to Commissioner Lees. After all, he had been removed from 21 Division and had other duties. But it was not just police who were turning to him. Just a week later he took a call at his station at Hornsby from an Opposition MP, who also wanted to pass on information. Beck agreed to meet him in Chatswood shopping centre.

The politician said businesspeople were most unhappy with the performance of 21 Division since Beck's departure. He also said there was talk of getting Beck back.

Beck believed the MP's motives were good. For the first time, he wondered if the rumours about him returning to gaming and betting might be true. Soon after he went to Police Headquarters to see Keith Paull, but Paull said he knew nothing about Beck being reappointed to his former position.

On Anzac Day 1981, Beck was in the city early to carry out his duties as commander of the police parade for the second time. He had thanked Commissioner Lees for allowing him that privilege, as Beck was close to retiring age and it would be his last Anzac Parade.

He also invited Lees to inspect the police on parade to give it added status, which Lees did. Lees said he was proud of their turnout, and Beck was gratified.

A few weeks later Beck had to go to court for the continuance of a case that had been partly heard. George Walker was finally going to trial for gaming offences dating back to his arrest by Beck at his second gaming premises in Bayswater Rd, King's Cross.

About 11am, while Beck was at the courthouse with the police prosecutor, Colin Spalding and other police witnesses, he got an urgent message to go to Mona Vale hospital as his daughter Elizabeth was having serious difficulties in childbirth.

With permission from the court, Beck raced to the hospital. While he was there, the problem was overcome and the birth proceeded. Although his daughter was seriously ill, she was going to recover and the baby was also safe. Beck hurried back to the court, where he gave evidence from almost two hours, until 4pm. The matter was then adjourned for a week.

To add to this dramatic day, two people approached Beck during the hearing. Both told him there had been a leak of confidential police information, which had benefited the defence. One of these sources was a solicitor who had known Beck for many years, who, sadly, was terminally ill at the time.

"Merv, there are evil people in the gaming squad," he told Beck earnestly. "They want to sell you out, to bring you down.

"There's talk that money is there for anyone who provides information that can be used against you, to damage your reputation."

Beck knew the real aim of any move to discredit him was to reduce the credibility of the crackdown on illegal gambling and prevent it recurring.

He had recently received similar advice from Detective Inspector Neville Stevenson of the CIB. Stevenson said he had heard that a plan was being hatched to interfere with Beck's official records, to destroy evidence. Strange as the plan sounded, it worried Beck. He knew that Bill Allen had accessed his official diaries while Beck was absent. Even though Beck had been off gaming and betting for almost a year, it was possible the Assistant Commissioner was working on a rewrite of history which was less flattering to Beck.

The following day Beck went to a police social gathering at Randwick Racecourse, where he was able to tell Commissioner Lees what he had heard.

"Let it go, Bill Allen is on the way out," Lees replied. Suddenly, Beck's spirits lifted.

When the George Walker trial ended and the verdict was delivered, however, Beck was again disappointed. Although Walker was found guilty, his 'punishment' was a two-year good behaviour bond. This was less than the two men who were the cockatoos and security guards received. Both had pleaded guilty and each was fined $200 or eight days hard labour. As was usual in these cases, Beck had no doubt that the fines were happily paid by their employer.

As if the penalties were not paltry enough, to Beck's disgust, Walker appealed the judgment. Once again there were lengthy delays and when the appeal was finally heard, after Beck's retirement, it was upheld and the conviction was overturned. Newspaper reports of the verdict carried photographs of Walker in company with his friend, the former Commissioner Merv Wood.

* * * *

It was around the time of the Walker trial, in early May 1981, that Justice Edwin (Ted) Lusher released his long-awaited report of the Commission to Inquire into New South Wales Police Administration. The inquiry had been triggered two years before by revelations of the suppression of the Criminal Intelligence Unit's report on George Freeman, which had also contributed to then-Commissioner Merv Wood's resignation.

Premier Wran had set the terms of reference for Lusher's inquiry. Although they notably excluded corruption in the NSW Police Force, Lusher did not stick with the script. While he was unable to make direct findings on whether corruption existed, Lusher did comment on the 'rotten apple' theory of corruption.

Removing bad apples would not stop rot in the barrel, he argued, because there was ample evidence that corruption in police forces was more likely to be institutionalised.

Lusher was a friend of Neville Wran and of his Government. Nevertheless, he strongly recommended the creation of an independent Police Board, including two people from outside the force. In a radical move, he also called for the Police Commissioner to be appointed from outside the force.

Both recommendations were in direct conflict with the Premier's stated views. In late 1979 Wran had pre-empted the report, insisting that control of the force would remain with a commissioner, who would come from within the force, and not a board.

Lusher also recommended that no one aged 57 or more be eligible for appointment as Police Commissioner, because of the compulsory retirement at 60. This was relevant to Bill Allen, who was 57 at this time, and showing every expectation of further advances in his career.

Beck and his friends were also getting closer to the magic retirement number. It was a somewhat sad occasion on 3 June 1981 when Beck farewelled his friend and head of Internal Affairs, Chief Superintendent Keith Paull, but it was also a reminder that there could be life outside the Police Force and that even the best would be replaced eventually.

The question was, how good would the replacements be?

When Beck had left gaming and betting, he was confident that the team on the squad there were highly competent and enthusiastic, and he could only praise the work they had done with and for him. But he also believed, as he had always, that men would go the way in which they are led, and the new leadership left a lot to be desired.

When Beck was in charge, his squad members had been unhappy about the interference from Bill Allen and would often angrily query his directions: "Who is running the place? Is it our boss or is it Bill Allen?" Beck of course shared their annoyance but he was bold and confident enough to stand up to Allen when he felt it was needed.

Ron Flood did not have that confidence. The squad members no longer had a bulwark between them and the Assistant Commissioner they did not respect. With enforcement of the law no longer paramount, many of the good men who had served under Beck became disillusioned and when they left, were replaced by others who found it easier to compromise.

At this time in mid-1981, the number of people contacting Beck about gaming and betting rose sharply. They shared a feeling that 21 Division was heading for a new crisis.

On 30 July Beck responded to one of many requests for a meeting about the issue. This request was from a group of Sydney city businessmen, one of whom was very prominent in the entertainment industry. The group told him that they were voicing the concerns of many in business about the Government's attitude towards gaming and betting and lack of police attention, in the city and the surrounding suburbs.

They asked Beck whether it would be prudent for them to make an appointment to see Premier Wran and ask him to reinstate Beck.

"I would go back," Beck said honestly. "But it's not that simple. There are rules and procedures and I am a superintendent now.

"I wouldn't be able to take that job because I'm too senior. I was pushed off the squad for that reason before."

As he had before, Beck suggested they take their views and whatever evidence they had to Commissioner Lees and ask him to sort out the issues.

But despite the technical hitch about his seniority, the suggestion that Beck was the only person who could do the gaming and betting job properly, would not go away.

On 13 August Beck was attending to district matters at Hornsby when he got a call from the *Sydney Morning Herald* asking for an interview on what the journalists described as "out of hand" illegal gaming and betting. Beck declined. It was outside his role to make any public comment, and he did want to be interviewed.

In addition, regardless of his disappointment about the return of illegal gambling in Sydney and across NSW, he did not want to give the media or the public the idea that he was positioning himself for a return to the squad. The truth was, he did not want the job.

"I didn't—because number one I didn't expect to be accepted and number two, I had had a gutful of what had taken place before," he recalled.

There was also a bigger issue at stake. Beck was 59 years old, only months away from his compulsory retirement at 60. Bringing him back, as far as he could see, was just not possible.

Two weeks later, Beck received another call about gambling matters. A man called Jack Furlong wanted Beck to know that SP betting was rife at Parramatta. Local businesspeople had asked him to do something as the situation was declining but the police appeared to be unconcerned. Once again, Beck could do nothing but direct him to Lees.

While Lees knew what was happening, he knew his own power was precarious. This was confirmed when he received a call from Police Minister Bill Crabtree, who was in Hobart at a conference. Crabtree rang to tell him that Bill Allen would be the new Deputy Commissioner.

Lees was furious. He told Crabtree he should give the job to Roy Whitelaw instead, but the Minister dismissed his objections.

Lees knew that just three days before the Lusher report was released, Allen, his wife Norma and 23-year-old daughter had flown to Hong Kong and Macau for a quick holiday. A month later, the family boarded another jumbo jet from Sydney Airport, this time taking them to the United States to visit San Francisco and Las Vegas.

On 21 July Commissioner Lees called Allen into his office to answer questions about this trip. It later emerged that Allen wore a hidden tape recorder to record the conversation.

When Lees asked about the cost of the trip, Allen claimed he had obtained 'cut price' or 'concessional' tickets. Lees was not fully satisfied but, despite his words to Beck, he took no action against the Premier's favourite Assistant Commissioner.

Now, on 27 August 1981 Allen was officially promoted from Assistant Commissioner to Deputy Commissioner. He celebrated with a party at a Chinese club.

The calls from the media and business for Beck to be brought back became even louder. Several people told Beck confidently that he was about to be reinstated, and many people were taking about it.

This time it was a journalist from *the Daily Telegraph* who rang wanting to know Beck's views on the state of gaming and betting. Did he feel the government was sincere in recent crackdowns on illegal casinos? the journalist demanded. Would he return to 21 Division, and what duties was he performing now?

Beck said nothing, directing the inquiry to police public relations. A senior constable there rang the journalist back and told her that Bill Allen had vetoed any interview with Beck.

* * * *

Public concern and commentary on organised crime and corruption in Sydney had been building for some time.

In his book, *Drug Traffic – Narcotics and Organised Crime in Australia*, published in January 1980, Alfred McCoy proclaimed that Sydney was more tolerant of organised crime than any other city in the world. He also remarked on the "disturbing instances" of close relationships between organised crime figures and influential NSW politicians from both sides of politics, in recent decades.

"During much of this century there has been a close affinity between leading vice entrepreneurs—sly grog traders, narcotics dealers, SP bookmakers and gambling school managers—and the Byzantine bureaucracy of the NSW Labor Party which has provided protection for these illicit enterprises...

"During the decade when Labor was out of power in New South Wales, Sydney's syndicates were able to negotiate a similar arrangement with elements of the Liberal-Country Party," McCoy wrote in an obvious but still veiled reference to Robert Askin's decade in power, 1965 to 1976.

Just a few weeks after Allen's promotion the veils came off when Robert Askin, succumbed to pneumonia. He died on 9 September 1981 and was due to be cremated five days later. NSW was in the last stages of an election campaign, with polling day to be held on Saturday 18 September.

NSW defamation laws deemed it impossible to defame the dead. Claims about Askin which could not be published whilst he was alive, for fear of a lawsuit, were now let loose.

So it was that the day before the cremation, *the National Times* carried a story by David Hickie with the no-nonsense headline: "Askin: Friend of Organised Crime", accompanied by a photograph of an ebullient Askin waving both hands and wielding a cigar.

It opened: "Sir Robert Askin was an underestimated man. The mark he left on this country was considerable—and has never publicly been discussed.

"While Sir Robert Askin was in power, organised crime became institutionalised on a large scale in New South Wales for the first time. Sydney became. and has remained, the crime capital of Australia."

The article included this statement: "According to a very reliable source in the old Percival John Galea empire, Askin and his police chief Fred Hanson were paid approximately $100,000 each in bribes a year from the end of the Sydney gang wars in 1967-68 until Askin's retirement." (Galea was the former owner of the Double Bay Bridge Club, one of Beck's targets.)

It was not so much the allegation which was new as the detail, but the article caused a storm of reaction. Some denounced it as an appalling breach of taste given that the former Premier was not even laid to rest yet. Others defended it, saying the truth often was in bad taste.

There were plenty of other journalists and media outlets prepared to speak ill of the dead.

The late Maxwell Newton, newspaper publisher and journalist, claimed that back in 1970, he had delivered $15,000 in brown paper bags to Premier Askin in his office. Newton said the money was from a Filipino businessman who wanted Askin's approval to build a new sports stadium.

"I told him who it was from and I have never seen $15,000 disappear so quickly in my life. He took the money and whipped it into the top drawer of his desk and said, 'That's very kind of him, I'm very grateful.'"

Newton, added, "I'm afraid Bob didn't deliver."

It was also claimed that Askin himself had operated as an SP bookie in the 1930s and 1940s and continued as a customer of SP and illegal casinos while he was premier.[25]

Despite broad brush allegations by Independent MLA John Hatton among others, under parliamentary privilege (which provided protection from being sued for defamation), the specific allegation that Askin was corrupt and associated with crime figures was a bombshell. Although Askin was from the other side of politics, Premier Wran joined others in denouncing *the National Times* report for lacking taste, while also admitting that allegations about Askin had circulated in Sydney for many years.

Wran claimed he himself had never been slow to investigate allegations of corruption, even if they were to the detriment of his own party, "but I am certainly not going to dig up corpses and engage in that sort of thing".

Other Labor politicians went further to defend Askin's memory, including Police Minister Crabtree, who said *the National Times* article was "out of taste with all Australians"[26].

Federal Labor MP Dr Dick Klugman said the NSW defamation laws (already among the toughest in the world) should be amended to protect the dead, by allowing the estate to sue. But another Federal Labor MP, Senator Nick Bolkus, who became a Minister in the Hawke Government

---

[25] https://www.afr.com/lifestyle/arts-and-entertainment/sydney-1960s-corruption-theproblem-lay-with-everyone-20170430-gvvk3p

[26] See Evan Whitton *Can of Worms* http://netk.net.au/Whitton/Worms28.asp

in 1988, suggested the Australian Taxation Office should perhaps take a hard look at Askin's estate.

The widow, Lady Mollie said *the National Times* journalists and editors were "utter curs". She claimed the story was a rehash of claims that had been made before and proved incorrect.

Advertising executive John Singleton took the allegations personally.

"I hope that sometime I get a chance to have a little yarn with that man from *the National Times*, that little cowardly person who wrote that attack on Bob Askin yesterday, free of facts, just smears and innuendos of a petty mind," he said.

"And to think the once mighty Fairfax empire would stoop to just utter gutter journalism is to me sickening and I'm sure that's the sentiment that will be shared by every fair thinking person."

Days later the voters of NSW not only returned the Labor Party to power, but increased its majority. The result became known as the second 'Wranslide'. Labor now held 69 of the 99 seats on the Legislative Assembly (the Lower House).

Later it was revealed that Askin had left an estate of $1,957,995, a huge sum in those days for a man who had no fortune before he took public office.

Independent MP John Hatton, who had been re-elected unopposed in his South Coast seat, followed up *the National Times* report on Askin, claiming in Parliament that what Askin had begun, Wran was condoning. NSW had become "the gambling state" and a hive of organised crime thanks to the legacy of Askin and then Wran.

"This is the honey pot," Hatton said. "Crime attracted to Sydney the worst criminals from the west coast of the United States….

"Do not tell me that organised crime is not protected. If it is not, why is it so visible, and why is it so successful?

"With prostitution, massage parlours, gambling casinos, starting price betting and between 7,000 and 10,000 heroin addicts on our streets, it must be visible…

"Blind Freddie knows that crime is organised. Hundreds of thousands of Sydney people know it. How much proof is needed? It goes from administration to administration and government to government."

But Wran was a hugely popular, newly re-elected Premier. Compared to the personal allegations against Askin, Hatton's comments on Wran barely created a ripple.

* * * *

On the same day *the National Times* published its story about Askin, 13 September 1981, Commissioner Jim Lees began to deliberately distance himself from Bill Allen and the Government which had appointed him.

Lees told senior officers that he had not been consulted about Allen's appointment as deputy commissioner and added that he intended to retire shortly. They were pointed remarks, highly newsworthy and immediately leaked to the media.

Lees had bitten his lip for years to maintain his place in the Police Force. His comments now, prompted by inside information about a storm blowing Allen's way, added to the atmosphere of suspicion surrounding the Government. Neville Wran, known as 'Nifty', knew he had to take action, and it came without delay.

On 30 September, the new ALP caucus (comprising all of its Members of the NSW Parliament) voted for a new ministry. Bill Crabtree was voted out, and Premier Wran appointed 34- year- old Peter Anderson, a tall, strong former police prosecutor, as Police Minister. A few weeks later, Premier Wran confronted Crabtree over allegations that he had taken bribes from unnamed police. Crabtree denied the claims, but Wran set up an investigation, purportedly to clear the air.

The choice of investigator by Wran and Anderson was interesting. Detective Inspector Joe Parrington had been investigating the death of anti-drug campaigner Donald Mackay, but took time off from the Mackay inquiry to investigate Crabtree. Obviously in no hurry on either investigation, he took six months to deal with the Crabtree matter. Around 50 people, including members of 21 Division and others associated with illegal gambling and casinos were interviewed.

Ultimately, in June 1982, Anderson announced that the investigation had found "no evidence whatsoever to substantiate claims of a criminal conspiracy involving police, Members of Parliament and/or the gambling fraternity".

(Just two years after the Crabtree inquiry was initiated, Parrington was asked to undertake another investigation of possible corruption— by Minister for Corrective Services Rex Jackson, who was forced to resign his ministerial portfolios on 27 October 1983. While Parrington found no criminal charges were warranted, the claims of corruption kept surfacing. Wran was succeeded as Premier by Barrie Unsworth in July 1986 and a month later Rex Jackson resigned from Parliament, He was charged with corruption and despite Parrington's findings, the following year was convicted of conspiracy to accept bribes for the early release of prisoners from NSW jails.)

While Crabtree was under fire, the Deputy Commissioner of Police he had recently appointed, Bill Allen, was also coming under scrutiny over his overseas trip to the US in June.

Allen's claim that he had bought the tickets to the US at a 'cut price' was not true. In fact he had paid nothing for the tickets. They had originally been offered by US airline Pan Am to Les McIntyre, chairman of Queanbeyan Leagues Club, as part of a promotion. McIntyre had suggested they be given to Allen instead. Allen later claimed that, although he was the senior NSW Police officer in charge of licensing, he was not aware that the Queanbeyan Club had applied to the Government in 1976 for a casino licence.

In Las Vegas, the Allens were treated like VIPs. Their luxury hotel accommodation was also free of charge—the bill being picked up by Australian Bally poker machine boss, Jack Rooklyn.

Rooklyn was a colourful businessman who was well-known to the public.

He had started his business empire in the 1950s, making Bally pinball machines and related products which were sold across Australasia and South East Asia. In 1964, Bally branched out into poker machines and quickly became dominant in the US gambling headquarters, Nevada.

In the late 1960s, Rooklyn formed a new company, Electronic Amusements in which he had a half share, to distribute Bally poker machines in Australia. In 1972 this was bought out by Bally America in a complex share deal which left Rooklyn as the head of a new company, Bally Australia. It was revealed in late 1971 that Rooklyn's secret partner in Bally America was Gerardo Catena, a senior figure in the Genovese Mafia crime family.

In his 1973-74 Royal Commission into organised crime—established by the Askin Government—Justice Athol Moffitt found that allowing Bally America or its subsidiary Bally Australia to operate in Australia offered a risk of infiltration of organised crime into or in relation to Australian clubs.

Despite these findings, Rooklyn continued to enjoy good business and high-level connections in his homeland. He enjoyed great success with his racing yacht Ballyhoo, and in 1976 won the Sydney to Hobart race.

This happy popularity did not, however extend to the US Federal Bureau of Investigation (FBI). The FBI regarded Rooklyn as a friend and associate of mafia leaders, and everyone associating with Rooklyn was of great interest.

When the FBI learned that Rooklyn was playing host to a senior Australian police officer, they thought the Australian Government might like to know too. They alerted the Australian Federal Police (AFP), which raised the issue with Liberal Prime Minister Malcolm Fraser. Fraser asked the head of his department to write to his NSW equivalent, the secretary of the Premier's Department, Gerry Gleason. This was happening just when Crabtree was pushed out of the police portfolio and replaced by Peter Anderson.

Peter Anderson's job was to reassure the public that all was well in the NSW Police Force, but it was going to be tough. Despite the 'Wranslide', many people had misgivings about the rule of law in Sydney. The focus was sharpened by a column in *the Sunday Telegraph* on 18 October by the Reverend Fred Nile, who had been elected to the Legislative Council with more than 9 per cent of the vote. For the first time, a link was publicly drawn between the poor policing of illegal casinos and the bungled investigation of Donald Mackay's 1977 disappearance.

The NSW Royal Commission into Drug Trafficking which arose from Mackay's death, conducted by Justice Philip Woodward, in 1979 had named Robert Trimbole as 'the practical leader' of an organisation engaged in marijuana production that was responsible for Mackay's death. But the NSW Police seemed unable to make any headway on the case. In May 1981, after a tip off that the Federal Government was about to act, Trimbole left Australia, raising immediate questions of why he had not been stopped at the border.

Fred Nile's article was headed, "Police Keep from Doing their Job".

"Political crimes in NSW are the crimes where there is no crime unless the political bosses have given the word. Under both Liberal and ALP Governments it is alleged this type of political interference in the police enforcement of the law has become a well-known fact.

"The procedure apparently is the police know there are 'no go' areas such as illegal casinos, brothels et cetera. They take no action except to monitor the activity until they receive specific orders from the Government of the day, usually the Premier or Attorney General or Minister for Police.

"Senior police officials know that if they take unilateral action, they will be carpeted, as occurred with Commissioner Salisbury in SA and a senior inspector in WA.

"Such a situation is a major reason for the growth of organised crime and the corruption of sections of the police force and for the low morale in other areas of the police force.

"It means police at both senior and junior levels have to ignore the clear and deliberate breaking of the law. They have to be selective in the laws they enforce.

"I believe the public of NSW want the police to do the right thing, to enforce the law without fear or favour, under the authority of the Police Commissioner and his senior officers. Political interference must stop. Police should not be turned on and off in response to political orders based on public outrage or unrest over the activities of criminals.

"The public is deeply concerned over the deliberate cover-up concerning Don Mackay's murder at Griffith. Why over four years and no inquest? Now the people of NSW demand an urgent and thorough inquest based on the new police report which is now under study by the Police Commissioner and the NSW Attorney General.

"The NSW Attorney General cannot keep passing the buck, saying it is up to the police. Police in response say they are waiting for the Attorney General.

"The buck stops at the Government's door. The Government must take full responsibility for the action or inaction over Don Mackay's death and other matters. The public is very concerned over reports that key witnesses (Trimbole) in a future Don Mackay inquest have simply left the country. Why no surveillance, why no court orders to stop these people leaving Australia for places unknown?

"Now the casinos are in the headlines again. To be or not to be. Illegal casinos can and should be shut down immediately for the good of the community. The current effort to close illegal casinos under the new Police Minister must be genuine and not simply a PR exercise with a view to the introduction of legalised casinos.

"Casinos must not be legalised. NSW is already saturated with gambling, with over $7000 million spent in (various) forms of gambling and thousands of millions of dollars through illegal gambling such as illegal casinos etc.

"The closure of the Playboy casino in London and the constant allegations of Mafia involvement in the legal casinos in the United States should be sufficient proof that legal casinos do not work, they simply become an adjunct of organised crime to launder and process the millions of dollars that flow in from drugs, extortion, prostitution etc. The people of NSW do not want casinos legalised."

Nile was considered an extremist by many. But his arguments on crime added to pressure on the new Police Minister to do something, or stand condemned with his predecessors.

The following day, Monday, 19 October 1981 the Wran Government bowed to the inevitable.

* * * *

Beck was about to go on leave to use up some accrued time. He was at Police Headquarters in the public relations office when Police Minister Peter Anderson and Commissioner Jim Lees spotted him through the doorway.

"Oh there you are, we've been looking for you everywhere," said Lees, and he invited Beck to come up to his office.

Once they were seated and the door shut, Anderson spoke up.

"I'm glad we found you Superintendent Beck. I've got a favour to ask," he opened.

Beck waited.

"As you know, the Government's in trouble over illegal gambling. It's out of control again and it's looking bad," Anderson continued.

"I want you to come back to gaming, as a matter of urgency.

"I'm sorry to have to call on you, but things have got out of hand again and you're the only one that I believe can do the job properly."

Beck was taken aback. The request was certainly not out of the blue, but it was still a surprise given all the circumstances.

"Thank you, Minister for the compliment," he replied after a moment.

"But in 1980 I was told that if I was a superintendent, that was a rank too high for the 21 Division position," he said. "I am a superintendent now as you know and I am not going to drop rank.

"As far as I can see, that means I can't go back to 21 Division."

Anderson smiled and shook his head.

"No forget that. It's not a problem, it doesn't matter!" he said forcefully.

It was clear that the Government wanted Beck back, as a matter of urgency. Bureaucratic rules which had once been important, no longer mattered.

Beck was flattered and he wanted nothing more than to put his broom through the illegal gambling outlets once again. But he was also hesitant. His 60th birthday was just three and a half months away, on 14 February 1982, and there was no way he could postpone his retirement. Even if he wanted to, that was one police rule which was never broken, and Elsie would possibly break him if he suggested it.

For most police about to retire, their last few months would be a time for winding down, completing files, writing up reports, returning equipment and generally tidying up, not to mention the round of official and unofficial farewells which would be expected.

Beck had to consider whether it worth going back to the extreme demands of 21 Division, for such a short stint. He also had no desire to battle the new Deputy Commissioner every day.

Anderson could read his silence.

"I know, you're very close to retirement. I understand, this puts you in a dilemma.

"But I'm asking you to take it on, as a special favour to me," the Police Minister said.

Beck was wavering.

"I have one condition, and it's not negotiable," Beck said very firmly. "I will not work with Bill Allen."

"You can forget him, he won't be anywhere near the scene," Anderson promised immediately.

As Anderson knew, Bill Allen was on a slippery slope. Beck was Anderson's best and in fact only hope for rekindling some public trust in the police force.

Anderson said Beck would be working to Assistant Commissioner Cec Abbott and Roy Whitelaw, which pleased Beck as he had always found Whitelaw a pleasure to work with. Anderson also promised that his own door would always be open to Beck.

Anderson's instruction was that Beck was to close the casinos and curtail SP bookmaking, just as it had been before.

The 21 Mobile Division, as it was then called, would be disbanded. Anderson insisted that he was a forming a new squad, the Special Gaming Squad. The name was a merger of the former names, 21 Special Division and the Gaming and Betting Squad, but the function was no different.

Because time was limited, Beck asked that most of the existing gaming and betting squad members be kept on, but Anderson refused to allow this. He said it was a new squad and Beck would have to choose a whole new team, once again. His advice was to get them from wherever he could.

For Beck's first appointment to gaming duties, this was appropriate, and Beck would have been a lot happier if the order had been carried out more thoroughly. But this time, most of the squad members were men who had worked under him and had proven their worth, when they had the right leadership, and Beck objected.

"Just a minute, those people worked well for me and I'm sure they would again," he protested.

"No," said Anderson, "I directed them to close all the places down and they didn't do it."

"You're not blaming the men for that are you?" said Beck.

But Anderson would not budge.

"I have already said it. You can't use any of them, you will have to find new people and do it."

There was one more problem. Beck was due for leave before he retired. Taking leave would cut even further into the meagre three and a half months he had left.

Anderson asked if Beck would agree to work through his leave and have it paid out at the end, and Beck agreed. Anderson shook Beck's hand, and Lees followed suit. Beck allowed himself a smile.

It was official. Beck was coming back.

In typical fashion, Beck wasted no time. He was already at Police Headquarters, so he found a desk and got on the phone, asking his trusted colleagues Deputy Commissioner William 'Barney' Ross and Inspector Norman West to help him put together a new team.

Everyone that Beck confided in told him that the directive to start with an entirely new squad was "crazy", as it would clearly set Beck back and make the huge task facing him even harder and even more time pressured.

They included several police of various ranks who told Beck the refusal to allow him to choose his squad members was deliberately intended to restrict him.

Beck himself could not understand the Minister's order. Why reappoint him, knowing that Beck would do everything possible to close the gambling outlets, but also hold him back? It made no sense.

Telling his wife was also difficult. Elsie was not pleased with the prospect of losing her husband again to 20-hour days at work.

"Not again! You're not going to do this again are you?" she asked him, incredulous and angry.

"Well look," he shrugged. "It's only for a short time."

Elsie knew she could not budge him.

She was concerned about whether she and the family, as well as Merv, would be subjected to threats and danger.

"We're not going to go through all that again with people coming here and the phone calls, are we?"

"I hope not," replied Beck. "But—it won't be for long."

In truth, Beck's feelings were mixed. He knew that he had been removed from gaming and betting in the first instance as a political move. Now he was being reinstated for political reasons. The job he was asked to do was worth doing, but the Government's motives were not straightforward.

Beck also knew that he only had three and a half months in which to attempt to clean up the gambling. The time limit only made him more determined.

Just after Beck agreed to take the gaming and betting job, as chronicled in Evan Whitton's book *Can of Worms*, Commissioner Lees told Anderson what the AFP and US FBI had passed on about Allen's Las Vegas trip. Anderson had no choice. He immediately asked Lees to investigate, and quietly moved Allen out of an active policing role and into administration, although at the same rank.

Within a week, the story of the Vegas trip was published in *the National Times*. Corruption was again front-page news. In the first week of November, the Liberal-led Opposition used new information on Allen to launch a three-day attack on Wran and the Government, proclaiming "organised crime is present within the Police Department (sic) of this state at a senior level".

On the third day, 4 November, National Country Party Leader Leon Punch and Opposition Leader John Dowd focused on the newly-appointed Deputy Commissioner of Police, Bill Allen.

Dowd asked whether 21 Division, then under Inspector Merv Beck, had in early 1980 been directed not to operate against illegal gambling in Newcastle, and whether the order had been given by Bill (W.A.R) Allen.

Police Minister Anderson said he did not know but would make inquiries. Punch then directed his question to Wran: "Did you say, in answer to a question from me yesterday, that the fact that the Deputy Police Commissioner's brother had been a prominent Newcastle SP operator was irrelevant?

"If that was irrelevant, is it also irrelevant that police internal affairs records show that senior police officers complained and forced the termination of frequent visits to Mr Allen at Police headquarters by a well-known Sydney crime figure?"

Punch then asked the Premier whether "your choice for Police Commissioner, Mr Allen, is not suitable for a senior position and in fact has been patronised by you because of his activities as a bag man for the Labor Party and for you personally?"

The Speaker of the Assembly ordered Mr Punch to withdraw the second half of the question, but Wran responded to it anyway.

"I feel that I cannot let this occasion go by other than to stamp the Leader of the Country Party as the purveyor of the most guttersnipe, most deceitful and most horrendous allegations. He is a person of no credit."

Wran said he had not known until it was raised by the Opposition that Bill Allen had a brother and defended his appointment as Assistant Commissioner over 22 superintendents.

"If he were appointed commissioner on Mr Lees' retirement and if some allegation were raised some time after that, is it going to be suggested that the Government has acted improperly by promoting him over the heads of other police?

"I have never heard such a baseless and foolhardy argument."

The Premier added that Commissioner Lees was investigating Allen's trip to Las Vegas and the Parliament would have to wait util the investigation was over and Lees decided what to do.

Four weeks later, Police Minister Anderson announced that the Crown Law office had advised him to refer Bill Allen's trip and associated matters to the NSW Police Tribunal, headed by Justice William Perrignon.

The following day, 1 December 1981, was a happy one for Merv Beck. Bill Allen was suspended from all police duties, albeit on full pay.

Inside the main room of C & B in George St showing the numerous phones for receiving bets.

Wardrobe in the front office, showing the hidden doors at the back of the wardrobe which led to the main room where bets were taken.

CHAPTER TWELVE

Hammer and Tongs

On his first day of duty on the 'new' Special Gaming Squad, 20 October 1981, Beck arrived at the Police Headquarters as he usually did at 7am.

Unfair and illogical as it was to start with no squad members, there was no time to waste in argument. Beck and his friends quickly put together a list of men who could be relied on to do their best and started to call them.

"So it was on again, and overnight I gathered around me a few police that I knew," recalled Beck.

It was harder to find new men for his squad the second time around. Moving to gaming and betting was not regarded as a great career move, as the squad had been cleaned out for the second time in a few years.

Beck also had to tell some of his Raiders, who remained in 21 Division, that they had to leave. He did this reluctantly, and with some sadness. Predictably, these men were insulted and Beck himself knew that they were more than equal to the task ahead, if given the right leadership.

"It wasn't the men that was the problem, it was the way they were led," he said, not for the first time. But his pleas were ignored.

One of those who had to go was a senior constable who said after Beck had left the squad, his wife had taken a number of indecent telephone calls on their home phone, referring to his work. Judging by his comments, the caller was himself a policeman. Both the senior constable and his wife had decided to ignore this harassment and he had remained on the squad, only to be removed when the man he most admired, Merv Beck, was reinstated. The story made Beck sad and embarrassed, but he was powerless.

Working with Beck, on the other hand, was an attraction for others. When he had secured a handful of experienced police, he filled out the numbers with young police who would be trained on the job in the fundamentals of gaming and betting duties.

As before, Beck was faced with the difficult task of training almost a whole squad, as he not been allowed to keep any of the experienced gaming police. This time, however, he was fortunate to be able to gather some very good senior police, who like Beck were dedicated and courageous.

Beck liked to surround himself with men who were similar to him in many ways. They did not have to be tall and heavily built, but they had to be physically and mentally tough. He looked for people who could work day and night without getting sick, who were prepared to use their bodies as well as their minds, and who combined cleverness with diligence and honesty.

One of the first he chose to join him was Sergeant Brian McIlvena, whom he considered to be an excellent worker. Beck had previously worked with McIlvena and was impressed by his dedication.

Another of the new recruits to the Special Gaming Squad was Bruce Trees, with whom Beck had worked first at North Sydney and later during his first period on 21 Division.

"He played very prominent part with the other members of our squad and to this day I look upon all those people as my friends," recalled Beck fondly. "That team was some of the best police that I have worked with. They showed their courage and they did the job, and I don't think any of them was ever caught up in moral issues. They were there to do a job, and they did it to the best of their ability – which was excellent."

Another key person to join Beck's team was Faye Barber, a public servant at Police Headquarters. Barber was between duties when Beck took on the job and he snapped her up to be his assistant and help with administration. Beck considered this "one of the greatest strokes of luck that we had".

Barber not only did her job with grace and efficiency, she changed the atmosphere on the squad. As Beck put it, she had a calming and stabilising effect on the team when they were working so intensely and under so much pressure. A mature lady, she went well beyond her duties to provide advice to the men personally and was known affectionately by the squad members as 'Mother'.

"I think a lot of our younger people found security and strength in the fact that there was a person like Faye there, with the motherly instinct that made them feel relaxed and supported despite the demands of the job," recalled Beck.

As well as the usual demands, Beck and the squad had to contend with intense media scrutiny. On the afternoon of that first day, the Sydney *Daily Mirror* ran an article about Beck's return: "Beck's Raiders Scare Casinos".

"Casino bosses reacted sharply to yesterday's announcement that Superintendent Merv beck was back on the gambling beat—only two dens were open last night.

"In recent weeks up to 10 casinos, dozens of smaller gambling dens have continued trading despite a pledge by the Police Minister, Mr Anderson, to close them.

"But it was a different story last night, with only two out of 10 casinos visited by the *Daily Mirror*'s investigations team open.

"These were the Goulburn Club in Goulburn St, City and one in Oxford St, Taylor Square.

"Supt Beck will be retiring in February so he and his raiders will be racing against time.

"Some casino operators were talking about taking a rest until Supt Beck retires.

"But the word was that some would tighten security and try to keep going.

"Last night most casinos seemed worried that the new Beck's Raiders would start a blitz immediately.

"Guests were being turned away from one of the biggest casinos in Forbes St, Darlinghurst."

It was also on that first day back on gambling duties that Beck received some very interesting information about one of his old foes, George Freeman.

At 5pm, he took a call from Superintendent Bob Blissett, the officer in charge of the Bureau of Criminal Intelligence (BCI, which had taken over from the CIU). Blissett asked Beck to come and meet him in his office in the Remington Building.

The BCI was responsible for undercover work, mingling with criminals to pick up information on past and future crimes. As became known later, they were also carrying out phone tapping on various criminals, although they did not have the legal authority to do so. Some tapping was allowed, for drug and murder inquiries, but a warrant signed by a judge was needed for each tap and in some cases the police considered this process to be too slow and unwieldy for their purposes.

The taps were proving to be very valuable and had already uncovered some startling connections.

When Beck arrived, Blissett informed him that the BCI had been tapping George Freeman's phone. Blissett said the tapes were part of a drug investigation, implying that they were being conducted legally. He then played a particular tape of the intercepted phone calls, which had been recorded by a Senior Constable Paul Hegg.

Beck heard a male person talking to George Freeman. The first man spoke with an exaggerated stutter, apparently to disguise his voice. He said he was ringing from NSW Parliament House in Macquarie Street Sydney.

The stutterer was trying to reassure Freeman about Beck's return to 21 Division. Freeman sounded very upset and nervous.

"The bastard will come straight to my place," he said anxiously, clearly referring to Beck.

The stutterer tried to soothe him. "The Boss said to tell you not to worry, and the young Minister said to tell you not to worry," he said, clearly referring to Peter Anderson.

"They said, tell George not to worry. Beck is only there for three and a half months."

But Freeman could not be placated. He sounded very upset. "The Boss said that this wouldn't happen," he said, making it clear he felt he had been let down and that the Boss had told lies.

Freeman complained even more bitterly when the stutterer told him that a cabinet minister had stated he could not do anything to stop Beck's return, as the orders to close the casinos had not been carried out while he was not on the squad.

The two men then discussed what was likely to happen and suggested a complete close down of the casinos and SPs for three and a half months until Beck retired.

The stutterer said Bruce Hardin, was having "a last go" that same night, presumably before closing down. He also claimed that Beck had made a raid in Chinatown and at 65 Darlinghurst Rd. Neither of these claims were true. While the Darlinghurst Road address had been visited by Beck's team during his first period on gaming, no raid had been made recently.

If the news was intended to stir Freeman up, it clearly worked. But then the stutterer changed his tune. He assured him that "Jimmy" had

had "an ear" in 21 Division during Beck's last stint, telling them about Beck's movements, and they could do it again. "I will know by 11.30 today who his new staff's going to be," he boasted.

This was not correct either, as it had not yet been established who would be joining Beck on 21 Division. Nonetheless, the whole conversation was extremely disturbing.

Beck returned to his office and immediately made notes of what he had heard, and then contacted Assistant Commissioner Abbott for a meeting the following day, 21 October.

The stutterer had mentioned a person called "Jimmy" who had been a pipeline into the squad during Beck's first period. Beck could not think who this might be, although there was an assistant commissioner at the time known as Jimmy.

When Beck read his notes to Abbot, he did not seem terribly surprised. He asked whether the stutterer had actually named all of the people on Beck's squad.

When Beck said no, Abbott suggested the claims were all made up. He assured Beck that Peter Anderson was completely sincere in wanting the new crackdown on illegal gambling.

But, he admitted, other elements in the Government might have different views.

Beck thought this was even worse, as it spread the blame.

"This is the job you want me to do?" he said angrily. "I am to put on this act and pretend the Government wants to enforce the law when in reality it's a farce?"

Abbott sighed. He tried to change the subject..

"I'll have to get that rubbed off," he said, referring to the tape.

"I think you can do a lot better than that!" Beck replied.

Four years later, in 1985, Lees and Abbott (who succeeded him as Commissioner in December 1981) were questioned in secret by the Stewart Royal Commission into drugs about this tape. They reportedly both said that they believed the stuttering person was a police officer but could not identify the voice.

Blissett told the Royal Commission that he had played the tape to Lees and Abbott and had then destroyed it on Abbott's instructions. However, he said, a copy might have been kept.

No other inquiries were made about the tape, despite the potentially explosive nature of its revelations, and the names that it contained.

Freeman himself was called before the Royal Commission at an in camera hearing on 6 December 1985 where certain tapes were played to him. Justice Stewart in his public report to Federal Parliament found that in numerous answers to questions, Freeman did not identify his own voice or that of others on the tape.

Justice Stewart stated in his report: "Having heard the voice of Freeman before, during and after the playing of various conversations recorded on the tape, the commission is satisfied that the tape records Freeman's voice and that Freeman was deliberately untruthful in stating that he did not recognise one of the voices on that tape recorded as his."

One tape provided to the Commission recorded a conversation between Freeman and a former police officer, Frank Charlton. In his evidence to the Commission, Charlton denied that the voice on the recordings was his and claimed he had never spoken with Freeman. Justice Stewart concluded that this was also a lie, and the tape did record a phone call between Charlton and Freeman.

The Royal Commission was told that all the tapes and transcripts of conversations from the second round of tapping on Freeman were also destroyed by police.

At the time he was on the gaming and betting squad, Beck had only a small insight into their explosive contents. Although the phone taps were largely illegal, Beck believed they were justified.

* * * *

As well as the disturbing evidence on the phone tape, and the repeated manpower issues, Beck discovered another annoying hurdle in his way. The records of 21 Division had again been destroyed.

As leader of the squad, Beck had instituted a filing system to record and maintain detailed records. But it appeared these records were burnt, dumped, and shredded before he came back. How this happened, remained a mystery.

This time however, Beck had his own accumulated knowledge. He was determined to do the job he had been assigned and to do it well, regardless of the difficulties, although he knew he was being used by Wran and his government.

This was spelled out in an editorial in *The Sun* newspaper reflecting on his re-appointment.

"Some policemen are better at catching illegal gamblers than others.

"That much is clear from the current gambling blitz and police reshuffle.

"But the latest move in the on-and-off mock war against illegal gambling seems to have more to it than a wish to close a few casinos and ethnic card clubs,

"Mr Wran has revenue problems. Legal casinos would yield him an estimated $40 million a year, and in his new Cabinet he may well have the numbers to push them through.

"Blitzing illegal casinos is a necessary condition for opening legal ones. It sets the right moral tone for those sections of the community which doubt the need for more legal gambling, and it defuses talk of corruption.

"Thus, the way seems clear for NSW to follow Tasmania, the Northern Territory and probably Queensland into legal casinos.

"The Government will then have to decide what to do about the gambling urges of all those who don't want to risk their money where the Government tells them to. It's a sure thing illegal casinos and SP betting will still pop up to serve them.

"Mr Wran or his successor will then have to decide whether police raiding is serious, a mere money raiser or just a move to make police and Government look good."

While less cynical, the *Sydney Morning Herald* editorial on Friday 21 October suggested Beck's return would pave the way for legal casinos.

It praised Peter Anderson for his sincerity in ordering a crackdown on illegal gaming, "displaying a refreshing refusal to be fobbed off by token police responses to his instruction".

"It is possible that Mr Anderson's crackdown on illegal casinos will clear the path for the licensing of legal casinos in NSW. Mr Wran has been a consistent advocate of this, on the grounds that, since casino gambling cannot be stamped out for any length of time, it would be preferable to legalise it, bring it under government control, and derive revenue from it—an estimated $40 million a year.

"Superintendent Beck will retire in February and his going may supply Mr Wran with the right time to act... Meanwhile, Mr Anderson would be wise to ensure that...Beck's Raiders concentrate on the big operators."

Regardless of the Government's motives, Beck was never going to be anything but serious about the job. He would have preferred to target big operators and not clients, but there was more than one way to hit the operators. The increase in TAB revenue during his previous stint showed that raids were a turn-off for the gamblers and losing clients would hurt the big operators.

With the small team of very experienced people he had managed to pull together, he quickly began training the new recruits.

"There weren't a great number that had experience in this form of work, but the people that I did get, they buckled down and picked up the threads," he said.

From the start, Beck was back to the very long days. He worked 17, 18 or even more hours a day to get things done, as he knew the time available was so limited. As always, he expected similar from his men.

Beck's concerns receded as he again became caught up in the excitement and adrenalin rush that came from overcoming the many obstacles in his way. The new team quickly learned to work together under his leadership, and the impact was almost immediate.

As before, the exploits of the squad under Beck attracted great media interest. Beck was already so famous that this attention was inevitable, yet there were police who criticised Beck for being publicity hungry.

Personally, Beck had nothing to gain or lose from media attention, as he was retiring in February regardless. But he did not avoid publicity, because he recognised its power. The media coverage encouraged members of the public to take their information about illegal gambling to the squad, and the tip offs were flowing in thick and fast. Nor were Premier Wran and Police Minister Peter Anderson unhappy about the highly positive media coverage, after so many police scandals.

After one week of Beck, *the Sun-Herald* reported that SP operators were refusing to pay their protection money of $100,000 a week, because they could no longer be guaranteed immunity. It did not specify to whom the money was paid.

One place Beck was pleased to revisit was George Walker's Goulburn Club. *The Daily Mirror* reported the raid on Monday 26 October.

"The new Beck's Raiders struck this morning, arresting 22 gamblers in a swoop on an illegal city casino.

"A team of almost 20 undercover detectives from the new Gaming Squad, personally supervised by Superintendent Mervyn Beck, made the carefully planned raid on the Goulburn Club at 2am."

On this occasion, the squad used cutting equipment to burn through the lock on an iron security door in the stairwell leading up to the club on the first floor of 51 Goulburn St. There was another security door and a video monitor to protect the gambling room, neither of which posed any problem to the Raiders.

Nor did the casino's safe, which contained $55,000.

Minutes after Beck had made it inside, the police paddy wagons had arrived to take the arrested gamblers to Central Police Station.

Within two weeks, Beck and his team had raided and closed casinos and SP bookmakers from one end of the state to the other. They also had confirmation that the new blitz was intended to reduce opposition to legalisation of casino gambling.

On 29 October, Premier Wran announced that he had asked Treasurer Ken Booth to report back to Cabinet on the most appropriate means of legalising both casinos and telephone starting price betting.

"The subject of illegal gambling in this State has plagued the administration of New South Wales for too many years," Wran's statement said.

"I have long believed that the most effective deterrent against illegal gambling is to set up legal alternatives. Apart from the deterrent effect, these forms of legal gambling will provide valuable revenue for the Government."

Under questioning from journalists, Wran conceded that licensing a casino would not automatically mean the end of the illegal operators. "The legal replacements must be attractive if the illegal operations are to be stamped out without a massive and continuing use of police manpower and resources."

The Totalizator Agency Board of NSW made a strong submission to Booth, arguing against the proposal to legalise SP bookmaking. One of its points was that bookmakers paid a lot less tax than the TAB; even when they paid it, they were asked for just 1.25 percent of their turnover, while the TAB had to pay 7.5 percent. The TAB also had to comply with award conditions and government policies.

In 1980-81, the TAB said, legal bookmakers had paid the NSW Treasury only $12.2 million on a (declared) turnover of $966 million, compared with $79 million paid by the TAB on its turnover of $1,032 million.

"Legalisation of telephone starting price betting by bookmakers would result in a loss of business by the TAB and would lead to a substantial loss of existing revenue to the Treasury," it argued. "In reality it would mean diversion of existing State revenue to subsidise the operations of such bookmakers. The subsidy could be as high as $37 million per annum if the legalised bookmakers were to attract 50 per cent of the TAB's existing business…

"The TAB could operate a starting price service as effectively and efficiently as bookmakers if given the same opportunities…

"Illegal SP bookmakers can be controlled by effective law enforcement and legal systems. Reports on the proposed legalising of SP bookmakers all state that the legalised system would be backed up by effective laws to prevent a continuation of illegal SP operations. It is obvious, therefore, that it is not necessary to legalise off-course bookmakers to make laws effective.

"The solution to the Government's problem with illegal betting lies in establishing an effective law enforcement and legal system. This would ensure the Treasury, the racing industry and the TAB's agents and staff throughout the State derived the maximum revenue to be gained from betting on the races. At the same time a satisfactory betting system would be available from the TAB for all off-course punters.

"The additional revenue derived from legalised off-course totes and on-course bookmakers would be far in excess of the additional costs incurred in maintaining an effective organisation to enforce effective laws."

The TAB submission noted that Justice Kinsella in his 1963 Royal Commission report on off-course betting in NSW had concluded that laws against illegal betting would only succeed if the penalties were much higher. He suggested that NSW follow Queensland where mandatory jail sentences were imposed for a second offence of telephone betting, and for a second person convicted of gambling in a premises where someone else had been convicted within the previous six months.

The TAB continued, "The Judge's view was that while an agent or employee may face the court with equanimity knowing that the worst that could happen was a fine which his principal pays immediately, he is unlikely to be willing to shoulder the burden of a term of imprisonment which he must serve in person. In short, the Royal Commissioner reported that the only effective remedy against illegal SP betting was to make the game not worth the candle.

"It is a matter of record that his advice was not followed in this regard and his forecast of continued illegal betting as a consequence has proven to be accurate. Even in 1981 courts are fining convicted persons sums of $200 or less (tax deductible). In such circumstances illegal operations are bound to continue even if SP betting is legalised."

Beck could only hope that Treasurer Booth would listen to the TAB's arguments about revenue, effective policing and effective laws, but his hopes were not high. In reflective moments he thought back to the illegal phone tap on George Freeman's phone, and the fact that he was not allowed to use experienced members of 21 Division with whom he would have been happy to work. It was an unhappily familiar feeling that steps were being taken to slow him down.

He enjoyed his work and his success, but his satisfaction was tempered by the knowledge that his work was paving the way for one or more legal casinos.

In melancholy moments he thought back to the illegal phone tap on George Freeman's phone, and the fact that he was not allowed to use experienced members of 21 Division with whom he would have been happy to work. It was an unhappily familiar feeling that steps were being taken to slow him down.

"They wanted me back there in name only, and to keep my operations at a confined level to keep down complaints from the operators," he surmised.

"Time and time again they (gambling operators) would tell us that they had been assured by various members of the Government, the Wran Government, that they realised I only had a short time to go and as soon as I would leave, they would be into it up to their necks and I would go into retirement and be disgusted by it.

"But I could not turn away from the job I had been given."

One of their early raids, on 3 November 1981 was unsuccessful, but yielded an unexpected bonus. By accident, the squad uncovered a large sum of money in Australian and US currency. They passed information on to the Bureau of Criminal Intelligence who arrested two men, involved in the US and Australian mafia. Beck and his team were thanked and congratulated by Commissioner Lees.

After this, a very fruitful raid was carried out on a major casino in Albury in early November. At that time there were still two large casinos in Albury-Wodonga servicing both sides of the state border, and it was well known that the Albury operators were also involved in casinos in the Wollongong area.

Beck had sent two detectives, Owens and Anderson, down to the town to make observations. Owens called in that morning and said that gaming had been going on in the Twin Towers Club the previous night, so Beck instructed Sergeant Ralph Lloyd to get warrants for further action. Beck went back to Lees the next day and obtained his approval to travel to Albury and direct a raid on the club.

Busy as he was, Beck was more than pleased to do a bit of extra work. Before he left for Albury, he gave Lees a report on Bill Allen's order in 1979 that 21 Division not go to Newcastle, which had subsequently been overturned by Roy Whitelaw. Beck was keen to assist the Commissioner with his inquiries into Bill Allen.

Beck briefed his staff and at 6 pm he set off for Albury with two cars. Sergeant McIlvena, Sergeant Lloyd, Sergeant Trees, Detective Beazley, and a policewoman were with him. They arrived in Wodonga at 1.30 am, where they met Owen and Anderson and discussed their detailed plans.

The raid took place just an hour later, at 2.30am. There was no resistance when Beck showed his warrant. They walked in to find the manager Peter Tomlanouvic, and groups of men and women playing blackjack and manila. The manager, staff and players were arrested and charged at Albury Police Station.

The local *Border Morning Mail* carried a large report on Monday 9 November about the raid, complete with a photo of Beck and three squad members loading confiscated gaming tables onto a trailer.

"Two blackjack tables, three manila tables, gaming chips, money and other furniture were seized in the raid," the article stated. "Members of the Gaming Squad entered the back door of the club at 2.30am and produced a search warrant. They found a group of men allegedly playing manila.

"Fourteen men and five women were arrested including two women alleged to be croupiers. One man was charged with having kept a common gaming house. The police found one man hiding between two cars in a car park behind the casino. Another man was taken to the Albury base Hospital for treatment for an asthma attack before being charged. Fourteen cars were parked behind the building.

"The casino featured a large bar stocked with alcohol and soft drinks, coffee and sandwiches were also available. Large windows facing Townsend St were blackened out. The well-lit rear car park was not visible from the street.

"A senior policeman later described the Twin Cities Club as a well fitted out, plush casino type premises. The policeman said the casino was of a standard equal to similar operations in Sydney.

"Seven members of the Gaming Squad and a Sydney policewoman took part.

"It is understood Albury police were given no advance warning of the raid. The local police (who had not been informed about the raids in advance, partly for their protection in case a leak occurred) were called in later to transport those arrested to the Albury Police station.

"The casino is believed to have been operating at the Twin Cities Club for about three weeks. *The Border Mail* first reported in September 1976 that the former warehouse in Townsend St was operating as a casino."

By the time all the people had been charged it was 8am. By then, Beck's team had been on duty for 24 hours and were exhausted. It was an eight-hour drive home (improvements to the Hume Highway were yet to be made), so Beck decided they should all have some sleep. He rented some rooms at a motel to let them sleep for a few hours, then they piled in the cars and drove back to Sydney.

It was 10 pm when they arrived at their squad headquarters, but Beck had no intention of going home. Instead he got busy on other matters that were waiting for him, and at midnight went out on patrol as normal. At 163 Norton St Leichhardt he and his team found what they were looking for and arrested 19 people playing unlawful games of manila and rummy. They finished duty at 2am, and Beck went home. In typical fashion, after a few hours sleep he back at his desk at 8am.

During Beck's absence from the gaming squad, Thommo's had restored its position as the most iconic Sydney gambling spot. It was still in the same premises where Beck had last raided it, in Little Oxford St, but had added a steel security door at the top of the internal stairs, which gave the players more time to organise their fake game of bowls before any police could enter.

On his first visit with his new team of Raiders, Beck had to leave empty-handed once again. But he kept calling and three more raids were successful. The gamblers became expert at hiding the kips, but Beck and his men were equally diligent in their searches.

The gambling room had an old fireplace, which had been used in the recent past. During one raid the squad found the pennies and the kip hidden in the ashes of the fire. Another time they found the gaming implements stuck down the hole of a small billiard table. The table had rattled when the police shook it.

Each time, the squad would arrest 60 to 80 people at the premises, who would be a mixed lot from a variety of backgrounds.

On the third raid, Beck recognised a man who had been there each time and asked him his occupation. The man replied that he was an accountant, and when Beck asked further, he said he worked for the charity, the Smith Family.

"We have arrested you three times here. What would the charity think if we found you here and, in your pockets, you have got envelopes with money for the Smith Family. Whose money are you gambling with?" asked Beck.

"Only my own," replied the man obstinately.

"What view would they take of you being here?" asked Beck.

"Oh they wouldn't care," he replied dismissively.

Beck decided to find out if this was true and rang the Smith Family and spoke to one of its senior managers. To Beck's surprise, he confirmed what the accountant had said.

"Oh, we trust that fellow implicitly," the manager insisted.

Beck was surprised and frankly a little disturbed by this attitude. It seemed to him to be only a reasonable caution for the manager to ensure that donated money was not being put at risk. Beck passed the information on to the CIB, but no action was taken because there was not enough evidence that donation money was being misused.

* * * *

Predictably, Beck's return to the fray was greeted with a anger, annoyance and anguish by the gambling interests who had prospered in his absence. Some tried to fight back, as they had done before, appealing to their supporters in the State Parliament.

When Beck raided one venue the operator snarled at him: "The pollies are going to get rid of you." But whatever complaints were made to the Government were ignored.

Others seemed to accept that Beck was just doing his job. Several gambling operators who had been arrested by Beck during his first period on the squad sought him out to have a private chat. They told him straight out that they were not going to carry out any gaming and betting until such time as Beck had retired and was gone for good—their good at least.

These people were disparaging of the police who had taken their money in return for protection, suggesting they had become too greedy.

Beck listened to these operators and was not unhappy that, for the time being, he was hurting their businesses, but the thought that he was also hurting the corrupt police gave him even more satisfaction.

"There'll be a price on your head again, Beck," one chatty SP operative told Beck with a chuckle. "Not from our side—the cops who were getting protection money.

"No one's going to pay while you're around. You're breaking the system mate."

Beck's journalist friends such as Andrew Watson and Graham Gambie gave him similar warnings.

Beck urged his squad to maintain their discipline and to be vigilant. He was not surprised when, only a month after his return, the anonymous phone calls began again at his home.

He reported this to Commissioner Lees on 23 November but Lees had no advice.

"I'm sorry to hear this Merv. I really appreciate the work you are doing, please keep up the good work."

"The thing is, Jim, I think these calls are coming from police," Beck insisted. "You know why—my crackdown is affecting some who are crooked or who are gamblers.

"It makes me uneasy. It's bad enough having crims after you but police can get access to information and to places that others can't. It's making Elsie nervous."

"I understand," Lees frowned. "I know this is especially hard for Elsie.

"But please, don't let it get to you. You're doing an outstanding job, as always, Merv and I really appreciate it."

"Well it won't affect the way I do my job, Jim. I am not going to be intimidated, but I want you to know what we're up against. And frankly, if anything happens, make sure Elsie is okay."

Beck's concerns were real. One of the menacing callers told Elsie, "We know you are all alone, we just saw you put the light on in the kitchen, and we will be there soon."

It was true, so the house was obviously being watched. Beck decided then to take action, but backing off or quitting was never an option.

He bought two "good, big" dogs, as he put it, which were more barkers than biters, but would make a row if anyone attempted to intrude. He also gave Elsie a shotgun and showed her how to use it.

Beck's initial worry was that shooting the gun would be too much for Elsie and the recoil would send her over backwards. But although Elsie was small, she was fit and very strong mentally, a keen tennis player and amateur swimming judge who also ran her own cake shop and delicatessen. She took up the challenge and quickly became very proficient in using the gun.

Beck then instructed her, "If anyone breaks in to get you, or you're under threat, shoot them.

"If you don't feel like doing that at the time, if you can't do it—fire it into the floor or the ceiling. But make sure the kids are not in the background when you let it off."

After this, when Beck arrived home at 4 am most mornings, he would have to remove the shotgun from the bed before he could climb in next to his wife

In 1982 Elsie told the *Sun-Herald*. "All the time I wished Mervyn wasn't doing that kind of work. I wasn't happy about it at all.

"The children were my main worry—the suggestion that their lives were threatened by something their father was doing.

"There was a whole series of threats. Mervyn knew more about them than I did. I guess I like to be a bit of an ostrich and stick my head in the sand.

"It affected me a great deal. I became irritable and depressed."

Elsie said the phone calls came at all hours. She would pick up, to hear either silence or threats or abuse.

"I think the threats and the tension got to me more the second time around. I felt they got closer to me then."

"The dogs were good and I felt comforted by them. I also had the shotgun, which Mervyn showed me how to use.

"The phone calls were a combination of threats and abuse. There were calls at all hours—at midnight, 2am, 4am, all the time. Often there'd be nobody there (on the line).

"I'm pleased for Mervyn that he saw the job through until his retirement. But when he was recalled, the children and I all wished he wouldn't go back on to it. He said it was another challenge and he wanted to take it.

"I don't have a part in any of Mervyn's decisions. He's a very strong man, he'll talk to me about things but I don't try to influence him. I know he won't be influenced, so I don't try."

Merv Beck himself was not fearless. He certainly knew what fear was, and he knew that he and his family were endangered by his refusal to compromise. But he never allowed fear or doubt to influence his actions.

When Beck was being interviewed for the Wood Royal Commission into police corruption in the mid 1990s, he revealed the menacing calls to Elsie.

The commission's staff were suitably concerned. They felt Beck and Elsie might again be targeted in view of his evidence, and offered to provide a silent telephone number. At the least, they suggested, they could provide an answering machine which would allow the Becks to screen all calls before answering.

After thinking it through, Beck once again declined both. Given the likelihood that police were responsible, he had no faith in the security of silent numbers. He personally knew a magistrate who was given a new, unpublished number after receiving threats. His number was changed on the Friday and the following Tuesday he received a threatening call on the new number.

As for an answering machine, Beck did not want to listen to ugly messages from hateful callers.

* * * *

Perhaps Beck's return emboldened the media to do more to expose the seamy underside of Sydney, known at this time as Australia's crime capital. The defamation laws still made it hard to run more than hints of scandal about persons who were still alive, but the dead were fair game. In November 1981 *the Daily Telegraph* did its best with a special two-part investigation into organised crime. Part 2 had the headline "The Bagman of Macquarie St". A breakout line stated: "Strange alliances prove that corruption knows no pollical allegiance".

The article focused on Christopher (Gus) Kelly, Premier Askin and former Police Commissioner Fred Hanson, all of whom were safely deceased by that time. Kelly, it noted, "was one of the old-style Labor politicians, amiable, generous, loyal, a man to have on side when the going got tough". But despite being the NSW Chief Secretary (a ministerial position) from 1952 to 1956, responsible for policing gaming, he was an active gambler and supporter of illegal casinos,

"Kelly was also a close associate of William Sinclair who was arrested in Bangkok in 1978 along with rugby league player Paul Haywood and hairdresser Warren Fellows on heroin charges," the article continued.

"The case of Gus Kelly illustrates the close links between politicians and crime figures, a tradition stretching back more than 50 years and one which has proved extremely beneficial to both sides.

"The links remain today and the latest scandal involves a prominent Labor politician who is said to be the bagman of Macquarie St.

"According to one senior police officer the politician collected $220,000 a week from such activities as illegal SP bookmaking and casinos, meeting each Wednesday lunch time with three policemen who helped divide the spoils.

"The politician has a long association with criminals. His entry into politics was made possible by an SP operator who was not without influence in the Labor Party machine. The sum of $220,000 may seem a staggering amount of money but it's almost small change to the crime syndicates.

"A secret police file estimates that one illegal casino on the Gold Coast was paying $5000 a week in bribes. It would therefore not be unreasonable to expect Sydney casinos to be paying similar or even larger amounts.

"And then there are the SP operators. Some are turning over more than $100,000 a week, which allows ample spare cash to be set aside for bribes."

Although the squad was making excellent progress, Beck was keen to get more manpower. On 10 November he raised the issue with Assistant Commissioner Cec Abbott, who was not sympathetic.

"You have a good team, Beck. There are many serious matters to police—murders, assaults, theft.

"We can't spare any men from those areas. What you're doing is all well and good but I don't consider gaming and gambling to be criminal offences."

Beck was floored. Was Abbott, who had been unofficially named as Lees' successor as Commissioner, saying he did not support the crackdown on gambling ordered by the Minister?

"The extra men are required because the Special Gaming Squad was directed to perform duties by the Minister and the Government," Beck replied curtly. Never good at toeing the line, with just three months to go until retirement, he found it hard to stomach Abbott's attitude.

Abbott realised his tone was wrong.

"Of course," he appeased. "It's not an area I'm very familiar with. Why don't you and Lees give me a detailed briefing on the anti-gambling operations? I'll get my assistant to make an appointment."

If Abbott did not think highly of the job Beck was doing, the feeling was mutual. As an Inspector, Abbott had been in charge of the investigation into the interference by former Police Commissioner Merv Wood and NSW Chief Magistrate Murray Farquhar in the notorious Cessna-Milner drug case. Morgan Ryan was the solicitor for the defendants. Abbott found "no more than suspicion" about collusion between Ryan and Wood, and no evidence that Farquhar was complicit.

Apparently, he did not have access to the material obtained from the illegal CIU phone tap on Ryan's phone which would make sensational reading many years later. Ryan was a friend and associate not only of Farquhar but of George Freeman and Abe Saffron. He was also described as "my little mate" by Lionel Murphy, the former ALP Senator, Attorney General in the Whitlam Government and, from 1975 to 1986, High Court judge.

This close relationship would become central to the dramatic events which followed publication of extracts from the transcripts of maerial gained from phone taps, in *the Age* newspaper in 1984. The phone tap transcripts subsequently became known as *the Age* tapes.

Beck of course did not know these details. He did know that Abbott was a favourite of the Wran Government. So much so, that the Government had proposed new terms of appointment which would give Abbott the option of remaining as the State's top police officer longer than any previous Commissioner— for eight years, until 1989.

This did not inspire Beck to greater trust of either Abbott or the Government. But Beck believed his personal public profile and authority would allow him to get the job done and he was not going to let anyone stand in his way without a fight.

As his new crackdown continued, on November 21, 1981 his public reputation and status reached a new high. The *Sydney Morning Herald's* lead editorial was headed, "Beck's Raiders".

"Elliott Ness and the Untouchables now have their local counterpart in Beck's Raiders," the paper proclaimed.

"So far the Raiders have not had to demolish the doors of gaming houses with a five-kg sledgehammer or drop in through a skylight as Mr Beck's men did when he was in charge of 21 Division from 1979 to mid 1980.

"But the raids have the stuff of television serials about them, nevertheless. In the tradition set by the redoubtable Mr Ness, Superintendent Beck often leads the raids himself...

"Superintendent Beck has shown twice that he is capable of doing what has been believed to be the impossible: to crack down effectively on illegal gambling in this gambling-mad State.

"For his success in his first stint as a Raider, Mr Beck was promoted to superintendent and transferred to Hornsby, an area not noted for its prevalence of crime.

"The Raider's successful return poses this question: what will happen to the crackdown when Superintendent Beck retires in February?"

The article also detailed the difference Beck's work had made to legal gambling. The on-course tote turnover at Rosehill the previous Saturday was $306,646 higher than the figure for the same meet the previous year, bookmakers' holdings for the day's meeting were up by an estimated $700,000 and the NSW TAB gain was $1,021,024 up on the previous year. The extra revenue to the State from the increase in legal gambling probably meant that the Raiders were paying their way, it speculated.

As the article suggested, despite their lack of experience and the various obstacles, the squad was already making impressive headway. Disciplined, polite and willing to work, they eased the burden on Beck. It was a comfort to him to know that there were still many police who were in the job to enforce the law.

This was especially the case as he was given a fresh warning about the group of former and current police who wanted him stopped. The source of this warning was a surprising one: Parramatta casino owner Graham 'Crocodile' Palmer.

Palmer contacted the squad and first spoke to one of the sergeants, Tomic. He said he had new information for Beck about the police barbecue set. There had been constant complaints about Beck at the last barbecue, and he needed to be careful.

At Beck's request, Tomic advised Palmer to come and see Beck himself. Palmer agreed but admitted he was nervous. He knew how many police were working against Beck and it could have been dangerous for him to be spotted visiting the squad. Beck promised he would be given complete confidentiality, as were all informants. Once you gave up an informant, Beck believed, you gave up your own credibility.

Palmer made an appointment to meet Beck, but did not show up at the appointed time, To Beck's surprise, on 25 November he rang back and apologised. While Palmer was later sent to jail for 16 years on drug offences, Beck felt he was not as bad as many of those he mixed with—both criminals and cops.

Moreover, Palmer may have made the right decision about the appointment. Shortly after this, Beck was informed by an electrician fixing faulty wiring in the CIB building that there were two bugging devices in the ceiling of his office. Although Beck did not get more detail from Palmer, he took the message on board—not by slowing down but by being extremely vigilant.

Numerous arrests were made all over Sydney. The gaming squad patrolled constantly in the well-known gambling hotspots of Chinatown, Matraville, Newtown, Crows Nest and Rozelle.

A typical day was 28 November when they made a large number of arrests throughout the city, and at 47 Dixon St in Chinatown. Another squad member rang to report that he had arrested four people at a busy SP premises at the Entrance on the Central Coast.

The Entrance raid revealed an interesting connection. In the SP operator's telex address book was the name and home phone number of Sergeant First Class Hermes, formerly of 21 Division, a close ally of Bill Allen. When Beck informed Lees a few days later about the Hermes connection, Lees was disgusted. As Hermes was no longer in the force, however, no action could or would be taken.

Sergeant Brian McIlvena, one of Beck's most experienced men, was due to go on leave in late November. But like Beck, he hated to leave a job half done, and he asked Beck if it would be possible to defer his leave until 1982. McIlvena said he had a great deal of information about gaming and betting which he wanted to follow up, without breaking the continuity by going on leave.

Beck was downright proud of McIlvena and others on the squad who displayed that kind of dedication. He was happy to support McIlvena's request to stay on, and several successful raids resulted from his further inquiries.

One of these was memorable to Beck for several reasons: firstly the nickname of the offender, 'Evil George', and secondly, McIlvena's dogged determination.

This incident took place on 9 December. It was a Wednesday, the normal mid-week race day, and acting on information received by the squad, a Special Search Warrant had been issued for an old brick house in Cowper Street, Glebe.

McIlvena and Senior Constable Norm Ellis entered the yard by the back gate. The back door was open and inside they found a woman in a small room. Inside the room was a counter with a large timber framed shutter that had been drawn up with a length of rope. The door they had come in through also had a metal roller shutter on the inside, attached to a brick wall in such a way that it could prevent entry to the house even if the back door was forced open.

The two police spoke to the woman and showed her the warrant. She denied any knowledge of the man named on the warrant, George William Thorpe, nicknamed 'Evil George', but they waited as an informant had said he was likely to be returning to the house from a nearby hotel. While they waited they found betting material and were satisfied the place was used for SP betting.

The following is McIlvena's account of what happened next.

"Shortly later we heard a person waking into the rear of the house. As we walked out to meet this person the woman yelled out to him that we were police. Our suspect turned and ran out into the yard and then along Cowper Street. We gave chase and shortly after we entered nearby Broughton St, continuing behind our man. After running about 100 metres along this street, Norm Ellis and I caught up with the man, who ran behind a parked lorry. I went to one side of the lorry, Ellis was on the other side and then we chased this man around and around the lorry. Finally he stopped, threw his arms into the air and yelled out, 'Fair go, I've had enough!' Then he was placed under arrest.

"Both Ellis and I were dressed very casually in T-shirts and shorts. From memory Ellis had a pair of joggers on his feet but I only had thongs, which I had kicked off back near the house in Cowper St. It was a very hot day, the temperature reaching around the mid-90s (Fahrenheit, equivalent to around 35 celsius). When we returned to the house I put my thongs back on and we returned to the Police vehicle which was parked nearby.

"We drove the offender to the nearby Glebe Police station, where Evil George was charged. After attending to these formalities Ellis and I drove back to our office at Police Headquarters. It was not until we reached the office that I noticed how sore my feet really were. When I inspected them, I found the ball of each foot had a blister about 2 inches (more than 5 cm) in diameter, no doubt caused by the very hot bitumen during our chase. I attended the medical centre where I was given treatment for the burns and some good advice about wearing footwear!"

After another raid led by McIlvena on a gaming place in Kings Cross, Beck received a note from a person who wished to remain anonymous, but said he was a union leader in a hotel. The writer wanted to congratulate McIlvena and his team for their good work, which Beck and the Raiders thought was high praise indeed, coming from a unionist.

Another highly valued sergeant, Ralph Lloyd, had been a police prosecutor and was seriously ill with a bone wasting disease. He was told that he had a life expectancy of five years. With his legal background, his main duty was to prepare warrants and other legal documents. But perhaps because he knew his life was going to be short, he asked Beck if he could go on raids. He insisted on taking on many of the physically challenging assignments that made the squad's work both exciting and successful.

He thrived on the adrenalin and the long hours and put more energy into his work than most healthy people ever would. He quickly won Beck's admiration and affection.

"He was a terrific fellow, he was most loyal and courageous," said Beck. "He did some wonderful work for us, and it was quite common at night time to see him running along the rooftops trying to get into places being raided. He was so keen. And yet in the daytime he was the adviser to the troops on their court briefs and legal matters."

The court results were often disappointing, as the paltry fines were easily paid by the major gambling businesses. But the loss of large telephone systems and gaming tables, the need to pay PMG technicians ever-higher fees, and dwindling clientele due to the fear factor aroused by Beck's return, hit the mark.

When the demands to the Government to stop Beck failed, more club and casino operators closed up their doors, including the Bridge Club at Double Bay. According to advice Beck received from an informant on 29 November, one or more were looking to hire rooms in city hotels as temporary premises to avoid Beck, with smaller numbers of players.

At least one operator gave up on Sydney permanently. A group of Chinese went to Western Australia hoping for an easier wicket. What they did not know was that Beck had been tipped off about their plans. He sent a message to the gaming and betting team in WA, advising them that he believed the Chinese were heading that way and to look out for them. The WA Police nabbed them as they came off the Indian Pacific and told them to get straight back on the train and head east.

The remaining operators tried to tough out Beck's assault using all the old methods and a few new ones. One of these appeared to be a trap. Beck received a phone call from a man who claimed he was ready to tell all about several gambling premises he was involved with.

The caller said he would be standing outside a certain hotel in the city, dressed in a plum-coloured suit. He wanted Beck's team to swoop on him on the street, push him into their car and drive off with him, so his associates would think he had been nabbed rather than volunteering information. Then, he claimed, he would tell them all about a certain location, which he named and which were known to the gaming and betting squad.

To Beck it sounded fishy. He did not want to knock back information from any source but swooping on men in plum-coloured suits on the street was more the style of the mafia than the NSW Police, or at least Beck's part of it. He sent a pair of experienced officers, and there was the man standing as arranged. But instead of grabbing him and pushing him into the car, as he wanted, one of the officers got close to him and asked him if he wanted to speak to the police.

The man denied everything, so the police left him. When the premises he had mentioned were checked, they were clear. Beck was glad he had not taken the 'informant' at face value. The criminals he was dealing with were well equipped and were quite capable of using tactics such as hidden microphones and tape recorders to gather false evidence to incriminate police they would rather be without.

Beck knew he also had to be vigilant against other police stealing information from the squad and giving or selling it to people facing charges, to assist their defence. He had reason to believe this had been done in the past with the squad's records, but he knew better than to expect any assistance from his superiors. With a few exceptions, he ignored the various difficulties and got on with the job.

"Our job was to enforce the law. The rule of law is an essential principle of our society. I and my men were asked to do that job by the law makers, so we did it as well as we could. Our satisfaction was doing the job we have been given," said Beck.

Cec Abbott, who had made it clear he did not rate Beck's job highly, was confirmed as the next Police Commissioner on 2 December, to take over from Lees on 29 December.

As before, Beck did not ignore the less glamorous side of the illegal gambling scene. There were many people on low incomes who had become caught up in gambling and growing debts through the ethnic clubs.

Despite the Government's nervousness, once the new squad had become established, Beck again turned his attention to these clubs.

A dramatic example was reported in *the Sun-Herald* newspaper on 6 December. A raid by his team on an ethnic club in Civic Parade, Auburn had resulted in the arrest of 22 Turkish gamblers. As it turned out, 19 of them were receiving either social security or workers' compensation.

"None of the out-of-work men was destitute," Graham Gambie reported. "Amounts ranging from $100 to more than $1000 was (sic) found on each of them.

"News of the arrests has shocked the migrant community and some organisations announced yesterday that the gambling dens should be raided by officers of the Social Security Department to discover how the unemployed men had so much money.

"Until a few weeks ago, the clubs had been considered untouchable

"The raids have caused widespread comment in political circles, especially as the gamblers traditionally have operated behind the front of 'ethnic clubs.'"

During his first term on 21 Division Beck had pressed to have casinos uncovered by his squad declared as common gaming houses under Section 28 of the Gaming and Betting Act, a move that effectively made that location a permanent target. Bill Allen had told him point blank that the Government did not support this and would not agree to do it. To Beck's chagrin, Commissioner Lees had washed his hands of it too, saying he could not do anything about it if Allen and the Government were opposed.

But when Beck returned, Bill Allen was under a cloud. This time he made the request directly to the Minister, Peter Anderson and was surprised and pleased that permission was granted.

Beck assigned Sergeant Lloyd to work on the legal processes required. By the end of November, he had prepared the paperwork for the Goulburn Club to be declared and the application had been submitted to the Government for approval. Several others were under way.

Beck pushed Anderson to complete the process and was delighted when the declaration was completed. He was now free to raid the Goulburn Club premises at any time, without a warrant, which made the club untenable.

Application for the Forbes Club and Thommo's to be declared were also signed, which was a great victory. The declaration put an end to Thommo's—for a while.

Beck was not sorry to see the end of a Sydney institution. He was convinced that Thommo's by then was controlled by a syndicate, no different from any of the other crime and gambling syndicates, which employed managers to control it while they stayed out of reach. It had to be closed, especially as it made a laughingstock of the police. (Shortly after he retired, Beck heard that Thommo's was looking for new premises and intended to open again soon.)

On 7 December 1981, Bruce Galea was arrested by Beck's Raiders on his way into the illegal casino at 77 Darlinghurst Road King's Cross. Galea and 48 others were charged with being in a common gaming house without legal excuse.

The charge was ironic. Bruce was the son of the notorious Perc Galea, bookmaker and proprietor of illegal casinos. Perc Galea was a 'colourful racing identity' who appeared in a photograph in December 1970 standing next to then-Prime Minister Robert Menzies and Pope Paul VI, the first Pope to visit Australia. After Perc's death in 1977, Bruce became a partner in his father's illegal casinos. The Forbes Club at 155 Forbes Street, Woolloomooloo, and the Telford Club at Bondi Junction had been closed by Beck in 1979 and never fully recovered, but Bruce was still making money from the Double Bay Bridge Club and 77 Darlinghurst Road, which he co-owned with Frank Armante.

(The premises were later used by Armante to run a famous strip club, Porky's, which opened in 1988. In 2003, after interviewing Armante, Neil Mercer wrote that he had "seen it all" in 34 years in the Cross (from 1969), "the Vietnam era boom, the drugs, the girls, the drunks, the fights and the corrupt cops who, until the Wood royal commission, took money from a lot of the clubs to turn a blind eye to what was going on".

"I actually opened Porky's, before that I had SPs (illegal bookmakers) up here," Mercer quoted Armante saying without shame. "I've done everything illegal up here, that's how I became rich. Now I'm becoming a pauper." Porky's closed in 2018.)

Whether it was the arrests or some other factor, Anderson changed his mind about common gaming house declarations. By February he had four more applications prepared by Lloyd on his desk, relating to premises in Chinatown and in the suburbs, but he did not sign them. They were still waiting for processing when Beck retired, and never proceeded.

After Beck's retirement, in 1982 Beck invited Lloyd and his wife to spend some time with him and Elsie at their new home in Dubbo. When Lloyd died not long after, Beck travelled to Sydney and joined a large number of police in bidding him a fond farewell.

* * * *

Knowing how important Telecom was to the illegal gambling businesses, on his return to gaming and betting Beck pushed hard for cooperation with his squad. He had previously complained to Telecom management about their staff involvement in SP bookmaking, but was each time met with claims that nothing could be done or it would upset the Australian Postal and Telecommunications Union.

While he was on his second period on the squad, Telecom began to come under public pressure over the issue.

In November, the federal Labor shadow minister for posts and telecommunications, Ted Innes, said he knew for certain that criminal elements had a strong influence with some Telecom employees. SP bookmakers were paying these employees to install banks of telephones, Innes said, enabling them to jump the queue ahead of about 20,000 people then waiting for their phones to be installed.

The following month Federal Communications Minister, Ian Sinclair ordered Telecom to consult with the NSW Police to crackdown on this type of abuse. Their consultation did not, however, extend to Merv Beck.

Later, it was revealed that Telecom technicians had been diverting phones from the State Department of Public Works for SPs for use in r their betting operations. The racket came to light when the NSW Government Review Unit ordered the Public Works Department to review the thousands of telephones on its book, to reduce wastage.

The department was responsible for installing, maintaining and paying accounts for about 7000 telephone services to all State government departments.

Investigators found phones had been installed during the final stages of construction of new public buildings, before the buildings were occupied, This included sites such as the new NSW Institute of Technology at Ultimo, where phones had not been used to make an outgoing call for up to six months, yet were constantly busy on race days.

Informers within the department and Telecom would alert the SPs to the existence of spare phones. Technicians in their pay would then redirect the lines to other telephones in the same exchange on which they could take incoming calls.

As there were no outgoing calls, there was no expense to show up in the department's accounts. The department paid the phone rental, so the SPs were not only getting secret lines, but getting them at taxpayers' expense.

Also in 1982, an inquiry into Telecom was set up under Justice F Xavier Conner. Before the inquiry, the acting federal secretary of the Australian Postal and Telecommunications Union (APTU), a Mr Arndt, denied that the union would ever interfere with either an internal or police investigation of criminal behaviour by Telecom employees.

Arndt claimed that Telecom management had never discussed the SP problem with the union. But as a former telephone technician of 13 years, Arndt had to agree that there was "no way" an SP who had been raided and closed down could set up again quickly with a new bank of phones, unless someone had access to a telephone exchange.

Justice Conner concluded it was likely "substantial bribes are paid to Telecom employees up to a high rank to ensure that the activities of the technicians in the exchanges who do the jobs are overlooked".

DAILY MIRROR 20 OCT 1981

22 HELD IN RAID ON CLUB

THE new Gaming Squad, "Beck's Raiders," arrested 22 people and seized a truckload of casino equipment in an early morning raid on the Goulburn Club in the city.

Six detectives swooped on the five-door club at 2 am after Goulburn Street, to Central Police Station.

At dawn police were still removing equipment and processing those they had arrested.

Of the 22 arrested six were women.

The police, members of the new Gaming Squad, charged a man, aged 55, with assisting in the conduct of a common gaming house.

The remaining 21 were charged with being found in a common gaming house.

A fleet of police cars and trucks took the men and women from the club, in Goulburn Street, to Central Police Station.

All 22 were granted unconditional bail to appear before Central Court next Monday.

The six detectives who made the initial raid were joined at about 2 am by Inspector Norm West.

"Open up... or we'll break in," the fellow let us in," the detective said later.

Police said that equipment seized for several games was seized in the raid.

The police removed a roulette wheel along with professional but Polaroid cameras, money, trays and game paraphernalia.

It is believed the police also seized a large amount of money.

The seized equipment was taken to Central Police Station.

It is expected that it will be used in evidence.

Four men caught playing a "dominoes-type" game at Glenville were each fined $50 in Parra-

matta Court today.

The court was told the men were arrested after the Gaming Squad raided a Friday night.

A woman is escorted from the Goulburn Club, City, by a policewoman after the Gaming Squad raid.

BECK'S RAIDERS SCARE CASINOS

MERV BECK ... retiring

CASINO bosses reacted sharply to yesterday's announcement that Superintendent Merv Beck was back on the gambling beat — only two dens were open last night.

By a Mirror reporter

In recent weeks up to 10 casinos and dozens of smaller gambling dens have been trading, despite a pledge by Police Minister, Mr Anderson, to close them.

These were the Goulburn Club, in Goulburn St, Sydney and one in Oxford St, Turner Bouvar.

But it was a different story last night, with only two out of 10 casinos visited by the Daily Mirror investigating team open.

a few until Supt Beck retires.

Last night one raided gambling den, the new Becky Raiders made a mass sweep.

Owners never know from one day to the next when the raiders will be hitting against them. Some casino operations were talking about taking.

a few until Supt Beck retires.

Last night one raid was made in Forbes St, Darlinghurst. At Kings Cross, another establishment was raided and another closed.

Other raiders traversed St, Bondi Junction, Roslyn Cross, Kings Cross and Double Bay.

Been Beck is being tipped to head the State's Special Gaming Squad.

Daily Mirror coverage of Beck's return.

CHAPTER THIRTEEN

To do what a policeman must do

This time around, there was no Christmas break for Beck or his squad. They knew their time was limited, and were determined to make the most of it.

Incoming Police Commissioner, Cec Abbott, formally took over from Jim Lees the day after Boxing Day. It was annoying to Beck that the change was reported as a victory in the fight against crime in NSW. As he well knew, what was seen in public as often different from the reality of policing.

"Out went retiring Police Commissioner Jim Lees, seemingly a man beaten by a difficult job, and in came Cec Abbott, fit and enthusiastic about his ability to fight crime," reported the *Sun-Herald*.

"Abbott quickly established that the ways of James Travers Lees (nicknamed the Clam) were not to be his.

"He declared that he wanted to be a people's commissioner, and that his number one priority was to fight violence in the street....

"Saying he did not believe corruption was widespread in the force he added: 'There should not be anyone out there paying police anything apart from their wages.'"

Ironically, the report commented: "Old reporters had to go back a decade, to the first days of Fred Hanson's commissionership, to recall such a determined, frank speech."

Adjacent to the report on Abbott was an article headlined, "Beck's boys boost TAB turnover to $538 million".

"TAB betting has risen to $538 million since June 30— up almost 9 per cent on 1980 figures.

"Beck's Raiders—the SP bookies' blight—are responsible for much of the extra revenue.

"It was feared that recent power cuts, which cancelled trotting and dog races, would reduce turnover. The strike by hotel employees was also expected to keep many punters at home.

"'But there is no doubt that the police drive against SP operators put a lot more money into the TAB,' a board official said yesterday. 'Last week's turnover was $2 million more than for the same period the previous year.'

"TAB officials) now expect the total for this financial year to be well above the $1 billion mark it reached in 1980-81.

"Meanwhile, Supt Merv Beck has not had a day or night off since his nocturnal gaming squad began swooping on Sydney's illegal casinos three months ago. His raiders have scared some big SP operators off to the Gold Coast and others are now frequently seen at Sydney races."

As the days ticked over in 1982, Beck's retirement was looming, The *Sydney Morning Herald* proclaimed that while all the casinos had been shut by Christmas 1981, the future was uncertain.

"While Superintendent Beck's Raiders have had great success, the question being asked in Sydney is what will happen when he retires on his 60th birthday in February.

"Will the crackdown continue or will the casinos open up once again? In a bid to ensure that the Beck approach continues, Mr Anderson has taken the unusual step of asking the Superintendent to choose his successor.

" 'I have got my eye on several and naturally I want to pick a man who's going to make a team,' says Supt Beck.

'I consider that when I go, despite all of what you hear, I will be very disappointed and surprised if they didn't (sic) carry on just the same as if I was here.

'If it doesn't, it won't be the squad that would be the cause. It will depend on the political leadership and the political climate.' "

Beck hoped to shame the politicians into enforcing the antigambling laws. He knew that the casinos would reopen if pressure was not maintained.

By now the Raiders' fame had spread. The Melbourne *Sun* on 16 January 1982 ran a weekend magazine article by Peter Rees on the Raider's exploits.

"In the crash through tradition of TV's Elliott Ness and the Untouchables, a 59-year-old police superintendent has done what previous police chiefs said was impossible," the report proclaimed.

"The sledgehammer in the corner of Superintendent Merv Beck's sparsely furnished Sydney office is not there for decoration. It's what might be termed a calling card, the sort of weapon Supt Beck takes with him when he visits illegal casinos to demolish fortified iron doors.

"If the sledgehammer proves inadequate, his armoury also includes bolt cutters and power saws. Such is the style of the man who leads the team of detectives known as Beck's Raiders, a latter day band of Elliot Ness and the Untouchables, who have earned a reputation for shimmying up drain pipes and dropping in through skylights to bust illegal casinos.

"In the past two months, Superintendent Beck, a non-gambler, has achieved what the former NSW Police Commissioner Mr Jim Lees said was practically impossible, closed Sydney's casinos.

"And to the amusement of cynical Sydneysiders who chortled when former Commissioner Colin Delaney and Norman Allan maintained, straight-faced, that the legendary Thommo's Two-up School didn't exist.

"Supt Beck has not only found it but closed it as well. SP bookmakers and scores of small clubs, mostly fronts for gambling houses, have also been hit.

"Since Supt Beck's campaign began in late October last year, most SP bookmakers have closed down. The result has been a huge lift in TAB turnover of around $3 million a week.

"Beck's Raiders hit more than 500 small clubs in Sydney, Wollongong and elsewhere in the state, but it was the scandal of the plush casinos with their ornate furnishings, glamorous croupiers and apparent immunity from prosecution which forced the gambling crackdown.

"There were 26 casinos in Sydney and NSW country areas, about half of which were major operations. Among them (were) the Double Bay Bridge Club, the Goulburn Club, the Rockwell Crescent Palace, the Bondi Telford and the Rozelle Club. All were goldmines which made their owners wealthy men.

"But with Superintendent Beck's crackdown successfully enforced, the casinos have been left in turmoil. The owners of one club for instance have even put the premises up for sale. (At) many others, the principals in most cases have been arrested and charged.

" 'They're all closed now, they're all out of business,' Superintendent Beck said this week."

The media were not the only Victorians paying attention to Beck. Beck was now working with the Victorian Police to jointly tackle the big gambling operators, whose organised crime networks operated nationally.

In November 1981, despite his huge workload, Beck had made a lightning visit to Melbourne at the request of the Victorian Police. On his advice they had set up a taskforce, known as Zebra, headed by Inspector Bob Pittaway. As well as advice, Beck provided a sergeant from his squad to the Task Force to give them support and insights into the methods which Beck had pioneered so successfully.

The task force's first major gambling target was a multi-million dollar SP betting syndicate with links in every state. Police investigations indicated the syndicate was also involved in race fixing, drugs and vice.

But on advice from Beck, the taskforce quickly branched out to help expose corruption within the Victorian Police itself. It worked with the Victorian Police Bureau of Internal Investigation which was probing allegations of corruption, pointing it to the gaming squad.

As detailed in a 2007[27] Victorian Government report on police corruption in the state: "In 1981, the Internal Investigations Bureau received information about corruption within the Licensing, Gaming and Vice Squad. It seemed that the entire unit was compromised by longstanding, systemic corruption.

"(Then-Victorian Police Commissioner Mick) Miller continued to take a keen interest in the progress of the matter and visited the team weekly. Although the investigators could not obtain sufficient evidence to prosecute the corrupt, their work nonetheless cleansed the ranks of the Licensing, Gaming and Vice Squad.

"Eighteen Squad members retired, resigned or went off on long term sick leave. One man was charged and received a short term of imprisonment…

"The Task Force soon identified networks of illegal bookmakers whose wealth and influence gave them a strong power base; it was estimated that a 'fairly good sized operator' might have an annual income of around $5 million per year.

"Apprehending offenders was difficult. Community demand for betting facilities and the large profits meant that there was always someone ready to take a risk. Despite driving many offenders out of business and forcing others to move interstate where lesser penalties

---

[27] "Past Patterns – Future Directions: Victorian Police and the problem of corruption of serious misconduct". Victorian Government Printer February 2007, Report to the Victorian Parliament by the Director of Police Integrity

applied, the Task Force soon found there was no 'quick fix' solution and that 100 per cent permanent eradication was unlikely.

"Nevertheless, by the end (1984), Zebra Task Force could legitimately claim that SP betting had been all but destroyed in Victoria. Zebra's work was not confined to SP bookies. It also included raids on Chinese gambling clubs where Triad involvement was alleged, and had a measure of success in charging people connected with a large 'place card' operation controlled by a prominent member of the Ships Painters and Dockers Union."

On 21 January 1982, the Victorian Police Commissioner's office issued a media statement about Taskforce Zebra.

"A special police task force is cracking down on organised crime based on SP betting syndicates. Raids in Melbourne had revealed that the SP business was highly organised, with interstate links and a multimillion dollar turnover, police said today.

"The task force, codenamed Operation Zebra, raided two city buildings last Saturday afternoon, and later passed on information which led to another successful raid in NSW.

"Task force police, who have become known as "the Z-Men" in illegal betting circles, had to use sledge-hammers to smash through a brick wall into a fortified office in one of the buildings.

"The head of the special squad, Det Inspector Bob Pittaway, said today his men had encountered specially built reinforced steel doors, with girders linking doors on either side of the room to prevent a forcible (sic) entry.

"But four men swinging sledgehammers took only 15 seconds to knock a hole in the wall from an adjoining room and burst into the SP office.

"Inspector Pittaway said some of the big operators had been using telephones expertly diverted from one floor of a building to another without Telecom knowledge or approval. Up to seven lines had been 'running hot' at some of the premises raided so far, he said…

"Off-course turnover on last Saturday's Moonee Valley meeting was up more than $1 million on the corresponding meeting last year.

"'The SPs don't pay any tax, of course, so the Government—and therefore the public—is being robbed of a lot of money that has been going through SP bookies rather than the TAB,' Inspector Pittaway said."

The statement added that police believed the heads of this multimillion dollar empire also coordinated other areas of organised crime, notably drugs and vice, and had branched out into legitimate business using 'black money' gained from illegal SP operations.. There was also evidence that the syndicates had the power to fix races, and thereby manipulate the betting prices,

"Interstate syndicates have organised Victorian SP betting, and it's obvious now just how big the problem is," Pittaway said. "It's a national operation, and that's the way we're treating it."

Discussions were held about expanding Operation Zebra. Merv Beck had retired before this came to fruition, but there is no doubt its work was part of his enduring legacy.

* * * *

Beck's own face was known by millions, thanks to his high media profile, and other members of the squad were also being very closely watched by the illegal operators and their friends in the force.

This high recognition became a liability as illegal gambling operators went to extraordinary lengths to detect and head off visits from the Raiders. This was vividly demonstrated when Beck asked one of his men to take a team to a large town north west NSW, as the officer recounted.

"About January 1980, Supt Beck requested me to take a team one weekend to a north western town some 400 miles (640 km) from Sydney with a view to making observations and the possible arrest of one of several SP bookies in the town. I was informed that the town had a very good intelligence system operating, and had thus far not been done over (successfully raided).

"Being the good soldier that I was, I arranged to go to this town with my team, after first requesting them NOT to shave or get a hair cut before we went away. Even they had no knowledge of our target.

"We left Sydney via the Great Western Highway instead of the Pacific Highway, thus avoiding the Sydney Harbour Bridge and certain of the toll collectors who, we had been told, had all of the registration numbers of the squad vehicles and particularly on Thursdays, Fridays and Saturdays if we were observed going north they would make a telephone call to their contact in Sydney, who would then relay the message up the coast advising all and sundry that the Gaming Squad was heading north.

"It was further alleged that for this service the toll collectors would receive certain gratuities. Funny thing that—nobody could ever nominate which toll collectors were involved, so to be on the safe side, we would always avoid the Harbour Bridge.

"On this occasion we travelled via Lithgow, Mudgee and Gulgong, finally arriving at Coonabarabran in the late afternoon of a very hot day.

"We stayed overnight in a local motel, where I had arranged to meet a friend of mine who owned several trucks. I organised the loan of one of his oldest, roughest looking trucks.

"The following morning my team and I arrived at my friend's property some 20 kilometres out of town and away from prying eyes we jumped into some pretty rough clothing—old oil and paint stained stubbies, blue working singlets or old shirts of varying designs and either bare feet or thongs. No one was wearing one piece of clothing which would be identified as Police issue.

"We secured the Police vehicle in a locked garage on the property, and then after securing a couple of oxyacetylene bottles on the truck we commenced a further journey of some 150 kilometres to the target town in the north west. On the way, we stopped the truck on a bush track and proceeded to obtain some diesel from the tank and washed our arms and legs with it and then rolled one another in the dirt. We even found some discarded oil and smeared some of that on our arms and patches of it on our faces.

"Upon arrival later in the day in the target town, we parked the truck right at the front doors of the first hotel we saw going into town. We entered the bar and ordered three schooners of beer, bearing in mind this was another very hot day! After having the first beer, we ordered our second and commenced our observations trying to locate the bookie.

"As we were part way through our second schooner, one of the lads thought he might have a look in the gents toilet for our quarry. While he was away a chap approached me and said in a low voice, 'You are wasting your time here boys'. I had not seen him approach, I turned to face him and said, 'Did you say something to me?' He then said, 'Youse coppers are wasting your time, there's nothing doing here today.'

"I said, 'What are you talking about?' This chap then said, 'Come on, you blokes are coppers'. I said, 'If you are worrying about bloody coppers then you must have been looking outside when we pulled up in our truck. What the hell are you talking about mate, we've been up in the Pilliga (a wild area, now a nature reserve) for a couple of days with a broken pig crate, we just come to town to get some more oxy. What's this about coppers?'

"With that, he pulled from his shirt pocket what appeared to be a bundle of cards, these turned out to be a bundle of photographs. They were photos of each member of the Special Gaming Squad, taken at various times and places, but nonetheless they were photos of us. The chap shuffled through the photos, identifying each one of us correctly.

"Of course, I was pretty upset at this, considering the trouble we had gone to disguise ourselves. I grabbed the photos off him and dragged him outside the hotel where I started to question him about how he came in possession of the photographs. He maintained I had no right to take the photos as they had cost him $1000 dollars, and he went on to say that they were freely available at that price throughout the north west. He never did get his photos back, I can't remember what happened to them!"

Despite some frustrations such as this, the casinos were under control. With his fixed term drawing to an end, Beck decided it was time to tackle an old enemy—no less than George Freeman.

Freeman was a very well-connected man. He was also well-known as a race fixer (and has been linked to the infamous 1984 ring-in scandal, the Fine Cotton affair, when a much better performed horse was substituted for Fine Cotton.) His 'reliable tips' on racing were eagerly sought by many who desired money more than clean sport or clean reputations, including some in politics, the media, racing, business and legal circles.

Beck had a keen interest in Freeman, which the phone tap material had done nothing to diminish. He had been warned by some very senior officers to be very careful of taking action against Freeman, and he knew about Freeman's connections in high places.

Freeman often boasted about the doors that would open for him, without notice, if he so desired. Many civic and social leaders and 'personalities' associated with him, despite the well-founded rumours.

Freeman was proof, if it was needed, that casino owners and SP operators were no longer 'Friendly Freds'. They were serious criminals involved in other areas of crime such as drugs and race fixing.

A racing identity had told Beck that Freeman was scared of Beck and knew he was a target. This person expressed the view that Freeman was very worried about being at the SP operation when Beck arrived. Beck believed every word because of what he had heard of the illegal phone tap recording.

These factors made Beck all the more keen to carry out a raid and nab Freeman himself. It was now or never to do this, and never was not an option Beck accepted easily.

He devised a plan for a raid literally on Freeman's home turf. Freeman's Yowie Bay mansion was the heart of his empire and included an SP operation with multiple phone lines and staffed by Freeman, a man named Evers and three women.

Two savage dogs patrolled the house grounds, making it difficult to get inside safely or quietly.

First, Beck consulted veterinarians about whether the guard dogs could be stunned, using a dart gun. This was not usual practice for suburban vets so Beck was directed to Taronga Zoo. He was well received and it was indicated that a staff member might be able to help to ensure the dogs were tranquillised humanely but effectively, and were not harmed.

Even without the danger presented by the dogs, getting to the house would be arduous. The wall around the property was a formidable barrier. After considering various options, Beck decided the best one was to get onto the house roof, using a helicopter.

As well as the logistics, there was the issue of how the raid would go down with the Police Commissioner, the Government, and the public. Given Freeman's high profile and the fact that his home was the target, Beck knew he would need explicit permission from the Commissioner.

With only weeks to go before his duties would come end, and the opportunity would evaporate, as soon as his plan of attack was ready he fronted Abbott.

The response was unenthusiastic. Abbott told Beck he did not want him to conduct a high risk raid, which would attract huge media attention, just before he retired.

"You'd be leaving the squad to clean up the mess," he claimed. "What if the raid goes wrong?

"I don't think the other squad members should have to take the blame for attacking a person's home and for doping the dogs. Just think, what if the dogs are hurt and don't recover quickly?

"That wouldn't look good, would it?"

Beck dismissed Abbott's concern for the dogs' welfare, but the Commissioner's other point made sense.

Time was running out. Beck was due to retire on February 13 and given the time lags in the justice system, the case would not be heard for some months. Beck would have to provide court evidence after his retirement, which raised a number of issues.

Seeing that he had hit the mark, Abbott presented a compromise. He told Beck to go ahead with his planning, but to be careful to keep it confidential. Beck was not to proceed with the raid without his approval, he ordered.

Beck did as he was asked. But when he returned to Commissioner Abbott with a more detailed plan, Abbott gave him a firm negative.

He repeated the same arguments. If the raid did not go according to plan, it would reflect badly on both Beck and Abbott, and if it did go well, Beck would not be available to follow up in court.

Although he knew this was the likely outcome, Beck was disappointed. He had been excited at the prospect of taking on Freeman head to head and confident that the Raiders would succeed. Freeman had got away with a lot over the years and Beck thought it was time his luck ran out.

"I think we could have done that and done it well. And I was very disappointed that we were never given the opportunity," he said.

While Beck was unable to put his into action, his strategy was effected two years later in January 1983 by some of his former team members.

The raid was a success. Freeman was charged, but told the court that he was a legitimate commission agent for on course bookmakers, and had only just started SP bookmaking for people in his local area. He was let off with a paltry $500 fine.

Several years later Freeman was raided again and in late January 1986 he was convicted of SP betting and given the maximum fine of $5000. The fine did not hurt him much either financially or socially: two days later, Freeman appeared on television on Channel Nine, owned and personally controlled by famous gambling high roller Kerry Packer, as a guest horse racing tipster.

Freeman's illustrious career and double life as a darling of the racing crowd on the one hand, and crime boss on the other, came to a premature end in March 1990. Only 55, he died from heart failure related to asthma and pethidine addiction.

Outside Freeman's funeral, his friend and rival Lennie McPherson claimed he "lived a really clean life". "He hadn't been in jail since we were both locked up (jn the late 1950s). George hadn't been arrested for years because he hadn't done anything wrong. You think these coppers are stupid?"[28]

* * * *

---

[28] Quoted in the *Sun-Herald* 25 March 1990, "The Freeman Dossier" by Candace Sutton, Steve Warnock, Anita Catalano and Cindy Jones,

During Beck's second period on gaming duties, the question of legal, government-licenced casinos became a federal as well as state political issue. The Federal Government, a Coalition of the Liberal and National Parties led by Prime Minister Malcolm Fraser was going through the same debate as New South Wales and other states.

At that time, the Australian Capital Territory was under direct control of the Commonwealth, as self-government was not granted until 1989. There was a serious push to establish a casino in the capital to attract tourism, a proposal which later went ahead.

The Sunday Telegraph's political commentator at the time, Laurie Oakes, wrote in his column on 24 January 1982 that fears of police corruption were the main reason why Fraser blocked the casino proposal. The Australian Federal Police were taking an active interest and it was AFP advice, passed on by the Fraser Government, which had forced an investigation into Bill Allen's trip to the US and his connections with gambling interests.

"Strong opposition from Prime Minister Mr Fraser was a major factor in the Cabinet decision on Tuesday to veto proposals for a legalised casino in Canberra," Oakes wrote.

"Officially, the reason for Cabinet's thumbs down was a view that a gambling palace was not an appropriate development for Australia's national capital.

"In fact, though, Mr Fraser was concerned that locating a casino in Canberra could lead to corruption in the Australian Federal Police force. He expressed this view bluntly at private meetings on the issue.

"When word of this attitude leaked out, members of the force were upset which led Administrative Services Minister Kevin Newman to say that fears of police corruption had not been relevant to the cabinet discussion, but they had certainly been relevant to the Prime Minister.

"At one meeting he even quoted figures relating to the kind of bribes paid to police in areas where gambling occurred.

"Mr Fraser is reported to have expressed the opinion that in some states, a policeman could be bought for $25,000 a year.

"His attitude was that police corruption led to political problems. He wanted those sorts of problems confined to state level and not brought into the federal arena.

"If Mr Fraser believes organised gambling does not already occur in Canberra, however, he is naive.

"There are three well-known illegal gambling establishments right in the centre of the city with a weekly turnover estimated by some authorities at $250,000. They specialise in card games and SP betting.

"One of them used to offer the full range of gambling activities available in any well-appointed casino. It was equipped with roulette wheels, attractive croupiers in low cut gowns— the lot.

"At about the middle of last year the roulette wheels disappeared and the croupiers returned to Sydney. The reason was competition from another big illegal casino across the border in Queanbeyan.

"The Canberra area, it was said, was not big enough for two fully fledged casinos.

"The Queanbeyan casino, incidentally, has suspended operations temporarily, It closed its doors recently when word leaked out from NSW Police sources that Beck's Raiders were about to pay a visit to Queanbeyan.

"Canberra business sources were disappointed when the cabinet's decision was announced by Capital Territory Minister Michael Hodgman on Tuesday, but the illegal operators were happy."

Beck read the report with interest. According to his information, the casino in Queanbeyan was connected to several in Sydney which he had previously raided. But there was no planned raid as Beck had already sent men to Queanbeyan to scout it. The casino operators knew this and had closed down as a pre-emptive move against a raid.

On the other hand the illegal premises in Canberra were out of Beck's province. The Federal Police often contacted him for advice on how to deal with them, which he provided, but their policing was not as effective as a raid from Beck would have been.

With the raid on Freeman vetoed, Beck turned his attention to another matter that had been on his agenda, but on the backburner, so some time. This was the rampant SP bookmaking at Broken Hill. He had previously been instructed by Bill Allen that it was too far away, but as far as he could see it was in NSW and should be treated like any other part of the state.

Beck's interest was sharpened when he was sent a copy of a report by a TAB agent in Broken Hill, written in response to an earlier request from the TAB management for TABs throughout NSW to provide advice about SP bookmaking in their areas.

The Broken Hill agent was despondent.

"It would be merely an academic exercise to once more provide these details," he reported to his headquarters. "Even before 21 Division was emasculated, Broken Hill was considered to be another state. I have tired of providing positive information in view of the masterly inaction of the police from various commissioners downwards.

"At least 40 per cent of all hotels and approximately 60 per cent of all registered clubs at Broken Hill have a bookmaker on the premises. Some operators leave at 12 noon and 12.30 pm on Saturdays, others stay on. Midweek activity is minimal except Wednesdays when coverage is in about one third of the localities which take $10,000 of the (TAB) agency's average weekly take.

"Several licensed bookmakers have their agents operating for them on Saturdays in clubs and hotels. However, the vast majority of illegal operators have little or nothing to contribute to the local racing industry. It seems blatantly obvious the present State Government would not countenance any action against illegal SP operators, especially in Broken Hill. SP is a widespread and deep rooted, business conducted in an open manner."

Beck was already keen to go to the west and the report made him keener than ever. But he knew there was little enthusiasm in Police Headquarters for him to raid Broken Hill.

As Anderson had promised that his office would always be open to him, Beck decided to put the Broken Hill question direct to the Minister. He rang Anderson's office and reminded the receptionist that the Minister had said his door was always open to Beck.

The secretary had no such instruction.

"The best I can do for you is an appointment in three weeks' time," she said.

Astonished, Beck said this was just not good enough, and again repeated Anderson's promise. He told her to try harder and get back to him.

But when the phone rang soon after it was not the Minister's office, but the Police Commissioner. Abbott wanted to know why Beck wanted to see Anderson. When Beck told him, Abbott was not happy. He told Beck he did not want him to go to Broken Hill.

Beck argued back. Poor policing in Broken Hill was a political issue for the Government, he said. Surely the Police Minister would want to have a say on what was decided?

"Yes it is an issue for the Government," Abbott reluctantly agreed. "Alright, you can go and see Anderson—but I will come with you."

An appointment was made for four days later. Beck and Abbott walked from Police HQ to Parliament House in Macquarie St. When they entered the Minister's office there were already three other people with Anderson: two men and one woman from the Police Department (at that time separate from the Police Force).

Abbott said nothing while Beck outlined his plan to raid gambling operations in Broken Hill, explaining he had been told that he needed approval from the Government to go there.

Anderson appeared to be keen to help.

"If you want to go there, I'll accept the political flak," he said.

Beck immediately wondered why there would be any political flak to the Police Minister for enforcing the state's law. But before he could say anything, Abbott spoke up.

"I think before any decision is made, it's a matter for two cabinet ministers and they should make the decision whether Beck should go there," he said firmly.

This statement also puzzled Beck. Anderson was a cabinet minister, in charge of police, and no other minister's approval was needed. Abbott must have been referring to the Premier, although Wran had officially handed over the Police portfolio sometime before. There was no legal reason for the Premier to be involved in approving a raid in Broken Hill any more than a raid in Newcastle.

Beck suppressed his urge to jump in as Anderson processed Abbott's statement. Anderson had every right to override the Commissioner. But in the face of Abbott's insistence, he wavered.

He turned his attention to Beck.

"Would you go there yourself? Would you lead the raids?" he asked. Beck said yes, he would, as he was in the habit of leading his men.

Anderson frowned at this idea. He told Beck he was not to go himself. He also wanted to know how the Raiders would succeed when other police seemed unable to tackle the Broken Hill gambling.

The Minister was fishing for details that Beck did not want to provide. He was acutely aware of the public servants in the meeting. Although he did not doubt their integrity, he felt it was unfair and wrong for him to be asked to give out confidential information when it would most likely be taken down and written up in minutes which would be available to an unknown range of people.

Knowing the intense interest in his activities, Beck had no doubt that any plan he might mention in that room, would be sure to find its way to gambling interests in Broken Hill. If a raid was to proceed, he would have to devise a new strategy.

Anderson had been a policeman but had very little experience on the street. Beck could only assume he was being naïve, but also wondered if Abbott and Anderson had decided in advance how to play him.

While Beck tried to be deliberately vague in his answers, he was uneasy that too much had already been said.

After a discussion, Anderson confirmed that Beck could send a team to the west, provided he did not go himself, and provided his ministerial colleagues agreed.

With the end of his service looming close, Beck believed that any chance of a surprise raid on Broken Hill was now blown. He decided not to send men to the west as any raid was likely to be a waste of time.

"I think this was a case of people looking after their own interests. I think it was a political thing settled many years ago by both parties and Broken Hill was out of our reach," he said a few years later.

(Some time after Beck's retirement, a raid by 21 Division was conducted on Broken Hill. It was not a great success and serving police passed on to Beck privately their suspicions that that the gambling operators had indeed been tipped off in advance.)

The exchange over Broken Hill left Beck annoyed and in doubt about which, if any, of his superiors could be trusted. He was also concerned by a call from a woman, who would not provide her name, on Tuesday 2 February.

This woman claimed police involved with gaming and betting operators were organising a smear campaign to damage Beck before he left the Police Force. Beck was not sure whether it was a nuisance call or a last hurrah by the gambling interests. The same day, Beck was told by a senior NSW public servant that certain politicians were looking forward to his retirement with the same relief as the gambling operators. While no surprise, it was also disappointing to hear this from a non-partisan source.

With less than two weeks to go to his retirement, Beck and the squad were working as hard as ever. One day in early February they acted on a tip off about an illegal telephone betting office in George St Sydney, near Quay St. This alleged betting office was located directly above a very prominent sporting equipment shop.

As it turned out, the premises were used by C and B.

As detailed in the following account written by one of the squad members, the raiding party first entered the sports store looking for no access to the upstairs office from the store. There was none, so they went back to the shop front.

"After a short time, it was found that a show cabinet had been attached to the front of a door, which when opened led into a narrow flight of stairs. The stairs were just wide enough to allow two persons to pass. At the top of these stairs we found our way was blocked by a very formidable looking steel security/fire door. The Det Inspector knocked very loudly on this door several times and also called out that it was the Police and we were seeking entry.

"After a period of almost 10 minutes, he gave the order to have our 'key' brought forward. Our key was in fact a fourteen pound (6.3 kg) sledgehammer. The door and the door frame were then attacked with great gusto, and after about 10 minutes of continual hammering entry was gained.

"Upon entering the door, we found that we had entered large room, which was bare except for a standard telephone switch board of the plug and line type with a considerable number of lines. This was situated behind a small counter fitting, and to one side in the corner was a double wardrobe.

"When I opened the two doors of the wardrobe, a close examination of the interior was made. I found what appeared to be a door cut into the rear panelling of the wardrobe. I pushed and at the same time had one of the other police pull on a large coat hook which was also screwed into the wardrobe rear panelling. Suddenly the panel gave way, or more or less swung away from me, it formed a door into another large room.

"Inside of this room we found an array of desks, counters and tables. On these we located about 40 phones. We located other evidence that indicated our information was 'good', but not current as the evidence indicated the premises had been last used some two months previous.

"During our search we found a small area that was used as a tiny kitchen. On a wall was what appeared to be tea towel rails affixed to the timber window surrounds. These we found could be removed, at which time a removable panel of Masonite sheeting fell forward to reveal a window. Under a bench which ran along the window we located a rope ladder. This obviously was the means of escape, should a police raid take place whilst the premises were being used for telephone betting."

As big as they were, it appeared C and B were not prepared to risk being raided and closed by Beck. Beck found it amusing that the operators had literally resorted to a rope ladder in case the Raiders had made a visit. Less satisfying was the thought that the closure was very likely temporary.

Around this time, by chance Beck ran into a sporting identity who had been arrested by Beck's team but let off by then-Chief Magistrate Murray Farquhar (Farquhar was jailed for four years in 1985 after a District Court jury found him guilty of attempting to pervert the course of justice). The sportsman was a talkative fellow and could not help making a comment to Beck.

If all of the gambling operators had stuck together and made a coordinated campaign against Beck, he claimed, they would have beaten him. Beck thought it might have been true, although his experience told him that, as formidable as some of the criminal organisations were, the greatest threat to his success was always within the NSW Government.

* * * *

Since the beginning of his first stint on gaming and betting, Beck had asked for another officer to bring the division back to the usual quota of three and reduce the pressure on himself and his new deputy, Norman West. It was typical of his experience that now, when he was on the cusp of retirement, his request was approved, but the third officer did not start work until after Beck had departed.

Shortly before he retired, Beck and Ralph Lloyd wrote a summary report on the job that had been done. As well as fulfilling its charter to close the casinos and curtail SP betting, its success had a wider social significance, they proposed.

"There is no environment more destructive of the Police Force than a situation where the law is seen by the public at large to be openly flouted, through criminal conduct involving large sums of money and where police are seen to be, or seem, to turn a blind eye. The inference is insidious and inescapable. It matters not, so far as its damaging effect is concerned, whether the corruption is real or merely apparent. It frightens and alienates good people. The spectacle of gaming establishments, some of which were fully fledged casinos, flourishing openly was a disgrace to every policeman.

"Putting aside for the moment any consideration of whether SP betting or gaming is good, bad or indifferent, every policeman can, to adopt an expression used by the Minister, hold his head that much higher because we can at last be seen to do what a policeman must do, to enforce the law. Anything less commands only public derision.

"(Likewise), any legislation which is recognised more in the breach than in its observance reflects equally badly upon the government and creates nothing but cynicism."

Beck had done his best and he had done an extraordinary job. Some of the damage he had done to SP and casino operators had been permanent, but he was aware that others could bounce back quickly, if they were allowed to do so.

Cynical though he was, Beck did not let up until literally the last moment. He made his last patrol of illegal premises late that night but found them all to be closed, then finally returned to the office to settle his shift at midnight.

His 60th birthday, Sunday 14 February 1982 (St Valentine's Day), was commencing as he drove home, without great joy, knowing that he was now retired and no longer a serving policeman.

In Beck's First period on gaming policing, 3350 arrests were made in 10 months. It was a highwater mark in policing of illegal gaming that was never to be met again.

In the month before Beck's reappointment in October 1981, 21 Division had made a total of five arrests for illegal gambling.

In November, Beck's newly-formed Special Gaming Squad made 158 arrests and in December this rose to 403. Altogether, in just three and a half months, he and his hastily-formed team of Raiders made 1055 arrests.

His greatest regret was that he was taken off the squad in 1980, after his promotion, when there was still so much to do. If he had been left in charge of 21 Division from 1980, and allowed to pursue all targets, the illegal gambling industry would have been destroyed.

"Harking back, I think it was a grave mistake that I was removed but I feel that we had left our mark.

"We did the job that was expected of us, for the community," he said. "But I know the squad was causing too much friction and pressure on the Government, because it was so effective."

The *Daily Telegraph* had run a large article on Beck's last day at work. As the clock ticked into Sunday and the retirement was official, *The Sun-Herald* also carried a full page article on his retirement, complete with a photo of him and the famous sledgehammer with the headline, "Merv Beck hands over the key".

"The tireless Mervyn Beck turned 60 at midnight, saying goodbye to the NSW Police Force and to the state's illegal gamblers, whom he had kept in check right through his last 18 hour day," wrote Graham Gambie.

"During these final hours, Supt Beck leader of Beck's Raiders, added further arrests to the anti-gaming squad's lists, taking the tally since he took over in October to more than 1000.

"The big question, what happens now? Will Beck's successor be as successful? Or will the SP and casino operators come out of hiding like some of them predict and like they did last time Beck left the job?

"Yesterday's 18-hour crusade was fairly typical for the Superintendent. He left home at 6am, to organise the day's activities, after getting to bed only 2 hours before.

"At 2am yesterday he had led his squad on a raid with other police on a city hotel, allegedly open after licensing hours. Forty people were arrested and charged with being on licensed premises without lawful excuse.

"As Supt Beck helped escort those arrested into the paddy wagons, he was amazed to find that several people recognised him, shook his hand and wished him well in his retirement.

"Home at 4am, he was gone again at 6.

" 'I think people sleep too much these days, if I can get 6 hours every couple of days I'm alright,' he said.

"At 6.45 he was in the eastern suburbs lining up details for several planned SP operations in the area for later in the day. Supt Beck left for home on the stroke of midnight, but not before he had spent some hours touring the old haunts to make sure the big casino operators did not beat the gun and open on his last night of duty.

"The deputy leader of the squad, senior inspector Norman West is tipped to succeed Supt Beck. In an unusual gesture on Friday, the Police Minister Mr Anderson and Police Commissioner Mr Abbott called Supt Beck to headquarters to say thanks for doing a good job.

"Supt Beck, the man who proved illegal gambling could be checked, said yesterday, 'Sydney's casinos still have their lights out'.

"But he said gambling bosses were rubbing their hands together and boasting 'things are going to be alright after that Beck goes'.

"Supt Beck said, 'They have been a bit desperate over the past few months and think the drought has broken (now), but I am sure the fellows in this squad will be equal to the task.'

"Several arrests were made yesterday for illegal betting. In one raid, police used the key, a 10 pound sledgehammer, to gain entry to premises in the city. Friends will farewell him at Epping RSL Squad on Friday night,"

Then Beck's police career, 36 years of duty, was over. He had investigated 17 murders, arrested countless criminals, many of them dangerous, and commanded the Australian Peacekeeping Force in Cyprus.

But it was the two periods between 1979 and 1982 when he was hand-picked to head the Gaming and Betting squad, that provided both his greatest test and his greatest achievements.

The rope ladder in the inner sanctum of C and B.

Merv puts down the 'key'

Merv Beck hands over "the key."

By GRAHAM GAMBIE

The tireless Mervyn Beck turned 60 at midnight, saying goodbye to the NSW police force and to the State's illegal gamblers whom he had kept in check right through his last, 18-hour day.

During these final hours Superintendent Beck, leader of Beck's Raiders, added further arrests to the anti-gambling squad lists, taking the tally since he took over in October to more than 1000.

The big question: What happens now? Will Beck's successor be as successful? Or will the SP and casino operators come out of hiding, like some of them predict and like they did last time Beck left the job?

Yesterday's 18-hour crusade was fairly typical for the superintendent.

He left home at 6 am to organise the day's activities, after getting to bed only two hours before.

At 2 am yesterday he had led his squad on a raid with other police on a city hotel, allegedly open after licensed hours.

Forty people were arrested and charged with being on licensed premises without lawful excuse.

As Supt. Beck helped escort those arrested into paddy wagons, he was amazed to find that several people recognised him, shook his hand and wished him well in his retirement.

Home at 4 am, he was gone again at 6. "I think people sleep too much these days — if I can get six hours

every couple of days I'm right," he said.

At 6.45 he was in the eastern suburbs, lining up details for several planned SP operations in the area for later in the day.

Superintendent Beck left for home on the stroke of midnight, but not before he had spent some hours touring the old haunts to make sure the big casino operators did not "beat the gun" and open on his last night of duty.

The deputy leader of the squad, Senior Inspector Norman West, is tipped to succeed Superintendent Beck.

In an unusual gesture on Friday the Police Minister, Mr Anderson and Police Commissioner, Mr Abbott, called Superintendent Beck to headquarters to say thanks for doing a good job,

Superintendent Beck, the man who proved illegal gambling could be checked, said yesterday Sydney's casinos "still have their lights out."

But, he said, gambling bosses were rubbing their hands together and boasting: "Things are going to be all right after that Beck goes."

Superintendent Beck said: "They've been a bit desperate over the past few months and think the drought has broken. "But I'm sure the fellows in this squad will be equal to the task."

Friends will farewell him at Epping RSL Club on Friday night.

Several arrests were made yesterday for illegal betting. In one raid police used "the key" — a 10lb. sledge hammer — to gain entry to premises in the city.

Beck puts down the key.

CHAPTER FOURTEEN

Not Fade Away

The respect and camaraderie which Beck enjoyed with the men and women working for him was demonstrated at his farewell. Beck had always pushed them hard in terms of work hours, physical fitness and appearance, and they responded with pride in their work and a strong team spirit.

A few days after his retirement, the squad took Beck and Elsie to dinner. Elsie was extremely relieved that Beck had in fact retired. The squad presented him with a unique memento—a decorative sledgehammer with a short handle on it, handmade out of New Guinea timber by a friend of the squad who had helped them in their work and sadly, died shortly after Beck's retirement.

The hammer head was chromed and rested on a tri-level wooden stand. It was engraved with two little keys—as the sledgehammer was always referred to as the key, one with the initial M and the other with B. Underneath the hammer was a small silver plate with the words, "To Superintendent Merv Beck, from your Raiders, 23.10.81 to 13.2.1982". Another strip of metal around the base of the hammer was also inscribed, "The Raider's key". Beck was delighted.

He had always promised some of the team that he would have a game of tennis with them, but the furious pace with which they worked had prevented that. In his retirement he had the time so some weeks later he kept his promise and organised a game at the Moore Park courts in Redfern.

When he went to play with them they presented him with a new tennis racquet, a kit bag, and a full set of tennis gear. Again, Beck was bowled over by their appreciation.

"You know, I was astounded, and they just did this on their own volition. No one of them was any more friendly to me than the others, and when we hark back on discipline, I certainly required firm Discipline— but I hope it was friendly enough. This certainly indicates it couldn't have been too bad. But by jove, I appreciated these things upon my retirement. A great lot of fellows!"

A large public farewell dinner was also organised by a committee of Beck's friends. An astonishing 350 people attended, including Jim Lees and his wife, squad members, other serving and former police with whom Beck had worked, politicians, journalists, businessmen and women, victims of crimes which Beck investigated, and even Air Force colleagues from World War 2 including the commanding officer of 3 Squadron, Bobby Gibbs and some mates from the desert air force (who served in the Middle East, Sicily and Italy).

It was another wonderful occasion which warmed Beck's heart and made him feel appreciated, putting the trials of gaming and betting into a broader context. Lees and others gave speeches in praise of Beck which might have brought tears to the eyes of many, and Mr Beck, now a civilian, was presented with a stereo record player, a symbol of his leisure time.

Beck also received a letter, dated 16 February, from the Victoria Police Chief Commissioner, SI (Sinclair Imrie, known as Mick) Miller. Typically, Beck had written to him on his last day at work to comment on some issues raised in Beck's work with Detective Inspector Bob Pittaway and his Taskforce Zebra.

"I have long been an admirer of your efforts in the extremely difficult area of suppression of gaming offences," Commissioner Miller wrote. "Having had the same responsibility, myself, years ago, I have an understanding of the problem with which you are confronted. I can also appreciate the difficulties you have had to overcome to achieve the outstanding success you have. This is a reflection on your intelligence, integrity and dedication….Only those who have worked in this area would understand the pressures.

"I have always thought that the measure of professionalism and integrity of any police organisation can be judged by the attention which it gives to problems of unlawful gaming and betting and the success which it achieves. You can be assured that your contribution has done much to promote the reputation and standing of the New South Wales Police."

Despite the media claim that Beck would be allowed to choose his successor, this had not happened. Police Minister Anderson had nominated Inspector Norman West, the deputy leader under Beck, to take over. West was a good officer, but not Beck's first choice for the job as most of his career had been spent in internal affairs and on divisional and traffic duties.

Beck did not object to the appointment, however, as West was considered to be a man of integrity, in particular by Assistant Commissioner Barney Ross whose opinion Beck respected.

When Ross advised Beck that West was going to take over from him, he also asked Beck to assist the new leader as much as possible before he retired, and Beck was more than willing to do that. He wanted the team to succeed after his departure, and gave West as much advice as he could.

West had seen how Beck operated, and Beck thought West should follow this example as closely as possible.

He advised West to maintain strong discipline over the squad, as Beck did, because if he did not do so he would find that some police would soon get out of hand, as had happened so often in the past.

Beck also recommended that West accompany the men on all important raids, to guide and encourage his men, as this was very important to their success. Beck knew from experience that questions would often arise during a raid, and by being on the spot he could deal with them immediately. The leader would also be able to respond to allegations of misbehaviour, and ove full support to his men.

Beck also nominated a squad member, Sergeant Wilson, as someone to whom West could turn if he needed help. He suggested that West should discuss the field operations with Wilson and be guided by his advice.

Of course, Beck also warned West to be on the lookout for trickery and deceit from within the Police Force, given the potential for corruption money to affect behaviour.

The team Beck had put together had proven itself time and again. By the time he left they had enough experience for Beck to be confident they could keep up the good work without him, provided West took the advice of his sergeants and maintained the squad's harmony. Beck also left enough information about various gambling premises and operations to keep them fully occupied for another 12 months.

Unfortunately, despite West's best efforts, the team's performance soon began to wane. For various reasons, within a few months some of the squad members were transferred, others left of their own volition, while some took early retirement to leave the Police Force altogether.

One of those who left contacted Beck and indicated he had left out of frustration that the squad no longer had the support they expected in carrying out their raids. It was not the same inspiring place to work without Beck, he lamented.

Beck was again disappointed that his winning team was torn apart. History was repeating.

"I was very proud of that team I had left, they were dedicated and very loyal to me," he recalled. "Unfortunately it didn't take long before that team was broken up. Whatever came of the old adage you don't change a winning team? To my way of thinking, I think they were too effective."

One of the senior members of the squad had been moved after Beck's departure. In 1984 he told Beck he had been asked to return to gaming and betting, but had refused. He was still bitter about what had happened after Beck's retirement.

Beck was often asked, after his retirement, how he had been able to make such a difference. The gaming and betting squad had twice, in 1979 and 1981, been dissolved by the NSW Government because of poor performance, and replaced by new and largely inexperienced police led by Beck. The squad had then done an outstanding job, only to falter as soon as Beck left.

Beck's answer was that it all came back to leadership and discipline.

"Those in charge must accept the responsibility when their command fails due to their ineptitude," he said. "In addition to the lack of leadership, one cannot dismiss other ingredients such as political policies, and those influences such as greed and the temptation and pressure that came with the involvement of organised crime with all its pressures. The failure of the gaming and betting squad despite three different sets of members was inevitable because men will go in the direction in which they are led."

It was Beck's view that vast majority of police were decent men who were happy to follow the directions of a strong, connected leader. But when they were uncertain about the morality of their leaders, they found it difficult to disobey until it was too late and they were caught up themselves. Once caught they were afraid to rebel and they knew that blowing the whistle could place them in serious trouble.

Beck discovered later that West had not completely followed this advice. Rather than being on the spot during raids he preferred to supervise from a safe distance, finding an observation post from which he could view the premises being raided. This did not allow him to see what happened on the inside when the police actually made their arrests.

It was somewhat ironic that, more than a decade later, Norman West supported Beck's views during evidence to the NSW Independent Commission Against Corruption (ICAC) inquiry into the relationship between police and criminals. Although he did not go as far as Beck, he said supervising work in the field was a vital responsibility of police leadership.

"I don't know how you can do your job unless you go out and supervise, unless you see it on the ground," West said.

In contrast, the head of the gaming and betting squad at that time, Inspector George Taylforth argued the opposite. The squad was again in difficulties and Taylforth was forced to defend his leadership style.

Taylforth told the ICAC in September 1993 that close checking on the men under his supervision amounted to 'spying' and was bad for morale—a claim in which he was supported by the then-Assistant Commissioner, William Donaldson. Tony Lauer was the Commissioner at the time.

Taylforth also revealed that he rarely worked at nights and weekends, the times when the gaming and betting squad was doing most of its work. His reason was that 'modern management procedures' dictated that the staff should be left to carry out their duties without being checked on all the time.

Taylforth criticised West, as his predecessor, for watching his men too much, which he claimed was counterproductive.

Taylforth's attitude ignored the history of the squad and the real temptations it faced. When Beck read reports of Taylforth's comments he did not know whether to tear his hair, or laugh.

"He overlooked the sound advice that you can't become an experienced police officer by reading a book," commented Beck at the time. "It's experience and what you do with the experience which will carry the day.

"I didn't agree with either of them, Taylforth or West. My choice as the officer in charge was providing leadership, by leading from the front, and giving support and confidence to my men."

Needless to say, Beck had no time for Donaldson's 'modern' views either.

* * * *

While the Victorian Police Commissioner was fulsome in his praise of Beck, the NSW Police Force and its Minister, Peter Anderson, seemed less sincere in their appreciation. While the right words were said, their actions said the opposite.

Because he had been working very long hours and refused to take days off because of the work to be done, by the time Beck's retirement day came he was owed a lot of time off. Being a commissioned officer, unlike the 'troops', he was not eligible to be paid for overtime but he was entitled to have time off in lieu.

A week before, Beck reminded Anderson that he had a lot of time off owed to him—an issue he had flagged when he accepted the appointment. There was his holiday leave, totalling three weeks, 12 rest days accrued through work hours as recorded in his diary, and normal days off that he chose to work.

Anderson seemed sympathetic.

"Well that is not right," he said. "You've done the job and that's what matters, you shouldn't be behind because you worked hard.

"I'll see to it, I'll make sure steps are taken so your leave can be paid out through an ex gratia payment."

He told Beck to submit a claim through the Police Department.

Anderson's promise was made in front of the Police Commissioner. Beck duly applied for the money, which was estimated by a senior public servant at $5000 in 1982.

On his last day of service, Anderson had made a show of thanking him on behalf of the NSW Government and the Police Department. Beck had accepted the praise, while also hoping for something more tangible. As it turned out, Whether or not Anderson was sincere, his promise proved to be s hollow.

Beck never received the payment. Anderson claimed it was stopped by the then-NSW Treasurer, Ken Booth, who in turn claimed the payment was not proper and could not be made. Booth made the proclamation immediately before his own retirement.

Although there might have been scope to have this decision reviewed by the incoming Treasurer, this never happened. Beck was rarely angry but when the Government's decision was relayed to him, he felt justifiably wounded.

"I think more than anything there is a principle involved," he wrote at the time. "My feeling is one of disappointment and my advice to all police in particular is, if any promises are made to you by any politician, obtain them in writing so you will have something to fall back on.

"I have since been reliably informed that if I pursue this matter I will have a bucket dropped on me. I don't know what they have in mind, but if it comes to dropping buckets on people, let's see who will drop the bucket!"

Beck had been warned by a former senior policeman when he first took over gaming and betting that, unless he was careful, he would be used by an ungrateful government.

"It was one of the great disappointments of my police career to learn that this caution was well-founded," he recalled in his later years.

Even more hurtful, Beck was also denied official recognition of his long and distinguished career. Throughout his career, his supervisors had praised his outstanding work. He had been handpicked for jobs that the Police Force's most senior leaders admitted could not have been done by anyone else, and had succeeded. Yet in 36 years he had never received an official honour, despite a number of recommendations.

Beck's father Launcelot had received the King's Police Medal, which was considered a great honour. It had made a large impression on Beck. Throughout his police career he had worked hard and at the back of his mind was the hope that one day he would reach the same heights as his father and be recognised with the Queen's Medal (as it had become under Queen Elizabeth). It was an aspiration shared by most dedicated police of Beck's era.

Beck had certainly attained the criteria for award of the medal, but even if Beck had been in political favour, history intervened.

Commissioner Lees before he retired had told Beck apologetically that he could not recommend him for the Queen's Medal. The reason was that the Wran Government, being Labor and pro republic, had decided it was no longer appropriate to issue a medal in the name of the British monarch. This became a very sore point with many police of Beck's era, including himself, but there was nothing they could do about it.

Several years later, in 1984 Victorian Police Commissioner Mick Miller (who remained in the position until 1987) publicly lamented the lack of the Queen's Medal and called for its reintroduction. Two years later the Australian Police Medal was instituted, but this was too late for Beck.

As no medal was available for police service at the time, a friend nominated Beck for an Australian honour, but it came to nothing. It was hard for Beck not to see it as part of a pattern of official disregard for his work.

On the other hand, he continued to have a lot of public support and regular mentions in newspapers and other media. It was ironic that, just five weeks after his retirement, *The Sydney Morning Herald* on 28 March 1982 ran an expose on the role of Telecom in the SP bookmaking industry. The article also speculated that the Wran Government was preparing to legalise SP betting.

"Who is Telecom helping more—the SP bookies or the SP raiders?" the headline asked.

The standfirst read: "SP bookmakers have fled the Haymarket but the game goes on, aided by numerous changes in operators' telephone numbers. Richard McGregor reports on the state of SP bookmaking which the NSW Government may legalise after the ALP State Conference in June."

"Looming legalisation of SP betting and police pressure has thrown the multi-million dollar industry into turmoil but it has not by any means wiped it out.

"The well-publicised successes of the Special Gaming Squad popularly known as Beck's Raiders has effectively changed the public debate over SP or off-course telephone betting in NSW.

"Instead of establishments being notoriously open they are now ruthlessly closed.

"But their successes have overshadowed one important fact, that many of the big betting shops with entrenched criminal connections have so far survived the crackdown."

Beck did not dispute the article's claim that some of the big organised betting outfits had survived. He had wanted to prevent this by having clubs and other premises declared as common gaming houses to put them out of action permanently, but had not received the Government's support.

Now the squad under West was able to target these operators better because firstly, there were so few SPs left, and secondly, they had the experience, information and reliable informants generated under Beck's command. The article also described Beck as "zealous" and quoted unnamed SP operators that he was "a bit of a maniac". Beck had been accused before of zealotry and did not like he term. After finding that the original meaning of zealous was "enthusiastic and keen", however, he decided to take it as a compliment.

More pleasing to Beck was McGregor's confirmation of Telecom's nefarious role in aiding and abetting illegal SP operators. As Beck had found, McGregor reported that SP bookies frequently changed their telephone numbers with the aid of Telecom technicians, changed premises, and used diverters and sophisticated alarm systems.

One SP operator told McGregor he had changed his number six times in three weeks.

But McGregor now claimed, somewhat optimistically, that governments were preparing to take action against rogue telephone technicians. He said Peter Anderson had raised it with the Federal Minister for Administrative Affairs, Kevin Newman, who was responsible for the Federal Police. Federal Communications Minister, Ian Sinclair, had also directed Telecom officials to cooperate with NSW Police in efforts to crack down on abuses of telephones in SP betting, McGregor wrote.

Despite this prediction, no action was announced. A few months later, in May 1982 the heads of all state police forces were concerned enough to issue a statement heavily criticising Telecom for not helping police stamp out SP betting rackets, which they estimated were turning over $1 billion a year at the time.

The commissioners' proclamation was made as various state governments were edging closer to legalising casino gambling. A few months later, in October, Queensland passed the Casino Control Act, resulting in the opening of the state's first legal casino in November 1985 at the Conrad Hotel and Jupiters Casino complex at Broadbeach on the Gold Coast.

In NSW, legal versus illegal gambling remained a contentious political issue, and the Wran Government was still equivocating over casino policy. The NSW Labor Party—the party machine, as opposed to the caucus of Labor Members of Parliament—had for some time supported privately run casinos, supervised by an independent board. It now changed its policy to support a casino or casinos owned and managed by the Government, like the TAB.

As it had with the previous policy, the Government still led by Neville Wran recognised the public controversy this would cause and declined to act on the party's policy.

Beck himself felt compelled to add fuel to the controversy. After leaving the Police Force, he was—for the first period of any length in more than four decades—again a civilian. The shackles of confidentiality placed on him and other public servants were removed, and he wanted to tell the public and remaining police some of his story in the hope that the truth might lead to improvements.

Kevin Perkins, who had worked with Beck on many previous stories, was then the news editor of *the Sun-Herald* newspaper. It was a natural partnership for him to offer Beck the chance to tell the inside story of his experiences in gaming and betting.

The result was a series of four multi-page spreads in *The Sun-Herald* published over several weeks under the title, "the Beck Dossier". It was no surprise that they generated a storm of interest. Nor was it a surprise that some police reacted badly, accusing Beck of betrayal and more.

The series opened on 30 May 1982 with a banner headline, "I could have made a Million", It continued: "By retired Superintendent Merv Beck. That's how much he thinks it cost him to be an honest cop—the leader of the famous Beck's Raiders, scourge of Sydney's illegal gambling bosses."

"As head of Beck's Raiders, Supt Merv Beck became the scourge of Sydney's underworld. He closed down Sydney's casinos and smashed the State's biggest SP rackets," Perkins wrote.

"Now, he's telling his astounding story for the first time…It's the story of an honest cop who did his job despite enormous pressure from criminals and colleagues…"

Beck was quoted at length.

"I'm telling my story in the public interest…. To explain the difficulties police have and how things work in the NSW Police Force, how organised crime can hamstring an honest policeman and enrich those who are corrupt. I'm telling this story to defend the great majority of honest police and as a guide to young policemen on traps to be avoided in their careers.

"A policeman's work is difficult enough without the risk of succumbing to bribes. The job has occupational hazards. It can also be destructive to the character, and there is often a social stigma.

"In recent years, young policemen complained to me that when they went to social functions they were careful not to say who they were because, if they did, there would be snide remarks about SP and gambling joints and insinuations they must be getting something out of it.

"The detective in particular must be careful whom he mixes with. People just don't realise what it's like to work in the area of big criminals. It's a jungle. The detective is on a razor's edge and it's so easy to get into trouble.

"As a servant of the community, the policeman is open to criticism from all quarters. He can be reported on, complained against anonymously and is constantly under the threat of internal investigation. Criminals make baseless accusations to put him out of action in an inquiry (criminals used this tactic against Scotland Yard and I've experienced it too).

"In court, he's open to vicious attacks and allegations used as a defence. He must stand up to the best legal brains as learned counsel explore his actions, which he usually has to take at short notice, even seconds.

"In all of this he suffers personal stress and anxiety as all people do, for he has the same pride and emotions as other people. He bleeds like any other person.

"The policeman is allowed no error without being sued, publicly admonished, interrogated by his officers and charged with neglect. He does his job, often despite inadequate laws, and is made to feel as if he, not the person charged, is on trial.

"I think more is expected of him than anyone else in the community, yet he's taken for granted. And when he's under attack, his family suffers with him.

"I know he must be strictly controlled because of his great responsibility and the effect his actions can have on people's lives. But it should be remembered (that) the policeman is the front line between the law-abiding citizen and the criminal, and needs all the support he can get.

"He should not be used as a political football. Politicians should not meddle or interfere in his duties and, when he does his job, he should not have to suffer the threat of political reprisal.

"I believe the Police Commissioner should be allowed to run the police force. In that regard I admired one former commissioner, Bill Mackay (1935 to 1948), for the way he stood up to the politicians.

"The political handicap under which police have to work was summed up recently when a detective told me he and his mates had to look for political aspects as a matter of self-preservation before they began any investigation.

"That's a bad situation and not in the public interest."

In the final instalment of the Dossier, Beck probably surprised many of his fans in the community by supporting legalisation of casino gambling.

"Casinos should be legalised because people will gamble no matter what others may think of it," he wrote. "But if privately owned, the

Government must thoroughly check the backgrounds of those obtaining the licences in order to keep criminals out.

"I'm not so sure about legalising SP operators, I can see serious problems in controlling SP operators' earnings.

"(At the same time) the clamp-down will have to be maintained on illegal casinos and SP, otherwise they'll spring up like desert blooms after rain."

If illegal gambling was under control, part of the proceeds of legal gambling could go towards victims of crime, Beck suggested.

He also recommended that a Federal Crimes Commission be established, which among other things could take evidence with immunity for whistleblowers and access Australian Taxation Office information.

A recurring theme of the Dossier articles was political interference hampering honest police, even at the highest levels. It was daring journalism, although thanks to the draconian defamation laws, names were scarce. According to Kevin Perkins in his book, *The Gambling Man*, the *Sun-Herald* editor reported to the board of John Fairfax Pty Ltd (publishers of the *Sun-Herald and Sydney Morning Herald*) that the Dossier series was the best story he could remember ever appearing in the paper.

Not everyone appreciated Beck's candour. Shortly after the Dossier was published, Beck attended the annual Police Association Officers dinner at Randwick Racecourse. As a matter of course, all police officers retiring in the previous year are invited to attend the dinner. Beck had received his invitation in the mail and did not hesitate to accept.

Before heading to the dinner, Beck dropped into Police Headquarters where he ran into Commissioner Abbott. Abbott made it clear he was not impressed by Beck's newspaper revelations.

"You'll regret some of those things you said the in the paper," Abbott said darkly. He also expressed surprise that Beck was going to attend the dinner, implying that he might find a hostile crowd. Beck brushed off Abbott's comments, as he felt he had nothing to apologise for.

The dinner was a very formal, large affair. The diners, all police, were sitting in rows along long tables. Beck was seated next to a very senior officer whom he knew, named Graham and was enjoying the food and chat when the room was called to attention to hear an address from the special guest, NSW Governor, Air Marshall Sir James Rowland..

While the Governor was speaking, a man got up and moved behind the chairs on Beck's row until he was at Graham's place. He then squeezed in between Graham and Beck, perched on Graham's chair, Graham was literally pushed out of his place but instead of reacting angrily, when he saw who it was, he just stood up and moved to another place.

Then Beck also turned and saw that his unexpected visitor was the former Commissioner, Merv Wood, who had received a large and highly unfavourable mention in the Dossiers.

The Governor was still speaking but as word spread through the audience that Wood was confronting Beck, few of them had eyes or ears for anything except what they expected to be a heated confrontation.

Wood put his left elbow on the table and lent his chin on his hand, leaning up close to Beck and staring at him in a menacing fashion. Beck could smell alcohol on his breath, he was so close. Beck responded in kind, putting his right elbow on the table and taking up a mirror image pose. They glared at each other, but neither said a word.

Beck was trying to work out how to respond if Wood decided to take him on physically, and decided he had the advantage as his right hand was already raised. If Wood went for him, Beck thought, he was ready to let him have it with a punch from his right hand.

Before it could come to blows, if that was the intention, another senior officer, Jim Black, appeared and took Wood by the arm, breaking the stalemate. Wood allowed himself to be led away, while Beck watched him go - glad that it had not come to a fight, but confident he would have met any challenge raised with him.

The Governor finished his speech and shortly afterwards the dinner concluded and the diners left the tables to mingle. There was almost a queue of people coming up to Beck to ask him keenly, "What was that all about?", although they knew the answer. Beck just responded, "I don't know, go and ask Wood."

A few minutes later Beck went off to the toilet. As he approached, Wood came out. Beck paused, ready for whatever Wood might throw at him, verbally or otherwise. It was a perfect opportunity, but Wood surprised him. In contrast to his former aggression, or perhaps thinking better about taking Beck on, Wood stepped back and held the door open for Beck to go in. He then closed the door behind Beck, and that was the last Beck saw of him.

* * * *

The Wran Government made no official response to the publication of the Dossier. Although Beck had done an extraordinary job, no more and no less than he was directed to do, it became clear that the Government's preference was that Merv Beck should fade away and be forgotten by the public and the media, and the sooner the better. If history had to be tweaked to make that happen, so be it.

Just over a year after Beck's retirement, in March 1983, Peter Anderson claimed the gaming and betting squad was doing better under Senior Inspector Norm West, than it had under Beck.

Anderson's comments followed another report in the *Sydney Morning Herald,* this one claiming illegal gambling interests had begun a smear campaign against West and Deputy Commissioner (Operations), Barney Ross.

After a question in the NSW Parliament about the article, Anderson claimed death threats had also been made, and praised West and Ross. It was a successful publicity grab, attracting attention and implying that the new brooms were so effective they were making enemies. No such supportive statements had been made when Beck and his family were under threat.

Anderson said: "The rumours, fairy tales, and innuendo would not be of great concern if they were not becoming linked to much more sinister aspects, such as death threats, as they have been in recent weeks.

"Since its inception in October 1981, the Special Gaming Squad has proved to be one of the most successful police units in this State.

"The success of its original officer in charge, Superintendent Merv Beck, is well known and Senior Inspector West has not only matched his predecessor's success but exceeded it. It is a classic tactic of the illegal gaming fraternity to adopt these sorts of smear tactics when they are getting a particularly hard time."

Nothing came of the rumours and "fairy tales", nor of the threats. Given his own experience, Beck could well believe that Ross and West and their families had received threats, and he hoped this meant they were hurting the criminals and their corrupt police mates. He had felt at the time that West was 'thrown to the wolves' in being asked to take over the job from Beck, on the frontline between the law and some of Australia's toughest, most ruthless and most powerful criminals at a time when they were poised to strike back.

Anderson's praise, on the other hand, seemed designed as much to dispel Beck's public status as a 'giant killer' as to bolster West. Beck did not like to see his squad's achievements downplayed, and his annoyance was amplified when the Premier ran with the same theme.

In an interview on *Willesee,* the most popular television current affairs show of the time, Wran repeated the claim that more illegal gambling was being cleaned up now than when Beck was in charge of the squad.

When Beck saw the interview he was dismayed. He liked to give people the benefit of the doubt, and decided that Wran had been misled and both he and Anderson were quoting from incorrect statistics given to them by the Police Force. Still, he was annoyed as he knew from his contacts and friends in gaming and betting and other areas of the force that the squad had slowed down and its success rate had dropped.

Approaching the media would have been too self serving. But when he was contacted by the ABC's flagship television current affairs program, *Four Corners* on another matter, he decided to set the record straight.

Beck was able to show that the figures quoted by two senior ministers were incorrect, and in fact it took more than 12 months for the team led by West to record anything like the number of arrests which he had carried out in less than one third of the time.

"These statements by politicians—if they weren't stupid and hurtful they would be amusing," Beck recalled.

"If the team did better after I left I would congratulate them. But they didn't—the figures didn't stand up."

Detractors in both government and the police kept up their attempts to undermine his reputation and legacy. It happened again in December 1985 when Beck was rated in a *Sydney Morning Herald* article as "Sydney's most effective crime buster". This prompted a letter to the editor from the head of the Criminal Investigation Branch from 1966 to 1968, Ray Blissett (not to be confused with Bob Blissett, who played the tape of Freeman to Beck).

Ray Blissett, nicknamed The Blizzard during his policing years, had retired in 1969, long before Beck first took over gaming and betting, but he continued to comment in the media on police matters for many years. He and Beck had private history which made his media comments on Beck's achievements less of a surprise to Beck, but no less a disappointment. Blissett had also made no secret at the time of his annoyance at the publicity Beck had received as head of the gaming squad.

Blissett now objected to the accolade given to Beck by the newspaper.

"It is simply not true," he wrote. "When I joined the police force in 1928 the late Joe Chuck was achieving headlines similar to those attained by Mr Beck. In the 1950s the late Ron Walden did likewise.

"They used the same tactics as Mr Beck—search warrants and a sledgehammer. They knocked down doors and locked up lots of people – for doing what? Gambling, a national pastime in this country, meriting a minimal fine.

"Admittedly there are rackets associated with organised illegal gambling but through the years crime, defined as a serious violation of human law, has covered a much wider scope. Therefore, how can you refer to a man who effectively slowed down illegal gambling for a short period as Sydney's most effective crime buster?"

Blissett's casual dismissal of the link between organised crime and illegal gambling was interesting. To add insult to injury, he named crooked cops Colin Delaney and Ray Kelly among others as "dedicated detectives who put gunmen and others away for years". He finished with a flourish: "their present day counterparts (are) fighting not only the underworld, but graft and corruption in the highest places."

Blissett had another go when he was joint editor of *Police News* magazine published by Tolan Printing in 1990. The magazine included a number of articles he had written, as well as newspaper clippings from Beck's period and a brief account by Beck himself.

"I, like many, could have claimed greater fame than Beck in the real world of crime because I believe, despite the enormous arrests rate quoted by Beck in the illegal gambling field, that I personally arrested as many real dinki-di criminals as any other NSW policeman," claimed Blissett. "I cannot recall arresting anyone for betting or gaming but that is not to say they should not have been arrested."

By this time, 1990, the NSW Government had changed. The Liberal National Coalition was in power and Labor was in Opposition. In an apparent concession to the new Government's anti-corruption focus, Blissett conceded that policing of gaming had not been genuine before Beck.

"My query is why we had to wait until 1979 for it to happen? Why was it not taken more seriously in prior years? The answer is in one simple word—graft."

In several later newspaper articles in 1993 and 1994, with a Royal Commission in NSW Police looming, Blissett admitted the corruption and criminal connections to the gaming squad were not as trivial as he originally suggested. But he refused to change his view of Beck.

He even named former Commissioner Fred Hanson as a cop who was probably on the take from the big SPs.

"There have been casinos and SP men here (in NSW) as long as I can remember," Blissett wrote in *The Sun-Herald* on June 13, 1993. "When I was around Number 21 Special Squad knocked these blokes off regularly. But politicians got some of the cream and I suppose a few policemen were getting a little of the cream on their coffee too."

What readers did not know was that Blissett and Beck went way back. Blissett had been on the consorting squad with Beck, although he was considerably older. Beck remembered well the occasion on which Ray Blissett was bawled out by the then-CIB Chief, Superintendent Jack Flint, after complaining to the Police Association about working long hours.

When Beck had been stationed at Camperdown and Blissett was CIB chief, Blissett had complimented Beck on his outstandingly high arrest rate. But when Beck was heading the gaming and betting squad, Blissett (then retired) had a different attitude.

Blissett had contacted Beck several times to ask favours. Blissett had been a detective on the consorting squad for many years, patrolling the Balmain-Glebe area. When Beck headed the gaming squad, Blissett asked him to go easy when raiding gambling places in Balmain. Some of his former informants were SPs, Blissett said, and they were "not bad people" and should not be targeted by the Raiders.

Beck suspected the relationship went well beyond the provision of information about other criminals.

"Give them a go in my old territory," Blissett had entreated, to no avail.

"Sorry Ray, I can't do that. One in, all in."

Given this history, Beck was not surprised that Blissett was less than fulsome in his praise for Beck's work. It did not pass him by that Blissett was another recipient of the Queen's Police Medal, in 1967.

"There's no competition in the cleaning up of crime," Beck commented. "You either do it or you don't, you do your duty or you don't.

"That was my view, and fortunately all these young people that I worked with, they responded handsomely and supported us and that's why we were able to get that large amount of criminal arrests."

It was not just Beck's record that was subject to historical revision. As astute as he was, Neville Wran was never one to cling to a sinking ship. As time went by and more information emerged, Wran began to distance himself from his predecessor, Robert Askin.

Less than six months after Askin's death, a link emerged between Askin and the notorious Nugan Hand Bank—an Australian merchant bank that collapsed in 1980.

In February 1982, Retired US Admiral Earl Preston 'Buddy' Yates, revealed that he had accepted the position as the bank's president on advice from Robert Askin and a senior Sydney bank officer. Yates said he had trusted Askin, who gave him a favourable opinion about the bank principals, Frank Nugan and Michael Hand. Askin knew them well and shared an office with them in Macquarie St.

On 9 November 2015 the *Sydney Morning Herald* reported that one of the bank's principals, Michael Hand had been found after being on the run from Australian authorities for decades.

"One of Australia's most wanted fugitives, Michael Hand, the cofounder of the Sydney-based international merchant bank Nugan Hand, has been found alive and well and living in small-town America.

"He vanished in 1980 amid rumours of CIA and organised crime involvement in the bank as the United States attempted to back anti-communist governments and anti-communist insurgents at the height of the Cold War.

"Hand disappeared in June 1980 after his partner, Griffith-born lawyer Frank Nugan, then 37, was found dead beside a .30-calibre rifle in his Mercedes-Benz outside Lithgow…

"Over the years, the two words Nugan Hand became shorthand for drug-dealing, gun-running, organised crime and clandestine intelligence activities.

"But nobody has been convicted. Governments, security and espionage agencies ran dead or appeared to look the other way. Many men associated with the bank's affairs in Australia, the US and Asia have died early or in mysterious circumstances."

With this link now in the open, around September 1982 Premier Wran tried to draw a contrast between Askin and himself.

He now agreed with claims that corrupt practices were allowed to flourish under the Askin Government.

In contrast, he claimed, his own government had taken strong action. It had set up an independent Police Board (a move Wran had personally opposed for years), cracked down on drugs, and set up a security unit to deal with corrupt police. When Wran said these measures should have been taken years ago he was undoubtedly right, but somehow he managed to avoid the obvious implication that his own government should have acted earlier.

Two years on, in May 1986, Wran put further distance between himself and Askin. Asked if he now believed Askin had been "a crook" he replied simply: "Yes."

* * * *

After his retirement, Beck and Elsie moved from Sydney to the western NSW town of Dubbo, where they lived a very different life on 30 acres.

They quickly fitted in to the Dubbo community. During their first summer there in 1982, Merv lent a hand to fight bushfires around Christmas, and the couple formed lasting friendships. They stayed there for 10 years, before they returned to the Sydney region for medical reasons.

Even when he was doing his best to enjoy a quiet retirement with Elsie, Beck could not escape from his old life. He was often rung for comment by journalists, which kept his name before the public and also his enemies alike. But when the phone rang in the Beck household and no one replied to Beck's greeting, Beck would just tell himself it was a wrong number.

The years after his retirement saw a series of dramatic revelations about corruption in NSW, which eventually culminated in the announcement of the Royal Commission into the NSW Police Service in May 1994. The Royal Commission, led by Justice James Wood, was both a turning point and a sign of change in broader society.

Before this, the scandalous revelations began only weeks after Beck's retirement. Justice Perrignon's inquiry into what became known as the 'Allen Affair' ran from January to March 1982.

Beck was of course keen to provide information to the inquiry into Allen. Chief Superintendent Ralph Masters, who was assisting Justice Perrignon, contacted Beck and told him he would be called as a witness. But although Beck had obviously relevant experiences to share, this did not happen and Beck did not have the opportunity to tell his story.

Despite this omission, Justice Perrignon delivered a damning report on 21 April 1982. It disclosed close relationships between Allen—the greatest thorn in Beck's side—and members of Sydney's organised crime elite including Abe Saffron, Perce and Bruce Galea, and George Freeman. These relationships had continued right throughout 1981.

Between March and September 1981—after he had been appointed Deputy Commissioner of NSW Police— Allen met Abe Saffron in his office in Police Headquarters, alone, on six occasions. Incredibly, each time he came, Saffron signed the visitor's book. It appeared neither man felt they had any reason to hide their association. Justice Perrignon described Saffron as "unsavoury" and "involved in illicit activities".

Allen also admitted that a few months before the inquiry began, in August 1981 he had attended George Freeman's second wedding and reception at the Sydney Hilton Hotel. Other guests included a collection of Sydney's leading criminals, as well as a director of the Sydney Turf Club and prominent journalists.

Allen also had an ongoing relationship with Bruce Galea (who had been arrested by Beck in December 1981). In February 1981, Bruce— who described himself as 'a reputable bookmaker'—had paid out $4200 to then-Assistant Commissioner Bill Allen for a 20 to 1 bet on the horse, How Apparent, at Rosehill Racecourse.

Galea told the inquiry he was aware that money could be laundered through bookmakers but claimed "it was never done with Allen". Allen told the inquiry in April 1982 that he had won more than $18,000 over the previous year gambling on horse racing.

Allen was asked if he knew that people often attributed large sums of cash found in their possession to "gambling wins". Somehow maintaining a straight face, he claimed he was not aware of the practice.

Bookmaker Bill Waterhouse also appeared before the Perrignon inquiry. He said he had first met Allen at the Gosford races in 1954. They were friends and Allen had visited his home a few times. He said Allen was not a large bettor and usually placed bets of $10 to $20 a time (which made his $18,000 in wins very lucky indeed). Waterhouse, father of Robbie Waterhouse, had also helped to organise the Allens' Vegas trip.

Sergeant Second Class Warren Molloy, chief of the Special Licensing squad based at King's Cross, gave damning evidence that Allen had tried to bribe him to influence his policing activities. Molloy said Allen had given him $500 in cash in an envelope on five separate occasions in 1981. His evidence was corroborated by John Avery, who would become Commissioner just three years later. Avery said in 1981, Molloy had told him that Bill Allen had tried to give him (Molloy) money, presumably to influence the way he conducted his licensing duties.

Molloy told the Police Tribunal, "If anything happens to me they'll never get another honest policeman to come forward."

Justice Perrignon accepted Molloy's evidence. He found that Allen had paid Sergeant Warren Molloy $2500 in an attempt to compromise him and to render him susceptible to improper influence, and had lied to the tribunal.

He also concluded that Allen's association with Jack Rooklyn in Las Vegas was likely to bring discredit on the force.

Justice Perrignon's report was referred to then-NSW Solicitor General Mary Gaudron (who later replaced Lionel Murphy on the High Court). Gaudron concluded in May 1982 that there were insufficient grounds to begin criminal proceedings against anyone as a result of the inquiry.

Allen's reputation was shot but he was not entirely without favour. On the day Gaudron's report came out, the Wran Government accepted Allen's proposal that he be demoted to Sergeant First Class and be allowed to retire instead of being dishonourably discharged.

The deal surprised and disgusted Beck and many others. It meant that Allen was eligible for a comfortable police pension for life, despite proven misconduct. Apparently, the NSW Treasurer had no qualms about this deal, in stark contrast to the refusal to honour the commitment to pay out the leave to which Beck had been entitled.

Other sergeants at the time were furious that being reduced to their level, which they had reached by years of hard work, was considered a punishment for a corrupt policeman who was then allowed to leave on his own terms.

In addition, Allen's legal costs for the tribunal inquiry were paid by the NSW Government.

In July 1982 Allen was finally replaced as Deputy Commissioner by John Perrin. Much like Allen himself, Perrin was appointed ahead of 12 more senior officers.

Allen's very soft landing drew the attention of journalists. A contrast was drawn with the treatment of whistleblower Phillip Arantz, who had been dismissed with no pension because of his 'misconduct' in exposing the long-standing deception practised by the NSW Police Force in relation to crime figures, through Paddy's Book.

The media pressure forced the Government to review the situation and in 1985 Arantz received $250,000 compensation, but neither an apology nor correction of his dismissal.

(This changed in 1989 when the Liberal-National Coalition NSW Government led by Nick Greiner, which had won power the previous year, passed special legislation to notionally reinstate Arantz. When Arantz died in 1998, the Sydney Morning Herald described him as "the archetypal whistleblower".)

Despite Gaudron's finding, in 1986 charges were finally laid against Allen for five counts of bribery relating to payments made to Molloy. On 29 February 1991, Judge Ducker in the District Court criticised the government prosecutors for taking five years to bring the charges to court, but said this would not prevent Allen from having a fair trial. He also refused Allen's cheeky application for a permanent stay on proceedings.

Later Allen was sent to the prison farm at Bathurst. He was also charged over two separate incidents—assault on a milkman, and breaking a radio aerial of a civilian's car, for which he received a $200 bond.

Beck always believed that Neville Wran's appointment of Bill Allen as Deputy Commissioner of Police was a prime example of the dangers of political interference in running of the force. Despite the evidence, he gave Wran the benefit of the doubt by suggesting the appointment was fuelled by lack of understanding—something of which Wran was rarely accused. Beck was undoubtedly closer to the mark when he added, "and politicians are inevitably pushing their own agendas".

A postscript to the Allen Affair appeared in 1991 when John Dowd, by then retired from Parliament, revealed what a nasty piece of work Allen was in a series of articles, "the Dowd Dossier", published in the *Sydney Morning Herald*.

Dowd referred to an incident dating back to when Allen was a detective inspector at Chatswood Police Station. Dowd had received word that he was a target and could be shot by a hitman because of his probes into crime and corruption in Sydney. He took the threat seriously because the criminal James McCarthy Anderson, who had given Dowd documents, had already been fired at.

In the article, Dowd said Anderson claimed he had been asked by Abe Saffron, on behalf of Bill Allen, to 'get some dirt' on Dowd so they could blackmail him.

Anderson confirmed this to a parliamentary inquiry. "Allen contacted Saffron who contacted me to find out what Dowd's preferences were. Does he like little girls, big girls, little boys, big boys, is his wife playing around?" he said.

Instead of carrying out the request, Anderson ratted on Saffron, his former employer, by giving Dowd a second set of nightclub account books. These became famous when, in a direct parallel to the downfall of American gangster Al Capone in 1931, Saffron was convicted and served 27 months in jail on tax charges.

CHAPTER FIFTEEN

A Larger Jigsaw

While the law moved slowly against figures like Allen and Saffron, public and political concern about corruption was changing rapidly. The two years after Beck's retirement proved to be a tumultuous time for the Wran Government, as it was caught up in a relentless series of scandals. In retrospect, it was a political miracle that Wran and his government survived this wave of allegations, especially given what is now on the public record.

For Beck, it was increasingly clear that his experiences were one piece of a larger jigsaw. As the focus was pulled wider, illegal gambling was revealed as a common thread behind corruption among three of the most essential pillars of NSW society—police, government, and the legal system.

The first inquiry which should have rung alarm bells in NSW was a Board of Inquiry into SP bookmaking and casinos, set up by the Victorian Government in 1982. Beck gave detailed oral evidence to the inquiry, chaired by Justice Francis Xavier Connor, about his experience in NSW, including SP betting operations which he had raided, as well as a written submission about the SP industry Australia wide.

Beck also told the inquiry candidly that his attempt to wipe out illegal gaming and betting in Sydney had been handicapped by lack of support by senior police officers and MPs. He revealed the offers of bribes and the threats and smear campaign against him.

Beck commented publicly then, "Let it be understood. Big-time gambling could not survive in this State (NSW) without corruption. Certainly not to the extent it does...

"But it does because of protection rackets, because of corrupt police, corrupt politicians and corrupt people at all levels in our society, even individuals in the media."

In his 1983 report, Justice Connor concluded that illegal SP bookmakers were turning over about $1000 million a year in Victoria, $1800 million in NSW and about $4000 million in total nationally. He also found that the major bookmakers who ran phone networks were part of Victorian organised crime, and had interstate connections.

Justice Connor expanded on his findings at a public conference on gambling. He said illegal bookmaking was a multi-million dollar industry run by organised criminals. Each outfit operated 40 to 50 phones, backed by enough technical resources to enable them to move the entire network to another premises within a week, if they were closed down in a police raid.

"The profits, it is a fair inference, are used to finance other organised crime or, even more insidious, to enable organised crime figures to go into legitimate business. Illegal bookmakers prosper, making millions of illegal dollars, simply because they do not pay income tax or betting tax," Connor said.

Political change was underway. The Labor Party swept into power at the federal level in March 1983, led by the hugely popular Bob Hawke. Although the NSW ALP and particularly its right wing held great power within the party, the new Hawke Government was focused on bedding down and starting its reform program. It could not afford to be seen to be providing favours to the struggling NSW Government or to Wran himself.

This conflict became intense when, only four weeks after the federal election, new allegations were levelled at Premier Wran.

The ABC's flagship public affairs program, *Four Corners,* aired an investigation by reporter Chris Masters and producer Peter Manning into the administration of rugby league in NSW.

This is how the ABC summed up the program and its aftermath in 2001[29].

"The resulting story, 'The Big League' outlines how the League's President, Kevin Humphreys, had misappropriated funds and been charged by police. The story alleges that NSW's Chief Stipendiary Magistrate, Murray Farquhar intervened to have those charges dismissed, at the behest of the NSW Premier, Neville Wran.

---

[29] https://www.abc.net.au/4corners/the-big-league---1983/2841712

"Given the defamatory nature of the program it is referred to the ABC's Managing Director who, in an unprecedented move, refers it to the ABC Board for approval. The program goes to air unchanged.

"Ten days later the NSW Attorney General announces a Royal Commission and Premier Wran stands aside while the investigation takes place. The Commission finds that Magistrate Murray Farquhar did influence the committal hearing, but exonerates Mr Wran, finding that Farquhar did not act at his behest.

"Farquhar is tried and found guilty, serving four years. Humphreys was also convicted of his original offence and fined $4000."

The Royal Commission into Certain Committal Proceedings Against K. E. Humphreys ran from May to July 1983. Led by Justice (later Sir) Laurence Street, it found that the basic allegations made by Four Corners were true.

The essential facts were that in 1977 Humphreys, then president of the NSW Rugby League was facing charges of fraud after allegedly 'borrowing' thousands of dollars from the Balmain rugby league club, of which he was secretary.

He needed the money to repay gambling debts.

On the morning of 11 August, the day of Humphreys' committal hearing in the Central Magistrates' Court, Chief Magistrate Murray Farquhar's secretary told him to take a phone call. "The premier is on the phone," she said.

Immediately after the finishing the call, Farquhar told his deputy to assign a compliant magistrate to the Humphreys case. "The premier has just phoned," he said. "Kevin Humphreys is not to be committed."

The new magistrate chosen for the case was Kevin Jones. After a two-day hearing, Jones dismissed the charges against Humphreys.

Premier Wran sued the ABC for defamation. *Four Corners* could not prove that the Premier had made the call, although it could prove that the Chief Magistrate had claimed this and that other magistrates believed Wran had intervened to save Humphreys.

The case was settled out of court, at the request of the ABC Board.

Veteran crime journalist Evan Whitton in his book *Can of Worms*[30] wrote of the Humphreys inquiry: "It is clear that, whatever it was called, the Commission marked a watershed in the history of public corruption in New South Wales: it established both a climate

---

[30] http://netk.net.au/Whitton/Worms16.aspn

in which automatic cover up of malpractice in public life would no longer suffice, and a momentum of disclosure which had far-reaching consequences."

Even while the Commission was running, another major scandal had erupted. There were claims that NSW prisoners were being routinely released from prison early, after paying corrupt officials. Only months after Wran was cleared by Laurence Street, his Minister for Corrective Services, Rex Jackson, was under a cloud.

In a sign of things to come, it was phone tapping by police which revealed the early release scandal. In April 1983, Federal Police had placed taps on phones while investigating drug trafficking, and stumbled on conversations relating to the early release scheme[31]. The following month the AFP advised the Hawke Government. The Prime Minister, Bob Hawke, asked his Special Minister for State, Mick Young, to contact the appropriate NSW Minister and "ensure, so far as it was within the Commonwealth's capacity to do so, that all necessary steps were taken to fully investigate the matters in issue"[32].

Jack Ferguson was the acting Premier as Wran had stepped down over the Humphreys affair. Despite the AFP concerns, and despite public complaints from five NSW judges in one week in June about early releases, Jackson was allowed to remain as Minister.

In an ironic twist, or perhaps just a sign of how powerful Beck appeared to some, in September 1983 Jackson took a swipe at him, accusing Beck of ordering a phone tap on the Minister's phone when Beck was heading the gaming squad.

Jackson claimed an anonymous caller had told him that Beck had ordered Telecom to bug Jackson's phone and, as a result of this, certain information had been passed on to "prominent members of the Liberal Party".

Beck found himself being questioned at his Dubbo home by a young Federal Policeman investigating misuse of Telecom property. Beck was so angered by the accusation and the fact that it was being taken seriously that he fired more questions at the young acting sergeant than the other way around. The claim was soon proven to be ridiculous: Beck had no authority to direct Telecom to do anything, and Telecom was not in the business of placing bugs on anyone's phone and certainly not a minister's.

---

[31] ibidem

[32] Statement to Federal Parliament, quoted in ibidem.

The Federal Police involvement was a double irony as it later emerged that there had indeed been a tap on Jackson's phone—placed by Federal, not NSW police.

It was not until late October that Jackson was finally forced to resign as Minister.

This occurred because of political and media pressure at the national level. Federal Opposition Leader Andrew Peacock asked a question in Parliament, and the *National Times* put questions in writing to Jackson after a briefing by Bob Bottom, who had obtained transcripts of the AFP tapes.

Even then, while Neville Wran cut Jackson loose at that point he was allowed to remain in Parliament for another three years. In August 1984 Jackson was finally charged with conspiring to corruptly receive money, after investigations showed that he had routinely taken bribes to organise the early release of prisoners serving long jail terms.

In the same pattern as Bill Allen, it was another three years before he was sent to trial and convicted. He was found guilty of accepting a bribe of $12,000 in 1983 and conspiring to organise the early release of three prisoners from Broken Hill Correctional Centre. He was initially sentenced to seven and a half years in jail but this was extended to 10 years in 1988. Despite this, he was released after just three and a half years.

Like Humphreys, he revealed that he needed the money to meet gambling debts.

Under political pressure after the Street Royal Commission and the Jackson allegations, the Wran Government reluctantly accepted Justice Lusher's recommendation—made two and a half years earlier—that the Police Force be accountable to a Police Board with a majority of nonpolice members.

As described by Evan Whitton: "One of the Board's first major decisions had the effect of forestalling a proposed Cabinet appointment to the post of Police Commissioner. Instead, John Avery was installed, and there followed a major assault on institutionalised corruption in the force."

Attention was also growing on the role of Telecom, the national telecommunications authority, in facilitating organised illegal gambling.

In early 1983 Bob Bottom wrote that Federal Police were extremely concerned about organised crime influencing Telecom, and had been pushing for a full judicial inquiry for nine months. Bottom said police had complained that their inquiries were frustrated by Telecom managers who did not want to get involved because they feared "union trouble".

Subsequently, Beck told the *Financial Review* in June 1983 that the big crime syndicates were flourishing with assistance from corrupt officials within Telecom as well as the Police Force.

"In my last three months (on gaming and betting) I raided thousands of places, I could have got heaps more in the years before if I had been allowed. There are still thousands of SP operators around, but now they are controlled by big syndicates," he said.

Beck was also quoted several times saying "Control telephones and you just about control SP betting."

A limited inquiry into Telecom and organised crime was commissioned in 1984, led by Victorian Queens Counsel Frank Vincent. Vincent contacted Beck in Dubbo and invited him to come to Sydney to meet him and his team. Beck was happy to assist and supplied detailed information about his experiences with Telecom.

In his report, Vincent found no evidence of links between Telecom's management and organised crime, but did find evidence of corruption and criminality by individual Telecom employees. He also criticised senior Telecom officials for lax attitudes towards disciplining staff involved in serious crime.

Rumours about Telecom's role in creating a huge national SP network persisted, fuelled by claims that sensational evidence presented to the Vincent inquiry in secret was never published.

According to the NSW president of the Telecom line staff union at the time, the secret evidence "would make reports emanating from the Costigan inquiry into the Painters and Dockers look like an afternoon tea party".

This was quite a startling claim. The Costigan Royal Commission, headed by Frank Costigan QC, had been set up in 1980 by the conservative Federal (led by Malcolm Fraser) and Victorian (led by Premier Rupert Hamer) Governments in September 1980, to investigate criminal activities, including violence, associated with the Melbourne branch of the Painters and Dockers Union after a series of media revelations. By following the money trail it had become a much wider investigation, exposing massive tax evasion (including the so-called 'bottom of the harbour' schemes), immense money laundering, organised crime, drug rings and murder.

While Wran and then Jackson were under fire, the new Hawke Government moved quickly to dissociate itself from the trouble in NSW. One of the key recommendations of the Costigan Royal Commission was a national law enforcement response to organised crime to overcome the legal barriers posed by the federal system. Legislation to establish the new National Crime Authority (NCA) was quickly introduced to Parliament and in 1984 the NCA opened for business under the leadership of its chair, Justice Donald Stewart.

Serious as they were, and despite Federal Police concerns, the allegations about Telecom were not further investigated. They were superseded by other allegations which emerged around this time, related to illegal use of phones— by the police, not the criminals.

The NSW police intercept material became the foundation of the so-called *Age* Tapes a affair. This escalated into one of Australia's greatest and most controversial constitutional dramas, questioning the actions of High Court judge and former Whitlam Government Attorney General, Lionel Murphy.

Murphy was a luminary and powerbroker in the NSW Labor Party. Like others at the time, he was fond of illegal gambling. That meant he was not fond of Merv Beck.

As a portent of things to come, in December 1982 *the Daily Telegraph* published a humorous snippet. It said Murphy had been a guest at a farewell dinner for his former ministerial colleague, Al Grassby at a restaurant in Rozelle the previous Friday night.

As it turned out, the restaurant had 10 years earlier been the venue for Bruce Hardin's illegal casino. According to the article, while they were eating Murphy asked about the restaurant's name. When he was told it was named after Beck's Raiders, Murphy, without eating another mouthful, got up and left.

The article seemed innocuous enough at the time. Less than a year later, the reasons for Murphy's dislike of Beck began to be revealed.

Pursuing his inquiries, Bob Bottom had obtained transcripts of a number of the tapes made by NSW police illegally putting intercept devices on the phones of leading crime figures. Bottom sent Beck a copy of a transcript of a phone conversation in which he was mentioned.

It was a call to Sid Einfeld, a close friend of Lionel Murphy and a member of the Wran Government from 1976 to 1981. The tape appeared to have been made in late 1979, when Einfeld was the very active and popular Consumer Affairs Minister. (Even after his retirement from Parliament, he continued as a commentator on consumer affairs on Radio 2GB.)

The caller was Morgan Ryan, a low grade solicitor with friends in the criminal underworld as well as in high places. On this occasion Ryan phoned Einfeld and said he had some good news.

"That bastard Beck has been moved."

The conversation continued. Then Einfeld said, "Well, now get busy on that place up near the railway."

In context, it was clear that Einfeld was referring to a gambling club or illegal casino.

Soon after Bottom had given this to Beck, the first media report appeared about the existence of a large number of illegal tapes made by police, featuring senior criminals in conversation with leading public figures.

Bottom had heard a rumour that the Wran Government planned to ban not only telephone tapping, but possession of illegally obtained tapes or transcripts. He left Sydney, leaving some of the material with *National Times* journalist Marion Wilkinson.

Wilkinson produced an article published in late November 1983[33] with the headline. "Big Shots Bugged". It attracted little public or media attention and was shrugged off by the NSW Police. In response to the article, the head of the Bureau of Criminal Intelligence, Robert Shepherd, formally advised Commissioner Abbott in December 1983 that "the only telephone intercepts (with) which this Department is involved are those where a combined operation is taking place with the Australian Federal Police". That statement was, at the very best, misleading, as both Shepherd and Abbott were fully aware.

Bottom knew what the police were covering up. Dissatisfied with the reaction to Wilkinson's article, he passed the material to the Melbourne *Age*, where it received the attention it deserved.

Age Editor Creighton Burns realised that material on the tapes was political dynamite—not for what it revealed about the targeted bookmakers, gamblers and drug dealers, but what emerged about their high powered connections.

After careful consideration, in February 1984 *The Age* published a three-part series of front page stories by Lindsay Murdoch and David Wilson, entitled "Network of Influence".

---

[33] Marian Wilkinson, 'Big Shots Bugged', National Times, 25 November – 1 December 1983, 3-5.

The first article[34] was headlined "Secret Tapes of Judge, Lawyer". The judge was revealed to be Lionel Murphy. Murphy was controversial, outgoing and flamboyant. He was a social and political reformer who had played politics hard before his appointment to the High Court by the Whitlam Government in 1975. He was also a very close colleague of Premier Neville Wran QC.

The series revealed a conversation between Murphy and NSW chief stipendiary magistrate Clarence (Clarrie) Briese in late January 1982. Murphy had phoned Briese to talk about the conspiracy charges against his friend, Morgan Ryan.

Murphy wanted to know whether Ryan would be committed to stand trial. After some preliminary chat he came to the point.

"And now, what about my little mate?" the High Court judge asked the magistrate.

Briese felt that he was being pressured to intervene and let Ryan off the hook. While Murphy denied this, it later emerged that other NSW judges had had similar conversations with Murphy where they believed he was trying to influence them.

Following hot on the heels of the Humphreys Royal Commission, the inferences regarding Murphy's behaviour could not be ignored.

"The systematic tapping of private telephones in Sydney has revealed an extraordinary network of organised crime and corruption in Australia," said *the Age* editorial on 6 February.

As the political storm over the article continued to build, a week later *the Age* again editorialised: "The matters raised in the transcripts are too serious to be waved aside as insubstantial or irrelevant or dismissed cavalierly as sordid weapons of a political assault."

Two weeks after the original *Age* story, the NSW Solicitor-General Mary Gaudron (who 18 months earlier had found no case for charges against Bill Allen, and would later follow Murphy onto the High Court), shifted the focus onto the police who had made the tapes, and *the Age* which had published the extracts.

She advised the NSW Government that disclosure of the illegally obtained material, even in Parliament, could constitute an offence under the Telecommunications (Interception) Act. She also opined that unless

---

[34] Lindsay Murdoch and David Wilson, 'Secret Tapes of Judge, Lawyer', The Age (Melbourne), 2 February 1984, 1, 5.

the material was authenticated, it was unlikely that inquiries would lead to any significant outcome in terms of convictions.

Premier Wran denounced *The Age*. "What purports to be and what's been described as a crime intelligence unit report is phoney, it's not genuine and if it's been fabricated then of course it opens up all sorts of questions as to who fabricated it," Wran thundered. Wran omitted to mention that Murphy was a very close friend and that Morgan Ryan was close enough to a friend to be the source of his own nickname, "Nifty" Neville.

A similar line was taken by Ministers in the Labor Federal Government, but the Liberal-National Opposition would not let the matter die. *The Age* insisted the transcripts were taken from genuine phone taps and warranted investigation.

During a hiatus on the *Age* Tapes, in March 1984 the ABC's *Four Corners* again stirred the pot with another investigation by Chris Masters, this time turning the spotlight on corruption and illegal gambling.

The program opened with Masters asking Merv Beck, "Were you ever asked by your superiors to ease off illegal gambling?"

"Well there were times I was told to keep away from various areas, and yes, I was told that."

Masters then asked a former SP bookmaker if he had ever made a payment to a politician.

"Yes I made a payment to a politician on behalf of the syndicate I was working for."

Masters singled out NSW as an SP betting haven, highlighting the low NSW penalties for SP betting.

"Victorian bookies operate on our side of the Murray, the South Australian boys make their headquarters in Broken Hill and the Queenslanders are in Tweed Heads," he said.

"They face a maximum fine in NSW of $5000 and that was only raised from $1000 two months ago. In Victoria, the maximum fine is $20,000 plus 12 months jail and in Queensland the maximum is $50,000.

"SP betting has been virtually eliminated in Western Australia where first offenders get an automatic six month jail sentence."

The program also looked at race-fixing and tax evasion. It quoted the Costigan Royal Commission finding that one interstate SP operator had an annual turnover of $120 million, representing lost government tax revenue of $2.7 million a year. Masters speculated that there were 100 similar SPs.

Merv Beck repeated his allegation that he was offered $500 a week to run dead when he was in charge of Darlinghurst in 1977; and that when he tried to broaden his investigations, he was soon after removed, allegedly at the request of Abe Saffron.

Beck said it was his belief that over the years, both sides of NSW politics had taken protection money from SP bookmakers.

"According to my information it would have to be Labor and Liberal Governments. I would have to say that money has been paid to politicians for use in election campaigns and also I believe that there are corrupt politicians who are receiving money from SP operators and the gambling syndicates."

The *Four Corners* program added to the widely-held impression that Sydney was the crime capital of Australia and a hotbed of corruption. The program had been several months in production, partly because of the legal sensitivities. By the time it went to air in mid-March 1984, a NSW state election campaign was underway with just a week remaining before polling day.

Beck's appearance was not well received by either political side in Macquarie Street, although nothing was said in public.

Still Neville Wran and his Government fended off the allegations, and continued to deny the existence of the *Age* tapes. In July 1984, it appeared that the scandal might conveniently go away when Commonwealth Director of Public Prosecutions, Ian Temby, agreed with Gaudron that the voices on the tapes could not be verified and there were no grounds for prosecution.

A few weeks after this, an in camera (secret) Senate inquiry provided its report, coming to the same conclusion after splitting on party lines. But in a dramatic turn of event, it became clear that new witnesses were available and a second Senate inquiry was called.

In the first week of October Clarrie Briese gave evidence, followed by two other judges. The new Senate inquiry found that on the balance of probability, Murphy had attempted to influence the course of justice.

This finding was rapidly followed by a new statement from Ian Temby which was tabled in Federal Parliament. The federal DPP confirmed that federal authorities had received material generated by phone taps not only of Morgan Ryan but also George Freeman, Frederick Paddles Anderson, Bob Trimboli and Abe Saffron.

Charges were laid against Murphy around Christmas 1984. Despite his emphatic denials he was convicted in July 1985 of one charge of attempting to pervert the course of justice and sentenced to jail. He immediately appealed and five months later the NSW Court of Appeal upheld the appeal, and ordered a retrial. In April 1986, Murphy was acquitted.

While this was going on, in March 1985, a new inquiry was established jointly by the Commonwealth, NSW and Victorian Governments. The Royal Commission of Inquiry into Alleged Telephone Interceptions: was led by the chairman of the new National Crime Authority, Justice Donald Stewart.

A former NSW Supreme Court Justice, Justice Stewart had impressive form. He had undertaken the Royal Commission of Inquiry into Drug Trafficking from 1981 to 1983, also a joint operation by the Commonwealth, Queensland, New South Wales and Victorian governments. This inquiry was tasked with investigating the drug trafficking and related criminal activities of Terrance John Clark and his associates, and made 40 recommendations to tighten the passport system to prevent abuse by organised criminals.

Beck had a hand in setting up the new Stewart Royal Commission. When it had just been announced, he was approached by a very senior member of the inquiry, who became a judge. This person asked Beck for his advice and assistance. Beck suggested that the inquiry would be better served if, for security reasons, it used police from outside NSW to make inquiries within that state, assisted by just one from NSW who was familiar with the geography. In other states, Beck suggested the same model apply, so that police from within a state force were not asking questions about their own operations.

Not only did the commission adopt this model, but it has been the model used by other commission inquiries since then.

Beck was also asked for recommendations of people who would be suitable for appointment to the inquiry. His advice was accepted and these people, by all accounts, did an outstanding job.

Premier Neville Wran threatened to sack all police found to have been involved in making the tapes, who numbered about 60. But Justice Stewart intervened, as the threat would prevent police from volunteering information to him.

The Hawke Federal Government was under pressure to authenticate or discredit the phone tap material because of its relevance to the allegations against Lionel Murphy. The Federal and New South Wales Governments finally agreed to shield individual police officers from prosecution which might result from their evidence to the Royal Commission. The NSW Commissioner of Police also agreed to protect these police from internal disciplinary action.

Beck watched all of this with great interest, especially as he knew he was mentioned on a number of the tapes. Journalist David Wilson in his book edited by Bob Bottom, *Big Shots 2* refers to the tape of George Freeman which was played to Beck when he first started back on 21 Division in October 1981.

The book claims this tape was mentioned in secret evidence to the Stewart Royal Commission in 1985. It was made by the NSW Police Bureau of Criminal Intelligence which had tapped Freeman's phone in April and October, 1981, Wilson said, under an assignment known as Operation Doncaster.

As usual with the illegal tapping, all the tapes and transcripts were destroyed by police; but Superintendent Bob Blissett had kept a cassette tape of a recording of Freeman speaking to a senior, unidentified NSW police officer.

"Blissett was obviously worried about its contents," Wilson wrote. "He had played it to two (then) senior officers, the Commissioner of Police, Jim Lees and an assistant commissioner, Cec Abbott, who was to succeed Lees. According to police, the conversation was a call made to Freeman from Parliament House in Macquarie Street, Sydney. The Stewart Royal Commission's secret report noted: 'The content of this conversation was such that the male speaker had undertaken to supply Freeman with the names of officers...' These officers were attached to the special gaming squad headed by Superintendent Merv Beck, since retired. Beck was regarded as one of NSW's most honest and forthright police.... During evidence to the commission, neither Lees nor Abbott could identify the male voice on the call to Freeman. Blissett told the commission he had erased the tape after meeting his superiors. Once again Freeman was not pursued[35]."

But the senior police officer was not the only public figure on the tape. Politicians were also mentioned, and Beck wonders whether they were ever questioned about the conversation on the tape and whether it accurately reflected their views.

"You would have thought it would be of some interest to the Stewart commission at that time," he reflected.

---

[35] Big Shots 2 page 57

Beck and a number of his former colleagues were disappointed that the royal commission did not reveal a lot more, and that it kept secret much of the content of the tapes.

"Those tapes were a Pandora's box. If that information had come out and been made public, more things would have come to light as people came forward with their own information.

"This is where I think the inquiry lost a great opportunity as so many of these inquiries do," Beck lamented.

"For the public only need some prompting. In some of the other tapes, individuals were mentioned and they have never been given the opportunity to respond, I am sure, although their names were on tape. I'm not necessarily talking about villains, I am talking about innocent people."

Beck himself was called to the Stewart Royal Commission and interviewed at length in private by one of its assisting counsels in relation to the problems he had encountered. He was disappointed that he was not called back to give evidence before Justice Stewart, as this would have allowed him to raise new information about the context of the tape.

Justice Stewart delivered the final report of his Royal Commission to the Governor-General and Governors of NSW and Victoria on 30 April 1986. The report was in two volumes, the second of which remained confidential in order not to jeopardise the ongoing investigation of various criminal matters.

The Commission confirmed that the tapes and transcripts were genuine and were drawn from phone intercepts made by NSW Police. It acknowledged that insights gained from the phone taps were "good information", although illegally obtained.

By this time Lionel Murphy had been acquitted. He could not be tried again on the same charges, but there was another way he could be removed from office.

Justice Stewart's findings now raised the question of whether he was fit to hold a seat on the High Court. Under section 72 of the Constitution, "proved misbehaviour" by a High Court judge could allow the judge to be removed from the court by an address to both Houses of the Federal Parliament.

Under intense political pressure, in May 1986 the Hawke Government set up a commission of inquiry to consider this question, comprising three retired Supreme Court judges. The commission was given a very limited time to reach its conclusion, with the report due in September.

It never delivered its opinion. In July it was formally abandoned after Murphy's close friend Neville Wran informed the Federal Government that Murphy had terminal cancer[36]. He died just three months later, on 21 October 1986.

While the inquiry was aborted, the documents it was considering were given to the presiding officers of parliament to be kept secret for 30 years. Time passed, and in September 2017 they were duly released, including secret phone tap evidence that had been presented to the Stewart Royal Commission.[37]

These files, which would have made fascinating reading for Merv Beck, revived public controversy over Lionel Murphy and made new revelations about the integrity if the NSW Police Force and the Wran Government.

Crime reporter for the *Sydney Morning Herald*, Kate McClymont wrote[38]: "On April 1, 1979, NSW police were physically monitoring Ryan as well as tapping his phones. Using a telephoto lens, police photographed then chief magistrate Murray Farquhar meeting Ryan in Sydney's Centennial Park.

"What was extraordinary was that, at the time, Farquhar was the magistrate assigned to hear the criminal case of Ryan's clients Roy Cessna and Tim Milner, who had been arrested only a fortnight earlier with 137 kilos of Indian hemp.

"The police listened as Ryan told Cessna that he was off to a 'very heavy conference' to see 'what can be done'. They also heard Ryan arrange to meet Farquhar at 4pm.

"After the meeting, Ryan reported back to Cessna that he was 'very, very happy' with the outcome.

"Four days after meeting Farquhar in the park, the visitors book at NSW Police headquarters in College Street showed Ryan turning up to see the then police commissioner, Merv Wood, who then intervened to see that the quality of the drugs (in evidence) was downgraded.

"On May 10, five days before the case was to be heard by Farquhar, Ryan hosted dinner at his Neutral Bay home. In attendance were Murphy, Wood and Farquhar.

---

[36] https://www.theaustralian.com.au/nation/inquirer/even-30-years-on-lionel-murphystill-divides-the-nation/news-story/9a76e9f6823542f139b3c5c5eaff3a21

[37] See the Australia, 15 September 2017

[38] Sydney Morning Herald July 23, 2017

"On the day the matter went to court, Wood instructed the (police) prosecution that instead of having a judge and jury, the chief magistrate alone would hear the case.

"Farquhar sentenced Milner to 18 months and Cessna received a fine."

The Australian published an equally interesting report on the newly released files, by associate editor Jamie Walker.

"After Sydney's Luna Park fire in 1979, (Abe) Saffron tried to position himself to acquire the lease (to the Luna Park site) from the NSW Labor government headed by Neville Wran.

"The phone intercepts show that Murphy was contacted by Ryan and asked to speak to Wran.

"Describing the (phone conversation) interplay, Sergeant P.L. Egge said: 'Mr Justice Lionel Murphy said, 'leave it with me' and then after a short time Mr Justice Lionel Murphy rang back Morgan Ryan and said that he had spoken to Neville ... and said that he's going to try and make some arrangements for Abe to get the lease and either the next day or shortly therein after Mr Wran said that the government is going to review the lease to Luna Park.'

"Sergeant Egge said the lease went to a 'front man' for a company owned or controlled by Saffron."

But Murphy and Wran still had their supporters. Both were fascinating, highly intelligent men who had made a positive difference to Australia in many ways. A day after the damning articles, the *Australian's* Editor-at-Large Paul Kelly (who was a political correspondent for more than 40 years from the 1970s) took a more tolerant view of Murphy and a more sceptical view of the released documents.

In an article headlined, "Even 30 years on, Lionel Murphy still divides the nation", Kelly appeared to forgive Murphy for any transgressions because corruption and sleaze was part of the world he lived in.

"Lionel Murphy was a charmer with a rich voice, a man of justice with a compulsion for danger, an ebullient visionary with nocturnal habits, a born reformer and a ruthless man of principle. Murphy remains forever at the centre of one of the great unresolved disruptions in our judicial life," Kelly wrote.

"Murphy came from the Sydney of the 1950s and 60s, when the cops were crooked, the races were fixed, industrial battles made legal and political careers, illegal gambling, grog and girls were fixtures in a milieu where established power met underworld figures, and lawyers, police and politicians mingled in a fog of deals and dinners. It was nothing remarkable; it was just Sydney."

Kelly seemed oblivious to the fact that his description was much more apt to Sydney in the late 1970s and early 1980s than earlier, and that the actions of corrupt people in public office had directly contributed to this grim reality.

He went on to detail a number of the allegations against Murphy as revealed by the documents.

The first of these, he said, was a claim by a Detective Chief Inspector of the Commonwealth Police (as it was then), Donald Thomas[39]. He said Murphy sought covert information from him and promised that if Thomas provided this, in return Murphy would arrange for Thomas to be promoted to assistant commissioner.

Thomas said the offer was made during lunch at a Kings Cross Korean restaurant in late 1979, attended by, among others, Morgan Ryan. The AFP was about to be formed by the merger of the Commonwealth Police and the federal Narcotics Bureau in October 1979.

Murphy allegedly told Thomas of the new force: "We need somebody inside to tell us what is going on."

The second allegation noted by Kelly was that Murphy in agreement with Ryan had made inquiries to find whether two AFP officers, David Lewington and Robert Jones, who were investigating alleged illegal activities by Korean nationals, could be 'influenced'. After making inquiries, Murphy allegedly told Ryan that both were very straight. Kelly said the inquiry of commission seemed to find this was at least "injudicious" behaviour but was not as certain that it was criminal behaviour.

Third, it was alleged that Murphy approached underworld figure Abe Saffron, either directly or indirectly, to 'lean on' Danny Sankey to drop his private legal action over the Khemlani Loans Affairs. Sankey had laid two charges each of unlawful conduct against former Whitlam Government Ministers, Gough Whitlam, Rex Connor, Lionel Murphy and Jim Cairns. (The High Court (excluding Murphy) dismissed Sankey's lawsuit as "bad in law" in November 1978.)

Kelly conceded the commission documents depicted this as an effort to pervert the course of justice and stated, "if an association with

---

[39] The AFP was formed on 19 October 1979 by the merger of the Commonwealth Police and the federal Narcotics Bureau.

Saffron could be proved contrary to any such denial, the Judge would be in difficulty".

Kelly did not comment on the other allegations linking Murphy to Saffron.

The release of the commission of inquiry documents prompted former Chief Magistrate Clarrie Briese to break his long silence on the Murphy affair. Briese told *Four Corners* in December 2017 he stood by his 1984 claims that Murphy had pressured him over the Morgan Ryan case, including the infamous "little mate" line.

Gareth Evans, who was Federal Attorney General in 1984 when *the Age* Tapes story broke, told *Four Corners* the Government had hoped the commission of inquiry would lay the issue to rest.

"At every stage of this thing I was just incredibly torn between my belief in the essential decency of the man (Murphy), my horror at the politicisation of the process, but on the other hand the need to demonstrate to a sceptical public and a sceptical media that we were in fact doing the right thing and we weren't defending the indefensible."

Former *National Times* editor David Marr said Murphy ignited passions.

"People loved Murphy. They really loved him. He was a rogue and he was known to be a rogue and his roguery was celebrated," he said.

Despite this, Marr said the illegal police tapes should have sparked a royal commission into corruption at the highest levels.

"There was never a proper in-depth inquiry with the powers required and the terms of reference needed," he said.

That was certainly Merv Beck's view. Most of the phone tap material revealed to Justice Stewart was never placed in the public arena.

While the Murphy affair ended without resolution, it consolidated the trend towards tougher anti-corruption laws and stronger powers to law enforcement agencies, in particular, the ability to use phone intercepts in major investigations.

In the end, it was Justice Donald Stewart who persuaded the Federal Government that telephone interception was too powerful a tool to ignore.

The public volume of Stewart's final report included a detailed account of the history and methods of illegal telephone interceptions by NSW Police.

It started in the late 1960s when Commissioner Norman Allan called two officers to his office at Police Headquarters in Phillip St Sydney. He wanted to know if it was possible to record conversations off a phone, via a tap.

There was no legal basis for phone tapping but this did not seem to worry Allan, who set up the new bugging experts in their own electronics section in a police building in Surrey Hills.

Tapping began and continued with the knowledge of successive commissioners, and occasionally by Commonwealth Police.

There were a number of incidents over the years[40] when PMG and then Telecom employees found devices on phone equipment. One of them occurred in 1977 when a device was found in a distribution pillar in Sydney's eastern suburbs. According to a 1989 account by Peter Grabosky of the Australian Institute of Criminology, the startled Telecom workers called the Army Ordnance Disposal unit, who assured them it was an interception device, not a bomb.

The device was delivered to the Acting Chief Investigating Officer of Telecom, who was quickly contacted by the NSW Police Technical Services Unit (the phone tapping unit). The Telecom official advised the officers that the device was illegal, returned the hardware to them, and warned that it should not happen again. He took no further action.

Following the 1973 NSW Royal Commission into allegations of organised crime connections with gambling in clubs, headed by Justice Athol Moffitt (triggered by concerns about links between Jack Rooklyn's Bally corporation and the US mafia), the NSW Police Crime Intelligence Unit, later renamed the Bureau of Criminal Intelligence was established.

By this time, detectives in Sydney knew about the phone tap facility and also knew to keep quiet about intercepts they were placing without warrants.

In 1979, not long before the AFP was formed, phone intercepts were explicitly outlawed by the 1979 federal Telecommunications (Interception) Act. According to one of his deputy commissioners[41], the first AFP Commissioner, Sir Colin Woods, "approved the receipt of tape recordings of conversations obtained but directed that AFP officers

---

[40] P N Grabosky Chapter 3: Telephone tapping by the New South Wales Police Published in: Wayward governance : illegality and its control in the public sector Australian Institute of Criminology 1989. https://aic.gov.au/publications/lcj/wayward/chapter-3telephone-tapping-new-south-wales-police

[41] Australia 1986b, Parliament, Joint Committee on the National Crime Authority, Second Report, Australian Government Publishing Service, Canberra.

should not themselves carry out the intercepts". Presumably the tapes came from the NSW Police.

Justice Donald Stewart strongly condemned the illegal phone tapping as criminal conduct.

"Members of the NSW Police who were guilty of breaking the law over a period of years, refused to tell the truth about what they had done unless they were indemnified," the report stated.

"Indeed not only did they refuse to co-operate with investigating authorities, but they deliberately and falsely denied knowledge of the illegal interceptions and covered up their illegal activities ...

"Police officers are sworn, however, to uphold the law—not just laws of which they approve. There can be no justification for their having taken the law into their own hands."

According to Justice Stewart, the illegal interceptions were not the work of a few 'rotten apples' or rogue police. The initiative for them came from the Commissioner of Police, and five successive Commissioners had condoned the interceptions. They were also common knowledge among experienced detectives.

He recommended that the NCA, which he chaired, should be granted powers to intercept telecommunications, and that state and territory police forces also be granted this power.

After consideration by a parliamentary committee, legislation was approved to allow phone tapping by a special unit within the Australian Federal Police, working through Telecom, with a warrant from a judge and only in suspected cases of murder, kidnapping and serious drug trafficking.

The debate today is only about how far these powers should be extended.

CHAPTER SIXTEEN

A Ripple of Hope

As all of this unfolded, Beck watched closely from the sidelines. His reputation as the doyen of gaming and betting policing may have been questioned by others, but not by those in the midst of it. For several years after his retirement, serving police and other interested parties contacted him to tell him of the latest developments and ask his advice.

At one point a young policeman came and visited him in Dubbo, seeking advice on a gaming and betting issue. Beck was happy to provide him with some tips, but also told him to go and see his own superintendent, which he did. Later the superintendent told another officer that Beck had been interfering and suggested that since he was retired, he should stop worrying about SP betting. This got back to Beck who was sad that his well-intended actions were again being misconstrued.

As an articulate and fearless former police officer, Beck's was also frequently asked by the media and community groups to comment on police-related issues.

He found himself in demand as a guest speaker at Probus and Rotary Clubs, business groups, charities and many other community groups and meetings. The varied audiences included community leaders, magistrates and Queen's Counsel barristers. He spoke at meetings across most of NSW including in Sydney, Canberra, country towns, and Newcastle.

His talks covered a range of topics, including all aspects of his own police duties and experiences, which helped him to revive and order his memories. Over a period of time he developed a list of 180 topics related to the law, law enforcement, and corruption on which he could speak.

The audiences loved to hear of his adventures and often he was called back for a repeat, or in some cases, four times. As late as 2005 he was fully booked up with 13 appearances scheduled for the second half of the year.

Beck never accepted a payment for his appearances, although it cost him personally to travel around the state. He was motivated by the desire to inform people and help them to be better and more understanding citizens. The enthusiastic response from his audiences also kindled his desire to record his story, in a book.

As the Lionel Murphy affair was unfolding, John Avery was appointed as NSW Police Commissioner on 7 August 1984. He came into office determined to give the force a better name and public image, even, to Beck's disgust, changing its name to the NSW Police Service. It was changed back to 'force' some years later.

Avery was to become one of the state's longest serving and most popular police commissioners[42], but he struggled to make headway against corruption and the illegal gambling that fuelled it.

At this time, Beck offered to help to raise the standards of policing by improving the training given to police recruits. Beck had heard a number of complaints from trainees at the Police Academy in Goulburn, including accounts of the way women trainees were treated. Beck was convinced that discipline needed to be imposed before the trainees started work as police constables.

Soon after Avery was appointed, Beck approached him to offer his services, free of charge. He told Avery he could give a talk or lecture to police in training, on a regular basis, about his experiences in all aspects of policing, the need and value of discipline, and the pitfalls waiting for unsuspecting young police.

Beck proposed to travel from Dubbo to Goulburn at his own expense and even stay there for a few days while he gave his lectures, without asking for any money.

But Avery rejected the idea, offering a lame excuse. "You might be seen that you were looking for a job, mate."

"I was just dumbfounded by that," Beck admitted. "If I was looking for a job it would be an unpaid job, it was in my own time, travelling to and fro, at my own expense! So that didn't eventuate. But, not long after, I read in the newspaper that former police had been used at the academy for the same purposes I had mentioned."

---

[42] Avery remained Commissioner until 1991

Beck may have been considered too controversial, at least in some quarters, to be teaching trainees. He certainly disagreed with some of the training and management principles of the time, especially the 'hands off' role given to many senior police. In his view, their job was to lead their officers in whatever law enforcement they were involved in, physically as well as mentally. This would give them direct experience of the problems their teams faced, including dangers and temptations.

"Weak and inexperienced senior officers have much to answer for in the final analysis as to why the Police Service failed the people of NSW. When we examine the strengths and weaknesses of Police Commissioners over many decades the service has been poorly served by the greater majority," he said.

"I have advocated officer presence in the field, particularly by more senior officers. I don't believe that because an officer attains rank he should be confined to a desk, I think this is a mistake that we should get over."

In more recent years, Beck's approach returned to favour and senior police were more involved in street work and even night work than ever before.

While Beck's offer was declined by Avery, he soon found himself very busy with a campaign for better policing and safer communities in his new home town of Dubbo. Always a magnet for people who wanted action on policing issues, Beck became co-chairman of the Orana Law and Order Forum (Orana being the central and north western region of New South Wales, including Dubbo in its south eastern corner).

Riots in Bourke and unrest in other towns had raised concerns about a law and order crisis. The movement grew as the direct impact of lawlessness was felt by more townspeople, especially local businesses. The forum's objective was to boost the local police presence and police powers to reduce the high rate of assault and robberies.

In late 1985, a public meeting of the campaign at Dubbo Town Hall was attended by 2000 people. The three speakers were the local Country Party MP, Gerry Peacocke; Merv Beck, and the local Mayor. The forum gave Beck an outlet for his belief that stronger police presence was needed on the streets, coupled with reform of the convoluted Offences in Public Places Act.

Beck did not condone police violence but he believe 'do-gooders' had gone too far in reducing police powers in the name of reducing brutality.

The meeting elected a 13-member committee, including Beck, which travelled to Sydney to meet Premier Wran. Wran (who did not comment on Beck's participation) agreed with their concerns and ordered a police taskforce under Chief Superintendent Don Graham to examine the area's problems. The taskforce's only recommendations related to police staffing. After a brief improvement, Dubbo began to slip back into lawlessness and the Orana Law and Order Forum was reactivated.

This time the response was even greater, with 3500 people attending a meeting by the river, including Opposition Leader, Nick Greiner[43], his police spokesman Ted Pickering and National Party Leader Wal Murray. The forum drew up a list of demands comprising:

- restoration of the Summary Offences Act to give the Police Force sufficient power to control lawlessness on the streets.
- reform of the penal system, with minimum jail sentences for serious offenders, to be fully served
- life imprisonment for all convicted drug dealers
- a minimum jail sentence of one year, with no early release except for first offenders, for robbery and assault
- double the sentence for repeat offences
- one legal aid system for all NSW residents
- legal aid to be repaid by people found guilty
- jail sentence in lieu of fines to be set at a rate of one day for each $5, not $50 owing.
- restoration of the Consorting Act
- more power for prison authorities to discipline prisoners
- an inquiry into financing of the prison system
- reinstatement of disciplinary authority of school teachers
- parents of juvenile criminals to face fines and damages
- the minimum age for adult punishment to be reduced from 18 to 16 years.
- juvenile culpability be limited to under 8 year olds
- allowing law abiding citizens to give sworn evidence at the time of a crime, by affidavit, with defence cross examination as determined by the court, without making their names and addresses publicly available.

---

[43] NSW Opposition Leader from March 1983 to March 1988

While some labelled the demands as reactionary, others saw them as a sensible restoration of punishment for crime. There was debate about consorting laws, for example, which drug smuggling investigator and author Dr Alfred McCoy called "one of the most authoritarian and effective measures against organised crime ever passed in a Western democracy"[44].

Beck was invited to speak at towns near and far.

* * * *

During this period, political debate about illegal versus legal gambling was continuing. In 1984 the illegal operators were handed a bonus by an official opinion from the state Crown Law Office that blackjack was not an illegal game, firmly tying the hands of the gaming police.

Journalist Warren Owens writing in *The Sunday Telegraph* noted that the Government had not taken action to stop the many illegal clubs in Sydney, which were back in force post Beck, from exploiting the blackjack loophole.

"Such is the lure of casino-style gambling, not to mention the cash flow, that a loophole in gaming laws exposed last year was soon exploited by dozens of gaming club operators, big and small, throughout the State.

"Almost overnight, every second Sydney suburb acquired a club offering gaming facilities on terms that kept it narrowly inside the newly-interpreted law.

"The Government could have amended the law, but chose instead to sit on its hands."

The Wran Government was still dithering about allowing one or more state regulated casinos, although this was the Premier's publicly stated preference. Tasmania had led the way with the Wrest Point Casino in 1973, followed by a smaller one in Launceston in 1982. The Labor Government in Western Australia had announced a casino would be built at Burswood Island but Premier Brian Burke's cabinet got cold feet over handing the project to one company, Tileska. A new tender process was ordered which Tileska won, but not without competition.

There were reportedly 11 illegal casinos in Perth at the time, and some of them also wanted a slice of the legal action. The casino eventually opened on 30 December 1985, but Burke and others were dragged into the mire through a royal commission into what became

---

[44] Sydney Morning Herald "Bring Back Old Consorting Laws, detectives say" 17 July 1985

known as WA Inc. The inquiry was told that individuals and companies associated with Tileska donated up to $600,000 to the Labor Party and Brian Burke's leadership fund[45].

As this was unfolding, NSW Police Minister Peter Anderson appointed the Commissioner of Public Complaints to undertake another inquiry into options for legal casino gambling in the state. In August 1985 Anderson released the inquiry's recommendations—supporting the licensing of legal gambling establishments, with strict controls— but not the report itself.

By this time, Beck had revised his own position on legalising gambling. "At one time I thought it was a great idea to legalise them (casinos). But in America where it was legalised there were still illegal ones about. There were also continuing concerns about organised crime links to the legal casinos," he said then.

Beck had every reason to be sceptical about the Wran Government's ability to keep criminal elements out of gambling, or to keep a check on police corruption. Around this time, he drove to Sydney to meet an old friend, Ernie Shepherd. Shepherd was then in charge of the Vice Squad, and told Beck that the old protection rackets were operating again. He said certain police were pushing for stronger action against brothels— not to get rid of the prostitution, but as leverage so they could increase their demands for protection money.

It was a familiar story to Beck, a direct parallel to the crackdown on illegal gambling that Allen and Wran had asked him to carry out. No matter how honest, determined and successful he had been, Beck was aware that he had been swimming against the tide.

He was not the only public figure concerned about the potential for a large scale gambling operation to provide money laundering for organised crime, as reported in the *Sydney Morning Herald* in October[46].

"The report of the State Government Committee on Gaming, which was released in August played down the likelihood of criminals laundering money through legal casinos, despite overwhelming evidence from the US that it is a major problem there.

"Recent evidence to a US House of Representatives Subcommittee on Crime has shown that although the American gaming industry is

---

[45] The West Australian Monday, 21 December 2015

[46] Andrew Keenan, Dirty Money Comes Clean, *SMH* 10 October 1985.

one of the most closely regulated in the world, criminals are turning more and more to casinos as the best way to launder their vast profits…

"According to the interim report of the President's Commission on Organised Crime, law enforcement agencies in the US had only recently begun to understand how important money laundering was to criminals."

A month after this report, in November 1985, Premier Wran, his Minister for Public Works and Ports, Laurie Brereton, and Police Minister Peter Anderson held a joint press conference to announce that a government-licensed casino would open in mid-1986.

They also announced that the Government would close not just the blackjack loophole, but all of what they called the state's illegal and 'semi-legal' casinos. What constituted a semi-legal casino was not spelled out.

"What we are doing is closing the loopholes, arming the police with powers and, to put it quite bluntly, it will be a test for the bona fides of the police," Wran told the media. "There will be no excuse whatsoever for these (illegal) places to remain open when the legislation goes through Parliament next week."

Wran's statement re bona fides prompted wry smiles from many Sydney insiders. A columnist in the *Sydney Morning Herald* commented anonymously, "Apparently they thought the journalists wouldn't dare to laugh so loudly if they said it together. The trio said that from the middle of next year, all the gambling in NSW (apart from Lotto, lotteries, racing, pools, poker machines and Footytab) would be concentrated in one Government-licensed temporary casino… How will the existing casinos be closed, given that no government in the history of NSW has managed to close them before? Harpo, Groucho and Chico said it would be done by Special Legislation. (Who would have thought) it would be so easy."

The *Sydney Morning Herald* also reported police reaction to Wran's announcement. The Gaming Squad, it claimed, was "exuberant at the prospect of resuming raids on NSW gambling dens".

"Isn't it wonderful," it quoted a senior member of the squad saying, with no reference to irony and no explanation of why the gambling dens were not being raided for other games than blackjack.

The squad member said there were up to 150 gambling establishments "dodging the law" in Sydney alone. He suggested they should close down voluntarily: "If they haven't, we will be only too happy to accommodate them. We know exactly where these places are and the people who run them."

The government-licensed casino did not materialise within six months as announced. But, on 24 June 1986, Brereton and NSW Treasurer Ken Booth unveiled a model of a legal casino which they said would be included in the new Darling Harbour development which had already been announced. Just before Christmas 1984[47], Wran and Brereton had announced that the derelict railway yards on the doorstop of the Sydney CBD at Darling Harbour would be the subject of a multi-million dollar redevelopment, but made no mention of a casino.

The casino was due to open in 1988 and, the ministers now said, would pay for the Darling Harbour project.

The announcement was one of Wran's last decisions as Premier. He shocked the NSW Labor Party conference the same week by announcing his resignation from NSW Parliament, effective from 4 July. It was the end of an unmatched political career, and of an era.

Wran had had surgery in 1980 to restore use of his vocal chords using teflon. The surgery was a success, although he had a gravelly, raspy voice for the rest of his life, and the 'teflon throat' became part of the Wran folklore. It has often been said that his reputation was also teflon, as none of the allegations against him were ever made to stick. Nifty Nev was able to retire unscathed. The only real damage from all the scandals was his inability to pursue his goal to transfer to federal politics and become Prime Minister.

In an interview a few days after his retirement, Wran audaciously painted himself as a victim of *the Age* Tapes affair who would happily have released the secret material.

"I made a mistake about *the Age* tapes," he said. "I was so concerned with the rights and liberties of other people that I forgot about myself. If I had my time over again, I would have taken the transcripts and tabled them in Parliament and to heck with the consequences. Any fair reading would indicate to the public that neither myself nor any member of the Government was answerable."

It was another example of Wran's brilliance at working an audience using some but not all of the facts, which had been so instrumental in his career first as a Queen's Counsel and then as a politician.

Despite his many friends in legal circles, the legal newsletter, *the Justinian*, was not kind to his political legacy after his retirement. Its list of the "best remembered features of the Wran years" included:

---

[47] 12 December 1984

"1. promoting the shonky copper Bill Allen to the highest reaches of the NSW Police Force

2. pushing for an extension of the term of office for the crooked Chief Magistrate Murray Farqhuar …

8. the attempts to sweep aside the exposures of corruption, case rigging, and influence revealed in the NSW Police tapes.

9. The establishment of whitewash Royal Commissions with hopeless terms of reference…"

Barrie Unsworth took over as Premier from Wran but the ALP was losing its appeal in NSW, despite the popularity of the Hawke Government at the federal level.

In a predictable cycle, Wran's final crackdown on the illegal casinos and gaming houses was so short lived that just 16 months later, in March 1987, the Unsworth Government was forced to announce the same thing. This promise again rang hollow, and was ridiculed in State Parliament at the end of May by Liberal MP Michael Yabsley (soon to become Minister for Corrective Services).

"Once again we are promised tough new legislation. Once again we are promised a tough police campaign. Once again we are promised that the illegal gaming houses will be closed," Yabsley said.

"This is the seventh time since this Government took office that it has taken 'decisive action' to close the casinos."

Yabsley noted that while Merv Beck had succeeded in closing the casinos during both his stints on the job, "by mid 1982 they were open and flourishing again".

"Honourable members will recall the strong words of the former Premier in November 1985, that led to the headlines, 'Wran vows to crush card dens'. Later in that year we had another blitz, and in November, more tough legislation that was supposed to close the clubs forever," Yabsley proclaimed.

"That legislation was a joke. Before the legislation had passed the crime bosses who run the prominent clubs had obtained legal advice, knew where the loopholes were, and were erecting steel security doors to keep the police out.

"In March this year there was another burst of concern from the Minister for Police, who began naming what he called the 'hardcore' gaming houses. As the Opposition was able to reveal within days, the Minister had missed several of the hardcore city clubs, and had managed to omit the biggest casino in Sydney, a casino that gaming police had been told all about.

"In spite of warm noises from the Minister, and periodic police raids, the harsh reality is that all of the hardcore clubs in the city remain open.

"Only the Double Bay Bridge Club has closed in recent weeks, and that is due to the competition from the Goulburn Club, not from the excessive police attention.

"Number 77 Darlinghurst Road, run by the Minister for Tourism's good friend, Bruce Galea, continues to operate. To my knowledge, it has not been successfully raided by the police for some years.

"Number 6 Kellett Street is open and offering one of the biggest Russian poker games in town. Number 20 Kellett Street is also open. Number 20 Bayswater Road is open. Number 26 has re-opened, being the new address of the operators of the Double Bay Bridge Club. The Barclay continues to thrive, offering one of the biggest games of Chinese dominoes in the city.

"…The Goulburn is now the biggest club in town, having drawn in some of the most prominent operators in Sydney. Following the latest police raid, in the early hours of Friday morning, the Goulburn Club was open for business as usual on Saturday night. And Sambo's, at 71 Dixon Street, continues to operate untouched."

It was, in other words, business as usual. The Minister for Tourism at the time was Mike Cleary, a former outstanding sportsman who was also Minister for Sport and Recreation and Minister for Racing.

The problems in the Criminal Investigation Branch had also continued, and in the late 1980s Commissioner Avery decided enough was enough. He gave the notorious branch one year to reform itself, but did not take steps to ensure this happened. Avery was serious and when the branch failed to perform, carried out his threat to shut it down, believing it to be hopelessly corrupt.

Ray 'Blizzard' Blissett again felt compelled to comment in a letter to *the Sun-Herald:* "I spent 40 years in the force, mainly on criminal investigation. I worked side by side with some of the finest men who ever joined, men of high principle and unblemished character.

"Through all those years there was a degree of corruption within the force, as there is today. Despite the efforts of Mr Avery, and others within his ivory tower, it will remain and for him to say that, with the help of a deity, he can overcome it is sheer nonsense."

One of the men most closely associated with the rot in the CIB was Detective Roger Rogerson. Rogerson had a number of bravery awards, but even more accusations—of corruption, heroin dealing, skimming the proceeds of armed robberies, and murder.

He had shot dead a drug dealer, Warren Lanfranchi, 'in the line of duty'. In 1984 Rogerson was accused of conspiring to murder his colleague, drug detective Michael Drury, who was shot twice through his kitchen window while feeding his three-year-old daughter. No charges were laid.

In 1986 Rogerson was dismissed from the NSW Police Force over comments made in an ABC interview, claiming Avery was campaigning against him. In 1992 he was jailed for perverting the course of justice and served more than three years before being released.

In 1993 he wrote to a journalist from prison:

"There are about 16 ex-coppers here, including former Deputy Commissioner Bill Allen, who is almost 71 years of age and a nice old bloke, so I have plenty of mates to talk to."[48]

Beck recognised the disbandment of the CIB was the logical result of the ongoing corruption it housed, but regarded Avery's solution as problematic. 'Throwing the baby out with the bathwater' left NSW Police as the only force in Australasia without a specialist CIB. Beck believed a better alternative would have been to replace the entire branch, in the same way that 21 Division had been cleaned out, appoint a strong commander, and enforce a limited period of service in the branch so people and habits did not become entrenched and open to corruption.

"The notorious and disastrous silence against corruption, ever present in the past, worked against numerous honest individuals whilst others of the force relied upon it providing the criminal element amongst police to finally bring the service to its knees. The CIB in particular suffered as a consequence until its end when it was discarded like a shabby garment not wanted for further use," Beck said.

In 2001 under Commissioner Peter Ryan, an import from the UK, there was talk of re-establishing the CIB as the focus for the new technology now available to policing, and with a new format of fixed tenure to prevent detectives from becoming entrenched and vulnerable to corruption, as suggested by Beck. This did not happen and NSW remained without a CIB.

* * * *

---

[48] https://www.abc.net.au/news/2016-06-15/the-life-of-roger-rogerson/7473306

In October 1987 the Orana Law and Order Forum produced a bigger movement. The first Sydney branch of the National Law and Order Forum was formed at the Guildford Bowls Club near West Ryde. The meeting was attended by more than 200 people and addressed by Merv Beck. The response from community leaders, academics and the media was enthusiastic.

Beck applied himself to his new cause. He read widely on approaches to law and order, crime and punishment, and spent much of his pension on travel expenses. He travelled by bus from Dubbo to Melbourne to meet the leader of the conservative Democratic Labor Party (DLP), B.A. Santamaria, who gave his complete support.

Beck's renewed public profile made it easy for friends and foes alike to find him. Former and serving police who had suffered in various ways as a result of his crackdown on gaming and betting had neither forgotten, nor forgiven. He received a steady stream of abusive anonymous phone calls from men accusing him of hurting other police personally and financially.

"Each time my name appeared in the press, practically the same calls would be received on my home phone at Dubbo, with the same threats, because of 'what you did to the boys on the job'—which I assume was about me stopping them making money illegally," Beck recalled.

As gutless as he considered the callers, he did not dismiss their threats completely. It was likely the barbecue set and its network were behind the continued harassment. He did not tell Elsie about the calls but he told his daughter Pauline, who was also living in Dubbo, about the worst of them. If something did happen to him, he wanted to make sure that it would be investigated, although he knew anonymous calls made this hard.

At this time, Beck was still pressing the Government to be paid the $5000 in leave pay due to him, without success. Another angry anonymous male caller, whom Beck suspected to be a police officer, told Beck he would have done better to look after himself and not depend on the Government to keep its word over the money due to him. This observation was sadly true.

Before the 1988 NSW state election, Opposition Leader Nick Greiner promised to 'get tough' on crime. The Liberal-National Coalition which he led was swept into power, and quickly introduced a raft of measures to control crime and corruption.

One of these was the reintroduction of the Summary Offences Act, as proposed by Beck's forum. Another was the creation of an Independent

Commission Against Corruption (ICAC), modelled on the Hong Kong agency of the same name. Beck was strongly in favour of such a body, to investigate politicians, police and public office holders. Headed by high profile former Federal Director of Public Prosecutions, Ian Temby QC, the NSW ICAC began operations in 1989.

The Greiner Government also introduced so-called 'truth in sentencing' legislation, banning early release of certain prisoners including 'life' prisoners. (While this was popular and well-intentioned, within three years the prison population had risen by 36 per cent to an unmanageable level, while the incidence of crime had not fallen.)

A committee of MPs was established to liaise with the Law and Order forum, and Beck would travel to Sydney to attend meetings. Often guests were asked to attend to give the MPs an insight into what was happening on the streets.

One of these meetings was very memorable to Beck. They were discussing firearms, and an MP turned up with a young female member of his staff.

The discussion turned to restrictions on firearms and the fact that police officers could take their weapons home. The young staffer spoke up to confirm this. She said she had lived with a police officer in a de facto relationship, and often he would allow her to fire his police issue revolver during day trips into the country. She also mentioned with amusement that the police officer had plenty of ammunition, so they never ran out.

The liaison committee was astonished by this revelation. As soon as the woman had finished her account, the embarrassed MP announced that he had an urgent meeting to attend and hurried out, taking her with him.

As welcome as it was, the liaison committee became a source of frustration for Beck and other Law and Order Forum members as their discussions did not lead to direct change. There was also the question of funding. The Government supported the forum in principle, but not financially. Travelling from Dubbo to Sydney for regular meetings at their personal expense became a drain on forum members, until they decided to abandon it.

The Orana Law and Order Forum remained very active, publishing its own newsletter which attracted advertising from local Dubbo businesses including McDonald's. Since its inception the forum had achieved a great deal, despite the predictable opposition from many senior police who were bound to support the status quo.

But Ted Pickering, now the Police Minister, was less supportive than he had appeared in Opposition. In February 1990 he publicly accused Beck and the forum of being out of touch with modern policing methods after they criticised the use of police on weekends to deliver Meals on Wheels. Pickering claimed there had been a 12.5 per cent drop in crime in Dubbo.

"These figures for the Dubbo Police District show conclusively that not only are police doing a first-rate job, but that community policing is also working," he said. "For Mr Beck to say there is too much emphasis on public relations and not enough on catching criminals is simply absurd."

Pickering did not comment on whether delivering Meals on Wheels was a good use of police time. The Dubbo *Daily Liberal* responded by reporting that on average, 2.65 homes were burgled in Dubbo every day, "a level described by Police Minister Ted Pickering as 'excellent'".

Beck was not deterred and remained the chairman and most prominent spokesperson for the forum. He was often quoted in the Dubbo newspaper calling on local businesses and residents to become more involved in reporting and attacking crime. He was also committed to the forum's manifesto, which he believed represented a common sense, practical approach to law enforcement.

There was no doubt that policing in NSW needed a shake-up. A 1990 report from the Australian Institute of Criminology, *The Size of the Crime Problem in Australia*, found that the NSW Police had the worst record of any Australian force in terms of the proportion of major crimes which were solved and for which offenders were tried. For home burglaries, the clean up rate was 4.8 per cent, less than one third of the Victorian rate (16.2 percent), although NSW per capita spending on police was more than one third higher.

Researchers Dr Satyanshu Mukherjee and Dianne Dagger also found that the incidence of most major crimes in NSW, relative to population, increased greatly between 1974 and 1989, including a fivefold rise in serious assaults.

At Christmas 1989, Beck was asked to become a member of a new committee to oversee the system for early release of particularly vicious criminals, the Serious Offenders Review Board. The payment was $2315 a year.

His appointment, predictably, attracted media attention. Beck made headlines claiming NSW Police were too soft on criminals. "People have to know who is in charge of the streets and it is not being made clear right now," he said. "The police must be allowed to go hard and that might rub some people up the wrong way but the criminals will soon learn who is in charge[49]."

Beck served on this committee for four years, together with two retired judges, a Queen's Counsel, a serving Chief Inspector of Police, Robert Treharne, prison officers and community representatives, one of whom was the father of Anita Cobby, who had been brutally murdered.

During that period, the committee visited gaols and spoke to people from all sides of the issue, such as families of prison inmates, serious offenders themselves and families of victims. Beck found it fascinating work. In September 1991 he received a letter of thanks from former Corrective Services Minister, Michael Yabsley. After the state election in May, Yabsley had been promoted to the State Development and Tourism portfolio.

"I was grateful for the professional manner in which the policies and directions of the Greiner Government were implemented in such a challenging and at times controversial area of public administration," Yabsley wrote.

"I acknowledge your contribution to the corrections systems in New South Wales and record my appreciation for your efforts in this area."

Ironically, the ICAC which he had created proved the downfall of Nick Greiner himself. The Premier became caught up in a 'jobs for the boys' scandal involving a public service position created for former Education Minister, Terry Metherell. The 'Metherell Affair' led to Greiner's resignation in June 1992.

He was replaced by John Fahey. In late 1993, the Serious Offenders Review Board was considering the release of two violent killers. Chief Inspector Treharne and Beck were strongly against their release, believing that they posed a threat to the families of their victims, and the general public. The board did not agree, and the murderers were subsequently set free.

Very soon after this, both Beck and the superintendent lost their positions on the review board when it was restructured by the Fahey Government in January 1994. To Beck and Treharne, their removal seemed more than a coincidence.

---

[49] Daily Mirror 28 December 1989

Administrative secretary of the Police Association, Lloyd Taylor, commented at the time: "It's quite obvious to me that the real reason (for dropping Treharne and Beck) is that they want smoother meetings than the ones they've been having with policemen upsetting things by offering practical advice."

Beck had a high regard for the board and believed it achieved a good balance in general between compassion for victims and for inmates, and the security of the public.

"Why does it upset authorities when a duty is performed in a sincere manner?" asked Beck. "Somehow I do not appear to please politicians of any party—and therein may be the answer!"

Beck certainly did not ingratiate himself with anyone. He was a frequent public critic of standards of policing and, where he saw the need, decisions by politicians.

An example of this had occurred in March 1991 when Police Minister Ted Pickering moved his ministerial office into police headquarters, ending 130 years of tradition which separated the Minister and the force. Pickering had created a $1.5 million office suite on the 20th floor of the police building in College Street Redfern.

Beck joined senior lawyers, criminologists, academics and even controversial Queensland Police Commissioner Ray Whitrod in criticising Pickering's move into the force's operational heart.

Pickering denied that he would involve himself in operational matters, but the location of his office—two floors above new Police Commissioner Tony Lauer—was seen as highly symbolic.

Labor Party spokesman Michael Egan said the minister's location would intimidate the Police Force, and Beck agreed

"I don't think it is a good move," Beck said. "I think it shows the political power is too close to the law enforcement agency. There should be two separate and distinct processes dealing with law enforcement in NSW, the law makers and the police enforcers."

In Beck's view, political intervention in the running of the police (and other essential services) was never helpful and inevitably produced bad results. He believed politics should be kept out of day to day police work and particularly administration. This included appointments. The appointment of Bill Allen as Deputy Police Commissioner in late 1981, over strong objections from Commissioner Jim Lees, was an obvious example.

Trouble also arose when police were requested to investigate matters involving politicians. The investigating police nearly always did the job properly, just as they did when investigating other police. "It's what happens when their reports go in. They tend to get nobbled further up the line," said Beck.

"I believe that if the Police Force was left alone with a team of good honest senior officers it would keep corruption in its ranks well in check. The sad truth is, however, that despite all the good honest people, corruption in and outside the Police Force is not being curtailed due to the growing influence of the major criminal elements. Conventional methods are not winning."

Even well-meaning politicians, Beck argued, were curtailed by the need to maintain good relations with their fellow MPs and with the public. Moreover, on most issues they were only as good as the briefs they were given by public servants, regarded by Beck as "a mixed complex group having too much power used to bamboozle their political leaders as in *Yes Minister*," a reference to the classic 1980s BBC television series.

As it turned out, whether it was the new office or other factors, Pickering's relations with the force were as bad as, and possibly worse than, any other police minister's. Within a few months of John Fahey becoming Premier, he was shifted from the Police portfolio to Justice, after a breakdown in his relations with Commissioner Lauer. Pickering lasted only a month in the Justice portfolio before he resigned over the treatment of Nick Greiner[50].

While Beck was busy with his work on the review board and the Law and Order Forum, in September 1991 he had a galling reminder of his work a decade earlier.

A warrant was issued for a character he knew well — Bruce Hardin, the operator of the casino in Darling St Rozelle (which was controlled by Freeman and Lennie McPherson). Hardin also ran an SP operation in Balmain and a small casino in King's Cross, called the Palace. His debts were reportedly collected by notorious hitman Christopher Flannery. McPherson once said Hardin was someone he "had known since babyhood and looked on as a son".

Hardin had been called to appear before the NSW Royal Commission into the Building Industry in NSW (1990-92) headed by Roger Gyles.

---

[50] See also First report : the circumstances which resulted in the resignation of the honourable E.P. Pickering, MLC, as Minister for Police and Emergency Services, New South Wales. Parliament. Joint Select Committee upon Police Administration, Duncan Gay, 1993.

The *Sun-Herald*' ran a story by Alyson McClymont and Susan Borham on 15 September under the headline "Gambler on the Run".

"A man with extremely prominent connections in the political, racing and criminal worlds, Hardin has apparently gone into hiding after failing to answer a subpoena to appear before the Building Industry Royal Commission."

Hardin had been missing since April. Two weeks after the article appeared he was tracked down in Ispwich, Queensland and arrested. He was promptly extradited and flew back to Sydney the next day, to attend a special late afternoon sitting before Gyles[51]. It then took half an hour of argument before Hardin would agree to take the oath.

After a night in the cells, Hardin gave explosive evidence the next day that he had loaned former Liberal MP, John Abel[56] $50,000 because "he was short of money". Hardin had also helped Abel to invest in a casino resort, Radisson Royal Palms, in Vanuatu.

In exchange for the favour, it was revealed, Hardin received a weekly retainer of $500 from Abel for "advice on the gambling industry".

Evidence was also provided to the Gyles inquiry that Hardin had collected $800,000 a year in protection money (equivalent to millions in today's money) from building companies as a 'security consultant'. The money went to Freeman and McPherson purportedly to make sure there were no problems in the building industry and scaffolding was not stolen, although no evidence was forthcoming that stealing scaffolding was, or ever had been, an issue.

Infuriatingly for all, including Beck, while Hardin was berated for his lack of cooperation with the inquiry, nothing seemed to stick and he walked away again without being charged.

While Hardin got away unscathed, the atmosphere in Sydney had definitely changed. The Government and the ICAC were keen to pin down allegations, and catch any public officials, including police, who were breaking the law.

One of the new ICAC's first investigations, in 1989, was of a complaint that senior police had fabricated evidence, including planting heroin on a person, during a search of premises in Redfern. The investigation concluded there was insufficient evidence to charge any of the five police involved, but called for changes to the ICAC legislation to make it more workable.

---

[51] See Tony Reeves The Real George Freeman: Thief, race-fixer, standover man and underworld crim By Tony Reeves [56] State Member for Evans 1975-77

The following year, Police Commissioner Avery referred allegations to the ICAC that harassing telephone calls made to an individual's residence in and after March 1990 had been traced to Mt Druitt Police Station.

In its report on this investigation, made public in December 1990, the ICAC made findings of corrupt conduct against five persons, including four NSW Police officers. It recommended prosecution of three of those persons for specified criminal offences and disciplinary action against four of them[52]. The contrast was stark with the official police response to the telephone threats received by Beck and his family, as well as the defamatory anonymous letters which had clearly been generated within the Police Force. Even in retirement, Beck was continuing to receive these calls.

As the ICAC's work began to attract more public trust and attention, in 1991 it investigated two claims regarding corrupt police behaviour, both of which resulted in action against police.

The first case related to claims that over an 18 month period in 1984 and 1985, a licensing police officer in the Sutherland district had asked for and taken weekly payments from the Caringbah Inn Hotel licencees. The ICAC recommended that the officer, since retired, be charged for common law bribery.

In late1990 and early 1991 the ICAC also worked with the NSW Police to investigate police in Wagga Wagga who were taking bribes to act as 'spotters' for truck repair companies. Three police officers were charged with serious offences. Further work by the ICAC resulted in a recommendation of criminal or disciplinary proceedings against two additional police.

These narrow investigations were important, but no one including the ICAC thought they were getting to the heart of the issue. In 1992 the ICAC began a much broader investigation—to examine "the relationship between police and criminals". This would focus on events since 1975, on detectives, and in particular, on illegal gambling and armed robberies. It would also consider how the NSW Police had handled complaints made by police against other police working in these areas.

The inquiry could have been tailor-made for Beck, who was keen to provide evidence. But many police felt differently as the hearings were public. When evidence was presented it was spectacular, as reported

---

[52] https://www.icac.nsw.gov.au/investigations/past-investigations/pre-2013#1993

in *the Sun-Herald* on 13 June 1993. Under the heading "Police and the gambling czars", Steve Warnock reported that the ICAC was "dealt a trump card when NSW Gaming Police admitted they were crooked".

"The ICAC was told that three former members of the squad had admitted engaging in 'various improper activities', including falsifying records and associating with alleged illegal gaming operators…Peter Neil, counsel assisting the ICAC, said former Gaming Squad officer Sergeant Graham Stockwell had 'admitted to soliciting and accepting favours from an illegal gaming operator.'"

"Last week's ICAC evidence set tongues wagging again about police, politicians and illegal casinos and SP betting in NSW over the past 30 years," Warnock wrote, before expounding on the 'glory days' of illegal gambling, marred only by Merv Beck.

Inspired by the ICAC inquiry, on Monday 5 July, *Four Corners* ran another corruption expose by Chris Masters. Masters' report on Queensland police corruption had been entitled "The Moonlight State". Now, he focused on NSW, "the Green Light state"—focused on its history of alleged entrenched corruption in the police service and attempts to clean it up.

Masters began the show by explaining the term. "In New South Wales, there has long been a practice known in the underworld as greenlighting. For decades, certain police have given certain criminals a green light to go about their business. Here is the closest we can get to an image of New South Wales corruption. The lines in this computer model produced by the Independent Commission Against Corruption link police and criminals. When all the lines are drawn, you see the Green Light State."

The following are extracts from the program transcript.

CHRIS MASTERS: In the last decade, an overdue clean up of the backyard was begun but there is a long way to go. You have to go back to the preceding decades to see why there is so much work to do, to fully comprehend the accumulated rotting weight of history.

What was the big money in say the '60s and the '70s?

UNIDENTIFIED: Definitely the SP and the casinos because there is no doubt, I don't think, to anybody, that it was well protected. In regard to the SP, there was those that weren't protected and the little fellows that was trying to get a quid in the pubs. They used to just pinch the fellows in the pubs and I suppose that is enough pinches—everybody is happy.

CHRIS MASTERS: A year ago it was easy to find the Forbes Club. The words 'Forbes Club' were painted in yard-long letters on the side of the building. Today, that is blotted out.

JOURNALIST: An illegal casino is operating in Kembla Street only a few hundred metres from the Police Station—is it or isn't it?

POLICE OFFICER: Yes.

JOURNALIST: Why isn't it closed down?

POLICE OFFICER: You had better ask people in another sphere other than police circles for that answer, the answer to that.

JOURNALIST: Isn't it your job as the senior policeman here, to close that casino down if it is against the law?

POLICE OFFICER: If I am able to, yes.

JOURNALIST: Why are you unable to?

POLICE OFFICER: I won't comment on that.

CHRIS MASTERS: Debate continues to this day, over who was more in control of the game—some politicians or some police.

RAY BLISSETT: I'd say the politicians had control.

MERV BECK: It is my belief and from the information that I have obtained, Chris, that it was a combined effort between the senior police of that era and the politicians, working together.

Masters went on to discuss the shooting of criminal Warren Lanfranchi by Roger Rogerson, who was lauded as a top detective but later found to be crooked and a close associate of hitman and drug dealer Neddy Smith. The shooting occurred on 27 June 1981, when Beck was on general duties in Hornsby.

CHRIS MASTERS: At the time of the Lanfranchi shooting, New South Wales was about as on the nose as you can get, to a range of other police services, notably the Victorians and the Federal Police. While the new Commissioner, Jim Lees, was trusted, the man directly below him, Bill Allen, and the man directly above him,

Bill Crabtree, were not. A month after the Lanfranchi shooting, the Victorians staged an extraordinary surveillance mission to prove their northern colleagues were crook.

Fran Martin was one of a small undercover team from the Victorian Bureau of Criminal Intelligence who arrived here, outside New South Wales police headquarters.

FRAN MARTIN: The information that we had at that time was that a member from the 21 Division was going to bring some money here, which he would take up to the Deputy Commissioner, Allen's office. And what our information was that he would then take that down to Parliament House and deliver it to a Member of Parliament, Mr Crabtree.

Four Corners also played a tape that had been revealed at the ICAC inquiry of a conversation legally taped by the AFP in 1983.

CHRIS MASTERS: The investigations revealed nothing. It was business as usual and if you want a good example of how business was done, listen to this conversation, revealed at the current ICAC inquiry. The ICAC contend one party was a Sergeant Ron Daly, the other was the gangster, Neddy Smith.

POLICE OFFICER: I have known you too long.

NEDDY SMITH: Oh mate, I am very generous to you, you know that.

POLICE OFFICER: You look after me all the time.

Masters concluded that corruption remained a huge problem in the overblown NSW Police Service (as it was then known). Yet the program had little impact as politicians and critics claimed it did not reveal anything new.

This was a sad indictment of the political culture in NSW at the time, but change was in the wind.

For Beck, his decision to speak out on police corruption yet again reminded his supporters and enemies alike of what he had done to the illegal gambling industry and the police who fed off it.

He and Elsie had moved to the Central Coast where they were closer to their children and grandchildren, and to hospitals. But, it seemed, Beck could still be tracked down. Three months after the *Four Corners* program, Beck received a phone call at 11.15 pm. The initial beeps told him it was an STD or long distance call, but this was not from a friend.

The caller sounded as though he had been drinking. Beck suspected he was a former or current member of the Police Force.

"You have not been forgotten for the troubles you caused the good blokes in the job!" the caller berated Beck. "You'll get yours before long!"

There was a string of indecencies and abuse, followed by "you won't recover from what's coming for you, you bastard".

As always, Beck kept his cool. "What's your problem?"

"You mongrel, you must know, you sent many of the good blokes broke." And then he slammed the phone down.

It was around this time that Beck decided that he should record what happened to him more fully, through a book. As with the Beck Dossiers, he wanted to record the difficulties which honest police often faced from corruption and from political pressure, as a warning and an aid to police finding themselves in similar situations.

He stressed that the 'bad apples' in the force were a minority, but also questioned the moral difference between people actively engaged in organised crime and corruption and the high ranked officials, elected and otherwise, who tuned a blind eye to their activities. Some of these were no doubt involved themselves but others were simply afraid of either failure or of making dangerous enemies. In Beck's view, all were equally guilty.

"Any police reading this, it's up to them to put themselves in the category in which they belong and enjoy or suffer from the contents, accordingly," he added.

The first report from ICAC's inquiry into police and criminals was released in February 1994. It examined several sets of circumstances including criminals paying money to police to avoid prosecution or conviction., making findings of corrupt conduct against 11 persons and recommendation prosecution or disciplinary action against 13.

The second report, made public in April 1994, focused on the administrative systems and management issues such as management of informers; conduct of criminal investigations; record-keeping; police and prosecutions; and misconduct and complaints. Sixteen recommendations were made to help prevent corruption.

The reports were worthy but far from earth-shattering. They proved that corruption existed in the NSW Police, but provided only snapshots, not the big picture.

As well as Beck, one of those most disappointed by the ICAC reports was NSW Independent MLA, John Hatton. Although the ICAC in many ways was comparable to a standing royal commission, Hatton believed its model was flawed and was not trusted by police whistleblowers. Police accused of wrongdoing were given enough advance notice to enable them to cover their tracks, and those giving evidence against them had to do so in public. The ICAC reports were also public. Serving police and others who could provide the most revealing evidence would be more likely to testify before a royal commission, he believed.

Hatton had been calling for a royal commission into NSW police involvement in growing marijuana crops (and the death of Donald Mackay) since 1987. He had renewed this call in 1990, linking the police-mafia drug connection to the murder of Assistant Commissioner of the Australian federal Police, Colin Winchester.

Under the Wran Government, after the 1978 'Wranslide' Hatton had no power apart from his ability to embarrass the Government through the media. Before the snap 1978 election called by Wran he had told Parliament, "The Government has a huge working majority. If they were serious about corruption they would appoint a wide-ranging royal commission, and ask it for an interim report by September, so they could go to the polls with clean hands[53]". His proposal fell on deaf ears.

But in 1991 he and other Independents took the balance of power in the NSW Parliament's Lower House. A few weeks after the ICAC inquiry fell flat, Hatton played this trump.

At 3,38 pm on 11 May 1994, he stood up in the Legislative Assembly, ostensibly to table a mundane report from a parliamentary committee. This done, he successfully moved to suspend standing orders and introduce a new topic. Dramatically, he moved "that the House calls upon the Premier, in consultation with the Leader of the Opposition, to establish a royal commission, staffed by personnel other than serving or former members of the New South Wales Police, to inquire into the operations of the Police Service."

The royal commission should have particular reference, he pronounced, to "entrenched corruption, the Professional Responsibility and Internal Affairs branches, the system of promotion, the impartiality of the service in pursuing prosecution including, but not limited to pedophile activity, the failure of the internal informers policy, and any

---

[53] Reported Sydney Morning Herald 14 March 1984

other matter involving criminal activity, neglect or violation of duty that was in the public interest".

Hatton had given notice of his intention and as a result, the public gallery was full of police officers who made clear their anger and dislike of what Hatton was saying as he alleged police involvement in criminal activity, surveillance by the Police Service on three former ALP Ministers, and other matters[54]. But Hatton was not intimidated.

At the end of the debate he summed up: "This motion is for honest police; it is for the vast majority of police. It is a watershed. There is now no doubt in New South Wales—and I have longed to reach this point for many years—that there must be a wide-ranging inquiry into entrenched corruption in the New South Wales Police Service."

After a lengthy debate, his motion for a royal commission was passed with the slimmest majority, by 46 votes to 45, with support from the Labor Party Opposition led by Bob Carr.

Although his call was for a royal commission into the NSW Police, in his last few comments on the debate Hatton referred to the murder of Colin Winchester, the most senior Australian policeman ever to be murdered on the job. Hatton had appeared at the 1990 inquest into Winchester's death but had been accused by the National Crime Authority and others of spreading "outrageous hearsay".

Now in 1994 under parliamentary privilege he claimed: "I had to be destroyed at the Winchester inquiry. I knew that when I went there. I challenge the Minister for Police (Terry Griffiths) to tell me how somewhere between $5 million and $10 million of marijuana can disappear; how his (Winchester's) police officers at the senior level can, with mafia figures, grow and harvest marijuana and have a large quantity of it disappear. That question was never addressed by Winchester; he never approached that question. It has never been answered. I challenge the Minister to answer it."

The following year, 1995, Canberra public servant David Eastman was convicted of Winchester's murder and sentenced to life imprisonment. Eastman always maintained he was framed. After a judicial inquiry and a retrial, on 22 November 2018 a jury found Eastman not guilty of murder. After 19 years in custody, he was awarded $7 million in compensation. No one else has been charged with the murder.

---

[54] See The Little Bloke: An Authorised Biography of John Hatton, Ruth Richmond, University of Wollongong, 2007

Following the NSW Parliament's consent to Hatton's motion, Premier John Fahey acted swiftly. On 13 May 1994, Supreme Court Justice James Wood was appointed to head the Royal Commission into the New South Wales Police Service as outlined by Hatton. The royal commission was due to report on 30 December 1996.

When Beck had suggested such an inquiry, the response from within the Police Force was horrified and the reaction in Macquarie St would have been even more negative. In the 1980s in particular, a phrase commonly used by NSW politicians in the corridors of power, both in Canberra and Sydney was "don't establish a royal commission if you don't already know the answer". When an inquiry had to be held under sufferance, as occurred under the Wran Government, damage could be limited by ensuring narrow terms of reference. In 1994, despite the obvious need for a major intervention into the NSW Police Force, it is likely the royal commission would not have gone ahead if the Government had held a majority in the State Parliament.

The powers granted to the royal commission were strong, even by the standards of royal commissions. As well as the usual powers to compel witnesses to appear and for production of documents, the commission was allowed to certify its own warrants for electronic surveillance and phone intercepts. On the other hand, without explanation, it was denied the power to make its own telephone intercepts, although this would have considerably boosted its ability to gather evidence of corruption.

Commission officers were permitted to carry firearms and were conferred the powers of a constable of the NSW Police Service. Lying to or misleading the commission was an offence carrying a sentence of up to 6 months imprisonment. In August 1994, Justice Wood asked the NSW Government for increased powers. The Australian Government also amended legislation to enable the AFP and National Crime Authority to conduct phone intercepts at the request of the royal commission.

In contrast to the usual structure of royal commissions, which are staffed primarily by lawyers and administrators, the commission had three investigation teams composed of lawyers, accountants, investigators and current and former officers from every Australian legal jurisdiction excepting New South Wales.

The commission also acquired the equipment and expertise for sophisticated covert surveillance capabilities so it could effectively monitor the activities of groups of corrupt police officers and organised criminals.

(In December 1994, the royal commission's terms of reference were expanded to include investigation into the protection of paedophiles by NSW Police.)

NSW Police Commissioner Tony Lauer initially belittled the inquiry and denied that there was systemic corruption in the force. But the royal commission found that the problems Beck had run up against from crooked cops were still around many years later.

When it began hearings, revealing the rich harvest of its electronic surveillance, it was not just the public which was shocked.

Even police who did not give evidence were emboldened to reveal corruption they encountered. Former first class constable Mark Tull claimed in the *Sun-Herald* on 11 August 1995 that the daughter of a prominent politician was caught four times driving without a licence, but was let off. Among other allegations, he said the son of an assistant commissioner of police was arrested for stealing a car, but had also been let off after a call to the assistant commissioner.

In the same month, Lauer had to stand down his own assistant chief of staff, who was named as corrupt in evidence to the royal commission.

Not all witnesses called to give evidence to royal commission were cooperative. In 1995 Justice Wood cited Bruce Galea, then 60, for contempt for refusing to answer questions, Galea was convicted and jailed. He served more than two years and three months, a record for a contempt charge.

In an article on the Galea clan in *the Sydney Morning Herald* in 2010[55], racing writer Max Presnell made it clear that he was one of the many media and public figures with sympathy for Galea and his colleagues, as he had himself been a client of the SP bookies and illegal casinos.

"Many old-timers figure Sydney in the Perce Galea heyday with the illegal games and SP betting was a better and safer city than now. Corrupt, yes, but the casinos had style, and Thommo's two-up school was still the best and fairest punt I've come across," he lamented.

"SP and two-up made way for the TAB and legal casinos—supermarket gambling, lacking the charisma of the Forbes Club."

Presnell also gave an insight into why Bruce Galea had not answered Justice Wood's questions.

---

[55] https://www.smh.com.au/sport/racing/galea-clans-mixed-fortunes-20100213-nyg2.html

"Galea went by the code of you don't give anyone up. Folklore has it he went to the commission with his toothbrush and said, 'You've got to do what you've got to do and I've got to do what I've got to do.' 7"

Undoubtedly, his self-sacrifice was appreciated by some who avoided considerable embarrassment, if not worse.

In February 1996, after months of evidence from corrupt former policemen describing widespread bribery, drug dealing and theft by police, especially in Sydney, Lauer resigned in humiliation.

Merv Beck was called to give public evidence in November 1996. He spoke again about Bill Allen's obstructionism and about the other obstacles he faced—the false allegations, circulated within the police and the media, and the anonymous phone threats, first to himself and then to his wife and daughter.

John Avery, who had left the role of commissioner in 1991, told the royal commission[56] that the 'high water mark' for syndicated police corruption was police involvement in gaming and betting in the late 1970s and early 1980s. In his final report[57], Justice Wood agreed with this assessment and identified three main factors that allowed corruption to flourish in this period.

Firstly, corrupt police were able to select and encourage junior officers who showed a willingness to participate in corrupt activities, to join up with them and then follow them through the ranks.

Wood cited Bill Allen's mentoring relationship with Warren Molloy, who in 1981 was Acting First Class Sergeant and head of the Special Licensing Branch. Evidence given to the commission alleged that Allen was passing corrupt payments to Molloy, but Abe Saffron was not happy about this. Saffron visited Allen at police headquarters six or seven times between March and September to discuss Molloy. This worried Molloy, who confided in two fellow officers—Ernie Shepherd of the Vice Squad and John Avery, who became Police Commissioner just three years later.

Wood concluded this mentoring initially meant that corrupt police tended to be concentrated in CIB; but later the corrupt networks were transplanted "across the regions as well as the specialist squads that remained".

---

[56] J.R.T. Wood, Final Report of the Royal Commission into the New South Wales Police Service, Volume 1, 1997, p 65

[57] Wood op cit p66

Secondly, Wood noted that corrupt or inept management ensured that there was nowhere an officer could safely go with a complaint about improper or criminal behaviour. Those in Internal Affairs were unable to protect whistleblowers, and the case of Phillip Arantz's enforced imprisonment in a psychiatric hospital for whistleblowing lingered in officers' minds. It was widely considered that speaking out about corruption was the end of one's career.

Thirdly, Wood observed, there was a general unwillingness or inability to target the corrupt police who had well-established links to senior officers.

Justice James Wood delivered the royal commission's *Final Report Volume II: Reform* in May 1997. It had 556 pages and made 174 recommendations. High up in its glossary of terms was "barbeque set— clique of senior and/or corrupt police in the 1980s who regularly socialised together".

A number of years after the royal commission, on December 2002, the NSW Parliamentary Committee on the Office of the Ombudsman and the Police Integrity Commission, chaired by Paul Lynch MLA, tabled a research report on trends in police corruption[58].

In his foreword, Lynch commented on the historical trend: "in general, police corruption has flourished at times when poor police oversight and poorly focused laws have combined to create extensive opportunities for police to engage in corrupt activities".

The Police Integrity Commission set up as a result of the Wood Royal Commission, and other mechanisms, ensured that the NSW Police Force had better oversight. But Lynch's committee echoed the findings of the royal commission, noting that corruption usually started with small acts and escalated over the years as the police officer's standards eroded.

It gave the example of two of the corrupt police who gave evidence to the royal commission, Trevor Haken and the witness known as JTF6.

"JTF6's corrupt activities revolved around planting evidence on those people he believed to be involved in the drug trade. At the end of his career, he was sharing in money stolen by officers from raids on dealers, but justified this as recompense for paying informants from his own pocket. On becoming aware of Trevor Haken's connections to the

---

[58] https://www.parliament.nsw.gov.au/ladocs/inquiries/1833/Research%20Report%20on%20Trends%20in%20Police%20Corruption.PDF

Bayeh group (a major drug organisation) and the involvement of other police with drug dealers, JTF6 reported Haken and the other officers to his patrol commander and the Professional Integrity Branch, urging the formation of a task force to investigate their activities," the report stated.

"JTF6 gave evidence at the Wood Royal Commission that he reported Haken and the others although he risked exposing his own corrupt activities because:

'I'd had enough of the corruption and that sort of corruption.... I could see a difference between helping a brief along or picking up some money here and there and the sort of allowing drug dealers to do what they do. I just couldn't see the morality of it.'"

But while it starts with small acts, it becomes hard to stop. As the Lynch committee noted, corrupt police "consistently believe that once they have committed the act, they are compromised" and therefore, unable to blow the whistle. It quoted Sergeant Ray Peattie, giving evidence at the Police Integrity Commission hearings into corruption in the Manly Davidson Local Area Command.

"I wasn't strong enough to stop. I remember every time I got money, I didn't really want it. But I didn't say no ... Once you are on the dark side, you are always on the dark side.'[59]

The committee agreed with Justice Wood, Justice Lusher who undertook the 1981 NSW Royal Commission, and the 1971 Knapp Commission into corruption in the New York Police Department, that corruption was the result of a systemic problem— the 'rotten barrel'— and not problem individuals—'rotten apples'.

"Clearly, in any large policing organisation it is impossible to ensure that all those recruited will have the strength of character and integrity required to resist, or will not be exposed to a situation where it will be easy to slip into corrupt behaviour. However, Knapp, Lusher and Wood all agree that it is dangerous for a police service to hold that any corruption that is exposed is a result of individual deviance. Dismissing such events as 'one offs' means that broader, underlying problems will remain unexamined and inevitably lead to greater damage."

The committee's report also included a sizable text box: "Merv Beck vs the Barbecue Set". It concluded:

"In 1981, with three months to be served before his retirement, and Bill Allen facing disciplinary hearings at a Police Tribunal, Merv

---

[59] Ibidem page 10.

Beck was again running the new Special Gaming Squad. Harassment of his family immediately began again. In three and half months Beck had closed down all the major gaming operations, arrested 1055 people and left enough criminal intelligence to keep his successor going for 12 months. But after he left, nothing happened. Even in his retirement, he continued to receive phone calls from members of the Barbecue Set, threatening reprisals for the damage he had done."

After the Wood Royal Commission, the NSW Police disbanded the Special Gaming Squad and the new SP Betting Task Force. Policing of SP bookmaking was given to the Licensing Enforcement Agency. Just 26 arrests for SP offences were made between January 1995 and July 1996.

During that period, in September 1995, the temporary Sydney Harbour Casino was opened. It was replaced on 27 November 1997 by Star City, later renamed the Star, a permanent casino for Sydney. The opening party featured a public concert with Diana Ross amongst others and in the first 24 hours, 45,000 people reportedly attended the new casino.

The heyday of SP was over. Although it had quickly bounced back from the damage caused by Beck's Raiders, the nature of gambling had changed. A high stakes punter commented in January 1997[60]: "The biggest challenge to NSW Racing isn't SP, it is the availability of interstate bookies. Who'd bother betting SP when you can check the price at home on the internet and then ring the Melbourne bookies and get on for $50,000 at the top fluctuation, no trouble."

In his 1999 book, *Scandals: Media, Politics and Corruption in Contemporary Australia*, author Rodney Tiffen noted: "In the 1990s there was probably less monolithic, institutionalised corruption than there had been a decade earlier. Under Police Commissioner John Avery[61] a determined assault had driven many corrupt officers out of the force and to a large extent destroyed the old cosy networks. However there were still many stories of police misdeeds and an apparent readiness by officers to turn a blind eye to them[62]."

* * * *

---

[60] *The Sun-Herald* The Gadlfy, 19 January 1997.
[61] Commissioner from 1984 to 1991
[62] Rodney Tiffen, Scandals: Media, Politics and Corruption in Contemporary Australia, UNSW Press, Sydney, 1999,

In the 21st century, there is more awareness of corruption and the damage it can cause. The activities that provide opportunities for corruption have changed, along with our social habits. Governments all around Australia have embraced legalised gambling as a way to raise revenue.

While some things change, others stay the same. In January 2009 the Tasmanian *Advocate* newspaper went right out of its comfort zone in terms of both locality and topic to report on "New places, some old faces for the Cross".

"The big illegal operations have been overtaken by legal casinos, poker machines in clubs throughout the suburbs and a huge variety of opportunities to bet on any type of sport— legally.

"Dynastic overtones are also apparent in Kings Cross. Bruce Peter Hardin, the one-time strip club and gambling identity, no longer features on business documents. Today his son, Christian Paris Hardin, runs the family business—three strip clubs and a Five Dock pub, the Illinois Hotel, with a strip club inside.

"Bruce's other son, Paul, has followed a different path, and is a successful criminal defence lawyer who runs his own Elizabeth Street practice.

"The brothers David George Freeman and Adam Sonny Freeman own the nightclub promotions company Freeman International, which is associated with numerous Kings Cross and Oxford Street venues.

"David and Adam are the children of George David Freeman, the former racing identity who was able to achieve a 98 per cent success rate in horse race tipping during his 30 years as a commission agent."

Freeman had long since passed away. On 20 April, 2014, it was Wran's time.

Amidst volumes of praise were a few articles suggesting that Wran's career was being viewed through rose-coloured glasses. Merv Beck was by then very old himself and nearing the end, but if he was able to read it, Andrew Rule's piece in the Melbourne *Herald Sun* on 27 April 2014 would have given him satisfaction.

Under the headline "Ex-NSW premier Neville Wran was Nifty by name, nifty by nature", Rule wrote:

"Wran predicted corruption allegations would surface as soon as he died. That wasn't a wild guess.

"He was just getting in first.

"He knew some allegations were true and that there were plenty more where they came from.

"Wran studied law in Sydney with people he would encounter for the rest of his life. They included his eminent contemporary Laurence Street, who would become a chief justice and end up in the same expensive nursing home where Wran died last Sunday.

"As a royal commissioner in 1983, Sir Laurence eventually cleared Wran of allegations he used his influence with the bent chief magistrate Murray Farquhar to nobble a fraud case against Rugby League chief Kevin Humphreys. Farquhar went to jail. So did Rex "Buckets" Jackson, who used his position as Wran's prisons minister to sell early releases to cashed-up crooks.

"Nothing stuck to the streetwise "Nifty" because the royal commissioner accepted he was in a meeting on the morning the chief magistrate's office took a call from "the Premier". That was just enough to beat the rap but the smell lingered.

"And Wran won another (nick)name: 'Premier Never Rang'.

"Just ahead of Wran and Street at university was 'Big Bill' Waterhouse, who ditched law to become a massive bookmaker before his disgrace with his son Robbie over the Fine Cotton 'ring-in' scandal of 1984.

"It's well-known that as a young man Wran was a 'runner' for the Waterhouses. Not so well-known is that the association continued after he became a powerful politician.

"Martin and David Waterhouse—Bill's nephew and younger son, respectively—noted Wran's involvement in the family's gambling enterprises.

"Martin worked for his uncles Bill and Jack at their headquarters in North Sydney early in Wran's political career. David also worked as a bookmaker—and at the family gaming house, The Palace, at the time in Rockwall Crescent, Potts Point.

"Martin took starting price bets from Premier Wran, which was unremarkable at a time when dozens of prominent citizens 'bet SP'. What interested him more was that a senior policeman called Bill Allen dropped in 'more times than I could count' to pick up cash.

"Martin Waterhouse once saw Allen pocket $2000 and he assumed the policeman picked up similar amounts on each brief visit.

"When Wran insisted on becoming Police Minister as well as Premier it raised eyebrows. But leapfrogging the dodgy Allen above many more senior officers to head the crime department (sic) and gaming and licensing was a scandal in waiting. The Waterhouses knew why Allen was chosen: Wran wanted someone he 'could trust'.

"It was a dangerous liaison for a cop who already had inexplicable spending power. Allen took free overseas trips organised by the notorious organised crime figure Abe Saffron, who visited his office at least six times for mysterious reasons. And he paid for his house in cash —from betting, he claimed."

On 23 April 2014, *The Sydney Morning Herald* also carried an opinion piece[63] about Wran, by Michael Pascoe.

"Praise for Neville Wran appears universal, from all factions and both sides of politics. The well-chronicled achievements were indeed immense. Mind you, so too were those of Sir Robert Askin when he died and was given a State funeral.

"…It would be wrong amidst the praise of Wran to overlook what he did not do, a sin of omission that would no longer be acceptable: clean up a notoriously corrupt state.

"At best, Wran was blind to the blatant organised crime and corruption that characterised Sydney during his time in politics. It is most unlikely anyone as intelligent as Wran could be that blind. Those close to him will swear that Wran was not himself corrupt and he was not found to be.

"So somewhere in between the possibilities of blindness and corruption there remains the suspicion that he was merely soft on corruption and organised crime, that permanently closing illegal casinos and cleaning up a rotten police force weren't high on his list of priorities.

"When the copious eulogies fade, Wran's leadership may be seen as a step in the evolution of government—the middle path of a politician not prepared to make powerful and ruthless enemies by pushing too hard against them when the electorate itself didn't seem to mind…

"We've come a very long way from the time of Premiers Askin and Wran. Many citizens have forgotten or weren't living here or were too young to appreciate just how crooked NSW was all those decades ago. The symptoms of corruption—most obviously, the numerous illegal casinos—were not even hidden.

"…That it could be so, that Neville Wran could be such a successful and popular politician in such a climate, now seems a mystery."

Pascoe concluded that, while Australia has come a long way in terms of defences against corruption, success cannot be taken for granted.

---

[63] https://www.smh.com.au/business/remember-failings-of-wrans-nsw-beforecurtailing-the-icac-20140423-373il.html

Winding back the powers of agencies such as the NSW Independent Commission Against Corruption, he concluded, would be an invitation to return to a dark past.

Police, and other powerful officials, will always be vulnerable to corruption. Beck's experiences and what he learned from them remain relevant today.

In December 2017, the Victorian Independent Broad-based Anti-corruption Commission (Ibac) released a report based on a survey of 1,172 Victoria police employees, of which 80 per cent were sworn police officers. It followed a series of investigations into corruption in the state's police force, including allegations of drug trafficking and abuse that were substantiated by an Ibac inquiry.

The survey report found that one in five Victoria Police employees would not report corruption if they witnessed it, and a further one in five believed they could lose their job if they reported corruption.

More than one in eight respondents said they felt Victoria Police "actively discourages the reporting of corruption".

One commented: "I have come across corruption and reported it. I was ostracised and bullied for doing so."

The survey results confirm that leadership and culture are key to resisting corruption. Beck never believed that corruption was endemic in NSW as it was, for example, in the New York Police Department in the late 1960s. In his view, the great majority of NSW police were always honest and capable, and performing under difficult circumstances, but did not feel capable of taking action against those who were corrupt, especially those of higher rank.

With the passage of time, the fears held by Beck, Bob Bottom and many others that organised criminals would find ways to use legal casinos for their own ends have also proven correct.

Despite their sophisticated appearance, legal casinos in Australia have now been linked to international drug traffickers and organised crime, including Chinse triads. Very serious accusations were levelled against Star Sydney, Star Queensland, SkyCity Entertainment Group's Adelaide casino and Crown Casino in Melbourne in 2021 and 2022.

It is also clear that the vast amounts of money involved in legal casinos have the potential to entrap not only individuals but governments, who find the revenue hard to resist.

Because money is usually at the heart of corruption, Beck approved of giving law enforcement agencies more power to follow the money trail, even at the expense of personal privacy. Since his retirement, federal governments have moved down this path and the organisation AusTrac has strong powers to access bank records of suspected major criminals such as drug traffickers.

The other side of law enforcement is the legal system. As Beck's story demonstrated, both law makers in Parliaments and legal decision makers in the court system can have a powerful influence on how the law is enforced, and whether laws are respected by the community.

Courts which impose only token punishments ensure there is little deterrent to breaking the law. Politicians who fail to update the law in line with community expectations leave police with the invidious choice of either enforcing unpopular laws, or failing to enforce them in disregard of their duties.

Far from an intellectual, Beck nonetheless understood how damaging it could be for a community to lose faith in its police force and justice system. His devotion to the rule of law, as the basis for a safe and fair society, was unshakable.

As summarised by the Australian Constitution Centre, the rule of law is the idea that every person is subject to the laws of the land regardless of their status. "It promotes justice, fairness and individual freedom. The rule of law provides a shield against the arbitrary exercise of power. It ensures that judges are independent from the people and institutions whose actions are challenged."

Despite the poor treatment he had received, Beck also remained loyal to the NSW Police. The values to be followed by every member of the Force, enshrined in section 7 of the NSW Police Act 1990 could have been modelled on his career: to place integrity above all, uphold the rule of law, preserve the rights and freedoms of individuals, to improve the quality of life by community involvement in policing, and ensure authority is exercised responsibly.

He also maintained personal links with the NSW Police. His grandson continued the tradition of policing within his family, creating a fourth generation of Becks to serve in the NSW Police Force.

From time to time, even in his old age, Merv regularly met with former members of his squad, whom he called "the Gamers" to enjoy their friendship, camaraderie and reminiscences.

"I would like to pay a tribute to all those people who I worked with, and who are my friends to this day," Beck said. "I only hope (my story) will be a guide to all police so that they will be alert to what can happen and what probably will happen in future. I think the best thing the police can do is get close to the people, the public, and drop those barriers, because everything they do should be for the people."

A quote from Robert F Kennedy became one of his favourites.

"Each time a man stands up for an ideal to improve the lot of others, or strikes out against injustice, he sends forth a tiny ripple of hope… And crossing each other from a million different centres of energy and daring, those ripples build a current that can sweep down the mightiest wall of opposition and resistance."

Mervyn Beck, one of Australia's most acclaimed policemen, died on 21 March 2018, aged 96. He was a fighter to the end. Never a vain man, he was buoyed in his later years by the knowledge that his full story would, eventually, be told.

www.ingramcontent.com/pod-product-compliance
Lightning Source LLC
Chambersburg PA
CBHW070456120526
44590CB00013B/661